# ANNUAL EDITIONS

# Human Resources  *05/06*

*Fifteenth Edition*

**EDITOR**

**Fred H. Maidment**

*Western Connecticut State University*

Dr. Fred Maidment is associate professor of management at Western Connecticut State University in Danbury, Connecticut. He received his bachelor's degree from New York University and his master's degree from the Bernard M. Baruch College of the City University of New York. In 1983 Dr. Maidment received his doctorate from the University of South Carolina. He resides in Connecticut with his wife.

*McGraw-Hill/Dushkin*

2460 Kerper Blvd., Dubuque, IA 52001

Visit us on the Internet

*http://www.dushkin.com*

# Credits

1. **Human Resource Management in Perspective**
   Unit photo—© Getty Images/Keith Brofsky
2. **Meeting Human Resource Requirements**
   Unit photo—© CORBIS/Royalty-Free
3. **Creating a Productive Work Environment**
   Unit photo— © Getty Images/Keith Brofsky
4. **Developing Effective Human Resources**
   Unit photo—© Getty Images/Duncan Smith
5. **Implementing Compensation, Benefits, and Workplace Safety**
   Unit photo—© Getty Images/Ryan McVay
6. **Fostering Employee/Management Relationships**
   Unit photo—© Getty Images/Ryan McVay
7. **International Human Resource Management**
   Unit photo—© CORBIS/Royalty-Free

# Copyright

Cataloging in Publication Data
Main entry under title: Annual Editions: Human Resources. 2005/2006.
1. Human Resources—Periodicals. I. Maidment, Fred H., *comp.* II. Title: Human Resources.
ISBN 0–07–310212–1       658'.05       ISSN 1092–6577

Fifteenth Edition

Cover image © Photos.com
Printed in the United States of America   1234567890QPDPD987654   Printed on Recycled Paper

# Editors/Advisory Board

Members of the Advisory Board are instrumental in the final selection of articles for each edition of ANNUAL EDITIONS. Their review of articles for content, level, currentness, and appropriateness provides critical direction to the editor and staff. We think that you will find their careful consideration well reflected in this volume.

# To the Reader

In publishing ANNUAL EDITIONS we recognize the enormous role played by the magazines, newspapers, and journals of the public press in providing current, first-rate educational information in a broad spectrum of interest areas. Many of these articles are appropriate for students, researchers, and professionals seeking accurate, current material to help bridge the gap between principles and theories and the real world. These articles, however, become more useful for study when those of lasting value are carefully collected, organized, indexed, and reproduced in a low-cost format, which provides easy and permanent access when the material is needed. That is the role played by ANNUAL EDITIONS.

The environment for human resource management is constantly changing. The events of September 11, 2001 are only just a preview of the global environment that may be developing for human resource managers. This terrorist act is certain to change the role of human resources in the future. At the very least, what has transpired will make the practice of human resources more difficult and more challenging. Meeting those challenges will be the task that will face human resource managers in the future and make it a key factor in the success of any organization.

Management must respond to these forces in many ways, not the least of which is the effort to keep current with the various developments in the field. The articles that have been chosen for *Annual Editions: Human Resources* reflect an outstanding cross section of the current articles in the field. The volume addresses the various component parts of HRM (human resource management) from compensation, training, and discipline to international implications for the worker and the employer. Articles have been chosen from leading business magazines such as *Forbes* and journals such as *Workforce, HR Magazine*, and *People Management* to provide a wide sampling of the latest thinking in the field of human resources.

*Annual Editions: Human Resources 05/06* contains a number of features designed to be useful for people interested in human resource management. These features include a Table of Contents with abstracts that summarize each article with bold italicized key ideas and a Topic Guide to locate articles on specific subjects. The volume is organized into units, each dealing with specific interrelated topics in human resources. Every unit begins with an overview that provides background information for the articles in the section. This will enable the reader to place the selection in the context of the larger issues concerning human resources. Important topics are emphasized and key points to consider, which address major themes, are presented.

This is the fifteenth edition of *Annual Editions: Human Resources*. It is hoped that many more will follow addressing these important issues. We believe that the collection is the most complete and useful compilation of current material available to the human resource management student. We would like to have your response to this volume, for we are interested in your opinions and recommendations. Please take a few minutes to complete and return the postage-paid Article Rating Form at the back of the volume. Any book can be improved, and we need your help to continue to improve *Annual Editions: Human Resources*.

Fred Maidment
*Editor*

# Contents

## UNIT 1
## Human Resource Management in Perspective

Twelve unit selections examine the current environment of human resource management with special emphasis on corporate strategy, disabled workers, sexual harassment, and the War on Terror following September 11, 2001.

*Part A.    The Environment of Human Resource Management*

*Part B.    Human Resources and Corporate Strategy*

The concepts in bold italics are developed in the article. For further expansion, please refer to the Topic Guide and the Index.

# UNIT 2
## Meeting Human Resource Requirements

The unit's four articles discuss the dynamics of human resource job requirements, planning, selection, recruitment, and information systems.

### Unit Overview      54

The concepts in bold italics are developed in the article. For further expansion, please refer to the Topic Guide and the Index.

# UNIT 3
# Creating a Productive Work Environment

The five selections in this section examine how to increase productivity in the workplace by motivating employees and developing effective communication channels.

**Unit Overview**                                                         **74**

The concepts in bold italics are developed in the article. For further expansion, please refer to the Topic Guide and the Index.

# UNIT 4
## Developing Effective Human Resources

Seven unit articles discuss how to develop human resources through employee training, career and staff development, performance appraisal, and diversity in the workforce.

The concepts in bold italics are developed in the article. For further expansion, please refer to the Topic Guide and the Index.

# UNIT 5
# Implementing Compensation, Benefits, and Workplace Safety

Nine articles address employee compensation, incentive arrangements, executive pay, health and safety considerations, and benefits.

The concepts in bold italics are developed in the article. For further expansion, please refer to the Topic Guide and the Index.

# UNIT 6
# Fostering Employee/Management Relationships

In this unit, six selections examine the dynamics of labor relations, collective bargaining, disciplinary action, temporary and part-time employees, and workplace ethics.

The concepts in bold italics are developed in the article. For further expansion, please refer to the Topic Guide and the Index.

# UNIT 7
# International Human Resource Management

Five articles discuss the increasing globalization of human resource management.

The concepts in bold italics are developed in the article. For further expansion, please refer to the Topic Guide and the Index.

# Topic Guide

This topic guide suggests how the selections in this book relate to the subjects covered in your course. You may want to use the topics listed on these pages to search the Web more easily.

On the following pages a number of Web sites have been gathered specifically for this book. They are arranged to reflect the units of this *Annual Edition.* You can link to these sites by going to the DUSHKIN ONLINE support site at *http://www.dushkin.com/online/*.

## ALL THE ARTICLES THAT RELATE TO EACH TOPIC ARE LISTED BELOW THE BOLD-FACED TERM.

# World Wide Web Sites

The following World Wide Web sites have been carefully researched and selected to support the articles found in this reader. The easiest way to access these selected sites is to go to our DUSHKIN ONLINE support site at *http://www.dushkin.com/online/*.

# AE: Human Resources 05/06

The following sites were available at the time of publication. Visit our Web site—we update DUSHKIN ONLINE regularly to reflect any changes.

## General Sources

### Bureau of Labor Statistics

*http://stats.bls.gov:80*

The home page of the Bureau of Labor Statistics (BLS), an agency of the U.S. Department of Labor, offers sections that include Economy at a Glance, Keyword Searches, Surveys and Programs, other statistical sites, and much more.

### CIBERWeb

*http://ciber.centers.purdue.edu*

This site of the Centers for International Business Education and Research is useful for exploring issues related to business ethics in the international marketplace.

### Economics Statistics Briefing Room

*http://www.whitehouse.gov/fsbr/esbr.html*

Easy access to current federal economic indicators is available at this site, which provides links to information produced by a number of federal agencies. Subjects are Output, Income, Employment, Production and Business Activity, Prices, Money, Transportation, and International Statistics.

### Human Resource Professional's Gateway to the Internet

*http://www.hrisolutions.com/index2.html*

This Web site has links to other human relations locations, recruiting-related Web sites, HR–related companies, and search tools.

### In the Workplace

*http://www.ilr.cornell.edu/workplace.html*

The Cornell School of Industrial and Labor Relations offers this Web site. It consists of a useful Work Index; a list of Centers, Institutes, and Affiliated Groups; and an Electronic Archive of full-text documents on the glass ceiling, child labor, and more.

### NBER Home Page

*http://www.nber.org*

The National Bureau of Economic Research engages in specialized research projects on every aspect of economics. Programs include asset pricing, economics of aging, labor studies, and productivity, among others.

### Society for Human Resource Management (SHRM)

*http://www.shrm.org*

SHRM is the world's largest association devoted to human resource management. Its mission is to serve the needs of HR professionals by providing essential and comprehensive resources. At this site, you'll find updates on methods, laws, and events as well as career information.

## UNIT 1: Human Resource Management in

## Perspective

### Employment and Labor Law

*http://www.lectlaw.com/temp.html*

This site offers wide-ranging Web resources and articles covering electronic privacy rights, sexual harassment, discrimination, Americans With Disabilities (ADA) statutes, the Fair Labor Standards Act, and employment law.

### Law at Work

*http://www.lawatwork.com*

From this site you can not only look at current labor laws, such as OSHA, but consider drug testing at work, unemployment questions, sexual harassment issues, affirmative action, and much more.

## UNIT 2: Meeting Human Resource Requirements

### America's Job Bank

*http://www.ajb.dni.us*

You can find employers or job seekers and lots of job market information at this site. Employers can register their job openings, update them, and request employment service recruitment help.

### International Association for Human Resource Information Management (IHRIM)

*http://www.ihrim.org*

IHRIM is a central network for its members to gain access and in-depth knowledge about HR information management and systems issues, trends, and technology.

## UNIT 3: Creating a Productive Work Environment

### Commission on the Future of Worker-Management Relations

*http://www.dol.gov/_sec/media/reports/dunlop/dunlop.htm*

The report of the U.S. Federal Commission on the Future of Worker-Management Relations, which covers many issues, including enhancement of workplace productivity, changes in collective bargaining practices, and intervention in workplace problems by government agencies, may be found here.

### The Downsizing of America

*http://www.nytimes.com/specials/downsize/glance.html*

The complete 7-week series on downsizing in America is printed on the Web by the *New York Times,* in which it appeared.

### Employee Incentives and Career Development

*http://www.snc.edu/socsci/chair/336/group1.htm*

This site states that effective employee compensation and career development is an important tool in obtaining, maintaining, and retaining a productive workforce. There are links to Pay-for-Knowledge, Incentive Systems, Career Development, Wage and Salary Compensation, and more.

# www.dushkin.com/online/

### Foundation for Enterprise Development
*http://www.fed.org/aboutus/aboutus.htm*

Access the Foundation for Enterprise Development files at this site. Their mission is to foster the development of competitive enterprises based on the premise that sharing company ownership and meaningful involvement with employees are effective ways of motivating the workforce in order to achieve business goals.

## UNIT 4: Developing Effective Human Resources

### Employment Interviews
*http://www.snc.edu/socsci/chair/336/group3.htm*

The importance of proper interview techniques to the building of a workforce is discussed here. The page has links to related sites and refers to a book by Alder and Elmhorst, *Communicating at Work: Principles and Practices for Business and the Professionals.*

### Feminist Majority Foundation
*http://www.feminist.org*

This site houses the Feminist Career Center, an Affirmative Action page, and information of interest to women.

### How to Do an Employee Appraisal
*http://www.visitorinfo.com/gallery/howapp.htm*

At this site learn online how to do an annual performance review appraisal and read a "horror story" of how one such appraisal went badly.

## UNIT 5: Implementing Compensation, Benefits, and Workplace Safety

### BenefitsLink: The National Employee Benefits Web Site
*http://www.benefitslink.com/index.php*

This link offers facts and services for employers who are sponsoring employee benefit plans and for participating workers.

### Executive Pay Watch
*http://www.aflcio.org/corporateamerica/paywatch/*

While keeping an eye on the issue of executive salaries, bonuses, and perks in CEO compensation packages, this labor union site offers suggestions to working families on what can be done to curb exorbitant pay schemes.

### Social Security Administration
*http://www.ssa.gov*

Here is the official Web site of the Social Security Administration.

### WorkPlace Injury and Illness Statistics
*http://www.osha.gov/oshstats/work.html*

The Bureau of Labor Statistics Web site presents links to many issues of occupational injury and illness and offers a great deal of statistical information.

## UNIT 6: Fostering Employee/Management Relationships

### Fair Measures: Legal Training for Managers
*http://www.fairmeasures.com/asklawyer/archive/*

All the questions in this Ask the Lawyer Archive are answered by Rita Risser, an employment law attorney. They cover a range of employee/management relations and are aimed at fostering out-of-court solutions to problems.

## UNIT 7: International Human Resource

### Management

### Globalization and Human Resource Management
*http://www.cic.sfu.ca/forum/adler.html*

Dr. Nancy J. Adler, a faculty member at McGill University, discusses strategic international human resource development in this thorough summary for the Internet.

### Labor Relations and the National Labor Relations Board
*http://www.snc.edu/socsci/chair/336/group2.htm*

From this site you can explore labor relations in today's international marketplace.

We highly recommend that you review our Web site for expanded information and our other product lines. We are continually updating and adding links to our Web site in order to offer you the most usable and useful information that will support and expand the value of your Annual Editions. You can reach us at: *http://www.dushkin.com/annualeditions/*.

# UNIT 1

# Human Resource Management in Perspective

## Unit Selections

1. **HR Is Dead, Long Live HR**, Shari Caudron
2. **The State of the Human Resources Profession in 2003: An Interview With Dave Ulrich**, Rich Vosburgh
3. **What Is an Employee? The Answer Depends on the Federal Law**, Charles J. Muhl
4. **Good As Gone**, Marianne Kolbasuk McGee
5. **7 Steps Before Strategy**, Bruce N. Pfau and Bonnie Bell Cundiff
6. **Strategic Human Resources Management in Government: Unresolved Issues**, Jonathan Tompkins
7. **Unquiet Minds**, Aliya Sternstein
8. **The Devil is in the Details**, Thomas Clark
9. **The ADA's Next Step: Cyberspace**, Suzanne Robitaille
10. **Not In My Company: Preventing Sexual Harassment**, Jim Mulligan and Norman Foy
11. **The Aesthetics of Security**, Ray A. Smith
12. **Aftershocks of War**, Linda Wasmer Andrews

## Key Points to Consider

• What social and economic trends do you feel are the most significant? Has downsizing gone too far? Are employees likely to bolt from their current jobs now that the economy seems to have turned around? How will these trends have an impact on the labor force as it continues into the twenty-first century? How does human resource management make a difference?

• What are some of the ways that firms can better utilize the skills and talents of their employees?

• What were the most important changes for the American worker during the twentieth century, and what changes do you see as likely in the next 20 years? How have changes in the family resulted in changes in human resource management?

• In the past 30 years, the government has taken a more active role in the struggle of minorities and other groups in the workforce. How has the ADA changed the workplace?

• Sexual harassment is a very important area of concern for most organizations. What do you think organizations can and should do about it?

• How do you think September 11 will affect organizations and their relations with their employees? Do you think that things will change significantly?

 **Links: www.dushkin.com/online/**
These sites are annotated in the World Wide Web pages.

**Employment and Labor Law**
*http://www.lectlaw.com/temp.html*
**Law at Work**
*http://www.lawatwork.com*

The only constant is change. Industrial society is dynamic, a great engine that has brought about many of the most significant changes in the history of the human race. Since the start of the Industrial Revolution in England, a little over 225 years ago, industrialized society has transformed Western civilization in a multitude of ways. Many great inventions of the last 200 years have significantly altered the way people live and the way they see the world.

At the time of the Declaration of Independence, the 13 colonies were an overwhelmingly agricultural society that clung to the Atlantic coast of North America. At the beginning of the twenty-first century, the United States is a continental nation with the world's largest industrial base and perhaps the smallest percentage of farmers of any major industrialized country. These changes did not happen overnight, but were both the result and the cause of the technological innovations of the Industrial Revolution. The technological marvels of today, such as television, radio, computers, airplanes, and automobiles, did not exist until after the Industrial Revolution, and a disproportionate number of them did not exist until after 1900.

Along with technological changes have come changes in the way people earn their living. When Thomas Jefferson authored the Declaration of Independence in 1776, he envisioned a nation of small, independent farmers, but that is not what later developed. Factories, mass production, and economies of scale have been the watchwords of industrial development. Industrial development changed not only the economy, but also society. Most Americans are no longer independent farmers, but are, for the most part, wage earners, who make their living working for someone else.

Changes in the American labor force include the increase in women and minorities working next to white males. The nature of most jobs has changed from those directly associated with production to those providing services in the white-collar economy. Many other changes are developing in the economy and society that will be reflected in the workforce. For the first time since the early days of the republic, international trade represents a significant part of the American economy, having increased greatly in the past 20 years. The economic reality is that the GM autoworker competes not only with Ford and Chrysler, but also with Toyota and Volkswagen.

The society, the economy, and the workforce have changed. Americans today live in a much different world than they did 200 years ago. It is a highly diverse, heterogeneous world, full of paradox. When people think of American industry, they tend to think of giant-sized companies like IBM and General Electric, but, in fact, most people work for small firms. The relative importance of the Fortune 500 companies in terms of employment in the economy has been declining both in real and percentage terms. Economic growth today is with small organizations.

Change has brought not only a different society, but a more complex one. Numerous rules and regulations must be followed that did not exist 200 years ago. The human element in any organization has been critical to its success, and knowing what the human resource needs of the organization are going to be 1, 5,

or even 10 years into the future, is a key element for continuing success as seen in "HR is Dead, Long Live HR."

Individual decisions have also changed. In the first part of the twentieth century, it was common for a worker to spend his or her entire life with one organization, doing one particular job. Now the worker can expect to do many different jobs, probably with a number of different organizations in different industries. Mergers, technological change, and economic fluctuations all put a premium on individual adaptability in a changing work environment for individual economic survival.

The changes in industrial society have often come at a faster rate than most people were willing to either accept or adapt to. Many old customs and prejudices have been retained from prior times, and while progress has been made with regard to certain groups—no American employer today would dare to end an employment notice with the letters "NINA" (No Irish Need Apply), as was common at one time—for other groups, the progress has been slow at best. Women represent about half of American workers but they are paid only about 70 percent of what men earn, and sexual harassment still represents a problem, as discussed in "Not in My Company: Preventing Sexual Harassment."

African Americans, and other minorities, have been discriminated against for centuries in American society, to the point where the federal government has been forced to step in and legislate equal opportunity, both on and off the job. People with disabilities have also sought protection as seen in "Unquiet Minds," "The Devil is in the Details," and "The ADA's Next Step: Cyberspace."

Finally, the clash of differing cultures seems ever more pronounced in our society. America has traditionally viewed itself as a melting pot, but it is clear that certain groups have historically "melted" more easily than others, a situation that is reflected in the workplace.

Human resource management plays an important role in industrial America. Business leaders recognize the value of their employees to the future of their organizations. Increasingly, competition in world markets is becoming based on the skills and abilities of people, not machines. Indeed, among major competitors, virtually everyone has essentially the same equipment. The difference is often what the people in the organization do with the equipment.

Of special consideration, are the recent events of 9/11. For the first time since The War of 1812, the United States was forcefully attacked on its home soil with a greater loss of life than at Pearl Harbor. These events will mean changes in the way the economy operates and the way organizations will treat their employees. HR professionals must address these issues as seen in "The Aesthetics of Security," and the "Aftershock of War."

Society, the workplace, and the way they are viewed have all undergone major changes. Frederick W. Taylor and Elton Mayo, early writers in management, held certain views about industry at the beginning of the twentieth century, while Peter Drucker, W. Edwards Deming, and others have different ideas now, at the beginning of the twenty-first century. The American society and economy, as well as the very life of the average American worker, are different from what they were 200 or even 100 years ago, and both the workers and the organizations that employ them must respond to those changes.

# HR is Dead
# Long Live HR

**In this era of human capital, HR is experiencing seismic change. Outsourcing is swiftly taking over. If HR stands still, it's doomed. But if it changes, its business clout can be more potent than ever.**

*By Shari Caudron*

The future of human resources has perhaps no greater champion than Kathleen S. Barclay, vice president of global human resources for General Motors. When asked if the function is becoming obsolete, Barclay is adamant. "I don't agree with that," she says. "I suppose it depends on the company that you're dealing with, but my view is that there has never been a more important time in any company to have a very strong, active HR organization. HR can have so much impact on the way the company works, how the culture feels, and the type of talent you have both now and in the future."

---

**Is it an HR reality to become indispensable and more vital than ever? Or do the job losses signify a different trend? Could HR be on its way toward obsolescence?**

---

In companies where HR has taken the reins and moved the function in a new direction, the financial results have been impressive. Research from Watson Wyatt's WorkUSA 2002 study indicates that companies with effective HR practices deliver shareholder returns that are three times higher than those of companies without such practices.

Despite the evidence and the firm belief in HR's potential among executives such as Barclay, the profession's rosy future is far from certain. In fact, the number of available HR jobs has dwindled significantly in recent years, and opportunities are not likely to increase anytime soon, says Frank Allen, president of Frank E. Allen and Associates in Florham Park, New Jersey. Allen, who has been in the HR recruitment field for more than 17 years, has placed thousands of HR professionals in jobs ranging from benefits manager to senior vice president. And right now, he's drowning in résumés. "I've got a database listing 18,000 HR professionals and out of that, somewhere around 7,000 active résumés," he says. "I'm also getting 200 to 300 résumés a week." The likelihood that Allen will be able to place all these people is pretty slim.

With the unemployment rate hovering around 6 percent, the same thing can be said of many jobs, including information technology, telecommunications, and marketing. But when the economy turns around, people in those positions are likely to find work again. That's not necessarily true for HR professionals, because the profession is enduring a wave of changes that by all accounts are likely to significantly reduce the number of people needed. David Ulrich, co-author of *The HR Scorecard: Linking People, Strategy, and Performance* (Harvard Business School Press, 2001), believes that the head count in HR will eventually plummet 25 percent—or more.

But wait. People like Barclay believe that HR is primed to lead knowledge-intensive companies into the future. Is she right? Is it an HR reality to become indispensable and more vital than ever? Or do the job losses signify a different trend? Could HR be on its way toward obsolescence?

## First, the bad news

If you are a pessimist who thinks that HR's cup is slowly draining, you'll find a lot of support for your position. The primary evidence comes in the form of outsourcing. Today, there are vendors available and champing at the bit to help with every single product and service offered by HR, including staffing, payroll, benefits administration, training, employee relations, and compensation. According to research by Gartner, Inc., 80 percent of companies now outsource at least one HR activity, and the number is swiftly growing.

---

## How will the HR profession look five years from now?

Steve VanNostrand, vice president, HR

The Raymond Corporation

(part of Toyota Industries Corporation) Greene, New York

"HR will take on more of a leadership role with the business units rather than a partnership role. I don't see radical change. I see continuous improvement. HR is now being held to the same standard as other functions such as marketing, manufacturing, and engineering. My expectation is that we will continue to deliver more value and our business expertise will continue to increase.

"I don't see HR becoming obsolete. I've got experience with both large and midsized organizations, and my network tells me our function continues to be valued more and more each year. In some cases, we'll see the line blur between historic HR and line management. But I see us becoming more relevant, not less."

---

Consequently, what started in the 1980s as simple payroll outsourcing has exploded into a $32 billion a year business involving all facets of HR. In the last two years alone, the value of the business-process outsourcing industry has grown 20 percent, and analysts from Gartner estimate that it will become a $55 billion worldwide industry by 2005. In just four years, one outsource provider—Exult—has grown from a start-up with a handful of people to an established company with 1,500 employees and more than $400 million in annual revenues. Other big players include Accenture HR Services, ADP, Fidelity, Hewitt, and Convergys.

"Right now, it is primarily large companies that outsource their HR activities," says Rebecca Scholl, senior analyst with Gartner. "But we're definitely seeing an uptick in the number of medium-sized companies that are looking for providers to take on more HR processes."

Outsourcing has become popular because companies are finding that external vendors—through technology and economies of scale—can provide more efficient and cost-effective HR services than in-house departments. In

---

## How do you envision the future of HR?

Lawrence B. Costello,

senior vice president, human resources

American Standard Companies, Inc.

Piscataway, New Jersey

"First off, [at American Standard] we're actively considering renaming the function. I think it's time. The typical image of HR is constraining and does not portray the visionary or leadership aspect we're trying to bring forward.

"That said, I think the future of HR is exciting because senior management is starting to look to HR for insight and perspective on how to guide the company. We're participating in the business process in a way we never have before.

"The new HR takes a different kind of person to succeed, and I'm having to do a lot more internal development work than I thought. The new HR takes people with business experience who are not afraid to state their point of view. Because of that, we in the HR community have to recognize that future HR leaders can't just come from HR. There is no reason we can't take people on a cross-functional basis and invite them into the profession."

---

1999, BP (formerly British Petroleum) contracted with Exult to take over all of its transactional activities in the United States and United Kingdom, including all payroll, recruiting, expatriation, records management, vendor management, and relocation services for its 63,000 employees. The only function that remains in-house is BP's learning and development program in the United States.

Over the last two years, the company has reaped many benefits from the arrangement. Payroll processing is more timely and accurate. Employees get their benefits questions answered sooner. HR processes have been standardized across the company. And for the first time, BP has measurable data on which HR activities are effective.

Because BP is no longer handling routine transactional work in-house, a lot of its HR employees were deemed unnecessary. As a result, its core HR staff has been slashed 65 percent—from 100 to 35 people.

This kind of staff reduction is fairly typical in outsource arrangements, says Jim Madden, chairman and president of Exult. "What usually happens when companies outsource with us is that one-half to two-thirds of the jobs in the HR department go away because the jobs are declared redundant."

External vendors have been so successful doing routine HR work that the list of companies handing over their HR activities continues to grow. In the last few months, Sony, Prudential, AT&T, and American Express have all inked deals with outsource providers. Chances are good that in the next few months, a lot of HR people in those companies will be looking for work.

## But what about strategy?

One of the primary arguments for downloading HR activities onto an external vendor is that getting rid of routine transactional tasks allows HR professionals to focus on the kind of transformational work that helps the bottom line. But despite all the talk about becoming strategic partners, research indicates that the majority of HR people still don't have what it takes to fulfill leadership roles.

Ed Lawler, director of the Center for Effective Organizations at the University of Southern California in Los Angeles, has been gathering data on the effectiveness of HR since 1995. In the last seven years, he's seen very little change in how HR professionals are spending their time. "It seems that instead of responding to this period of business turbulence by playing a central strategic business partner role," Lawler says, "HR has responded by maintaining the status quo."

His findings are supported by a recent survey of HR professionals conducted by the Society for Human Resource Management. When respondents were asked to identify two or three HR/workplace trends they believe will affect the HR profession, only 7 percent identified "HR as a strategic business partner" as a key trend. Much higher on the list were such things as managing diversity and administering health care. Clearly, HR professionals will never be able to transform the function—and hold on to their jobs—if they cannot embrace this new role.

Part of the problem is that many HR people simply don't understand what it means to be strategic. In a separate SHRM study entitled "The Future of the HR Profession," eight leading consulting firms shared their thoughts on the current and future state of HR. One of the themes that emerged is that few HR professionals possess both the business acumen and functional expertise necessary to move their companies and the HR profession forward.

Frank Allen, who's frequently given the task of finding high-level HR people for companies, estimates that of the 18,000 people in his database, "I'd say less than 1 percent of them are A players." And who are those A players? They are the people who not only have a solid understanding of HR, but also are conversant in finance, sales, marketing, and manufacturing, and know how HR can help companies meet their goals.

The dearth of business talent within HR is causing more and more companies to look outside the profession when seeking to fill top HR slots. Today, 75 percent of top HR executives have come up through the traditional ranks of HR. Four years ago, that number was 79 percent. What this means is that today, fully one quarter of the top HR jobs are going to people with backgrounds in marketing, manufacturing, finance, and other operational ar-

---

### What are the competencies needed for next-generation HR professionals?

Wayne Broadbank, clinical professor of business at the University of Michigan, Ann Arbor, has been studying HR competencies for the past 15 years. Over the course of his research, more than 27,000 HR professionals and their line management associates have participated.

Broadbank's most recent research, conducted last year (2002), revealed that HR professionals in high-performing firms demonstrate the following competencies:

1. **Strategic contribution:** HR professionals in high-performing companies manage culture, facilitate "fast change," are involved in strategic decision-making, and create market-driven connectivity.

2. **Personal credibility:** These HR professionals are credible to both their HR counterparts and the business line managers whom they serve. They also have effective writing and verbal skills.

3. **HR delivery:** Strategic HR people focus traditional HR activities in four key areas: staffing, development, performance management, and managing and measuring the impact of global HR practices.

4. **Business knowledge:** The most important areas of business knowledge for an HR professional include a keen understanding of how the firm creates wealth, how the firm is horizontally integrated (e.g., how sales and marketing relate to manufacturing), and what the industry challenges are.

5. **Knowledge of HR technology:** HR professionals must be able to leverage technology for HR practices and use e-HR/Web-based channels to deliver value to customers.

---

eas—and the number is growing. What hope does the profession have for its future if it is increasingly being managed by people from the outside?

To be fair, HR isn't solely to blame. Senior leaders have to recognize the role HR can play and give its HR team the time and resources necessary to make lasting changes. Unfortunately, not all CEOs understand that strategic workforce planning and management is an ongoing effort. Allen knows of some companies that have hired strategic high-level HR people only to let them go once they think they've achieved their objectives. "Either that, or a new chair will come in with a different idea of HR," he says. "Instead of viewing HR as an asset, they'll view it as an administrative function and fire the person who was trying to make strategic changes."

Fortunately, corporate leaders who do understand the role HR can play also realize that it takes time and a lot of serious effort to make changes.

---

**The dearth of business talent within HR is causing more and more companies to look outside the profession when seeking to fill top HR slots.**

---

Four years ago, when Barclay was promoted to vice president of global human resources at GM, it was the first time in the company's history that an HR person reported directly to the CEO. Barclay launched a company-wide HR transformation effort that involved standardizing processes, creating HR centers of excellence, and outsourcing routine activities. In a company with 362,000 global workers in 58 countries, a change of this magnitude obviously takes time. Barclay has already been at it for three years and says it will take three more years to fully complete the process—but that the CEO is committed to the change.

A key part of GM's global HR transformation involves developing HR people so that they understand and can take on the role of internal consultants. "We have a global HR curriculum that helps our people understand what we are attempting to accomplish in HR, what the transformation means to them, and where we're going as an HR community," Barclay says. "We have 15 to 20 courses out there now, and they are mandatory for all HR professionals." Among other things, these courses help HR professionals acquire business acumen, change-management skills, and the ability to forge relationships across the organization. As a result, in the not-too-distant future when a business unit is having trouble achieving its goals, GM's HR people will be able to work with that unit to diagnose its problem. It might be because the talent makeup is not adequate, the incentives are wrong, or goals have not been properly communicated. By training its HR people to understand—and address—such business issues, Barclay is slowly transforming the way the function operates.

In addition to training the HR people, her team has to train line managers to understand that HR is now there to help with strategy, not transactional work. "We have a global HR Web site that houses materials our HR people can use with their operating leaders to help those leaders understand how HR is changing, why it needs to, and why the value equation is better for the company," she says.

As in many other companies, a key part of the HR transformation at GM involves transferring responsibility for HR activities to line unit managers with the help of technology. For example, GM recently instituted a compensation plan for 40,000 employees that was implemented by managers entirely over the Web without any intervention from HR. "This experience helped managers understand how HR is working differently now," Barclay says.

However, this kind of change isn't always easy for organizations to accept, Lawler notes. "Line managers typically like the close, hand-holding type of relationship they've always gotten from their friendly HR person," he says. "The idea that transactional work might take place in an outsource company or disappear entirely because of employee self-service technology is unattractive and anxiety-producing for many managers."

But blaming anxious line managers or noncommittal CEOs for presenting obstacles to HR's transformation does not a strategic, fully employed HR person make. The fact remains that the HR profession itself has a long way to go in developing the skills, competencies, and focus necessary to become internal business consultants. Until that happens, the slow decline of HR jobs and stature is likely to continue.

## Finally, some good news

If you're an optimist who sees an unlimited future for HR, there's plenty of reason to celebrate.

Let's revisit the idea of outsourcing. Yes, it is reducing the number of HR jobs available in companies that choose to outsource. But those jobs tend to be lower-level administrative and technical positions. The good news is that outsourcing is finally giving higher-level HR professionals the time they need to tackle strategic workforce challenges. Even better, the demand for such strategists is higher than ever, for several reasons.

To begin with, demographic changes are making it harder and harder for companies to find and keep qualified employees. It will be up to HR to determine what kind of talent is needed to meet company goals and then devise

---

## Is HR becoming obsolete?

**Kathleen S. Barclay, vice president, global human resources**
**General Motors**
**Detroit, Michigan**

"I don't agree with that. I suppose it depends on the company that you're dealing with, but my view is that there has never been a more important time in any company to have a very strong, active HR organization. HR can have so much impact on the way the company works, how the culture feels, and the type of talent you have both now and in the future. HR has a huge role to play in helping senior leaders shape the culture and make sure that culture is driving business outcomes."

recruitment and retention programs based on that need. Second, technology is making it possible for companies to become more and more decentralized, with employees distributed across wider geographic regions. HR people will be the ones who determine how to keep widely dispersed employees connected to corporate goals.

Third, although outsource vendors have proven their ability to handle routine transactional work, internal HR consultants will still be needed to determine what combination of pay, benefits, and learning opportunities is necessary to keep employees engaged. Finally, even if outsourcing does remove all the transactional work, someone with a solid understanding of HR and business will be needed to manage the multimillion-dollar vendor contracts. HR will always be responsible for ensuring the speed and accuracy of employee transactions, regardless of who is doing the work.

"Essentially, what's happened is that the field of HR has begun to split into two parts," Ulrich says. One half consists of administrative and transactional work, which is becoming more automated and routine and is increasingly being turned over to employee self-service or outsource providers. The second half consists of transformational work, in which HR develops organizational goals, determines what capabilities are needed to meet those goals, and then creates HR practices that make those capabilities come to life.

Put all of this together and you realize that the field is in the midst of an enormous transformation and its final form is not yet clear. However, the function is likely to be smaller and very different from what it is now. And there will be no shortage of challenging work. HR professionals can have an impact on their companies. And obviously, the need is there.

Is HR up to the task? In companies like General Motors, the answer is a definite yes. But as research shows, there's still a huge chasm between desire and reality when it comes to the future of HR.

Is HR becoming indispensable—or obsolete? Only the people currently working in the profession know the answer to that. If they are able to forge a link between HR initiatives and corporate goals, their indispensability is all but assured. If not, a lot more HR résumés may be circulating in the near future.

---

*Contributing editor Shari Caudron lives in Denver. E-mail editors@workforce. com to comment.*

# The State of the Human Resources Profession in 2003: An Interview with Dave Ulrich

Interviewed by Rich Vosburgh

**Rich Vosburgh (RV):** Dave, you have been such a terrific friend of The Human Resource Planning Society that we appreciate your taking the time to do this interview before taking your three-year sabbatical from the University of Michigan. I also understand you have been reviewing some of your current thinking with a group of professionals whom you hold in high regard.

**Dave Ulrich (DU):** Yes, Rich, I have been giving this some thought, almost as a "teaser" before I leave on sabbatical. I presented some of this thinking at the SHRM conference in mid-2002. I am grateful for the input provided to me by Wayne Brockbank, Ralph Christensen, Bob Eichinger, Paul McKinnon, and Norm Smallwood... people whom I admire greatly and am privileged to consider friends.

**RV:** I understand you have eight challenges and seven indicators of progress that kind of counteract the challenges. So how would you answer the question: "What is the state of our profession?"

**DU:** I am clearly one voice of many, but as an interested and informed eyewitness of the HR profession for the past 20 years, I would like to offer a few observations. The challenges ahead are great, but the opportunities have never been greater. Let me start with eight challenges I believe we face as a profession. Challenges may be framed as what we need to pay attention to.

*First, we need to let go and move forward.* We in HR continue to be our own worst enemy. We keep seeking respect rather than acting as if we had respect. Respect comes from within the profession, not from the validation of line managers, customers, employees, or any other group who sanctifies our work. We need to find internal, not external, validation for the work we do. We need the self-confidence of a successful athlete, musician, author, or leader. We need to do what we think is best and right

## EIGHT CHALLENGES

- Let go and move forward.
- Use what we have.
- Develop new models and theories that push us forward.
- Align more of what we do with external stakeholders.
- Do better succession planning in our own profession.
- Have a strong voice in legislative affairs through professional associations.
- Find new delivery channels for our work.
- Keep the "human" in human resources.

## SEVEN INDICATORS OF PROGRESS

- The HR profession has made progress and continues to make progress.
- We have begun to bridge some gaps that have existed (academic vs. practitioner, doable vs. deliverable, strategic vs. operational, individual vs. organizational, compassion vs. competitiveness, past vs. future).
- We have the attention and resources to do what is necessary.
- We have pockets of exceptional innovation.
- We have become good at building companies with work environments, cultures, or identities that go beyond any individual leader or practice.
- We have networked better than ever.
- We have become a field of ethical, concerned, and caring professionals.

because we know it is based on theory, research, and best practice, not looking to or depending on others for validation of what we do.

**RV:** Sounds like you want to counteract what we sometimes see as a functional inferiority complex.

**DU:** Absolutely. Our forward-looking self-confidence must be rooted, however, in value created for others. Our standards should always be to define and deliver exceptional value to employees, customers, and investors. Our self-confidence should come because we strive for the best, because we acknowledge our shortcomings, and because we are committed to learning what is required to make progress.

**RV:**  So internal confidence along with an external-customer-serving focus?

**DU:**  Yes, and by so doing, we create value for others because of our confidence in ourselves. Our purpose should be to have impact, not merely to be heard. When we give up our need for control, we gain influence. When we set high standards, our self-image is one of excellence and competence. When we remove from our lexicon and actions any feelings of being second-class, any vestiges of the HR profession as the dumping ground, and any images of HR as anything less than the best of the breed, we are able to let go, move forward, and have impact.

**RV:**  OK, and the second challenge for the profession?

**DU:**  *We need to use what we have.* The science, research, and best practices are now sufficient for any skilled HR professional to become the ever-lauded partner in running the business. It's there for the taking. Unfortunately, too often those of us in the HR field either don't know and/or don't deploy well-researched findings and practices from the past (e.g., Maslow, Drucker, Argyris) or present (e.g., competency work and its rich and rigorous theory and database). While we need new findings and new science, even more we need solid aligned implementation of what we already know. Too many in the HR profession are blissfully unaware of the classics that never change.

**RV:**  Should we be content with simply mastering what has gone before us?

**DU:**  I'd say that first, we should learn and implement what we already know and probably won't ever change. There is always the need for listening skills to ensure we are picking the right facts. Then, you have earned the right to look for new insights. The problem is that people come into our field and believe we are based solely on common sense when in fact we are based on solid theory and research for over 50 years. Those of us in the profession need to know the research, be advocates for it, and use it in our work. Then, when we extend the body of knowledge, we make even more progress.

**RV:**  And the third challenge for our profession?

**DU:**  *We need new models and theories that push us forward.* This is almost paradoxical to what I just said about using tested research. We need to keep pushing new intellectual agendas at a macro HR profession level, and within each

of the HR practice domains. At the macro level, we have tried to shift a focus from HR practices to organization capabilities as a way to define deliverables from HR. Within the HR practice areas, we need a constant stream of innovation about competencies, recruiting, talent flow, training and development, performance management, communication, organization design, physical facilities, and others. I worry that we are not pushing ourselves hard enough to learn and cumulatively move the profession forward.

**RV:**  One great statement is that there is nothing so applied as a great theory. Models can help explain complex things in a simple way. What do you think about the "HR toolkit" approaches?

**DU:**  Well said. This should be a profession of ideas first, tools second. Great ideas will lead to great tools, but focusing on tools without great ideas may inhibit the full impact of what we can potentially offer. Let's not jump to panaceas, quick fixes, or tools for today's needs, but let us be a font of good ideas that will then lead to new behaviors.

**RV:**  The fourth challenge for the profession is what?

**DU:**  *We need to align more of what we do with external stakeholders.* Some of this has occurred when HR practices are connected to customers and some is occurring when we are connecting our work to investors. More here is necessary. We may still tend to focus too much internally and see what is happening inside a firm versus externally, and seeing how what we do inside adds value outside.

**RV:**  This reminds me of some excellent employee-value-chain and linkage research that shows the connections between leadership talent, employee commitment, customer satisfaction, and financial outcomes. Is that what you had in mind?

**DU:**  Yes. We need to continue the work of value chain management and seeing how our work within a firm connects to desired results outside a firm. We should keep pressing what Norm Smallwood and I call the "so that" query in all that we do. We need to keep asking the "so that" question, for example: benefits *so that…*; action learning *so that…*; physical facilities *so that…*

**RV:**  This reminds me of great advice my major professor, Herb Meyer, gave me 25 years ago: It is not enough to just present data, but you must also answer the "so what" question! I understand the fifth challenge for the profession really strikes close to home.

**DU:**  *We need to do better succession planning for our own profession.* We need a deeper bench for top and near-top positions. Senior HR positions for the overall function or for key roles like chief learning officer go open for too long because the talent pool is not where it should be. The bar is being raised faster than the talent pool is rising. Bench depth also occurs at all HR levels. Building top bench will require a more consistent sense of what leadership in the field looks like. Too often top HR leaders end up as independent cowboys doing their own thing with little consistency or learning across companies. Building top bench will filter throughout the profession.

**RV:** In addition to organizational leaders, don't we also need a continued focus on next-generation thought leaders in the academic world?

**DU:** Absolutely. We need to keep nurturing and investing in the next generation of HR thought leaders. The field has exploded in the past decade in the level of attention and number of ideas. Hopefully, this curve will not flatten, but will continue to grow as the profession attracts some of the best and brightest beginning their careers. We need to make sure that those who are the most talented come our way.

**RV:** When you talk about thought leaders, in what areas do you see the need?

**DU:** Some of these thought leaders will be generalists who are gifted at organizational diagnosis, at amassing resources to solve organizational problems, and at consulting with client line managers to deliver value. Some of these thought leaders will be specialists who develop deep expertise in their chosen topic area, create menus of choices from which leaders make choices for their specific business requirement, and who share knowledge across organizational units. Equally important, the next generation of HR professionals needs to find the whole more than the sum of the parts. Generalists, specialists, and HRIS technicians are on one team, bringing their own unique skills, but collaborating seamlessly to deliver value.

**RV:** Sounds like it is time for more senior people to mentor and grow some more junior people.

**DU:** Yes. Current senior HR leaders need to make a commitment to appear and present on campus to motivate and enlighten students who are selecting careers. Without strong and successful HR role models, the top students will select other majors. Even more, we need to create professional career paths where we can attract the best and brightest. We need HR to be a career of first choice for the very best. We want to build a profession where our children would be proud to work because of the challenges, opportunities, and relationships. This means serious attention to the next generation. Those of us who are more senior in the profession have the obligation of preparing a new generation who is more qualified,

more insightful, and more able to do the work of the future. I fear we are not investing enough in our own profession and that our pipeline is not full enough.

**RV:** I have to mention that The Human Resource Planning Society is largely made up of senior and strategic HR professionals and we have recently made networking down deeper a clear priority. Moving on, what is the sixth challenge for HR?

**DU:** *We need to have a strong voice in legislative affairs through professional associations.* Examples include HRPS, SIOP, SHRM, ASTD, and World at Work. Collectively the HR professionals in these associations represent millions of employees and should have a position on policies and legislation that affect all aspects of employee work life. And this legislation becomes less ethnocentric within one country because in our global village what goes on in one country affects and is affected by others. We need to have a collective voice on employee rights, organizational requirements, managerial ethics, and management processes. We need to find ways to build alliances across government, industry, and academia where each serves the other and helps the other succeed. We need to have a collective point of view on targeted issues that have profound impact on employees.

**RV:** OK, and the seventh challenge?

**DU:** *We need to find new delivery channels for our work.* Examples include web-based HR, employee and manager self-reliance, and outsourcing. Rather than fighting and quibbling about how this does or does not work or how "my program is better than your program," we need to see new approaches as experiments and learn from both successes and failures. There are many innovative and creative ways to deliver HR work being tried. Not all will work. But all should be sources of insight and progress.

**RV:** And the final challenge for our profession?

**DU:** *We need to keep the "human" in human resources.* Our legacy of "human" resources is a good one. We cannot always make organizations safe for people, so in some ways we have to make people safe from companies. We need to be the employee advocate, sponsor, and champion through the policies we create.

**RV:** There is a razor's edge here. Don't we also have to keep the interests of the organization at heart?

**DU:** Yes, but in so doing, we have to balance the paradox of being both compassionate and competitive, of caring about people and about profits, of creating a great place to work and a great place to invest. We should identify and face these paradoxes. The best way to serve the employees is to serve the business. Failed businesses are not employee-friendly. We have learned recently that business and integrity should not be an oxymoron, but go together. If we don't build ethics and integrity into the "human" side of the enterprise, businesses flail and flounder. As HR professionals, we should not only stand for, but also represent and advocate actively a moral code. We cannot legislate integrity and we cannot remove agency from business leaders who act in self-interests, but HR professionals can and should identify and confront ethical abuses that will ultimately impair organization success.

**RV:** Great advice for this time in the history of business! Dave, you have just summarized eight challenges for our profession. I understand you have also thought through seven indicators of positive progress, and your prognosis is really good for our profession.

**DU:** Yes. These challenges are great… but the profession is poised to respond. I have enormous confidence in the present and future state of the profession because of the things we have available to us. So my first statement would be simply that *the HR profession has made progress and continues to make progress.* Daily progress is almost invisible, but quarterly, annual, and decade-long annual progress does show up. The topics of discussion have evolved in the last decade. We now talk about business issues more than programs; about value and impact and measurement more than activities; about the external impact of HR on shareholders and customers, not just the internal impact; about how to define the purpose of change, not just facilitate change process; about being players, not just partners; and about the seriousness of ethics in a business setting. Progress is steady.

**RV:** Can you think of some examples that illustrate this progress?

**DU:** If we looked at the table of contents of our journals and the content of professional conferences, we would find a shift that while subtle in the short term is significant in the long term. We don't come to a conference merely to be entertained, but to master concepts that matter and to leave not just feeling good, but being able to do good by implementing new ideas. Think back to what you were doing 5, 10, 15, and even 20 years ago. What is different? What are your new vocabulary words, ideas, tools, and practices? Again, we are making progress. We are leaving the shadow of our legacy that confines us to administrative and procedural concerns and finding new opportunities in business, organization, and employee challenges.

**RV:** Do you have any suggestions for us in claiming this progress?

**DU:** Clearly, and sadly, some CEOs and business leaders still see an old HR focused on administrative programs or use HR to further their self-interest. So, while we are making progress, we need to continue to push forward harder and faster than ever.

**RV:** OK, and what is the second indicator of progress in the profession?

**DU:** *We have begun to bridge some gaps that have existed.* Too often we deal with either/or dilemmas and we are now beginning to bridge such paradoxes with an "and/ also" game. Let me give several examples:

- *Between academia and practice.* The best theoretical work is being done in the field and the best field work is being driven by good theory. "Ideas with impact" bridge the gap between what we know and what we do. For example, the "theory" of culture change has now been translated into actions for culture change in many organizations.
- *Between doable and deliverable.* We are beginning to see the impact of what we do. Our programs, practices, and HR activities have an impact on customers, investors, and employees. We are now beginning to bridge the gap of doing and delivering. HR outcomes are being defined in business terms and acted on in daily ways.
- *Between strategic and operational.* We have debated the shift "from" operational "to" strategic for years. Now we are learning to be strategic in operational ways and putting day-to-day operations into a strategic context.
- *Between individual and organization.* We are learning that we have to serve both the individual and the organization for both to win. The relationship between competencies for individuals and capabilities for organizations is being made by innovative work on both dimensions.
- *Between compassion and competitiveness.* We don't just care about people; we care about helping people be successful. We sometimes make fun of ourselves by saying we go into HR because we like people. While sometimes a bit of self-deprecating humor is appropriate, the fact is that many of us have entered the HR profession because we do have an underlying care and concern for people. We need to recognize, however, that competitiveness and compassion are not opposite sides of an issue, but can be combined into the same issue.
- *Between past and future.* We need to learn from, rely on, and honor our past, but we are more able now to focus on problems, opportunities, and challenges in our future. We can honor our

HR heritage while focusing on moving on for the future.

**RV:** Dave, great list of the paradoxes we are learning to handle. What you are saying is striking home with me, having just been directly involved with the HP-Compaq merger. It strikes me that during times of great change, like large-scale mergers or acquisitions, then all assumptions are open to question and some of these paradoxes become even more apparent. Can you say more about this issue of dealing with paradox in a far more complex and ambiguous world?

**DU:** Certainly, and yes, when the environment is "disrupted" for any reason, then many of these gaps that had been smoothed over become apparent and need to be worked again. Examples of other gaps include: global versus local, specialist versus generalist, policeman versus partner, employee self-sufficiency versus HR service provider. We are more able to live in the inevitable world of duality and paradox when we can handle simultaneously two or more issues and find ways to resolve them. Think of the paradoxes you confront in the next few days, weeks, and months. Now, instead of taking an advocacy position for one dimension of the paradox (e.g., advocating for employee rights, diversity programs, or HR budgets), we are more able to bridge what we advocate to what needs to be done, e.g., employee rights so we can retain talented employees, diversity programs so we innovate faster than a competitor, HR resources so we build customer and investor value.

**RV:** So, Dave, what is the third indicator of progress in the profession?

**DU:** _We have the attention and resources to do what is necessary._ We matter, not just to ourselves, but also to employees, line managers, customers, and investors. As business conditions shift, our work becomes ever more central. We don't need to spend energy justifying, but delivering. And, with perceived value, we have resources like money to invest in innovation, time to make things happen, management attention to do what we need to do. As the administrative legacy of our profession becomes delivered through technology, service centers, outsourcing, and employee self-reliance, then we open up vast new vistas for HR and are having our time freed up. This enables us to focus on building capabilities that add value.

**RV:** This sounds like it relates to busting the "HR inferiority complex" you discussed earlier, and HR's ability to get the resources needed to make an impact.

**DU:** Rich, I really believe that financial resources will not be the constraint in our new roles. The constraint will be the quality of ideas we bring to bear on business problems. If and when we solve real problems in real ways, we

will find access and opportunity. Our fight is not for money, but for ideas that will have impact. We must not fall into the trap of finding value in how smart we sound, but in the results we deliver.

**RV:** I think your fourth indicator of progress in our profession is my favorite. Could you speak to it?

**DU:** _We have pockets of exceptional innovation._ With bright folks in the profession, dozens of new and innovative ideas are being tried in known and visible companies and in unknown and less-visible companies. Innovation is occurring throughout our profession. We have innovation in defining HR accountabilities and the competencies and requirements for people, innovation in how to design and deliver training programs with impact, innovation in team-based incentives, innovation in shaping culture through external realities, innovation in engaging employees, innovation in defining and building a leadership brand, innovation in making change happen fast, innovation in learning, innovation in high-performing teams, innovation in linking strategy to HR practices through capabilities. We are a profession realizing the richness of innovation of both ideas and practices.

**RV:** That really is an exciting list of innovations. What do you see as the fifth indicator of progress in the profession?

**DU:** _We have become good at building companies with work environments, cultures, or identities that go beyond any individual leader or practice._ These efforts help make organizations better places for individuals to develop their talents and skills and to find meaning in their work. We have changed policies where employees are used and misused by the company to where employees are assets that must be nourished and developed. One of my friends had a father who was a miner. He suffered physically because of the working conditions, leading to premature death. Because of the work we have done, these cases of employee abuse are fewer and far between. As a profession we have made the workplace a better place. And, the cultures we have helped create go beyond any one individual.

**RV:** Classic case of working up the Maslow hierarchy from basic food, shelter, and safety all the way to self-actualization! And the next indicator of progress in our profession?

**DU:** _We have networked better than ever._ We are more willing to share than hoard ideas, putting the profession ahead of personal interest. Think about your own network of professional colleagues. These are people you know, can contact, and are willing to share ideas with, both as giver and receiver. These communities of practice within the profession make us stronger. The HR federation we create across organization and industry boundaries enable us to share and to learn. Learning becomes a standard for the profession and the formal and informal networks we create then enable such learning to occur. This learning becomes an enduring value of conferences when we can renew relationships.

**RV:** I understand that your final indicator of progress in our profession really strikes at the heart of current concerns in business.

**DU:** *We have become a field of ethical, concerned, and caring professionals.* We are a profession that gives back through service to each other. The willingness to serve creates an ethos that underlies this profession. This is a field I would be proud for my son or daughters to work in… people care about people and are kind. I have had a few minor health problems in the last year and clients where I was focused on HR inevitably put health before profit. It is nice to be in a field and profession where we can look around and see people we like and care about. I think about the group of people who may read this interview and I have enormous confidence that good people will eventually produce good services. The goodwill in this profession is high. The affect for each other is legitimate and positive. We want to help others succeed. In the long run, such warmth creates energy that produces results that matter most.

**RV:** It really sounds that as a profession we are "growing up." Do you have any final words for us? And can you share what you will be doing on your sabbatical?

**DU:** What I propose is only my view. I am sure others would have different lists of opportunities and challenges for the profession. But, I would like to emphasize that I see the profession as healthy… intellectually, emotionally, and socially. It is a privilege to have been a small part over the last 20 years of a noble profession. Wendy, my wife, and I have been asked to do a three-year missionary assignment (until July 2005) for the Church of Jesus Christ of Latter-Day Saints in Quebec and Ottawa. In this assignment, we will have our opportunity to give back and our challenge to put into practice our beliefs. Over the next three years, we will work with about 500 missionaries (mostly age 19–25) and thousands of church members in the area helping them strengthen their faith in God and commitment to serve humanity. This will also be a time for reflection and renewal for us. At the end of the assignment, I envision returning to my professional home in HR and reengaging with both people and ideas that mean so much to me.

**RV:** Thank you, Dave, for sharing these thoughts with us. We will miss you during your sabbatical, but a more well-deserved one I cannot imagine. Best wishes from HRPS.

---

From *Human Resource Planning Journal,* Vol. 26, Issue 1, 2003, pp. 18-22. © 2003 by Human Resource Planning.

# What is an employee? The answer depends on the Federal law

*In a legal context, the classification of a worker as either an employee or an independent contractor can have significant consequences*

Charles J. Muhl

In the American workplace today, a full-time, 40-hour-a-week employee who stays with the same employer performing the same job over the course of an entire worklife would be viewed as a rarity, or at least as a person found in lesser proportion in the U.S. workforce than in decades past. Today's workplace includes a variety of workers in contingent arrangements—independent contractors, leased employees, temporary employees, on-call workers, and more—perceived to be a result of employers' desire to reduce labor costs and employees' desire to increase their flexibility, among other things. The Bureau of Labor Statistics recently reported that in February 2001 the contingent workforce, or those workers who do not have an implicit or explicit contract for ongoing employment and who do not expect their current job to last, totaled 5.4 million people, roughly 4 percent of the U.S. workforce.[1] According to the BLS survey, millions more were employed in alternative work arrangements:[2] 8.6 million independent contractors (representing 6.4 percent of total employment), 2.1 million on-call workers, 1.2 million temporary help agency workers, and 633,000 contract company workers. The Bureau treats these contingent workers and workers in alternative work arrangements as part of total U.S. employment, and although they are in a typical employment situation, most of the general public would probably consider them employees.

But how does Federal law treat workers in contingent and alternative work arrangements? That is, are such workers viewed as employees who are entitled to legal protections under Federal legislation? As is frequently the case with legal questions, the answer depends—in this case, on the Federal law at issue. In general, though, courts evaluate the totality of the circumstances surrounding a worker's employment, with a focus on who has the right—the employer or the employee—to control the work process.

The question "Is a worker an employee?" may seem like a simple one to answer on its surface. The dictionary definition of "employee" says succinctly that an employee is "a person who works for another in return for financial or other compensation."[3] Under that definition, independent contractors would appear to be employees. However, the legal definition of "employee" is concerned with more than the pay received by a worker for services provided. *Black's Law Dictionary* defines "employee" as "a person in the service of another under any contract of hire, express or implied, oral or written, where the employer has the power or right to control and direct the employee in the material details of how the work is to be performed."[4] In contrast, an "independent contractor" is one who, "in the exercise of an independent employment, contracts to do a piece of work according to his own methods and is subject to his employer's control only as to the end product or final result of his work."[5] This legal distinction as to how a worker must be classified has broad implications—and potentially negative consequences for mischaracterization—for both employers and workers alike.

This article examines how the legal determination is made that a worker is either an employee or an independent contractor, beginning with a discussion of why the determination is important and then discussing the tests used by courts to make the determination and the laws pursuant to which each test applies.

## Employee or independent contractor?

Employers have used independent contractors and other contingent workers more frequently in recent times for a variety of reasons, including reducing the costs associated with salaries, benefits, and employment taxes and increasing the flexibility of the workforce.[6] Under U.S. law, employers are required to pay the employer's share, and withhold the worker's share, of employment taxes for employees, but not for independent contractors. Employment taxes include those collected pursuant to the

Federal Insurance Contributions Act (FICA)[7] for the U.S. Social Security system; those collected pursuant to the Federal Unemployment Tax Act (FUTA),[8] which pays unemployment benefits to displaced workers; and income tax withholding.[9]

U.S. law imposes other obligations on employers with respect to employees that are not imposed on independent contractors.[10] The Fair Labor Standards Act (FLSA)[11] requires employers to meet minimum-wage and overtime obligations toward their employees. Title VII of the Civil Rights Act of 1964[12] prohibits employers from discriminating against their employees on the basis of race, color, religion, sex, or national origin, while the Age Discrimination in Employment Act (ADEA)[13] prohibits employers from discriminating against employees on the basis of their age. The Employment Retirement Security Act (ERISA)[14] sets the parameters of qualified employee benefit plans, including the level of benefits and amount of service required for vesting of those benefits, typically in the context of retirement. The Americans with Disabilities Act (ADA)[15] prohibits employers from discriminating against qualified individuals who have disabilities. The Family and Medical Leave Act (FMLA)[16] requires employers to provide eligible employees with up to 12 weeks of unpaid leave per year when those employees are faced with certain critical life situations. The National Labor Relations Act (NLRA)[17] grants employees the right to organize and governs labor-management relations.

Clearly, then, some incentive exists for employers to classify their workers as independent contractors rather than employees, in order to reduce costs and various legal obligations. However, the failure of an employer to make the proper determination as to whether workers are employees or independent contractors can have dire consequences. Employers who are careless in their labeling of workers as independent contractors risk exposure to substantial liability in the future under Federal law if the workers are mischaracterized. The U.S. Government—in particular, the Internal Revenue Service (IRS)—can seek to recover back taxes and other contributions that should have been paid by the employer on the employee's behalf,[18] and the workers themselves can seek compensation for job benefits that the employer denied them on the basis of their supposed status as independent contractors.

One of the most striking examples of the danger of mischaracterizing workers as independent contractors rather than employees occurred in *Vizcaino* v. *Microsoft*,[19] a case in which the U.S. Court of Appeals for the Ninth Circuit held that a class of workers for the leading U.S. computer software company were employees who were entitled to participate in Microsoft's various pension and welfare plans, despite the fact that the workers had signed an agreement that labeled them as independent contractors.

Prior to 1990, Microsoft hired "freelancers" to perform various services for the company over a continuous period, in some cases extending in excess of 2 years. Upon joining Microsoft, the former freelancers executed agreements which specifically stated that they were independent contractors and not employees and that nothing contained in the agreement would be construed to create an employer-employee relationship. Despite the agreements, the workers were fully integrated into

Microsoft's workforce, working under nearly identical circumstances as Microsoft's regular employees. The erstwhile freelancers worked the same core hours at the same location and shared the same supervisors as regular employees. The only distinction between the freelancers and regular employees was that the freelancers were hired for specific projects. Microsoft neither paid the employer's share, nor withheld the worker's share, of FICA taxes and did not allow the workers to participate in the company's pension plans, on the basis of the agreements the workers had signed stating that they were independent contractors.

The IRS investigated Microsoft and determined that the workers were employees, not independent contractors, and that Microsoft should have been withholding taxes for them.[20] Accepting the IRS' determination, Microsoft conferred employee status on certain of the workers, but dismissed others from employment. Those who were dismissed then filed a class-action suit seeking to have the court declare that they were eligible to participate in Microsoft's pension plans. The district court determined that the workers were employees, not independent contractors.[21] On appeal, Microsoft conceded that the workers were employees, but argued (1) that they had waived their right to participate in the company's pension plans by executing the agreements which specifically stated that they were independent contractors and not employees and (2) that nothing contained in the agreement could be construed to create an employer-employee relationship. The court of appeals rejected Microsoft's argument, finding that the company's pension plan administrator had acted arbitrarily and capriciously in denying the workers' claim that they were entitled to participate in the pension plans. The court found that the administrator should have focused on the actual circumstances surrounding the freelancers' employment and not the labeling of the workers by the agreements. In December 2000, Microsoft settled the case for $97 million.

There are circumstances in which the classification of a worker as an independent contractor is detrimental to employers and beneficial to workers. When the services being performed result in a copyrightable work, employers may wish to establish that a worker is an employee in order to obtain authorship of the copyright. The U.S. Supreme Court, in *Community for Creative Non-Violence, et al.* v. *Reid*,[22] held that an employer is the owner of a copyright if the employer had contracted for a creative "work for hire"—that is, if work prepared by an employee is within the scope of employment. If the worker is an independent contractor, the worker, and not the employer, is the owner of the copyright for the work performed. Thus, in the context of intellectual property rights, employers are protected by establishing an employer-employee relationship with a worker.

## Determining a worker's status

The potential benefits to both employers and workers of the proper characterization of the working relationship raises the question, How is the legal determination made as to whether a worker is an employee or an independent contractor? Generally,

## Exhibit 1.  Tests for determining whether a worker is an employee

| Test | Description | Laws under which test has been applied by courts |
|---|---|---|
| Common-law test (used by Internal Revenue Service (IRS)) | Employment relationship exists if employer has right to control work process, as determined by evaluating totality of the circumstances and specific factors | Federal Insurance Contributions Act<br>Federal Unemployment Tax Act<br>Income tax withholding<br>Employment Retirement and Income Security Act<br>National Labor Relations Act<br>Immigration Reform and Control Act (IRS test) |
| Economic realities test | Employment relationship exists if individual is economically dependent on a business for continued employment | Fair Labor Standards Act<br>Title VII<br>Age Discrimination in Employment Act<br>Americans with Disabilities Act<br>Family and Medical Leave Act (likely to apply) |
| Hybrid test | Employment relationship is evaluated under both common-law and economic reality test factors, with a focus on who has the right to control the means and manner of a worker's performance | Title VII<br>Age Discrimination in Employment Act<br>Americans with Disabilities Act |

the totality of the circumstances—that is, all the conditions under which a person is working—governs the characterization of that person as an employee or an independent contractor; the label a company places on the worker has no bearing on the matter. Again generally, a person is an employee if the employer has the right to control the person's work process, whereas a worker is classified as an independent contractor if the employer does not control the process, but dictates only the end result or product of the work. Note that the employer does not actually have to control the work process: the mere *ability* of the employer to take control is sufficient to create an employer-employee relationship.

The courts have developed three tests to be used in determining a worker's status: the common-law test, the economic realities test, and a hybrid test that incorporates various elements of both of those tests. Because the tests have been applied to different Federal statutes, the characterization of a worker as an employee or an independent contractor can vary, depending on which statute is being applied. As a result, the same person can be classified as an employee under one test and the relevant Federal laws to which that test is applied, but as an independent contractor under another test and its relevant Federal laws. Furthermore, different tests are applied to the same Federal law, depending on which jurisdiction a case is heard in. However, because each of the tests evaluates the totality of the circumstances behind the employment relationship, the overlap in the tests is substantial. Exhibit 1 offers a brief summary or the three tests.

*Common-law test.* The common-law test was developed on the basis of the traditional legal concept of agency, which, in an em-

ployment context, consists of a relationship wherein one person (the employee) acts for or represents another (the employer) by the employer's authority.[23] The common-law test involves the evaluation of 10 factors to determine whether a worker is an employee, with no one factor dispositive, but with the determination centering on who has the right to control the work process. Exhibit 2 shows the 10 factors used in the common-law test.

The IRS uses a derivation of the common-law test in assessing whether a worker is an employee, taking into account some of the common-law test's factors as part of the IRS's own 20-factor test.[24] In addition to evaluating employment tax obligations under the Federal income tax law, FICA, and FUTA, the common-law/IRS test has been applied to the National Labor Relations Act, which governs labor-management relations and collective bargaining for unionized employers, and to the Immigration Reform and Control Act. Furthermore, in *NationWide Mutual Insurance Co.* v. *Darden*,[25] the U.S. Supreme Court ruled that, for Federal laws that do not contain a clear definition of "employee," the relationship between employer and worker should be evaluated on the basis of the common-law test, focusing on who had the right to control the worker.

In a vast number of cases throughout the U.S. Federal court system, some going back several decades, the common-law test has been applied to determine whether workers are employees or contractors. For example, in *Walker* v. *Altmeyer*,[26] decided in 1943, the U.S. Court of Appeals for the Second Circuit found that an attorney who was given office space at $100 per month in return for services performed was an employee pursuant to the Social Security Act, because his landlord, another attorney, had the right to control what the worker did and to supervise the

| **Exhibit 2. Factors used to determine a worker's status under the common-law test** | | |
|---|---|---|
| **Factor** | **Worker is an employee if—** | **Worker is an independent contractor if—** |
| Right to control | Employer controls details of the work | Worker controls details of the work |
| Type of business | Worker is not engaged in business or occupation distinct from employer's | Worker operates in business that is distinct from employer's business |
| Supervision | Employer supervises worker | Work is done without supervision |
| Skill level | Skill level need not be high or unique | Skill level is specialized, is unique, or requires substantial training |
| Tools and materials | Employer provides instrumentalities, tools, and location of workplace | Worker provides instrumentalities and tools of workplace and works at a site other than the employer's |
| Continuing relationship | Worker is employed for extended, continuous period | Worker is employed for specific project or for limited time |
| Method of payment | Worker is paid by the hour, or other computation based on time worked is used to determine pay | Worker is paid by the project |
| Integration | Work is part of employer's regular business | Work is not part of employer's regular business |
| Intent | Employer and worker intend to create an employer-employee relationship | Employer and worker do not intend to create an employer-employee relationship |
| Employment by more than one firm | Worker provides services only to one employer | Worker provides services to more than one business |

method used to complete the work. John E. Walker rented office space from another attorney, Pliny Williamson, beginning in 1927 and was also hired by Williamson to perform legal services for a fixed monthly salary. In April 1938, the two attorneys established a new compensation arrangement under which Walker would pay his rent by providing legal services and would receive additional compensation when his services were valued at more than $100 per month. Upon reaching the age of 65 in 1938, Walker applied for Social Security benefits, including monthly insurance benefits, under the Social Security Act. Although the Social Security Administration initially paid Walker the insurance benefits on the basis of his representation that he was not an employee making more than $15 per month, the Agency subsequently ceased payments upon learning of Walker's arrangement with Williamson. The court found Walker to be an employee because, despite the change in the manner of compensation beginning in 1938, the kind of work that Walker did for Williamson did not change at all. Walker still performed work as an attorney at the direction of Williamson. That right to control was dispositive for the court.

Similarly, in *United States v. Polk*,[27] the U.S. Court of Appeals for the Ninth Circuit found that an employer could be convicted of a criminal offense for failure to pay FICA employment taxes, despite the employer's declaration that its workers were all subcontractors. Polk was notified by an IRS agent that he was required to establish a separate bank account to be used to deposit employees' tax withholdings. Prior to receiving this notice, Polk paid his workers on an hourly or weekly basis, had

them work fixed hours, supervised the workers, and supplied them with the tools and materials necessary to perform their work. Furthermore, with the exception of one individual, all of the workers worked exclusively for Polk. These conditions did not change after the IRS served Polk with notice that his workers were employees, but thereafter, Polk represented to the IRS that he no longer had employees and employed only subcontractors. Polk was convicted of a criminal offense for failure to withhold wages to pay FICA taxes. The appeals court sustained Polk's conviction, finding that the jury had properly considered, under the common-law test, the totality of the circumstances of the working relationship between Polk and his workers and also had properly focused on Polk's right to control the workers, both with respect to the product of the work and the means by which the product was produced.

To summarize, then, under the common-law test, an employee is a worker whose work process and work product are controlled by the employer. In determining who has the right to control in a particular case, courts look to such factors as supervision, skill level, method of payment, whether the relationship is ongoing, who supplies the tools and materials for the work, whether the relationship between the worker and the employer is exclusive, and the parties' intent, as well as other, related factors.

*Economic realities test.* The economic realities test, which is most significantly applied in the context of the Fair Labor Standards Act[28] governing minimum-wage and overtime obligations, focuses on the economic relationship between the worker

17

## Exhibit 3. Factors used to determine a worker's status under the economic realities test

| Factor | Worker is an employee if— | Worker is an independent contractor if— |
|---|---|---|
| Integration | Worker provides services that are a part of the employer's regular business | Worker provides services outside the regular business of the employer |
| Investment in facilities | Worker has no investment in the work facilities and equipment | Worker has a substantial investment in the work facilities and equipment |
| Right to control | Management retains a certain type and degree of control over the work | Management has no right to control the work process of the worker |
| Risk | Worker does not have the opportunity to make a profit or incur a loss | Worker has the opportunity to make a profit or incur a loss from the job |
| Skill | Work does not require any special or unique skills or judgment | Work requires a special skill, judgment, or initiative |
| Continuing relationship | Worker has a permanent or extended relationship with the business | Work relationship is for one project or a limited duration |

and the employer. A worker is an employee under the test if the worker is economically dependent upon the employer for continued employment. The test examines the nature of the relationship in light of the fact that independent contractors would typically not rely on a sole employer for continued employment at any one time, but would work for, and be compensated by, many different employers, whereas most employees hold a single job and rely on that one employer for continued employment and for their primary source of income. The economic reality test is generally applied to laws whose purpose is to protect or benefit a worker, because courts view the protection of a worker who is financially dependent on a particular employer as important.[29] Because of its broader scope, the economic reality test has a greater likelihood of finding workers to be employees than does the common-law test. Accordingly, a worker could be classified as an employee for the purposes of dealing with one Federal law, such as the Fair Labor Standards Act, but as an independent contractor under another, like FICA. In evaluating whether a worker is an employee under the economic realities test, courts look to the factors listed in exhibit 3, some of which are similar to those considered under the common-law test.

In *Donovan* v. *DialAmerica Marketing, Inc.*,[30] the Third Circuit Court of Appeals demonstrated the precise application of the economic realities test, as well as the different results that can be reached regarding workers of the same corporation, even when just one legal test is applied. DialAmerica's principal business was the sale of magazine renewal subscriptions by telephone to persons whose subscriptions had expired or were nearing expiration. In pursuit of renewing subscriptions, the company hired workers to locate subscribers' phone numbers by looking names up in telephone books and calling directory assistance operators. In certain years, DialAmerica operated a program in which these workers were permitted to work from their homes. When they were hired, DialAmerica made the workers, called "home researchers," sign an "independent contractor's agreement" that supposedly established their status as

independent contractors. A worker would be given a box of 500 cards with names to be researched, and the company expected the cards to be returned within 1 week. The home researchers were free to choose the weeks and hours they worked; DialAmerica had little supervision over the workers, but placed certain conditions on how the work process was to be conducted, including stipulating the method for reporting back the results on each card and the ink to be used when doing so. DialAmerica also employed workers as "distributors," persons who gave the cards with names to the home researchers. The Department of Labor sued DialAmerica for paying the home researchers and distributors less than the minimum wage for the work they did, arguing that they were employees under the Fair Labor Standards Act.

The court of appeals ruled that, under the economic realities test, the home researchers were employees. First, the court found that the workers did not make a great investment in their work, they had little opportunity for profit or loss, and the work required little skill. Second, the court ruled that DialAmerica's lack of control over the manner in which the home researchers did their work did not support a finding that they were independent contractors, because the very nature of home work dictated that the times worked would be determined by the workers and they would be subjected to very little supervision when working. The fact that a person works from home does not, on its own, determine whether the person is an employee under the Fair Labor Standards Act, the court said. Third, the court found that the home researchers had a continuous working relationship with DialAmerica under which they did not work for other employers. Finally, the court held that the home researchers were an integral part of DialAmerica's business because they did the very work—locating phone numbers—that was essential to DialAmerica's ability to renew subscriptions, despite the fact that they located only approximately 4 percent to 5 percent of the number of phone numbers the company sought to be retrieved. After analyzing these factors, the court ruled that the home researchers were economically dependent on Dial-America for continued employment and, therefore, were employees under the economic realities test.

In contrast, the appellate court held that the distributors of the research work were independent contractors under the Fair Labor Standards Act. The court found that DialAmerica exhibited minimal control over the distributors' work providing cards to the home researchers, because the distributors maintained records of the work and were permitted to recruit home researchers. The court also noted that the distributors risked financial loss if they did not manage the distribution network properly, because their transportation expenses could exceed their revenue. The transportation expenses also required the distributors to make an investment in the business, the court found. Finally, the distributors required somewhat specialized managerial skills in operating the distribution network, according to the court. Although the distributors were typically employed for a long period, the Court found that factor insufficient to overcome the weight of the remaining circumstances indicating that the distributors were independent contractors.

In *Brock* v. *Superior Care, Inc.*,[31] the U.S. Court of Appeals for the Second Circuit found that an employer had violated the Fair Labor Standard Act's overtime-pay protections by not paying overtime to nurses who were employees under the Act. Superior Care referred nurses for temporary assignments to hospitals, nursing homes, and individual patients. The company would assign nurses as work opportunities became available, and the nurses were free to refuse an assignment for any reason. If a nurse accepted an assignment, the nurse reported directly to the patient, and Superior Care provided minimal supervision through visits to job sites approximately once or twice a month. Patients contracted directly with Superior Care, which paid them an hourly wage. The nurses could hold other jobs, including jobs with other health care providers.

The court found that the nurses were employees under the economic realities test. As a preliminary matter, the court rejected the company's contention that the trial court had used evidence outside of the six factors that make up the test. Superior Care had two sets of payrolls, one for taxed employees and one for nontaxed employees, despite the fact that the nurses on both payrolls did exactly the same work. The workers on the nontaxed payroll did not receive overtime pay for their work. The trial court relied in part on that evidence in finding that those workers were not independent contractors. The appeals court noted that the factors of the economic reality test are not exclusive and that *any* relevant evidence can be considered as part of the totality of the circumstances surrounding the employment relationship. The court also stated that an employer's "self-serving" labeling of workers as independent contractors is not controlling. Turning to the application of the economic reality factors, the court found that (1) the nurses had no opportunity for profit or loss, because Superior Care set their wages and prohibited them from entering into privately paying contracts with patients, (2) the nursing services that were provided were the most integral part of Superior Cafe's business of providing health care personnel on request, and (3) despite a quantitatively calculated lack of visits by Superior Care supervisors, the com-

pany retained the right to supervise the nurses and exerted control over them in that regard. Although the nurses obviously were skilled workers and also had the opportunity to work for other health care employers besides Superior Care, the court found those factors nondispositive. According to the court, the weight of the evidence indicated that when all the circumstances of the employment relationship were considered, the nurses were employees and not independent contractors.

In *Brock* v. *Mr. W Fireworks, Inc.*,[32] the Court of Appeals for the Fifth Circuit found that operators of fireworks stands in south Texas were employees under the economic realities test, subject to the protections of the Fair Labor Standards Act, because (1) Mr. W controlled the method of selling fireworks and made a substantial investment in the business operations, (2) the operators lacked skill and independent initiative, and (3) the duration of the employment relationship was lengthy. According to the parties' testimony, Mr. W acquired land for fireworks stands, procured materials to build the stands, hired workers to construct the stands at its warehouse, recruited operators to run the stands during the two short periods in each year that Texas permits the sale of fireworks, employed workers to supply the stands with fireworks, and advertised the sale of fireworks through the stands. Mr. W paid the operators of the stands on a commission basis.

The appeals court rejected the trial court's finding that the operators were independent contractors, ruling that Mr. W exerted control over the operators by determining the location and size of the stands, by suggesting the retail price of the fireworks and preprinting price tags, by requiring operators to attend to the stands for 24 hours a day to avoid the loss of inventory, by providing display instructions that were almost uniformly followed by the operators, by supplying a substantial portion of advertising, and by determining how the operators would be paid. The court also found that the operators had little opportunity to determine their own profit or loss, because the commission for the sale of the fireworks was set by Mr. W; that the operators made little or no investment in the operation of the stands, whose construction was always financed by Mr. W; and that the operators, while good salespersons, did not exhibit a degree of independent skill or initiative sufficient to conclude that they were independent contractors. Finally, the fact that the fireworks stands were seasonal was simply an operational characteristic unique to the particular business, and the permanency of an employment relationship could accordingly be determined by whether the operators worked for the entire operative period of a particular season. Because the operators were economically dependent on Mr. W for their continued employment as sellers of fireworks, the operators were deemed employees under the economic realities test, entitled to the protections of the Fair Labor Standards Act.

In conclusion, the economic realities test, while similar to the common-law test, focuses on the ultimate concern of whether the economic reality, as illuminated by several factors, is that a worker depends on someone else's business for his or her continued employment, in which case the worker is an employee. If a worker operates an independent business, the worker is classified as an independent contractor under the economic realities test.

*Hybrid test.* The hybrid test combines elements of the common-law test and the economic realities test, in keeping with the accepted view of all courts that the totality of the circumstances surrounding the relationship between worker and employer should be examined to determine whether the worker is an employee or an independent contractor. In practice, the hybrid test considers the economic realities of the work relationship as a critical factor in the determination, but focuses on the employer's right to control the work process as a determinative factor.

The hybrid test is applied frequently in cases brought under Title VII of the Civil Rights Act of 1964, which prohibits employers from discriminating against employees on the basis of race, color, religion, sex, or national origin. For example, in *Diggs* v. *Harris Hospital—Methodist, Inc.,*[33] the U.S. Court of Appeals for the Fifth Circuit held that Jacqulyn Diggs, a black female physician, could not sustain a claim under Title VII for discrimination on the basis of race or sex or in retaliation for a prior charge of discrimination against the hospital. The court found that, although she was appointed to the hospital's provisional medical staff and enjoyed the privileges associated with that appointment, including the ability to treat patients through hospital facilities, Diggs was an independent contractor, not an employee, of the hospital under the hybrid test.

Noting first that the hybrid test takes into account both the economic realities of the working relationship and the extent to which the employer is able to control the details and means of the work being done, the court then specified additional factors to be considered under the test. Certain of those factors, including supervision, skill level, method of payment, who supplies the tools and materials, the duration of the employment relationship, the extent to which the work is integrated into the employer's business, and the intention of the parties, are considered under both the common-law test and the economic realities test. Beyond these factors, the court also considered the manner in which the work relationship was terminated (that is, by one or both parties and with or without notice or explanation), whether annual leave was provided to the workers, whether retirement benefits were provided to them, and whether the employer paid Social Security taxes for the workers.

In concluding that Diggs was not an employee, the court found that physicians' privileges at Harris Hospital were not necessary to Diggs' practice; that is, if Diggs were denied those privileges, her ability to obtain them at other area hospitals would not have been restricted. Focusing on the control factor, the court also found that, although the hospital both supplied the tools and materials to make it possible for Diggs to provide medical care and imposed standards of care upon those with privileges, the hospital did not, in fact, direct the manner or means by which medical care was to be provided by the physician. Diggs treated patients without direct supervision and merely required the presence of a sponsor during surgical procedures to attest to the physician's qualifications. Furthermore, the hospital did not pay a salary to Diggs, nor did it pay her li-censing fees, professional dues, insurance premiums, taxes, or retirement benefits. These considerations cemented the court's conclusion that Diggs was an independent contractor who was not protected by Title VII.

The hybrid test seeks to combine the general and specific factors of both the common-law test and the economic realities test, recognizing that, in each legal determination of whether a worker is an employee or an independent contractor, a court may consider each and every circumstance of the employment relationship.

THE PROPER CLASSIFICATION OF A WORKER as an employee or independent contractor at the beginning of an employment relationship is important to both employers and workers with respect to their obligations and protections under Federal law. Although the classification does depend on the Federal law being applied, the overriding factor is who has the "right to control" the work process, and the relationship is based upon all of its characteristics, regardless of what label the employer applies to the worker.[34]

# Notes

1. The figures reported are for the broadest of the Bureau's three measurements of the contingent workforce. For additional information, see the BLS news release, "Contingent and Alternative Work Arrangements," February 2001.
2. By the criteria of the survey, a worker may be in both a contingent and an alternative work arrangement, but is not automatically so, because contingent work is defined separately from alternative work arrangements.
3. *American Heritage Dictionary of the English Language*, 1978.
4. Henry Campbell Black, *Black's Law Dictionary* (St. Paul, MN, West Publishing Co, 1991), p. 363.
5. *Ibid.*, p. 530.
6. See, for example, Mark Diana and Robin H. Rome, "Beyond Traditional Employment: The Contingent Workforce," 196 APR, NJ Law 8, * 9 (April 1999).
7. 26 U.S.C. 3101 *et seq.*
8. 26 U.S.C. 3301 *et seq.*
9. 26 U.S.C. 3401 *et seq.*
10. In many cases, an independent contractor's true employer is the contracting agency, which would be subject to these Federal laws. In addition to the Federal laws that protect employees, additional State laws, including those which provide workers' compensation benefits, typically protect employees, but not independent contractors.
11. 29 U.S.C. 201 *et seq.*
12. 42 U.S.C. 2000(e) *et seq.*
13. 29 U.S.C. 621 *et seq.*
14. 29 U.S.C. 1001 *et seq.*
15. 42 U.S.C. 12101 *et seq.*
16. 29 U.S.C. 2601 *et seq.*
17. 29 U.S.C. 151 *et seq.*

18. Federal law provides employers with a safe-harbor provision to avoid a retroactive IRS reclassification of workers as employees where an employer had a "reasonable basis" for treating a worker as an independent contractor. An employer's good faith in making the determination is required for the safe harbor to apply.

19. The case has an extensive procedural history throughout the 1990s. For the opinion of the Ninth Circuit Court of Appeals regarding the status of the Microsoft workers focused on in this article, see 120 F.3d 1006.

20. The IRS used its "20-factor test" in making its determination regarding the employees' status. (For details of the test, see next section in the text.)

21. The District Court used the "common-law test" in making its determination regarding the employees' status. (For details of the test, see next section in the text.)

22. 490 U.S. 730 (1989).

23. *Black's Law Dictionary*, p. 62.

24. See IRS Revenue Ruling 87-41; see also "Summary of ms 20-Factor Test," from HRnext.com, on the Internet at **http://www.hrnext.com/tools/view.cfm?articles_id= 1470&tools_id=2**.

25. 112 S.Ct. 1344, 1348-49 (1992).

26. 137 F.2d 531 (2nd Circuit 1943).

27. 550 F.2d 566 (9th Cir. 1977).

28. The Fair Labor Standards Act uses the following uninformative definition of "employee" in the statutory language: "any individual employed by an employer." However, Congress and the courts have recognized that, because of its primary focus on protecting workers, the definition of "employee" under the Act is the broadest one used pursuant to the economic realities test.

29. See Myra H. Barron, "Who's an Independent Contractor? Who's an Employee?" 14 Lab. Law 457, 460 (winter/spring 1999).

30. 757 F.2d 1376 (3rd Cir. 1985).

31. 840 F.2d 1054 (2nd Cir. 1988).

32. 814 F.2d 1042 (5th Cir. 1987).

33. 847 F.2d 270 (9th Cir. 1988).

34. For additional discussions of the classification of workers as employees or independent contractors and the ramifications for employers, see John C. Fox, *Is That Worker an Independent Contractor or Your Employee?* (Palo Alto, CA, Fenwick and West, March 1997); Barron, "Who's an Independent Contractor?" Diana and Rome, *Beyond Traditional Employment*; and William D. Frumkin and Elliot D. Bernak, "Cost Savings from Hiring Contingent Workers May Be Lost if Their Status Is Challenged," *New York State Bar Journal*, special edition on labor and employment law, New York State Bar Association, September-October 1999.

Charles J. Muhl is an attorney in the firm of Goldberg, Kohn, Bell, Black, Rosenbloom & Moritz, Ltd., Chicago, Illinois. E-mail: charles.muhl@goldbergkohn.com

From *Monthly Labor Review*, January 2002. © 2002 by US Department of Labor.

# GOOD AS GONE

Frustrated managers are ready to bolt if the economy heats up.
Companies must work to retain them or get ready to replace them.

By Marianne Kolbasuk McGee

**A**S CIOs DIGEST RECENT NEWS from the Labor Department about improving U.S. productivity, they should consider another factor: Many of their employees are working with one foot out the door.

Technology professionals, like many U.S. workers, have been dealing with increased workloads, job uncertainty, salary freezes, and pay cuts for so long that they're poised to jump ship to new jobs at the earliest opportunity. While job alternatives are scarce, company execs need to do what they can now to prevent a brain drain as soon as the economy improves.

Managers are particularly at risk of bolting. Almost half, 48%, across all business functions say they're looking for new jobs or plan to do so once the economy picks up, according to an Accenture survey. Fifty-five percent of business-technology managers say workloads have increased in the past 12 months, according to a recent Robert Half Technology survey. And median pay for IT managers remains flat this year, according to *InformationWeek* Research's National IT Salary Survey.

"Resentment is approaching unprecedented levels among mid-managers," says Marc Lewis, North American president of IT executive recruitment firm Morgan Howard Worldwide. Lewis predicts a "mass exodus of mid-managers" when the economy solidly recovers.

Business-technology workers have it tough, but many with jobs aren't about to complain, given how hard it is to find work these days.

Last December, Andy Baumel, who has computer science, math, and MBA degrees, plus 17 years of IT experience, lost his job as an IT manager supporting traders at an investment firm in San Francisco when the firm went out of business. After eight months of searching, Baumel landed a job last month as a consultant. The pay is about half what he was making before, he has less responsibility, and no direct reports. And the job is in Los Angeles,

so he's commuting weekly from his San Francisco home. "If you look at all my skills and experience as a big pie, I'd say this new job uses about 20% of my skills," Baumel says. Like others in this article, he asked that his employer not be named.

Still, Baumel considers himself fortunate. "I'm definitely lucky," he says. "I have a job that pays my bills and is still interesting, even if it's not exactly what I was looking for."

Smart companies are looking for signs of dissatisfaction and taking steps to head it off. For example, mutual-fund company Vanguard Group does regular employee-satisfaction surveys and charts changes over time. Hewitt Associates, the human-resources consulting and outsourcing firm, takes similar steps and has increased internal communication since deciding to hire IT staff in India, a hot button in many IT shops. Companies that take steps like these have been rewarded with lower turnover.

Losing management talent could be costly. Research by the HR consulting firm Towers Perrin suggests IT workers value leadership and management more than employees in other business disciplines. Four of the top 10 factors that motivate tech employees relate to management, compared with just two in other professions. The same research shows management performance deteriorating, comparing surveys done in April 2001 and in January 2003. In the 2003 survey, only the leadership attributes "supporting teamwork" and "acting with integrity" got positive responses from more than 50% of employees.

Though productivity and economic-growth numbers suggest the economy is improving, the job market is still weak. Employment figures released last week showed companies shed 93,000 jobs in August. A survey of 148 senior executives by recruitment firm Christian & Timbers shows almost half say they're short-staffed but have no plans to hire substantial numbers of employees in the next year.

Brian Hencey, an E-commerce IT manager at a Texas financial-services company, found out what it's like to look for a job. His company recently reduced overall head count by 10% and IT staff by 20%. Every employee—including the CIO—had to reapply for a job. Like most of his colleagues, Hencey started looking for work just in case, sending out 200 to 300 resumés and applying for about 100 jobs. "I only got about five call-backs," he says. Many of the hiring companies had long lists of job requirements that seemed to Hencey to combine the responsibilities of several positions. Hencey feels fortunate to have been rehired at the same pay, responsibilities, seniority, and title.

The most-surprising finding in the Accenture survey is the top reason managers give for looking for new jobs: money. Ed Jensen, partner of Accenture's Human Performance Service Line, says compensation is always among the reasons people look, but it's never been No. 1. Middle managers seem to feel that "even if the [work] situation isn't better somewhere else, the pay might be better," he says. Managers, whose pay is more often tied to bonuses and company performance, are less likely than staffers to have received raises this year. While median total cash compensation for managers was flat at $89,000, median IT staff pay rose 3.2% to $65,000, according to *Information-Week* Research's salary survey.

No matter who you are, the road to raises is difficult these days. Companies reward IT professionals less generously for key skills and certifications than in the past, research suggests. In the last six months, professionals in 57 certification categories saw average bonus pay for certifications fall to 7.7% of base salary, down from about 8.2% last year, says David Foote, president of IT-consulting and research firm Foote Partners LLC. Foote blames the slow economy, in part, but also points to offshore outsourcing, which puts pressure on U.S. IT workers' wages. For the same reason, Morgan Howard's Lewis calls outsourcing the "Achilles' heel" of the recovery of IT employment in the United States.

Software-quality professional George Bedarf has seen the results. While looking for work the past several months, he received calls from Indian-based services firms seeking U.S. workers at about $30 an hour. That's about 50% less than Bedarf was used to getting from American companies for the same work.

With 20 years IT experience and an MBA, Bedarf spent a year looking for a job after he was laid off as a software-quality engineer. He found one at a software company, only to be laid off again in April. Sending out 500 to 600 resumés yielded little response, and he's been driving a special-education school bus to make ends meet.

Bedarf tinkered with 23 versions of his resumé until a recent iteration, highlighting the five years he worked in biotechnology, seemed to do the trick, resulting in 24 job interviews. "That's a lot in this type of economy," he says. The payoff: Bedarf is due to start at Abbott Laboratories Inc. on Sept. 15 in a temporary job, with the possibility for it to become a full-time position.

Bedarf's success indicates there may be hope for unhappy IT managers. One IT recruiter goes as far as to say the things that have workers most discouraged—heavy workloads, tight resources, increased outsourcing—may be their tickets to success. Umesh Ramakrishnan, a partner at Christian & Timbers, says if hiring picks up, the best candidates will be those who can talk about how they've successfully done more with less. "Those people might be miserable in the conditions they've been working, but that group is a desirable one to hire from," he says.

All the more reason for people running IT departments to figure out who's unhappy, how much they need them, and how to keep them.

# 7 Steps
## Before Strategy

**In the rush to get a seat at the corporate table, some HR professionals skip the basics. That ruins HR's credibility and holds it back. Here's what to do before you strategize.**

*By Bruce N. Pfau & Bonnie Bell Cundiff*

"HR deserves a seat at the table."
"HR must be the champion of change."
How many times have we heard these tired phrases?

In recent years, human resources professionals have been told that their rightful place is as a senior company officer at the top of an organization. Tasks associated with what once was known as "personnel administration" have become the objects of scorn, while activities thought to position HR managers as "strategic partners" have been encouraged and applauded.

Many in HR have taken this message to heart. They are striving to focus on strategy, to participate in decision-making at the highest levels of their organizations, and to elicit respect from other members of the senior management team.

> **While HR managers ultimately should be focused on strategy, they must make sure that the basics of the job are taken care of first.**

Unfortunately, they are failing. Despite their best efforts, many are still blocked from the head table or only grudgingly given a seat. They find themselves too weak politically to be champions of organization transformation. And they find themselves in a constant battle to prove their worth and to have any influence in key decisions. While this is due, in part, to slow-to-change attitudes toward HR from other areas of the organization, HR also must accept responsibility.

The recent emphasis on strategy at the expense of operations has hurt HR. In their rush to become strategists, HR executives and managers have dropped the ball on some fundamental as-

pects of HR. This has allowed those predisposed to diminishing the role of HR to point to shoddy basics as evidence of limited abilities.

Does this mean that HR professionals should abandon strategic activities and return to the days of "administrivia"? No. It simply means that HR executives and managers must try harder to find the delicate balance between day-to-day operations and big-picture initiatives. While HR professionals ultimately should be focused on strategy, they must make sure that the basics of the job are taken care of first.

Ultimately, there is a hierarchy of roles and priorities that must be followed—moving from the smooth execution of the basics of HR to the assumption of a seat at the table to, finally, becoming a champion of change. Following this path lets HR professionals avoid the fate of one executive who tried to advise an internal client about manpower issues. The line manager reacted with scorn, asking, "How about getting my open-position requisitions filled before giving me advice on strategic staffing issues?"

## The seven steps

Taking care of the basics means taking steps to increase efficiency, streamline operations, link individuals and activities to organizational objectives, and establish sound relationships with multiple stakeholders. The following seven steps will help assure that both the basic and strategic HR needs of organizations can be met:

1. Get rid of what's unnecessary
2. Automate
3. Assess stakeholder satisfaction

4. Communicate regularly with stakeholders
5. Redefine "strategic"
6. Practice what you preach
7. Spread the word

## Step 1: Get rid of what's unnecessary

A common complaint from HR managers juggling basic HR operations and strategic thinking is that there isn't enough time to do both. With staff and budget cuts forcing organizations to do more with less, this balancing act is becoming even more difficult.

The solution is simple. Get rid of HR programs and practices that aren't adding value to the organization's bottom line.

We recognize that this is easier said than done. Jettisoning HR programs and practices requires HR managers to know which activities are contributing to shareholder value and which are not. It means they must have the courage to admit that certain practices do not work. And it means recognizing that just because a program is touted by conventional wisdom as a "must-have," that doesn't mean it's right for their organization.

The availability of new research is making this process less complicated. The Watson Wyatt 2001 Human Capital Index establishes exactly which human-capital practices have the greatest impact on shareholder value. For example, effectively implementing a specific set of recruiting practices is associated with a significant increase in shareholder value. Among the practices included in this category are those associated with hiring people who can hit the ground running, involving employees in the hiring process, treating people evenhandedly, and approaching recruiting and retention as mission-critical.

On the other hand, the HCI study also throws a cautionary flag in front of some popular HR practices. Three practices in particular—360-degree reviews, developmental training, and the use of HR technologies with "softer" goals in mind such as culture change and enhanced communication—were associated in the study with a decrease in financial performance. While there may be nothing inherently wrong with these practices, many organizations implement them in ways that decrease, rather than increase, shareholder value.

HR executives and managers must take a hard look at their programs and practices to evaluate which ones are adding value and which ones are not. By focusing only on core practices proven to add value, HR professionals free up time and resources previously invested in delivering programs that bring marginal returns.

## Step 2: Automate

Forty years ago, HR staffers kept employee records on index cards. Fortunately, those days are gone. Today, HR should be using technology to automate administrative transactions and to provide efficient, user-friendly self-service systems to employees and managers alike.

Achievement of these goals is dependent on good execution of carefully crafted HR technology plans. When HR technologies first became widely available several years ago, many com-

panies implemented as many eHR applications as they could and made them available to as many employees as possible through e-mail, voice mail, Interactive Voice Response systems, the company intranet, the public Internet, and HR service centers. The assumption was that the faster an organization moved its traditional HR services into an eHR environment, the more efficient HR would become and the more satisfied employees would be with HR services.

However, our research shows that getting results has more to do with a properly focused eHR strategy than with the speed or extent of an organization's eHR progression. Technology must be implemented with a clear objective in mind, and that objective must be tied to hard business outcomes. Using HR technologies to reduce costs is associated with an increase in shareholder value, for example. Similarly, using HR technologies to upgrade service or improve transaction integrity or accuracy also can boost the bottom line.

Unfortunately, implementing HR technology for "softer" reasons has the opposite effect. Using HR technologies to enhance communication, for example, is associated with a *decrease* in shareholder value, as is using technology to promote culture change.

The task for HR is to figure out what can and should be automated, establish quantifiable objectives, draw up a plan to meet them, and carefully execute the plan. Specific steps in this process should include:

- **Understanding and leveraging the link between eHR and business strategy.** HR services and systems must be viewed in the context of helping to achieve company objectives.
- **Quantifying the current cost of delivering HR services.** HR groups must know where they are today before they can identify opportunities for cost control and project expected cost-savings.
- **Defining how eHR will change the delivery of HR services.** This means establishing a vision and articulating what that vision will mean in terms of people, process, and technology.
- **Working closely with the finance side of the organization to develop the required analysis.** Typically, this includes a business case containing a combination of measures, such as net present value, rate of return, and payback period.
- **Establishing measures/targets to maintain focus and assess progress.** As the saying goes, "What gets measured gets done."

## Step 3: Assess stakeholder satisfaction

Just because an HR group believes its activities are going well, that does not mean others share the same view. Consider data from the Watson Wyatt WorkUSA 2002 study of employee attitudes and opinions. Only half—48 percent—of participants rated the effectiveness of their organizations' HR functions favorably.

HR executives and managers at every organization should know where they stand in the eyes of their stakeholders, including senior executives, line managers, and employees. What are they doing well? Which areas need work? How are they viewed by the majority? As administrative implementers? Strategic planners? Facilitators? Obstacles to progress?

Armed with this information, HR professionals can evaluate their roles in the context of what their organizations want and need from their HR departments.

## Step 4: Communicate regularly with stakeholders

The truth is that most stakeholders in an organization don't really care whether HR has a seat at the table or not. They just want their HR needs met.

Consider line managers. They want to see their staffing requirements fulfilled. They want the HRMS to be accurate and up-to-date. They want a compensation system that is easy to understand and lets them reward (and keep) their key talent. In short, they want to see the trains running on time.

When you make changes to the HR process that appear to eliminate HR duties, you might at the same time create confusion and concern among line managers and others in the company. Who will take care of the duties? How will the work get done? In addition, line managers often are unaware of the importance of specific HR processes. A program or practice they dismiss as a waste of time may actually bring significant value to the organization.

The solution is frequent and effective communication. By communicating regularly with stakeholders, HR executives can show them why certain practices and programs are essential. They can explain to stakeholders why changes such as automation of the performance-management system or introduction of self-service benefits administration are being made. And they can make the business case for them—pointing out advantages related to cost, efficiency, accuracy, and ease of use.

By making communication with stakeholders about proposed changes de rigueur, HR managers and executives can alleviate any concerns the stakeholders might have and develop a contract with HR's customers that covers the organization's human-capital priorities.

Ultimately, the key to establishing trust in the HR function is helping stakeholders understand the competitive and strategic human-capital issues facing their organizations and explaining the rationale behind change-related decisions.

## Step 5: Redefine "strategic"

Let's face it. It's just not realistic for every person working in HR to be focused solely on strategy. If every HR executive, manager, associate, and assistant eschewed administration for strategy, the result would be certain disaster.

Still, everyone wants to be seen as a strategist. With the mantra "think strategic" echoing in their ears, few HR managers are willing to define themselves as anything but strategic partners.

The solution to this problem lies in broadening the definition of "strategic" to encompass both the formulation of strategy and the execution of strategy to accomplish organizational goals. During the past few years, many of the people who focused on

---

## About the Human Capital Index Study

The Watson Wyatt Human Capital Index is an ongoing study that quantifies the link between specific human-capital practices and shareholder value. Conducted every two years, beginning in 1999, it has a four-pronged objective: 1) to provide HR with financial-performance metrics; 2) to test the belief that it pays to manage people right; 3) to help managers assess their human-capital investments; and 4) to determine whether some HR practices offer a "bigger bang for the buck" than others.

Seven hundred and fifty large publicly traded companies in the United States, Canada, and Europe took part in the 2001 study. Human resources executives at the companies were asked a wide range of questions about how the organizations carried out their HR practices, including pay, people development, communication, and staffing. Their responses were matched to objective financial measures, including market value, three- and five-year total return to shareholders, and Tobin's Q, an economist's ratio that measures an organization's ability to create value beyond its physical assets.

The 2001 survey linked 49 specific human resources practices to a cumulative 47 percent increase in market value.

To view the results of the HCI study, go to www.watsonwyatt.com/hci.

---

strategy at the expense of operational success did so because they saw no connection between their operational duties and the success of their organizations. They wanted to "make a difference" and believed the only way to do so was to become part of the decision-making process.

To solve this problem, organizations must clearly define roles and expectations for people in HR-related positions. The percentage of each person's time likely to be spent formulating strategy versus executing it should be calculated, and it should be made clear that meeting operational objectives is considered a top priority.

At the same time, steps should be taken to clarify for HR professionals in all positions how their work affects the bottom line. We call this "line of sight"—showing employees that their individual contributions do have a measurable effect on their companies' ability to meet business goals.

The best way to accomplish line of sight is through a strategy-mapping process. In the first stage, assess the primary business strategies. What are the business objectives of the organization? The division? The department?

Next, identify the operational plans necessary to execute these objectives. How will the business strategies be carried out? By whom? With what resources? In what time frame?

After the objectives and processes have been established, you can determine the human-capital requirements for executing the plans. Questions to ask include: What type of culture will we need? What type of work experiences will we have to offer in order to acquire top talent? How will our compensation and benefits practices change? Once you know the HR requirements, technological resources can then be evaluated and allocated to support the needed HR programs by reducing administration and maximizing existing resources.

With this knowledge, HR executives can show members of the HR staff where they fit in and how they can contribute to the achievement of business objectives.

## Step 6: Practice what you preach

Getting the HR house in order is important from an efficiency standpoint, but it also is crucial for establishing credibility within the company. Few line managers are going to be willing to test out new practices such as flexible work arrangements or automated performance-management systems if the HR group exempts itself from practices it asks others to accept.

By modeling behaviors and processes that can be implemented throughout the company, HR can be a testing ground to work out the kinks in new activities and as a showcase for good employment practices.

## Step 7: Spread the word

While the HR literature may be filled with articles and editorials celebrating the importance of human capital and its management, few people outside the field of HR are widely exposed to that message.

There are some signs that this is changing. Key newspapers and national business magazines regularly feature pieces on the handling of human-capital issues. And companies are finding that it pays off to position themselves publicly as good places to work.

HR executives and managers should emphasize this growing respect for human capital by showing line managers, senior management, and investors the strong link between superior human-capital practices and increased shareholder value. Three key findings from the HCI study can be used to make this case:

- **Superior human-capital practices are leading—not lagging—indicators of financial performance.** This means that effective human-capital practices drive positive business outcomes more than positive business outcomes lead to good HR practices. Changes made now will help companies recover more quickly and emerge stronger when the economy rebounds.

- **Shareholder returns are three times higher at companies with superior human-capital practices than at companies with weak practices.** During the boom years of the late 1990s, that difference was significant, but not nearly as large. It's even more important to focus on human-capital superiority in tough times.

- **Not all human-capital practices are created equal.** Some create a lot of value. Others actually diminish it. Companies must examine programs and practices to ensure they are adding to shareholder value.

Just because HR experts say HR executives and managers deserve a seat at the table, that doesn't make it so. HR professionals must evaluate for themselves their track record in meeting stakeholders' operational expectations. No matter how brilliant their strategic thinking, unless the basic HR needs of their organizations are satisfied, HR professionals will not be viewed as full members of the organizational team.

---

Bruce N. Pfau, Ph.D., *is national practice director, organization effectiveness, for Watson Wyatt Worldwide and a co-author of* The Human Capitol Edge: 21 People Management Practices Your Company Must Implement (or Avoid) to Maximize Shareholder Value *(McGraw-Hill, 2002).*

---

Bonnie Bell Cundiff, Ph.D., *is Watson Wyatt's national practice leader for HR excellence. To comment on this story, please write to editors@ workforce.com.*

# Strategic Human Resources Management in Government: Unresolved Issues

## *Jonathan Tompkins*

The concept of strategic human resources management (SHRM) holds considerable promise for improving government performance. However, to realize this promise, it is necessary to invest the concept with clear meaning. This article explores unresolved issues regarding the meaning of SHRM and its relevance to public organizations. Arguing that the value of the concept is undermined by tying it too closely to strategic planning, the article offers an expanded, two-pronged understanding of SHRM. The personnel office, in addition to helping the agency implement strategic initiatives, also carries out an integrated personnel program guided by a coherent theory about what it should be doing and why.

The concept of strategic human resources management (SHRM) is well established in business literature.[1] It refers to ongoing efforts to align an organization's personnel policies and practices with its business strategy. The recent interest in SHRM reflects a growing awareness that human resources are the key to success in both public and private organizations. Yet, despite this growing awareness, the relevance of SHRM to public organizations is far from clear. Government agencies rarely operate in competitive markets and thus do not develop business strategies in the same sense that private organizations do. And because they function within larger systems of authority, they do not enjoy the same degree of autonomy that private organizations do to alter their personnel policies or provide performance-based incentives to employees. Given these inherent differences, SHRM cannot be transferred successfully from the private to the public sector without tailoring its design and implementation to the unique characteristics of public organizations.

At present there remain many unresolved issues about what modifications are required and the probabilities of their success.

If SHRM is to succeed in fundamentally altering the role of the personnel department and the practice of public personnel management, greater clarity is required regarding the concept of SHRM and how it is to be implemented in public organizations. Accordingly, this article examines unresolved issues regarding the relevance of SHRM for government agencies and closes with an argument for an expanded understanding of what it means to manage human resources strategically.

## Procedural and Structural Prerequisites: Unresolved Issues

Figure 1 presents a conceptual framework representative of the kind found in the business literature. It depicts SHRM as a process that merges strategic planning and human resource management. Specifically, it views SHRM as a continuous process of determining mission-related objectives and aligning personnel policies and practices with those objectives. The personnel department plays a strategic role to the extent that its

Figure 1
**SHRM: A Conceptual Framework**

| Analysis of Internal Environment | | Analysis of External Environment |
|---|---|---|

Statement of Agency's Mission
and Strategic Objectives

VERTICAL
INTEGRATION

HR Objectives and Strategies

Function-Specific HR Policies and Practices

| Classification & Pay | Recruitment & Selection | Training & Development | Employee Benefits | Performance Management | Employee & Labor Relations |
|---|---|---|---|---|---|

HORIZONTAL INTEGRATION

---

policies and practices support accomplishment of the organization's objectives. Key components include analyzing the agency's internal and external environments, identifying the agency's strategic objectives, developing HR objectives and strategies consistent with the agency's goals (vertical integration), and aligning HR policies and practices with each other (horizontal integration). For this conceptual understanding of SHRM to be implemented successfully, certain structural and procedural requirements must be satisfied. These core requirements include the following:

1. An established strategic planning process.
2. Involvement of the HR director in the strategic planning process and full consideration of the personnel-related implications of the strategic objectives or initiatives under discussion.
3. A clear statement, written or unwritten, of each agency's mission and the strategic objectives to be achieved in pursuit of mission.
4. The vertical alignment of personnel policies and practices with an agency's mission and strategic objectives, and the horizontal integration of personnel policies and practices with each other.
5. A personnel office whose organizational role and structure are consistent with and contribute to the attainment of the agency's mission and strategic objectives.

These prerequisites capture what is required to integrate strategic planning with human resources management in a way that enhances organizational performance. Such an integration is difficult to achieve, for example, if there is no strategic planning process in place, no participation by the personnel director, and no subsequent development of personnel initiatives designed to support identified objectives. These prerequisites are explored

below, along with unresolved issues about how to fulfill them in governmental settings.

## An Established Strategic Planning Process

The role of strategic planning is to provide agencies with a clear sense of direction by clarifying mission, setting priorities, and identifying goals and objectives. NAPA's *Guide for Effective Strategic Management of Human Resources* recommends a short and simple planning process, five to seven days in length, which establishes five or six key objectives to be accomplished during the next few years.[2] A short and simple process has the advantage of providing a clear sense of direction to line and staff officials without becoming an overly elaborate and ultimately hollow planning exercise.

Most federal agencies engage in strategic planning because they are required to do so by the Government Performance and Results Act of 1993. The extent of its use among state and local governments, although somewhat less clear, is indicated by the results of two studies. Of those responding to a national survey of state agencies conducted by Berry and Wechsler, 60 percent said they had strategic planning processes in place.[3] Similarly, in a study of municipalities with populations between 25,000 and 1,000,000, Poister and Streib found that 60 percent had adopted strategic planning in at least one department or program area.[4] These findings indicate that a large and growing number of state and local agencies are using strategic planning as a basic way of doing business.

One unresolved issue is whether the goals of SHRM are best achieved through a single, top-down, jurisdiction-wide strategic planning process or by separate agency-level planning processes. The business literature promotes strategic planning as a company-wide process in which top executives identify strategic objectives for the entire organization and managers develop their operational plans accordingly. But however appropriate this may be in the private sector, it is less so in the public sector. The essential task of government agencies is to execute public law. Because each agency has a unique mission and set of mandates to carry out, a single, top-down strategic planning process is less appropriate for purposes of SHRM. As Poister and Streib observed in their study of municipal governments, strategic planning may be "more useful for major organizational units with a unified sense of mission rather than a highly diversified and fragmented municipal jurisdiction as a whole."[5] While it is true that states such as Oregon[6] and communities such as Rock Hill, South Carolina[7] have engaged in strategic planning, such efforts are typically short-term exercises designed to resolve jurisdiction-wide problems or policy issues rather than institutionalized processes designed to enhance agency performance. Enhanced performance is the purpose that SHRM is intended to serve. Because each agency has a unique mission and set of mandates, SHRM logically requires agency-level strategic planning processes guided by legislative intent as well as the chief executive's policy or political agenda. The subsequent integration of agency plans into a jurisdiction-wide strategic plan is not required for purposes of SHRM.

A second unresolved issue is whether SHRM requires a particular kind of strategic planning to deliver on its promise of enhanced organizational performance. Strategic planning may be practiced in a variety of ways.[8] It may be externally-oriented, bringing together a diverse range of stakeholders to resolve issues of mutual concern, or internally-oriented, bringing together a cross-functional team of agency officials to set internal priorities and objectives. It may be mandated from above for purposes of accountability, or adopted voluntarily by an agency to establish a clear sense of direction. It may comprise a temporary, problem-specific process that ends when the immediate problem has been resolved, or an ongoing, institutionalized process for goal setting and issues management. Lastly, it may follow the Harvard policy model and call for extensive analysis of the agency's internal and external environments, or it may avoid lengthy analyses, opting instead for simple goal-setting exercises.[9] Process characteristics are important because they affect how seriously strategic planning is taken by agency staff, its perceived value as a management tool, and how much it ultimately contributes to organizational performance.

Advocates of SHRM tend to assume an institutionalized, internally-oriented strategic planning process adopted by agencies to clarify their missions, set priorities, and decide upon strategic objectives. There are, however, two contrasting approaches in current use. Little attention has been given to which of these is best suited to SHRM. The **performance management approach**, which is typically mandated by law or executive order, aims to ensure accountability. Under this approach, strategic objectives are stated in terms of desired results, such as a ten percent increase in the number of criminal cases closed successfully, and appropriate performance measures are identified to track success in achieving identified objectives. Although touted as an important governmental reform by members of the managing-for-results movement,[10] this approach relies upon several problematic assumptions. Among

these are that agencies do not and will not pursue meaningful results on their own initiative, that rational planning models are appropriate for use in the public sector, that agencies can in fact translate their missions into measurable outcomes, and that agencies should be rewarded and sanctioned according to their degree of success in achieving their stated objectives. Despite the difficulties inherent in this approach, it has been mandated for use in the federal government as well as in many states. By contrast, the **issues management approach** is undertaken voluntarily to address emerging issues, internal or external to the agency, that are likely to affect its ability to carry out its mission.[11] Its primary purpose is adaptability rather than accountability. Under this approach, strategic objectives are stated in terms of the actions required to achieve a desired future state. Although the planning process is sometimes institutionalized and ongoing, in many cases it is undertaken on a limited basis to address emerging areas of concern. Examples of the latter include a federal agency seeking to maintain program quality in the face of budget cuts, a suburban school district wishing to explore educational reform initiatives, and a public library struggling to maintain employee morale as demand for its services continue to rise.[12] The issues management approach tends to emphasize political rationality (doing what is politically acceptable to powerful stakeholders) over formal rationality (utilizing objective criteria and cost-benefit calculations to determine how best to attain agency goals). Key stakeholders are often brought together to negotiate an agreement about what to do and how. This approach also tends to be more pragmatic than ideological, reflecting the assumption that strategic planning is a valuable management tool for adjusting an organization to its external environment and keeping it focused on desired future states. Although tracking success with quantitative measures is not excluded under this approach, emphasis is placed on addressing issues affecting the agency's ability to carry out its mission rather than managing performance through the use of outcome measures.

Although this issue remains unresolved, it is possible to cite three reasons why the performance management approach is less suited to the purposes of SHRM. First, its underlying assumptions are difficult to satisfy in practice, potentially leaving participants frustrated and undermining their commitment to the process. As Bryson and Roering have cautioned, "a strategic planning system characterized by substantial comprehensiveness, formal rationality in decision making, and tight control will work only in an organization that has a clear mission; clear goals and objectives; centralized authority; clear performance indicators; and information about actual performance available at reasonable cost. Few public-sector organizations—or functions or communities—operate under such conditions."[13] Second, performance management systems are usually mandated from above and monitored by budget and planning offices. The problems associated with mandating strategic planning for purposes of control are well established.[14] Such systems tend to create an underlying air of distrust, which undermines commitment to the process. They tend to skew goal statements, choice of performance measures, and actual behaviors towards those results that are easiest to achieve, whether or not they truly enhance organizational performance. Third, the model of SHRM presented in Figure 1 calls for the alignment of personnel policies and practices with strategic initiatives designed to help the agency adapt to or cope with internal and external pressures. It does not call for their alignment with performance measures as such. Managing issues and measuring program results may be complementary processes, but planning for action and planning for control are two very different things. In the final analysis more research is required to determine whether the issues management approach is best suited to the purposes of SHRM or, alternatively, whether it is possible to integrate the two approaches successfully.

## Involvement of the Personnel Director in Strategic Planning

SHRM as conceptualized in Figure 1 requires more than an established strategic planning process. It also requires the full involvement of the personnel director in that process. This is necessary to ensure that the strategic initiatives under discussion are evaluated in terms of their implications for human resources. When a new program initiative is under consideration, for example, the personnel director can offer an analysis of the gap between current human resources capabilities and projected needs. Similarly, if an agency wishes to adopt a customer-service orientation, the personnel director can explain the difficulties inherent in changing an organization's culture and the kinds of training and incentives required to accomplish it successfully. Involvement by the personnel director is also necessary so that the personnel staff can obtain a better and more complete understanding of the agency's mission and the issues confronting line managers.

Although examples of strategic partnerships are increasingly heralded in professional journals and at management conferences, many jurisdictions still do not include human resource professionals in strategic deliberations. An unresolved issue here is how to forge such a partnership. Traditionally, agency executives have tended to view the personnel office as a staff agency performing relatively routine functions and occupying a relatively low status in the organizational scheme of things. Consequently, they have not been inclined to involve personnel directors in strategic deliberations. At the same time many personnel directors have been slow to insist upon a strategic role because their professional training has not prepared them to perform such a role. Training in personnel management tends to emphasize the administration of personnel systems rather than general management or organizational development.

## A Clear Statement of Strategic Objectives

Strategic goals and objectives, key products of the planning process, are often stated in a written plan. This plan provides a useful guide to the personnel office as it seeks to align existing policies and practices with strategic objectives. A written plan

is not, however, an essential requirement of SHRM. As noted in NAPA's *Guide for Effective Strategic Management of Human Resources*, "the absence of a written plan developed at the agency level does not mean that SHRM cannot exist. The HR office can develop its own plan for linking its goals to the agency's goals, or the staff can be reminded of the need to factor the agency's strategic goals into its daily operations."[15] For purposes of SHRM, all that is required is that members of the personnel staff know and understand the agency's strategic objectives so that they can contribute to their attainment.

Although this requirement appears straightforward enough, most discussions of strategic planning fail to define what the term strategy or strategic objective means in a public context. In private sector firms practicing SHRM, a business strategy is designed to give them a competitive edge over other firms in their industry. They have three basic strategies from which to choose.[16] The **innovation strategy** involves developing a unique product or service, or concentrating on a specific market niche; the **quality enhancement strategy** involves offering products or services that are superior in quality; and the **cost reduction** strategy involves reducing costs so that the firm can offer goods and services at the lowest possible price. Firms may also explore different growth strategies, such as those involving mergers and diversification. Once business strategies are selected, specific objectives are identified and the task of aligning personnel policies and practices begins.

Because public agencies are embedded in authority networks rather than economic markets, what it means to select a "business strategy" is much less clear. As Wechsler and Backoff have noted, the "strategies of public organizations, unlike business strategies, are produced in response to a variety of competing signals that emanate not from markets but from complex political, economic, legal, and organizational structures, processes, and relationships."[17] Whereas business executives are relatively unconstrained in making strategic decisions, the constraints encountered by public administrators often cause them to make strategic choices other than those they believe are best suited to mission attainment. Factors influencing choice of strategy include the political goals of elected officials, demands of powerful stakeholders, judicial mandates, budgetary constraints, the organization's capacities and resources, and its relationships with other organizations. Agencies are more likely to engage in strategic planning and more likely to succeed in implementing their intended objectives when they possess internal capacity for performance (adequate funding, personnel, and management systems), a supportive political environment, and a weak or divided external influence field. Conversely, strategies tend to be shaped by external demands rather than internal intentions when an agency experiences a hostile environment and low internal capacity.

An agency's strategy may be understood as the basic pattern reflected in its policy decisions and actions. Wechsler and Backoff's analysis of state agencies in Ohio revealed three basic patterns. **Developmental** strategies involve actions taken to enhance the agency's resources, status, influence, and capacity for future action, presumably as it relates to mission attainment. Developmental strategies are often products of a formal planning process in which strategists and planners deliberately seek to develop capacity so as to maintain internal control and enhance organizational performance. **Political** strategies involve actions taken either to balance competing stakeholder demands or to reward supporters of the administration by moving the agency in specific policy or programmatic directions. For example, control over internal operations may be tightened in order to further a specific political agenda. Such strategies are adopted where political and partisan pressures are high. **Protective** strategies involve actions designed to accommodate external pressures or appease external stakeholders while maintaining the organizational status quo. It is a reactive strategy more or less forced on an agency by an overtly hostile environment and weak internal capacity for strategic action. It is a pattern that is highly frustrating for agency staff.

Steeped in the rationalistic assumptions of planning theory, discussions of SHRM tend to envision agencies pursuing developmental, capacity-building strategies rather than political or protective strategies. In practice, however, a developmental strategy requires widely shared objectives, the capacity to plan and carry out strategic initiatives, extensive discretion, adequate resources, and relatively weak or divided external forces—conditions which often cannot be satisfied. Although Backoff and Wechsler do not address issues relating to SHRM, their analysis strongly suggests that SHRM may look very different in agencies engaged in political or protective strategies. Rather than helping an agency develop its capacity for mission attainment, the personnel office may be asked, for example, to help the agency secure the political loyalty of career civil servants, recruit and reward based on partisan or political criteria, or tighten control over employee performance. In short, although the concept of SHRM, with its emphasis on linking means and ends, strongly implies an institutionalized process utilized by agencies pursuing a developmental strategy, it must be kept in mind that agency performance can be defined in terms of political and protective objectives as well, and that SHRM, as it is generally understood, may be undermined or derailed as a result.

## Alignment of HR Policies and Practices with Strategic Objectives

Although their mandates are set by external actors, agencies still must interpret their mandates, clarify their missions, and seek agreement among key stakeholders regarding how their missions will be carried out. Statements of strategic objectives, written or unwritten, emerge from these decision processes. The core requirement of SHRM is the alignment of personnel policies and practices with the agency's strategic objectives. Although many examples of alignment have been reported in the literature, no classification system has yet been proposed to capture how alignment is accomplished. In general, the reported examples tend to fall into one or more of the following categories:

**1. Adapting to environmental change.** This category includes actions taken by the personnel office in response to external events or trends, such as budget cuts, tight labor markets, changing demographic characteristics of workers, and new

technologies. During a period of retrenchment, for example, the personnel office can help managers communicate to staff members the reasons behind staff cutbacks and how they will be accomplished, develop and introduce an early retirement incentive program, counsel those who must be laid off about alternative job opportunities, provide stress management programs for those anxious about their jobs or struggling to cope with increased workloads, and explore the use of temporary or contract employees to ease workload burdens. Adaptive responses of this kind may or may not be guided by a formal statement of agency objectives.

**2. Building human capacity to support strategic initiatives.** Human resources planning is a traditional personnel function. It involves forecasting future staffing needs and taking steps to recruit new employees or train existing employees to meet the forecasted demands. What is unique in the context of SHRM is analysis of the gap between current and required capacity for each new strategic initiative. If an agency has decided to serve a new clientele group, expand services into new areas, or take on an entirely new program, the personnel office can play a strategic role by recruiting new employees with the requisite skills or enhancing the skills of existing personnel through training and development.

**3. Changing organizational culture.** Many public organizations have followed their private sector counterparts by reinventing and reengineering themselves. Major reform initiatives often require new organizational cultures, cultures driven by different values and requiring different behaviors. Adopting a "customer-service" orientation, for example, has become a common strategic objective in both the private and public sectors. The personnel office can help develop a shared commitment to service quality and customer satisfaction through its employee orientation sessions and training programs. It can also redesign performance appraisal and incentive systems so that employees are rewarded for emphasizing quality and customer service. The personnel office can undertake similar efforts in agencies seeking to move from a process-oriented to a results-oriented culture.[18]

**4. Preparing employees for change.** Staff members often resist the implementation of major reforms because of implicit or explicit threats to personal security. Thus, in addition to taking steps to develop a new organizational culture, the personnel office can also take steps to prepare employees for impending changes. It can, for example, encourage managers to involve employees in the design and implementation of the new program or reform initiative, help communicate the purposes behind the changes and the benefits to be derived from them, and provide additional training opportunities so that staff members are prepared to function successfully under the new order.

**5. Supporting a specific "business strategy."** This category, which overlaps with the preceding ones, is distinguished by the selection of a specific business strategy for success. Many of the examples of alignment in the business literature envision this kind of situation. When Marriott, for example, decided to gain a competitive advantage by being "the employer of choice," the personnel office altered its policies and practices so as to attract and retain the very best workers available.[19] Another business strategy is to become "a high commitment" organization. In this instance the personnel office is charged with altering its policies and practices to encourage employee development and empowerment. Indeed, some advocates tend to equate SHRM with the adoption of "progressive" policies designed to boost employee commitment and performance.[20] The common denominator in these business strategies is the belief that human resources are the key to organizational success.

These five kinds of actions are undertaken to achieve vertical integration. Vertical integration is a measure of how well personnel policies and practices, individually and collectively, contribute to organizational objectives. As indicated in Figure 1, horizontal integration is important as well. This is a measure of how well personnel policies mesh with each other in contributing to organizational objectives. The goal is to develop an integrated personnel program in which policies and practices in one functional area do not work at cross purposes with those in other areas.

## Changing the Role and Structure of the Personnel Office

The first four requirements of SHRM cannot be satisfied unless the personnel office fundamentally alters the way it does business. An unresolved issue is how to do so. Advocates of SHRM have offered several recommendations in this regard. First, the personnel office must develop the capacity it needs to support strategic initiatives. This means it must develop staff expertise in job design, organizational development, change management, employee motivation, and human resource theory. The personnel staff must also develop knowledge of general management, agency mission, and the specific personnel problems facing managers. Whether this strategic role should be assigned to a special unit within the personnel office or should be expected of all personnel staff remains an unanswered question. Because the strategic and operational roles of the personnel office are contradictory in many respects, performing both roles in an integrated fashion will remain an ongoing challenge.

Second, the traditional control orientation must be superseded by a service orientation. The required line-staff partnership cannot be forged as long as the personnel office is perceived by agency managers as an enforcer of rules and a source of suffocating red tape. According to SHRM advocates, a service orientation can be established by assigning primary responsibility for human resource management to managers and creating service teams comprised of personnel generalists to assist managers in achieving mission-related objectives.[21] Under this proposal, personnel generalists are to perform a service-oriented role both when administering personnel systems such as classification and pay and when consulting with managers about specific personnel problems or objectives. Adopting a service orientation does not require that the personnel office abdicate its responsibility for safeguarding merit, employee rights, and equal employment opportunity. Rather, it means carrying out this responsibility as legal counselors rather than police officers. If the personnel office is to contribute more directly to an agency's mission, shifts in role orientation are important. For SHRM to be implemented successfully, according to NAPA, "the HR staff must believe that their mission is helping the agency accomplish its mission by assisting supervisors in managing their human resources."[22]

Lastly, many advocates of SHRM believe that highly centralized personnel systems must be decentralized and deregulated. Perry and Mesch argue, for example, that the implementation of SHRM is incompatible with highly centralized personnel systems.[23] Possessing unique missions and mandates, and facing unique situations, agencies must be able to tailor their personnel policies and practices to their strategic needs. Centralized personnel systems deny them the flexibility they need. Structural reforms may include reducing the number of centralized personnel regulations to the bare minimum needed to enforce statutory requirements, devolving responsibility for classification and applicant screening to the agency and bureau level, and delegating policy making authority downwards so that agencies can establish personnel policies suited to their individual needs. Advocates of structural reform believe that certain positive effects will follow, including greater flexibility and timeliness in personnel decision making and improved line-staff relations.

In fact, however, decentralization and deregulation may not be a prerequisite for the successful implementation of SHRM. Structural reform efforts tend to encounter serious obstacles and create new problems. For example, devolution of authority means that agency personnel must be trained to handle personnel transactions formerly handled by a central personnel office and new ways must be found to coordinate the efforts of all line and staff officials engaged in performing the personnel management function. Some of these obstacles may prove insurmountable, creating additional redundancies and waste and further undermining agency performance. From the perspective of SHRM, structural reform may not be necessary as long as each agency has sufficient authority and flexibility to align its personnel policies and practices with its strategic objectives. This, too, remains an unresolved issue.

## An Expanded Understanding of SHRM

What it means to manage human resources strategically can be understood in more than one way. The difficulty with the understanding discussed above is that it lacks an integrated and sustained focus on the organization's human resources. Because it is closely tied to the practice of strategic planning, it envisions the personnel office taking only those actions necessary to support a specific strategic objective. In this instance the role of the personnel office may be strategic but it is also somewhat ad hoc and reactive. In actuality there is much the personnel office can do to advance an agency's strategic interests other than, or in addition to, supporting the initiatives that emerge from a strategic planning process.

An alternative understanding of what it means to manage human resources strategically has been suggested by Eugene McGregor.[24] The role of the personnel office, according to this

**FIGURE 2 Human Resource Strategies**

| HR Strategies | Underlying Values | Desired Outcomes |
| --- | --- | --- |
| Cost Containment Strategy. Containing labor costs by setting salaries at or below market levels, adopting wellness programs and managed care to reduce benefit costs, and using part-time, temporary, and contract employees whenever possible. | economy | cost-effective staffing |
| Performance Management Strategy. Setting measurable objectives for employees and making rewards contingent upon performance. | productivity | mission-related results |
| Involvement Strategy. Providing employees, individually or in teams, with considerable work autonomy, decision-making authority, and responsibility for a "complete" task. | empowerment | sense of ownership; enhanced motivation and contribution; employee commitment and retention |
| Retention Strategy. Providing the conditions necessary to retain valuable human resources, including generous benefit packages, pay that is at or above market, positive work environment, and family-friendly policies such as flextime and day care assistance. | need satisfaction | job satisfaction; employee commitment and retention |
| Investment Strategy. Increasing individual competence and organizational capacity by investing heavily in training and development. | human development | personal competence; agency adaptability; employee commitment and retention |
| Cohesion Strategy. Establishing a sense of community and strong social bonds through agency newsletters, picnics, and recreational activities, and by fostering open and trusting relationships between employees and managers and retention | comradeship; openness; trust. | job satisfaction; cooperative relations; employee commitment |

understanding, is to help "manage strategic resources strategically." It begins from the premise that many, if not most, government jobs are knowledge-intensive, involving the creation of knowledge or the creation of "smart products" through the application of "trained intelligence." Where this is the case, the intellectual capital stored within the workers becomes the critical resource for the organization and must therefore be viewed as a strategic resource. Managing this strategic resource strategically involves determining essential knowledge, skills, and abilities; improving recruitment and selection methods; developing the capacities of all employees so that the agency can respond to any opportunity or threat appearing on the horizon; and fostering employee commitment so that human capital is not lost to other employers. In short, this alternative understanding envi-

sions a personnel office pursuing an ongoing, integrated program for enhancing organizational performance by acquiring, developing, and managing human resources strategically.

With these observations in mind, it is possible to suggest an expanded, two-pronged approach to SHRM in which the personnel office, in addition to helping the agency implement strategic initiatives, also carries out an integrated personnel program guided by a coherent theory or philosophy about what it means to manage human resources strategically. A theory or philosophy of this kind specifies how human resources must be treated, how much money must be invested in developing human capital, the kind of culture and work climate that must be established, and the specific attitudes and behaviors that must be elicited if the agency is to achieve its vision of success.

That personnel offices are rarely guided by such a theory has been cited as the primary reason for their low institutional standing.[25] If the personnel office succeeds in developing such a theory in consultation with agency officials and legislative bodies, the next step is to identify and implement appropriate human resource strategies. Six human resource strategies are identified in Figure 2. Although these strategies are neither exhaustive nor mutually exclusive, they nonetheless serve to illustrate the connections between values and vision, desired outcomes, and the programmatic means by which to realize them.

The cost-containment strategy tends, in practice, to serve as a default strategy. Although it is antithetical to McGregor's understanding of what it means to manage strategic resources strategically, it is often the strategy of choice among elected officials concerned with holding the line on labor costs and budget increases. Where there is no agreed upon vision of success, nor any theory regarding the strategic importance of human resources to agency performance, other strategies tend to receive little attention. However, the convergence of several factors in recent years, including tighter labor markets, a growing proportion of high-skill and knowledge-intensive jobs, a better educated workforce with heightened growth needs, and political pressures to improve government performance, has turned attention to alternative strategies. The performance management strategy, for example, has been adopted in jurisdictions where the values and assumptions of the managing-for-results movement have gained sway.[26] Similarly, because most government employees are knowledge workers who can sell their intellectual capital on the open market, many agencies are turning to a combination of the investment, involvement, and retention strategies to attract, develop, and retain the human resources they need to provide knowledge intensive services in an ever changing environment. The investment strategy in particular reflects a growing awareness that human competence is the engine behind the creation of value.[27]

The strategies or combination of strategies chosen, if any, depends on situational factors such as the nature of the work performed by agency staff, the agency's capacity for pursuing excellence, and the priorities of its leaders. Political and practical factors often divert attention from developing a human resource philosophy or expending funds to put it into practice. Indeed, as McGregor has noted, "in the minds of many a case-hardened practitioner, the idea of strategic public-sector human resource management may well be an oxymoron."[28] But if the prospects for implementing SHRM in the public sector are uncertain, the concept itself represents a valuable goal toward which to strive.

## Conclusion

The concept of SHRM as outlined above calls upon the personnel office to adopt a strategic role in addition to its operational roles as rule enforcer and guardian of the integrity of personnel systems. For the personnel staff, adopting a strategic role means being more responsive to agency goals by acting as consultants and service providers to line managers; supporting

the attainment of the agency's strategic objectives; and carrying out an integrated, philosophy-driven personnel program. Although the concept of SHRM is steeped in problematic, rationalistic assumptions, it nonetheless holds considerable promise for enhancing government performance. Its success depends on whether the personnel office can integrate its strategic and operational roles successfully and whether it can satisfy the norms of political and formal rationality simultaneously. Too much is at stake for this potentially valuable concept to become a label for yet another failed management initiative.

## Notes

1. Tichy, Noel M., Charles J. Fombrun, and Mary Anne Devanna, "Strategic Human Resource Management," *Sloan Management Review* 23 (Winter 1982): 47–61; Cynthia A. Lengnick-Hall and Mark L. Lengnick-Hall, "Strategic Human Resources Management: A Review of the Literature and a Proposed Typology," *Academy of Management Review* 13 (July 1988): 454–470; Randall Schuler, "Strategic Human Resource Management and Industrial Relations," *Human Relations* 42 (No. 2 1989):157–184.

2. National Academy of Public Administration (NAPA), *A Guide for Effective Strategic Management of Human Resources* (Washington D.C.: NAPA, 1996).

3. Berry, Frances Stokes and Barton Wechsler, "State Agencies' Experience with Strategic Planning: Findings from a National Survey," *Public Administration Review* 55 (March/April 1995): 159–168.

4. Poister, Theodore H. and Gregory Streib, "Management Tools in Municipal Government: Trends over the Past Decade," *Public Administration Review* 49 (May/June 1989): 240–248.

5. Poister and Streib, "Management Tools," 244.

6. Kissler, Gerald R., Karmen N. Fore, Willow S. Jacobson, William P. Kittredge, and Scott L. Stewart, "State Strategic Planning: Suggestions from the Oregon Experience," *Public Administration Review* 58 (July/August 1998): 353–359.

7. Wheeland, Craig M., "Citywide Strategic Planning: An Evaluation of Rock Hill's Empowering Vision," *Public Administration Review* 53 (January/February 1993): 65–72.

8. Bryson, John M., *Strategic Planning for Public and Nonprofit Organizations: A Guide to Strengthening and Sustaining Organizational Achievement* (San Francisco: Jossey-Bass, 1995).

9. Bryson, John M. and William D. Roering, "Applying Private-Sector Strategic Planning in the Public Sector," *Journal of the American Planning Association* 53 (Winter 1987): 9–22.

10. Osborne, David and Ted Gaebler, *Reinventing Government* (Reading, MA: Addison-Wesley, 1992).

11. Bryson, *Strategic Planning*; Paul C. Nutt and Robert W. Backoff, *Strategic Management of Public and Third Sector Organizations* (San Francisco: Jossey-Bass, 1992).

12. Bryson, *Strategic Planning*.

13. Bryson and Roering, "Applying Private-Sector Strategic Planning," 15.

14. Mintzberg, Henry, *The Rise and Fall of Strategic Planning* (New York: Free Press, 1994).

15. NAPA, *A Guide for Effective Strategic Management of Human Resources*, 17.

16. Porter, Michael E., *Competitive Strategy: Techniques for Analyzing Industries and Competitors* (New York: Free Press, 1980); Schuler, "Strategic Human Resource Management and Industrial Relations."

17. Wechsler, Barton and Robert W. Backoff, "The Dynamics of Strategy in Public Organizations," *Journal of the American Planning Association* 53 (Winter 1987): 34–43.

18. Popovich, Mark G. (ed.), *Creating High-Performance Government Organizations* (San Francisco: Jossey-Bass, 1998).

19. Ulrich, Dave, "Strategic and Human Resource Planning: Linking Customers and Employees," *Human Resource Planning* 15 (June 1992): 47+.

20. NAPA, *A Guide for Effective Strategic Management of Human Resources*.

21. Perry, James L. and Debra J. Mesch, "Strategic Human Resource Management," in *Public Personnel Management: Current Concerns, Future Challenges* edited by Carolyn Ban and Norma M. Riccucci (New York: Longman, 1997), 21–34.

22. NAPA, *A Guide for Effective Strategic Management of Human Resources*, 53.

23. Perry and Mesch, "Strategic Human Resource Management."

24. McGregor, Eugene B., *Strategic Management of Human Knowledge, Skills, and Abilities* (San Francisco: Jossey-Bass, 1991).

25. Christensen, Ralph, "Where is HR?" *Human Resource Management* 36 (Spring 1997): 81–84.

26. Lawler, Edward E., *Strategic Pay: Aligning Organizational Strategies and Pay Systems* (San Francisco: Jossey-Bass, 1990); Popovich, *Creating High-Performance Government Organizations*.

27. Christensen, "Where is HR?"; Lee Dyer and Gerald W. Holder, "A Strategic Perspective of Human Resource Management," in *Human Resource Management: Evolving Roles and Responsibilities* edited by Lee Dyer (Washington D.C.: Bureau of National Affairs, 1988): 1–46.

28. McGregor, *Strategic Management*, 33.

Jonathan Tompkins is Professor of Political Science at The University of Montana. His primary teaching responsibilities include courses in human resources management, strategic planning, and organization theory. He has published several articles relating to human resource management and a text entitled *Human Resource Management in Government*.

From *Public Personnel Management,* Spring 2002, pp. 95-110. © 2002 by the International Personnel Management Association (IPMA), 1617 Duke Street, Alexandria, VA 22314; www.ipma-hr.org.

# Unquiet Minds

**A growing population of adults is being diagnosed with attention deficit hyperactive disorder. Bosses and workers are seeking ways to cope.**

ALIYA STERNSTEIN

ON A FRIDAY EVENING IN SEPtember Deborah Hoyt, a 46-year-old chief financial officer of a fundraising organization in Atlanta, sat at her desk frustrated with a financial analysis, still tackling other tasks. "My brain was in total meltdown," says Hoyt. She gave up 15 minutes later, only to walk through a fog of self-doubt on Saturday. She could not get the numbers swirling through her head to make sense. Finally, early Sunday morning, with *Saturday Night Live* on in the background, the pencil hit paper.

This kind of frustrating paralysis followed by flashes of insight is common for Hoyt. Five months ago she was diagnosed with adult attention deficit hyperactive disorder (ADHD), an affliction that hits 3% to 7% of U.S. adults. Hoyt now takes one pill a day, a potentially addictive stimulant called Concerta, to help her run the finance and administrative functions of a 50-person company. "I'm working on many things at one time," she says, echoing the mantra of the afflicted.

ADHD, long associated with boys who say and do whatever comes to mind, has been recognized among adults only in the last ten years. The people who make a career of treating this problem will tell you that only 20% of adults with ADHD know

they have it. (The disorder used to go by the shorthand ADD, but ADHD is now its official name.)

As with children, adults with ADHD range from the mildly affected, inattentive employee who needs constant reminders to keep from missing deadlines and meetings to the severely inattentive hyperactive who flies out of the office in a tantrum. Without treatment the acutely afflicted fail to divide work from home life, winding up losing both their jobs and marriages.

Misdiagnosis is common, as psychiatrists sometimes mistake ADHD's symptoms for depression or anxiety. And ADHD adults, notoriously bad self-reporters, often don't see their shortfalls. Oddly enough, ADHD can be a performance booster, as those afflicted can concentrate and work nonstop for hours when they are vitally interested. Studies cited in the Journal of the American Medical Association found that one-third of ADHD adults become entrepreneurs by their 30s. One case in point is Jet-Blue's idea-spinning chief executive, David Neeleman, who has admitted to having ADHD, though he no longer discusses it in interviews.

As adult ADHD has come into sharper focus, the disorder has become a growth business. Drug sales

are booming, as is the nascent industry of workplace coaches. Sales of medications for the child and adult markets were $1.7 billion in 2002, up 39% over 2001, according to IMS Health. This year's numbers will likely exceed that by 50%. And the percentage of adults on ADHD meds went from 11.4% in 2002 to 19% in 2003.

Ritalin gets all the headlines as the drug for the treatment, or overtreatment, of ADHD, but it is no longer the market force it once was. Sales have fallen, from $260 million in 1998 to $54 million last year. Those sales have been more than made up for by newer ADHD drugs. The top three are powerful stimulants: Alza's Concerta, Shire's Adderall and Cephalon's Provigil. They're followed closely by Strattera, Eli Lilly's new pill that was the first nonstimulant approved for adult use by the Food & Drug Administration. Strattera has captured 13% of the market since its debut in January.

ADHD's causes are still being determined, but they are likely genetic. A link has been found between ADHD and faulty regulation of dopamine, a brain neurotransmitter regulating movement and emotional response. Low dopamine activity may cause undiagnosed ADHD sufferers to self-medicate, first with sugar in childhood, then with caf-

## ADHD Survivors Guide

### Getting diagnosed

There is no single test, but doctors can run a comprehensive evaluation to rule out other disorders and coexisting conditions such as depression, drug/alcohol abuse and anxiety and sleep disorders. They'll want a history from parents and teachers, including old report cards and psych tests. For some self-assessments check out med.nyu.edu and then go to the psychiatry department's site.

### Coping at work

- Ask for a private place to work or arrange to work from home on occasion.

- Let fellow workers and managers know how to get your attention.

- Seek out opportunities to work in teams to help ensure structure and accountability.

- Exercise. Try yoga.

- Create a cutoff time each night for voice mail and e-mail checking.

- Engage in functional fidgeting by taking notes or making lists during meetings.

- Join a support group at chadd.org or add.org.

feine, cigarettes or cocaine—whatever helps them focus. Stimulants such as Concerta and Adderall keep dopamine in the brain synapses longer, but these pills can be addictive. Strattera takes a slightly different approach: preventing the reuptake of norepinephrine, another neurotransmitter in the brain.

Like depression or anxiety, ADHD is often a closet sickness. Deborah Hoyt told her employers only recently, after ten years on the job. Most big companies, like Ford Motor, have tucked confidential counseling for their employees with ADHD into their employee-assistance programs.

For others, a cottage industry of some 1,000 ADHD coaches has sprung up in response. Coaches are something like long-distance pseudotherapists who understand the ADHD mind. Phone sessions cost between $50 and $400 an hour but aren't covered by insurance. No standards or guidelines yet exist for coaches to live up to, and the coaching process can last for weeks or months. David Giwerc, a former Young & Rubicam marketing director, was diagnosed with ADHD in 1994 while training as an executive coach. He tells clients to find work that gets them moving around, to guard against the tendency to reply

to every last e-mail or voice mail, and, as he does, squeeze a grip ball to stop from interrupting people on the phone.

Employers who don't accommodate ADHD-diagnosed workers can be sued under the Americans with Disabilities Act, but good luck winning. Employers win ADA cases—all disability claims included—nine times out of ten, according to Patricia Latham, a Washington, D.C.-based attorney. Fred J. Calef Jr., a former production mechanic at Gillette, sued the company in 2001, claiming it failed to accommodate his ADHD. He lost the suit; Gillette says it fired him for threatening co-workers. "Even if ADHD does account for his behavior, it doesn't mean you can behave that way," says attorney Richard Ward.

Experts worry that some adults are getting swindled. Arthur Caplan, director of the Center for Bioethics at the University of Pennsylvania's medical school, says drug companies may throw pills at everyone, while physicians, without agreement on how to diagnose, will play along, over-prescribe and hype the disease. "I have no doubt that there is ADHD in adults—and undiagnosed ADHD in adults, but if you go looking for the disorder, you're going to find it," he says.

# THE DEVIL IS IN THE DETAILS

## More than a decade later, the ADA is still a tricky law to follow

Thomas Clark, Contributing Writer

After 13 years, the Americans with Disabilities Act still cause facility owners to stumble.

It's been more than a dozen years since the Americans with Disabilities Act became law, guaranteeing those with a variety of handicaps the right to work and access to public buildings. While the landmark civil rights legislation has had a profound impact in many ways, its myriad rules and standards still pose a problem for all institutions, including long term care facilities.

Cynthia Leibrock—a Livermore, Colo., interior designer who now specializes in universal design and aging, and the author of *Design Details for Health* (John Wiley & Sons)—says she's still never found a nursing home that is ADA compliant.

But that doesn't mean that Leibrock finds problems in the form of steep staircases and inaccessible bathrooms. The problems for most facilities are usually in the smaller issues that muddy the ideal of being fully compliant with the ADA.

"People don't get the nuances of the ADA," says Leibrock. "They get the basics right, but they miss the details."

It's those details that Leibrock closely examines when she surveys a nursing home. When she does, she can be sure that she'll literally find "hundreds of violations"—even in facilities built since the ADA became law.

"Not many [of the violations] are life-threatening," she says. "They are smaller matters."

A typical example, Leibrock said, is a Dutch door. Many facilities use these divided doorways to give residents a view of a room or hall without fully opening the door. But ADA restrictions say that any object that is lower than 80 inches above the floor and higher than 27 inches can't protrude more than three inches. The top half of the Dutch door is therefore non-compliant.

But "even the smaller details can disable someone," says Leibrock. The height requirements are to protect blind people who use a cane to sweep the landscape in front of them: They would have no way of knowing that the top half of the Dutch door would open in their path.

## States of inconsistency

Perhaps the biggest obstacle to a facility being 100 percent compliant with the ADA is the lack at consistency in regulations and restrictions from state to state. Federal ADA standards and state building codes differ, and state building codes aren't uniform from place to place.

Jim Terry, a Birmingham, Ala, architect and chief executive officer of Evan Terry Associates, P.C., routinely hears the complaint from clients who operate facilities throughout the United States. "They tell us it would be great if there were one national standard so they could have a national model to duplicate." But, says Terry, "that's not possible. Something that one state requires, another won't allow."

## THE ACT ITSELF

The AMERICANS WITH DISABILITIES ACT of 1990
**S. 933**
One Hundred First Congress of the United States of America at the second session

Begun and held at the City of Washington on Tuesday, the twenty-third day of January, one thousand nine hundred and ninety

**An Act**
To establish a clear and comprehensive prohibition of discrimination on the basis of disability.

**Sec. 2**
*(b)* Purpose.—It is the purpose of the Act—
*(1)* to provide a clear and comprehensive national mandate for the elimination of discrimination against individuals with disabilities;
*(2)* to provide clear, strong, consistent, enforceable standards addressing discrimination against individuals with disabilities;
*(3)* to ensure that the Federal Government plays a central role in enforcing the standards established in this Act on behalf of individuals with disabilities; and
*(4)* to invoke the sweep of congressional authority, including the power to enforce the fourteenth amendment and to regulate commerce, in order to address the major areas of discrimination faced day-to-day by people with disabilities.

# SWEATING THE SMALL (AND NOT SO SMALL) STUFF

Long term care facilites typically provide good patient care, but they fall down in providing good visitor care, according to Jim Terry, and Alabama architect specializing in accessibility and ADA issues.

The places that are good at it are making accommodations for visitors as well as patients, according to Terry. They know that the people who are deciding where to place a spouse or family member may need some type of accommodations themselves. "Their first impression is going to be, 'Hey, I got a parking spot,' " Terry says. "You can let them decide whether to go or not, rather them shooing them out of your building."

Terry tells building managers to "look out your window and see if your handicapped places are full most of the time. If they are, you need more spots." Other building details Terry suggest looking at:

- **Water fountains.** Some low for people in wheelchairs, others high for people who have trouble bending
- **Furniture.** Firm, raised (18–20) inches) seats, with armrests that extend to the chair's edge.
- **Signage.** Visual impairments make low-contrast, high-glare and warm colors hard to read.
- **Bathrooms.** "The ADA doesn't require grab bars in every room, but the more you have, the better," says Terry.
- **Easy-to-operate hardware.** Try to operate any hardware with your fingers taped together or your hand balled into a fist. That's why levers are better than knobs.
- **Door forces.** Non-fire rated doors shouldn't require more than five pounds of force.
- **Floor surfaces.** Walk the route from the parking lot to the rooms. Pay close attention to thresholds and to transitions between different flooring types.
- **Curb ramps.** Keep the slope gentle and never paint them (the paint is slippery). If they aren't right, says Terry, "rip 'em out. It's cheaper to rip out 100 ramps than defend one lawsuit."

"None of these are really expensive," says Terry, "and they serve a huge portion of the population. They also say a lot about your care of people who need these accommodations. They pay off in goodwill, new business and references."

—T.C

One state, for instance, requires a bathroom grab bar to be 33 inches off the floor. Another mandates a height of between 34 inches and 36 inches. Even toilet paper holders defy uniformity: In California and many other states. The holder must be 7 inches to 9 inches in front of the water closet. The ADA regulations say the holder may not be more than 36 inches from the rear wall. "So, in a 30-inch water closet," says Terry, "the holder would be too close for the state standard."

States are making an effort to align their accessibility standards to at least be compatible with, the ADA standards, says Terry. And, a revised set of combined ADA/ABA (Architectural Buildings Act) regulations now open to comment may help down the road. But it's unlikely that all the involved parties will ever get together on a single code.

"There's so much politics involved," says Terry. "These issues are emotional and critically important to people. Advocates have worked hard to win battles, and they don't want to give them up to harmonize with standards won by other people with different agendas."

"Everyone's pulling for their own needs on different sides of each issue," Terry continues, "and there may be three or four sides to the issue. Politics don't even land in the same place twice. We don't wind up with the same sorts of compromises."

## Courts of enforcement

The result is that litigation has become the chief enforcer of the ADA. "There are lots of advocacy groups out there," says Terry, "and they're saying people aren't doing anything until we sue them. So we're going to file as many suits as possible."

"These groups' members are saying the law's been in place a long time now. It's time for these places to be compliant."

Terry believes most lawsuits could be stopped through preventive work. "Ninety-nine percent of the companies that call us have a lawsuit because they had a problem with patient care. After that, the plaintiffs began looking for everything they could find."

Leibrock and Terry advocate hiring ADA specialists to survey a facility and identify non-compliance issues. Services vary: Terry's architectural firm performs five types, ranging from a "high-speed walkthrough" to a "standard barrier survey." Costs increase with thoroughness, says Terry. The simple walkthrough costs as little as $2,000, but may identify only 25 percent of the issues noted in the most detailed survey. The barrier survey—which also prioritizes problems and suggests solutions—can run between 25 and 40 cents per square foot.

For all its complexities, the ADA "has done a lot of good," says Leibrock. "The United States is the most accessible nation in the world." Still, she believes the law could be improved. "There are many problems that actually work against older people."

Leibrock cites Japanese research that led to the development of angled bathtub grab bars. These bars don't demand the same upper-body strength as the horizontal bars mandated by the ADA, making them more appropriate for older, weaker residents. But in some places, the angled bars aren't compatible with what's required by the ADA and state codes.

"You can claim [the modified bars] are a conditional equivalent to what's required," says Leibrock. "The law allows that. But no one will sign off on it—no state inspector and no one in the federal government."

"In the future," says Leibrock, "the regulations should be based on performance specifications. We need to stop giving lip service to the idea of meeting people's needs and really design an environment that allows people to do things for themselves."

# The ADA's Next Step:
# *Cyberspace*

The landmark law that ensures the disabled access to public facilities
and workplaces needs to be extended to the Net and e-commerce.

By Suzanne Robitaille

Entrepreneur Kevan Worley, blind since birth, relies on the World Wide Web for his livelihood. As president of Blackstone/Worley Consulting, a contractor of military food-service facilities, he regularly gets access to his e-mail and food-service industry research using a screen reader that speaks the text of the messages to him. He also operates a Web site and e-mail list service in his role as president of the National Association of Blind Merchants, a division of the National Federation of the Blind (NFB).

"The Internet is an indispensable tool," says Worley. Yet, he notices that screen readers still don't work well with many sites because they haven't been designed to be compatible with assistive technologies for the disabled. "There's clearly much more work to be done," he says.

That's for sure. The Americans with Disabilities Act marks its 13th anniversary on July 26. Plenty of progress has been made since enactment of this landmark law, which was intended to make public facilities and workplaces accessible to people with disabilities.

**SALES FORCE.** Yet, no mandate exists yet for companies doing business on the Web. Why? Congress enacted the statute in 1990—light years before the Web become the economic and social force it is today. Back then, e-commerce on a nascent Internet was prohibited. Imagine that.

With the Net and e-business now a vital part of commerce, it's time for companies to take the next step—and ensure that the Web is accessible, too. The Commerce Dept. estimates that retail e-commerce accounted for $45 billion in sales in 2002, up 11% from the prior year. In the first quarter of 2003, online retail sales jumped 30%, to $11.9 billion, from the first quarter of 2002, while total retail sales grew just 4.4% in this same period.

The ADA has done some of its job well, leading to hard-won improvements like Braille on banking ATMs and more restaurants with wheelchair-accessible ramps. The act has encouraged —in some cases forced—employers to make workplace accommodations for people with disabilities. And it has raised consciousness nationwide that people with disabilities can perform as ably and professionally as other workers if just given a chance.

**EVERYBODY WINS.** Now, disability groups are pushing for better Web usability for the blind, deaf, and mobility-impaired, and they're seeing improvements. "Executives are saying, 'O.K., now we get it. We don't want to discriminate against persons with disabilities,'" says Judy Brewer, director of the Web-accessibility initiative for the World Wide Web Consortium (WC3), which develops technical standards for the Web.

Disability advocates target top brass by translating the Web-accessibility issue into a language that corporate types can understand: the large, untapped market of 54 million Americans with disabilities. If that doesn't work, they can try threats of legal exposure. Accessibility-software makers spread awareness by packaging their products with other Internet tools coveted by CEOs and CIOs, like security and privacy.

With the Net playing an ever-increasing role in employment, education, commerce, and even social and family life, Web accessibility removes barriers to equal opportunity. As a side benefit, an aging population also benefits from many kinds of Web accessibility, including larger font sizes and computers that speak text.

**MUDDLED MEASURE.** PC maker Dell (DELL) says its online presence accounted for 50% of its $31.2 billion in revenues last year. At FleetBoston Financial (FBF), online banking is its fastest-growing business. Fleet is relaunching its Web site this summer with a new user interface, and it has hired blind and visually impaired people to test the site using screen readers and keyboard-only commands. The results? "We smoothed out all the bumps to make it fully accessible," says Neal Wolfson, director of Fleet's interactive banking group.

IBM (IBM) calls Web accessibility a great marketing tool. It sold that concept to Sprint PCS (PCS), the wireless-phone maker, which has made its Web site easier to use for the visually impaired, deaf, and hard-of-hearing. "What we're finding are different motivators. Companies aren't required by law, but this is a great way to market and to appeal to the community," says Cindy Drummond, director of IBM's Accessibility Solution Center.

While it's a huge advance, the ADA isn't perfect. One flaw: It's ambiguously written. Title III is the section that forbids discrimination in public places and places where commerce is affected. This includes restaurants, banks, hospitals, movie theaters, museums, and schools — but not cyberspace. Mucking things up further is a separate, unrelated federal workplace law called Section 508 that requires the U.S. government and its agencies to make their Web sites accessible. Adopted in 1998, Section 508 has helped to create the perception that the private sector needs to make the same accommodations under the ADA.

**CAN'T SURF? NO DISCOUNT.** An unclear law often leads to lawsuits but also to groundbreaking and constructive settlements. The NFB sued America Online unit of AOL Time Warner (AOL ) in 1999, saying the Interet service's proprietary software interfered with the ability of blind people using a screen reader to access the AOL system. The NFB withdrew its lawsuit in 2000 after AOL said it would develop an accessibility policy and make its newer software (version 6.0 and higher) compatible with screen readers.

In another high-profile case, a disability group and a Southwest Airline (LUV) customer, who is blind, sued the airline for refusing to sell him a Web-fare special over the phone because the site wasn't accessible with his screen reader. A U.S. District Court judge in Florida threw out the case, saying nothing in the ADA includes the Internet.

However, the WC3 filed a brief saying its guidelines allow for an acceptable standard to be developed for companies. The case is now on appeal. Meanwhile, Southwest says it's exploring possibilities to make its site more user-friendly. Sensitivity and common sense go a long way when it comes to disabilities law.

**COMPREHENSIVE POLICY?** The National Council on Disability has issued a report, recommending that the ADA be amended to cover the private-sector Net. "If the Internet is excluded from coverage under Title III because it isn't a physical location, or if Internet-only commerce is excluded from coverage for lack of a nexus, then under what logic can telephone, postal, or any other form of non-face-to-face interaction or commerce be covered?" the report asks.

Good question. Web accessibility must go beyond content and be extended to operating systems, hardware, and info-tech training. Microsoft (MSFT), IBM, and Macromedia (MACR) are all to be applauded for creating products to support Web accessibility. Disability advocates know it'll take more time to create comprehensive guidelines. Some groups, like the W3C, would like the U.S. to have a national policy for the Net, similar to policies in Britain and Australia.

However, after advocates pause to celebrate the ADA's anniversary, they should then hit the refresh button—and get ready for the work that still must be done.

---

# Not in My Company

## Preventing Sexual Harassment

### By Jim Mulligan and Norman Foy

"ABC Co. was convicted of sexually harassing female employees." Does that sound like the kind of free advertising that would help your organization? No, we wouldn't like to see our businesses get that kind of new exposure, either. As business managers we have many issues to confront, and sexual harassment in the workplace is one of them.

Sexual harassment isn't a problem for human resources and the lawyers to solve. They are just responsible for cleaning up the mess and paying the lawsuit awards after the fact. We, the organization's managers, are responsible for preventing sexual harassment.

Sexual harassment is bad business: The Equal Employment Opportunities Commission has shown a 150 percent increase in sexual harassment charges filed since 1992. Poor morale, decreased productivity, and increased absenteeism, along with financial and legal costs, are just some of the negative aspects of an ineffective or nonexistent sexual harassment prevention program. With these potential costs and hazards in mind, companies must take proactive steps to protect themselves.

The $34 million Mitsubishi case and the recent $10 million Dial settlement got headlines, but sexual harassment is also a major problem for the small business community. We conducted a survey of companies that have between 15 and 100 employees and found that one out of every five companies reported having had sexual harassment claims filed against them.

The purpose of this article is to describe the relevant legal framework and provide you with a management system to make sure you aren't one of those companies. While our recommendations apply to larger firms, we have found that it is the smaller companies that have the strongest need to increase their focus on sexual harassment prevention.

### Sexual harassment law

While you don't need to be a lawyer, you do need a basic understanding of sexual harassment law. The major pertinent legislation is Title VII of the Civil Rights Act of 1964. This federal law applies to organizations with 15 or more employees. Title VII never mentions the term "sexual harassment." Instead, it prohibits job discrimination based on race, gender, color, religion, or national origin. The Supreme Court has ruled that sexual harassment is a form of gender discrimination. The courts have issued many written definitions and interpretations of sexual harassment, which we will describe in this section. The courts have defined two forms of sexual harassment:

* **Quid pro quo harassment.** A common definition is "this for that." In operational terms, some condition of employment such as salary or promotion is dependent on the employee submitting to sexual advances or conduct. This type of harassment also applies to the negative form—if you don't submit, you will be fired. In some ways this is the hardest form of harassment to prevent. That is because it takes only one instance of quid pro quo harassment to make the organization liable. In addition, the Supreme Court has ruled that the threat doesn't have to be carried out for harassment to have occurred.

* **Hostile environment harassment.** These situations relate to the workplace environment and are more subject to the court's interpretation than quid pro quo harassment is. A hostile environment consists of such things as sexually explicit photos or telling sexual stories or making lewd suggestions—actions that are "unwelcomed" by the person complaining. Since what is unwelcomed will differ by person, management should set fairly strict rules

as to what materials are displayed in the workplace and what actions are permitted.

## The Equal Employment Opportunities Commission has shown a 150 percent increase in sexual harassment charges filed since 1992.

We need to know that even if the harassment is caused by a low-level supervisor or group of employees, the responsibility rests with the organization. Keep in mind that the law protects employees against sexual harassment from members of the same sex. Since sexual harassment relates to gender, not necessarily sex, a person can be guilty of harassing someone (male or female) even though a demand for sex was not made.

In addition, people can be victims of harassment even though they are not directly harassed. For example, suppose Supervisor Al promises Employee Carol a large raise if she has sex with him. Carol submits and gets the raise. Carol tells another employee, Sarah, who received a normal raise. Sarah is the victim of sexual harassment and can file a third-party complaint against the organization.

Getting worried? In addition to compensatory damages, a victim can receive punitive damages as described in the Civil Rights Act of 1991.

But instead of focusing on those details, let's look at the results of some 1998 Supreme Court decisions that will help us minimize sexual harassment liability. The court ruled that in cases where the employer hasn't taken some tangible employment action against the victim (such as firing or demoting the person being harassed), the organization may protect itself using the affirmative defense. That defense is that the employer exercised reasonable care to prevent and promptly correct any

sexually harassing behavior and that the complaining employee unreasonably failed to take advantage of preventive or corrective opportunities provided by the employer. You can provide an affirmative defense by developing an effective management system to prevent sexual harassment.

These are the high points of federal legislation and court rulings related to sexual harassment. There may be state or local legislation in your area that also must be considered.

## You can provide an affirmative defense by developing an effective management system to prevent sexual harassment.

For example, in New York State the law appears to parallel the federal approach, but the New York law applies to firms with four or more employees versus the federal minimum of 15. Thus, many firms that are exempt from the federal law are covered under the New York State law. The complexity of the federal sexual harassment law and specific state and local legislation make it particularly advantageous for companies to use the advice of a competent employment law attorney

Now let's take a look at a management system for preventing sexual harassment. Before disseminating a policy and program in your company, we recommend that you review them with an employment law attorney.

### Managing to prevent sexual harassment

The management system is a proactive way to be in compliance with all of the sexual harassment laws. This system includes simple steps that businesses can take to address the problem of sexual harassment in the workplace while taking into consid-

eration their lack of resources. This management system entails four important steps.

1. **Create and circulate a sexual harassment policy.** The policy should outline the company's position against sexual harassment: "ABC Co. will not tolerate sexual harassment." A good policy should also provide a definition of what is and what is not sexual harassment. By defining sexual harassment, a policy will become easier for employees to understand. If a policy already exists, this is a good time to review it to make sure it reflects any recent changes in the law. The policy should also state the company's procedure for filing a complaint. A strong and effective policy may be able to deter potential harassment.

The policy cannot be effective unless employees are made aware of its existence. In the past, many companies claimed to have sexual harassment policies, but the employees were not always informed about the existence of this policy. If a policy exists but is not published to the employees, the policy is not effectively preventing sexual harassment in the workplace. One effective way to circulate a sexual harassment policy is to publish it in an employee handbook, therefore distributing it with all other company policies. This seems to be the most popular method used by companies. If you don't have an employee handbook, another method of publicizing a company's sexual harassment policy is to post a memo from top management informing all employees or the policy. To be more effective and provide reinforcement, companies should periodically redistribute this policy to their employees. Many companies provide two copies of the policy to each employee, with the requirement that one of the copies be signed and dated, acknowledging receipt, and returned to management.

2. **Evaluate for the presence of sexual harassment.** The intention of this step is to uncover inappropriate workplace behaviors. A company

that evaluates and deals with sexual harassment is minimizing the costs of harassment while acting proactively to prevent it.

Organizational managers can use anonymous employee questionnaires or workplace inspections to evaluate for the presence of sexual harassment. These methods will often uncover inappropriate behaviors or items, which is the whole objective of this step. By implementing this step, employees will see that the company is serious about preventing sexual harassment. This will encourage employees to help keep the workplace free of all sexual harassment by following the lead of management.

If a policy exists but is not published to the employees, the policy is not effectively preventing sexual harassment in the workplace.

Firms can be proactive by using this approach to confront sexual harassment in their workplace. If the evaluation does show the existence of harassment, the employer needs to act to correct this illegal behavior. By acting immediately, the company is acting reasonably to protect its employees from sexual harassment and therefore might not be held liable in hostile work environment cases.

**3. Make training a priority.** Many organizations do not make sexual harassment prevention training for all of their employees a priority. There are a number of reasons for smaller companies not providing sexual harassment prevention training. Many of these companies wrongly believe that sexual harassment does not affect them. Another reason used by small companies for not providing sexual harassment prevention training is limited resources. However, harassment prevention training for all employees does not have to be expensive. Just because a firm cannot afford to hire

an expensive consultant to train their employees does not mean effective training cannot take place. The purchase of a $100 video combined with a discussion of the company's sexual harassment policy and procedures will display the "reasonable care" that will aid in complying with the affirmative defense. There are also programs from the U.S. Small Business Administration and local chambers of commerce available to train employees on this topic.

**4. Develop a procedure for complaint resolution and investigation.** Many employees will not report sexual harassment because there are no effective procedures lot reporting it. In the affirmative defense, the lack of an effective procedure leaves the employer open to liability. The second part of the defense states that the employee needs to fail unreasonably to use the procedures offered by the employer. The courts will find in favor of the employee it the company does not have an effective procedure.

# HARASSMENT STATS

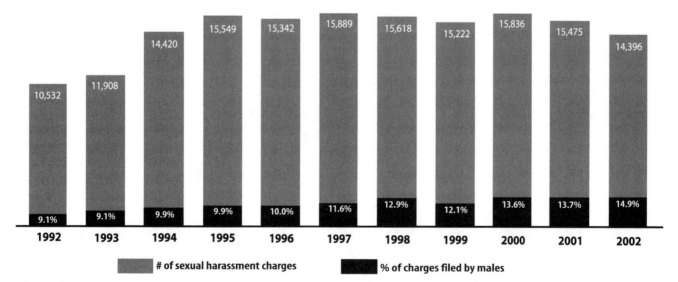

The statistics represent the total number of charges filed and resolved under Title VII alleging sexual harassment discrimination as an issue. The data reflect charges filed with EEOC as well as state and local fair employment practices agencies.

SOURCE: U.S. EQUAL OPPORTUNITY COMMISSION.

An effective complaint procedure allows an employee a method of reporting sexual harassment. This procedure should encourage employees to come forward with any complaints. Research shows that employees will turn to litigation only if they cannot get relief from within the company. A clear and effective complaint procedure should state to whom an employee can report a complaint. An employee's supervisor should not be the only person available to hear an employee's complaint since that person could be the harasser. In order to be effective, multiple people of both genders, if possible, should be selected to hear reports of sexual harassment. In addition, a complaint procedure should state that the employee will be free from retaliation for filing a complaint.

An effective complaint procedure should also outline an employer's intention to investigate all harassment complaints. An employer should investigate sexual harassment complaints in a timely and thorough manner. Investigating sexual harassment complaints is not always easy. The employer should attempt to keep the information about the complaint private but should not offer any guarantees of confidentiality to the complainant. An effective investigation may not be able to keep all information about a complaint private.

> Research shows that employees will turn to litigation only if they cannot get relief from within the company.

The presence of an effective procedure for complaint resolution and investigation can help organizations use the affirmative defense. If an employee unreasonably fails to use the methods provided by the employer, the employer will not be held liable for hostile work environment harassment.

Sexual harassment does occur in organizations of all sizes and its dangers should not be ignored. If you follow the advice provided here it will help minimize the chances that it will occur in your business.

---

**Norman Foy** is a professor in the Graduate Business School, Mercy College. He has 30 years of management experience in the information processing and semiconductor industries. Foy has a B.S. in business and an M.B.A. along with a doctorate from Columbia University. He is certified as a senior professional in human resources management and holds additional financial certifications.

---

**Jim Mulligan** is the human resource manager for Ludl Electronic Products, a manufacturer of precision automation equipment and accessories for microscopy. He has a B.A. in sociology and an M.S. in human resource management from Mercy College. Mulligan wrote his master's thesis on sexual harassment prevention in small companies. He is certified as a professional in human resource management.

---

From *Industrial Management*, Vol. 45, No. 5, September/October 2003, pages 26, 28-30. Reprinted with the permission of the Institute of Industrial Engineers, 3577 Parkway Lane, Suite 200, Norcross, GA 30092, 770-449-0461. Copyright © 2003 by Institute of Industrial Engineers.

# The Aesthetics of Security

Building owners, architects seek to make properties safer without the look of a fortress

## By RAY A. SMITH

How do you design a building that is people-friendly and pleasing to look at but is also as safe and secure as a fortress?

It is a challenge that building owners, architects and engineers are struggling to meet as they seek ways to protect their tenants and visitors from terrorist attacks. As the nation stands on high alert, building-design plans across the country are being updated or redone. The moves entail myriad compromises to reach a middle ground between security and aesthetics. After all, no matter how clear the threat, no one wants to live or work in a bunker.

Aside from structural strengthening to better equip buildings to withstand blasts and impacts, part of the designers' creative balancing act lies in what building designers call "transparent security"—protective measures that are hidden or blend in with the landscape and surroundings. Barriers to keep terrorists at bay are either unobtrusive or pleasing to the eye. Entrances, lobbies and halls of office buildings, sports stadiums and performing-arts centers are being designed wider and longer to accommodate turnstiles, security checkpoints and metal detectors.

Some examples of heightened security measures:

- At Times Square Tower, a 47-story, 1.2 million-square-foot office tower going up in New York, contractors have strengthened connections between steel columns with welded plates to stiffen joints between structural beams, people familiar with the matter say.
- At Ground Zero, design plans for a $700 million, 52-story tower to replace the destroyed 7 World Trade Center call for using reinforced concrete to surround the building's core, which contains such essential components as stairs, elevators and antennas for emergency communication.
- The Houston Multi-Purpose Arena, which will be the new home for the Houston Rockets, is among the stadiums and convention centers planning to feature new protective encasements made of concrete around vents to keep people from being able to release chemicals and toxins into the vents.
- The CIBC Tower, under construction in Manhattan, will have higher-grade, more-durable glass windows to minimize potential shattering. Such laminated and tempered glass is being considered for a number of other existing and planned facilities across the country, from schools to hospitals.

"We want to design buildings that reflect the values of our culture of openness and freedom," says architect Barbara A. Nadel, a former vice president of the American Institute of Architects. "We don't want to build bunkers. We don't want to live in a series of fortresses."

While there is consensus among building owners, architects and engineers that something must be done, there is little agreement on exactly what. No one is sure what to protect against.

"You can sit around and make a list of potential threats and the risk that they pose and never finish the list," says architect Roger K. Lewis. "Given this list of threats, how do you decide what you can do to protect yourself and minimize risk?"

Mr. Lewis, who is also professor of architecture at the University of Maryland in College Park, Md., says real-estate professionals have to make judgment calls about how far to go with security. "We're spending a lot of money doing this stuff to give people a sense of security and psychic comfort but in fact some of these security measures are really placebos. They're not necessarily going to do much if a terrorist cooks up some other crazy way to attack a target besides the one we planned for," he says. With most of these measures, says Mr. Lewis, the chance of damage to the building is "diminished, not eliminated."

Frank T. MacInnis, chief executive of **Emcor Group** Inc., a facility-management company based in Norwalk, Conn., credits some of the efforts being made to secure buildings but says a lot more has to be done. "Many owners are reluctant to spend money on measures without clear guidelines from the Department of Homeland Security on what practical steps they should take … especially in a recessionary environment," he says. He says the government should create a standardized security system for commercial buildings.

A homeland-security spokesman says the department has a working relationship with the Real Estate Roundtable, a Washington-based lobbying group whose 200 members include real-estate owners, developers and managers, and is using that forum to assess the real-estate industry's needs.

Roger Platt, senior vice president at the Real Estate Roundtable says, "Before there are comprehensive federal guidelines on how to develop new buildings, it would be valuable for the federal government to review its experience with hardening measures it is taking with its own portfolio. It would be a good test run for what sorts of hardening measures are practical."

Absent such guidelines, a number of owners have turned their attention to including more-attractively designed posts and planters in front of buildings to block vehicular access and avert car and truck bombings.

At the Citigroup Center at 53rd Street and Lexington Avenue in Manhattan, the building's owner, **Boston Properties** Inc., plans to replace some of the standard concrete planters installed outside just after Sept. 11, 2001, with concrete posts three feet tall and nine inches wide that are covered with stylish stainless steel, designed by **JJ Falk Design** LLC.

Architectural firm **HOK Sport + Venue + Event** of Kansas City, Mo., is designing security planters at sports stadiums with teams' logos to make them look like natural parts of a thematic landscape.

"The challenge is to create an environment where expectations of security are met but [visitors'] experience isn't like they're going into a prison," says Russ Simons, a principal at the firm. "If you're going to see a game and you get out of the car, and there are lights everywhere, razor wire, dogs, you'd be like, 'Maybe we should watch this at home.'"

Transparent security can also involve less-obvious measures, such as roadway access. Architectural firms **HKS** Inc., of Dallas, and Pickard Chilton, of New Haven, Conn., are studying the feasibility of "stair-stepping" roadways at Washington Hospital Center in Washington, D.C., so that less secure, nonemergency vehicles would be rerouted to a lower, more distant roadway to limit vehicular access to the entrance of the building. The study is part of a federal initiative called Project ER One.

Even building and site plans themselves have become more secure. In Massachusetts, an emergency, terrorism-related law enacted last September calls for the restriction of access to records, including but not limited to blueprints, plans, policies, procedures and schematic drawings of buildings, structures, facilities, utilities, transportation and infrastructure.

# Aftershocks of WAR

Soldiers returning from Iraq are likely to need HR's help in coping with delayed emotional trauma.

Linda Wasmer Andrews

Dan is a true hero of the war in Iraq, and he has the Bronze Star to prove it. A staff sergeant in the Army Reserve, Dan is part of a psychological operations unit that helped lead the way to places most of us know only as exotic names from the evening news: Nasiriyah, Baghdad, Tikrit.

It was near Nasiriyah that Dan earned the Bronze Star for meritorious service. He and his team were shepherding about 30 Iraqi civilians to safety while U.S. Marines were setting off explosives nearby. Suddenly, Dan's group came under enemy fire. Refusing to leave the civilians defenseless, Dan climbed onto the hood of a slow-moving Humvee and started firing back, shielding the civilians as they moved up the road to the safe area controlled by the Marines.

It was only after Dan returned home to Maryland that things began to fall apart. The company where he had worked as director of sales and marketing was gone, so he had to find a new job. He also had to adjust to married life since, in the long tradition of soldiers shipping out, he had married his girlfriend just four days before leaving for Iraq.

On top of that, there was the emotional residue of war. One of his unit's missions had involved broadcasting surrender appeals over loudspeakers, which led to many harrowing moments. "As soon as we cranked that thing up, we were immediately a target," Dan recalls. In a place where the days were punctuated by gunfire and grenades, a constant state of vigilance served him well. Back home, though, it was hard to let his guard down again. Something as innocuous as the banging noise of a trash truck was enough to set off alarm bells in his brain.

Dan went through a series of jobs in his first months back. He had trouble concentrating, and he showed up late for work. To make matters worse, he was plagued by back pain from an injury he sustained in a Humvee accident. Fortunately, Dan has since found a half-day sales job with an understanding employer. But he has yet to seek counseling, and he still seems to be struggling to grasp how his life could have changed so dramatically in such a short time.

## To Iraq and Back

Dan's struggle is far from unique, and stories such as his are apt to be repeated many times over this spring, as the military completes a massive rotation of troops into and out of Iraq. Of course, not everyone goes through a difficult readjustment period when they return. Dan himself had an easier time after coming home from an earlier deployment to Bosnia. For some, though, the stress of wartime service continues to exact a harsh toll long after the last shot has been fired.

For HR professionals, this presents a two-fold challenge: first, to understand what returning war veterans have been through—and may still be experiencing—and second, to be alert for signs that a little outside help might ease their transition back into their civilian jobs. Fortunately, we now know more than we ever did about how to spot war-related problems early and how to provide people with the emotional and practical support they need to heal.

Making use of that information will be particularly important in the coming months because many experts expect the war in Iraq to lead to more postwar psychological fallout than other recent conflicts. For one thing, there is the magnitude and duration of the war. "To put it in perspective, this has been the largest and longest-lasting mobilization [of the reserve and National Guard] since the Korean War," says Col. John O'Shea, U.S. Army (ret.), director of education for the Reserve Officers Association.

Then there is the high-anxiety nature of the combat. "This has been a much more difficult operation than the first Gulf War," notes John Thompson Jr., a former military psychiatrist who now teaches at Tulane University School of Medicine in New Orleans. This time around, our forces have had to contend with more exposure to traditional warfare as well as the injuries and fatalities that go with it. Add to that the ever-present threat of terrorist attacks and the unpredictable risk of conducting door-to-door searches, factor in difficult living conditions, and you have a recipe for fatigue, stress and possible trauma.

Among troops still in the field, this stress has manifested itself in a suicide rate that appears to be higher than peacetime military rates. (As of February, there were at least 18 suicides among service members in Operation Iraqi Freedom, according to the Department of Defense. The actual number may be higher and is a source of some controversy. As of this writing, additional information from the Defense Department is expected shortly.) In veterans who have returned home, such stress may lead to a host of adjustment problems.

At times, it may turn into full-blown post-traumatic stress disorder (PTSD)—an anxiety disorder that can develop in survivors of any terrifying ordeal in which there was a threat of serious bodily harm. In general, about 30 percent of individuals who spend time in a war zone go on to develop PTSD, according to data from the National Institute of Mental Health. Among those who spend extended periods of time in a high-risk situation, however, the odds of developing at least a few PTSD-like symptoms may rise to between 50 percent and 70 percent, says Thompson.

## Explosive Mind-Fields

They called it shell shock after World War I and combat fatigue after World War II. Since Vietnam, PTSD has been the term du jour. Whatever you call it, people have long recognized that soldiers returning from battle frequently have lingering emotional and behavioral reactions to the trauma they've endured. Sometimes, the reactions are limited and go away on their own.

"The only problem I had after I came back was trouble sleeping," says Derrick Smith, a senior supervisor at New York utility company KeySpan, who was deployed to Iraq with his Marine Corps Reserve communications unit. "After a couple of weeks, though, slowly but surely, I got back to normal."

For other people, however, problems persist, interfering with their lives at home and at work and often causing considerable distress and confusion.

Some veterans with war-related stress reactions are bothered by unwanted memories, flashbacks or nightmares. Others are troubled by emotional numbness, depression or self-blame for something they did or failed to do in combat. Still others are unable to let their defenses back down, even though the threat of imminent attack has now passed. Instead, they live in a continuing state of high alertness. This may show up as insomnia, irritability, angry outbursts, difficulty concentrating, anxiety, panic attacks, being easily startled or being constantly on the lookout for danger.

Such symptoms usually appear within the first three months after a traumatic event, although occasionally they may lie dormant for years. About half the time, the symptoms go away within a few months. The rest of the time, they stick around for longer. Even after the symptoms seem to have vanished, however, a recurrence may be triggered by reminders of the traumatic event or by new sources of stress in the person's life.

**In Iraq, constant vigilance served him well. Back home, though, it was hard to let his guard down again.**

### Injured But Not Broken

Thanks to modern advances in body armor and medical science, more soldiers are surviving injuries that would have been fatal in the past. That's undeniably good news, but it also means that some employees may be battling pain and disability long after they've returned home. Soldiers who have been injured in battle also are at high risk for developing post-traumatic stress disorder (PTSD).

"The military medical centers are already treating a lot of orthopedic injuries, and they're seeing that almost half of those people have PTSD," says Patrick Calhoun, a staff psychologist at the Durham VA Medical Center in North Carolina.

Health care coverage for injuries incurred while serving in the military is provided by the government. Nevertheless, the return of these soldiers raises some issues for employers.

"Developing work opportunities for those who have been injured will be a challenge," says Robert Ursano, director of the Center for the Study of Traumatic Stress in Bethesda, Md. "These individuals need to be given an opportunity to succeed. Feeling that they are contributing at work is critical to their self-esteem, and that may require some job accommodation."

If you have employees returning from Iraq, a little sensitivity to the stress they may be experiencing can go a long way. Joseph Mancusi, a psychologist, speaker and consultant who formerly was national director of the U.S. Department of Veterans Affairs (VA) psychology program, suggests that you watch for the following warning flags:

- Personality changes such as irritability, anger, anxiety or withdrawal.
- Tardiness or absenteeism.
- Trouble completing work on time.
- Conflict with co-workers.
- Increase in accidents or close calls.
- Drop in motivation or performance.
- Evidence of alcohol or drug abuse.

There's nothing unique about such signs, of course. They're similar to the signs of many other psychological and behavioral problems. PTSD isn't exclusively an issue for veterans, either. It can affect anyone who has been through a traumatic ordeal. Nevertheless, the horrible events that are the everyday stuff of war—such as firing a weapon at another person, being fired on, sustaining a serious injury, witnessing the maiming or death of others, or living in constant fear of attack—are powerful risk factors. It's little wonder that some vets take a while to heal.

Reaching out to these individuals is, first and foremost, an act of caring. However, it also makes sound financial sense. PTSD affects a number of physiological systems that are involved in the body's stress response, which can give rise to a host of physical symptoms. It also increases the risk of depression and hostility, both of which have been linked to poor health. In addition, people with untreated PTSD tend to abuse alcohol and other drugs at high rates. The bottom line is that PTSD raises the risk for a broad range of medical conditions.

"There is an increase in circulatory, digestive, musculoskeletal, nervous and respiratory diseases," says Patrick Calhoun, a staff psychologist at the Durham VA Medical Center in North Carolina. Although hard data aren't available yet, it seems logical that the cost of employee reintegration and assistance services might be more than offset by future health care savings, says Calhoun.

## Defusing the Stress

Two keys to helping your returning employees cope are common sense and compassion, says Elaine Weinstein, PHR, senior vice president of human resources at KeySpan. The company has had 28 employees, including Smith, mobilized since Sept. 11. Twenty have since returned.

"I try to anticipate what they might need to help them come back and readjust well," says Weinstein. If supervisors see that an employee is not 100 percent yet, "we might work out a gradual re-entry process or a flexible work arrangement. We'll do whatever it takes to make sure the reservist is integrated back in a sympathetic way."

She offers this advice to other HR professionals: "Although your policies and practices may not explicitly state what you should do, treat them as you would wish to be treated after leaving your family and supporting your country."

Brace Blythe, CEO of Atlanta-based Crisis Management International—which provides consulting and mental health services to companies whose employees have been affected by crises such as Sept. 11, the Oklahoma City bombing and Hurricane Andrew—seconds the need for an individualized approach. "We suggest that the person who is returning have some say-so in how the workplace responds to them," he says. "Have a meeting with the person before he or she comes back to work. Say, 'Let's talk about your re-entry—what you can expect, what you'd like from us, how'd you like it to be handled, and what you want communicated to others.' "

Some people are eager to move full-speed ahead. "I jumped right back in," says Steve LaBarbera, a supervisor in the retirement services group at Merrill Lynch in New York, whose Marine Corps Reserve unit patrolled cities in Iraq.

However, others need a more gradual transition. In that case, it may help to brainstorm with the supervisor about

---

### 'Welcome Back!'

Employers large and small are finding unique ways to welcome back their employees who are returning from military duty.

• GE Energy, the energy arm of General Electric Co., has had about 130 employees mobilized since Sept. 11. Susan Kratch, the company's human resource manager for military programs, is working on individualized reintegration plans for several employees who have been gone for more than a year. For one reservist due back soon, she plans to provide a full year of extra training.

• The Link Agency, a marketing firm in Providence, R.I., had just six employees when one was called up in early 2003. That employee is due back soon, and Joanne Sourial, who manages both communications and human resources, has devised an elaborate three-week re-entry plan. In addition, she has prepared a scrapbook that includes photos of staff and samples of recent work, and she has alerted clients so that those who wish to send welcome-back cards can do so.

• PG&E Corp., the San Francisco-based energy company, recently was one of five national winners of the Freedom Award, established by the Arlington, Va.-based National Committee for Employer Support of the Guard and reserve in recognition of the company's support of the National Guard and reserve. To celebrate, the company held large assemblies at its headquarters facility, where employees in the Guard and reserve were honored. Says Brent Stanley, the company's senior vice president of human resources, "We made it clear to them that we appreciated what they did for us."

---

possible ways to ease the person back into his or her job, says Blythe.

Robert Ursano, director of the Center for the Study of Traumatic Stress in Bethesda, Md., adds that a training course is often a good way to bring employees back up to speed gradually without expecting them to assume a full workload immediately.

Managing the reception from co-workers is another sensitive issue. "Co-workers often feel unsure about how they're supposed to behave," says Blythe. "They think, 'There's no telling what this person has been through. Should I ask about it or not? Can I still joke around, or do I have to watch everything I say?' " The veteran, meanwhile, may have no idea why everyone is acting so awkward and stilted. All the vet knows is that people aren't treating him or her the same as before.

You can help the returning employee understand what's going on and suggest possible strategies for handling the situation. Since everyone is different, though, let that individual guide you in what feels comfortable for him or her.

**'Co-workers often feel unsure about how they're supposed to behave' around returning veterans.**

"The No. 1 rule is, when a person wants to talk, he will," says Mancusi. Until then, respect the person's silence. Trying to force disclosures too soon can do much more harm than good.

If the person is ready, however, one option might be to call a meeting of the workgroup where the veteran can share stories and photos. Some may want to say, "I'm going to tell this once, and then I don't want to discuss it again." Others may say, "If you have any questions, feel free to ask at any time." The only rule is that the veteran should help define how other people interact with him or her.

"People are naturally resilient," says Blythe. Many are able to fully resume their old jobs in a matter of weeks. If a returning employee seems to be struggling, however, a prompt referral to the employee assistance program (EAP) can help smooth out a bumpy re-entry and possibly avert future problems. War veterans who seem to have PTSD-like symptoms may also benefit from a reminder about the specialized counseling provided by the U.S. Department of Veterans Affairs through its VA medical centers and Readjustment Counseling Service vet centers.

## The Rest of the Vets

Of course, not everyone who is called up for military service winds up on the front lines. Thankfully, many mobilized members of the National Guard or reserve have not had to face great danger to life and limb. Still, virtually all have had to contend with the substantial stress of leaving their ordinary lives behind on short notice.

Take Angee Linsey, a senior consultant in the Walnut Creek, Calif., office of career services firm Lee Hecht Harrison. Linsey, who is also a lieutenant commander in the Naval Reserve, was deployed to a post in Italy in the aftermath of Sept. 11. Although she had been told the deployment would last a year, she was sent home after only five months.

"With four days notice, I was literally plucked out of my life and all that was familiar to me," she says. "Then, with four days notice on the other side, I was dropped back into my life here."

While she felt fortunate in her military assignment and grateful to be sent home earlier than expected, it was still disorienting. Her work team had assumed she would be gone longer, and someone else was temporarily doing her job. "I felt a bit disconnected," Linsey says.

While returning employees such as Linsey aren't at risk for PTSD, they can still experience plenty of garden-variety stress caused by the disruption in their lives. They, too, may need time to take care of personal business and get reacquainted with their loved ones before returning full-time to work. Once back on the job, many may require a gradual reorientation period as well.

"It's like time stopped for them in terms of their organizational history," says Cynthia McCabe, a managing consultant in the Cleveland office of DBM, a global human resource firm. Meanwhile, back at the office, tasks that the person used to do have been redistributed, and changes in co-workers, clients, hardware, software, products and services have all continued apace. It's easy to see why a little catch-up time is often necessary.

For any returning members of the National Guard or Reserve, whether they were stationed across the country or across the globe, simply taking time to say "welcome back" and "thank you for the sacrifices you've made" can make a world of difference.

"If somebody is coming back, let the company or work team know," says Ursano. "You might have a small gift, a cake or ribbons on the person's chair and desk. The boss could make a special point of reaching out to say, 'We're glad you're back.' "

**'With four days notice, I was literally plucked out of my life and all that was familiar to me.'**

Once again, though, the exact form this takes needs to be tailored to the culture of the workplace and the personality of the returning individual. Some may be embarrassed by a lot of hoopla, while others may appreciate the attention.

If you have several mobilized employees, it might be a good idea to create standard information packets to give them on their return. The packet could include information about their rights and responsibilities under the Uniformed Services Employment and Reemployment Rights Act. The packet could also describe services provided through the EAP for veterans who are experiencing trouble readjusting. In addition, it could offer guidance on which health care services are covered by the employer's plan and which by the government's.

In general, "if they come back after serving and report within the approved time, they go right back into the employer's health plan just as if they had never left," says John Wirtshafter, an employee benefits attorney at the law firm McDonald Hopkins in Cleveland. "But if they were injured while serving, that injury would be covered under the government's plan, not the employer's."

## The Few, the Proud, the Employees

Of course, Blythe points out, no packet can ever take the place of simply sitting down with returning employees and discussing their personal needs and concerns. It's a scene HR professionals will play out many times in the years to come if, as some experts say, our military continues to rely ever more heavily on the National Guard and Reserve.

The payoff, says Ursano, is the retention of mature, dedicated employees who have received valuable leadership and job skills training courtesy of Uncle Sam.

For most, the transition back to everyday life will probably be relatively painless after the first few hectic weeks have passed. For some, however, the stress of wartime service may last longer. Early recognition of trouble signs and prompt referral to appropriate counseling or other resources may mean the difference between continued distress and fast recovery for many of these individuals.

"If there's one thing we've learned from research," says Blythe, "it's that a strong support system is highly correlated with resiliency and recovery."

---

LINDA WASMER ANDREWS IS A FREELANCE WRITER IN ALBUQUERQUE WHO HAS SPECIALIZED IN HEALTH AND PSYCHOLOGY ISSUES FOR TWO DECADES.

---

# UNIT 2

# Meeting Human Resource Requirements

## Unit Selections

13. **Too Old to Work**, Adam Cohen
14. **Can You Interview for Integrity?**, William C. Byham
15. **Does HR Planning Improve Business Performance?**, Bill Macaleer and Jones Shannon
16. **Tomorrow's World**, Carol Glover

## Key Points to Consider

* Job requirements and working conditions have changed over the past several years. What new changes do you foresee in the workplace in the next 10 years? How do you see the impact of the 24/7 work schedule on employers and employees? What impact do you think telecommuting will have on the workplace? Do you think you will be working in the same kind of position as your parents? Do you think there is such a thing as age discrimination?

* The first step in the process of working is getting hired. The last step is termination, whether for cause, leaving for a new job, retirement, or a "reduction in force." What trends do you see in the workforce concerning individuals and their careers? What do you think the impact of race or diversity in the workforce is? Do you see any changes coming?

* How do you see computerization being applied to human resources, and how will this change human resources?

 **Links: www.dushkin.com/online/**
These sites are annotated in the World Wide Web pages.

**America's Job Bank**
  *http://www.ajb.dni.us*
**International Association for Human Resource Information Management (IHRIM)**
  *http://www.ihrim.org*

Organizations, whether profit or nonprofit, are more than collections of buildings, desks, and telephones. Organizations are made of people—people with their particular traits, habits, and idiosyncrasies that make them unique. Each individual has different needs and wants, and the employer and the worker must seek a reasonable compromise so that at least an adequate match may be found for both.

The importance of human resource planning is greater than ever and will probably be even more important in the future. As Thomas Peters and Robert Waterman have pointed out in their book *In Search of Excellence*:

> Quality and service, then, were invariable hallmarks of excellent firms. To get them, of course, everyone's cooperation is required, not just the mighty labors of the top 200. The excellent companies require and demand extraordinary performance from the average man. Dana's former chairman, Rene McPherson, says that neither the few destructive laggards nor the handful of brilliant performers are the key. Instead, he urges attention to the care, feeding, and unshackling of the average man. We labeled it "productivity through people." All companies pay it lip service. Few deliver.
>
> —Thomas Peters and Robert Waterman,
> In Search of Excellence,
> New York, Warner Books, 1987

In the future, organizations are going to have to pay more than just lip service to "productivity through people" if they want to survive and prosper. They will have to practice it by demonstrating an understanding of not only their clients' and customers' needs but also those of their employees. The only way they will be able to deliver the goods and services and achieve success is through those same employees. As explained in "Does HR Planning Improve Business Performance?" companies are faced with the difficult task of finding the right people for the right jobs—a task that must be accomplished if the organization is going to have a future.

Organizations are trying to meet the needs of their employees by developing new and different approaches to workers' jobs. This means taking into account how society, the labor force, the family, and the nature of the jobs themselves have changed. Training and development will be key in meeting future human resource requirements. Employers will have to change the way they design their positions if they are to attract and keep good employees. They must consider how society has changed and how those changes have affected the labor force. They will have to consider how the labor force has changed and will change in the future. Learning from experience that there are fewer young people and more middle-aged employees, who are no longer "Too Old to Work," as well as dual-career couples struggling to raise children, and dealing with aging parents in the workforce. They will have to consider how the very nature of jobs has changed in society, especially from predominantly blue-collar to white-collar jobs, from "9 to 5" to "24/7".

Human resource planning, selection, and recruitment are going to be even more critical in the future. Companies will have to go to extraordinary lengths to attract and keep new employees. There is no mystery about the reasons for this situation. America is aging, and there are fewer people in their late teens and early

twenties to take the entry-level jobs that will be available in the future. Women, who for the past 20 years have been the major source of new employees, now represent almost half the workforce. As a result, new groups must be found, whether they are retirees, high school students, workers moonlighting on a second job, minority group members, people with disabilities, or immigrants. One thing is certain: the workforce is changing and organizations will need to unlock the potential of all their employees. Other means of recruitment will need to be employed in the future, and old ideas and prejudices will have to go by the boards in all industrialized societies.

Another aspect of human resource planning involves both the selection process and the termination process. The days of working for only one company and then retiring with a gold watch and a pension are over. People are going to change jobs, if not companies, more frequently in the future, and many of the tasks they will be doing in the next 10,15, or 20 years do not even exist today because of technological change. Midlife and mid-career changes are going to be far more common than they have been in the past, requiring people to change and adapt.

As seen in "Tomorrow's World," human resources information systems offer important tools in managing human resources. The ability of computers to handle large amounts of data is now being applied to human resource management with very interesting results. These practices, applied to hiring and internal information management, promise much greater automation of human resources in the future as well as reduced costs.

Meeting the human resource needs of any organization in the future is a difficult task. Assuming that the economy continues to grow at an acceptable rate, the need for workers will continue to increase, but many of the traditional sources of supply for new workers will be either exhausted or in decline. For example, human resource professionals know that there will be fewer workers available in the early twenties age group in the next 10 years because there are fewer teenagers today than 10 years ago. Management must plan for this shortage and consider alternative sources of potential employees. In turn, the individual employee must be ready to adapt quickly and efficiently to a changing environment. Job security is a thing of the past, and workers must remain flexible in order to cope with increased uncertainty.

# Too Old to Work?

## If you're over 40 and work for a big company, your future may well be tied to the fate of 6,400 Allstate agents who refused to be 'streamlined.'

By Adam Cohen

Allstate recruited new insurance agents in the 1980's with a brochure aimed at the dreams of time-clock punchers everywhere. The cover, which featured tidy-looking offices sporting the company's iconic blue-and-white logo, promised that signing on was "better than being in business for yourself." Inside, it offered prospective agents nothing less than a piece of the American dream. "Have you ever wanted a proprietary interest in a business?" the brochure beckoned. How about "unlimited income potential"? And "job security"?

Ron Harper, the son of a tractor salesman from Gainesville, Ga., wanted all of those things. A 38-year-old father of two, he had worked his way up in the supermarket business, starting as a bagger at 16 and rising to district sales manager in charge of 17 stores. But the supermarket industry was hurting, and after trying out a couple of other managerial jobs, he was looking for something more stable.

That was when he heard that Allstate was hiring. Its Neighborhood Office Agent program offered just the mix of opportunity and security he wanted. Allstate would give him policies to sell, money to run his own agency and a brand whose slogan— "You're in Good Hands"—was a marketing legend. He understood that the money would not be great at first. He would have to hustle to build a "book of business," and Allstate's commissions were less than he could earn as an independent broker. As an Allstate employee, though, he would receive generous benefits, including a pension. If he honed his skills and worked hard, he figured, there was no limit to what he could earn. And once

he got past the preliminaries, he was told, he could be terminated only for dishonesty.

In August 1989, Harper was assigned to the small town of Thomson, Ga., and he uprooted his family and began hunting for customers in difficult terrain. Most of Thomson's older residents already had car and home insurance, and the younger ones were clearing out for better jobs in Augusta and Atlanta. But Harper "bled blue," as the company's saying goes. He lived off savings at first, pouring his commissions back into the agency, and used his own money for rent, an assistant's salary and ads in the Yellow Pages. After a few years, he had his book of business and was making a modest living. Then, in 1998, Allstate reduced the commissions it paid its neighborhood agents. To make up the lost revenue, Harper's wife quit her job and worked for him at below-market wages.

In November 1999, just past Harper's 10-year anniversary with Allstate, his supervisor called him in to his office in Augusta. Harper and about 17 of his fellow agents were handed a box of documents—the "job in a box," they would come to call it—radically redefining their relationship with Allstate. Harper and the others would now be independent contractors. Their benefits, pensions included, would end.

The box also contained what Harper now calls the "damnable release," which guaranteed that the agents would not sue. They didn't have to sign, but if they refused, their days selling for Allstate were over. "I read that thing, and honest to God, I felt nauseous," Harper says. The agents were filled with questions. Prime among them, What happened to the job security they were promised? But the managers were "on transmit, no receive," Harper recalls. "All they wanted to do was read to us from the script."

The same meeting was being played out in Allstate offices nationwide. The company, which had more than 15,000 agents of various kinds, was offering all of its 6,400 employee agents—the longest-serving agents, and those with the best benefits—the same unrelenting terms. They could keep their jobs by forfeiting benefits that were, in some cases, worth hundreds of thousands of dollars. Or they could give up their benefits and their jobs.

Allstate's reneging on its promise was, Harper insists, "totally wrong." But he also knew that he couldn't afford to walk away. In the end, he did what all but a handful of the employee agents did—he signed the release. Then he sued for age discrimination.

ACCORDING TO the federal government, age-discrimination complaints filed with the Equal Employment Opportunity Commission are up more than 24 percent over the past two years. Pick up the paper, and the cases are everywhere. Ford Motor Company is paying more than $10.5 million to settle suits by older managers who claim that its evaluation system discriminates against them. A Pennsylvania judge has cleared the way for 5,665 employees over 40 in the state Department of Transportation to bring a discrimination class action. McDonnell-Douglas is paying $36 million in partial settlement of a suit by about 1,100 older workers who say that the company laid them off to save on pension costs and medical benefits.

It's an odd time for age bias to be on the upswing. With the vast improvements in medicine, nutrition and lifestyle in recent years, old simply isn't what it used to be. The problem is that workplace culture has, for the most part, stuck to old ways of thinking about older workers. In many elite job markets—investment banking, computer programming, publishing—youth is celebrated, and regardless of how young older workers may feel, they only have to look around to realize that they represent the old school, not the new wave.

Hollywood has been rocked by a recent round of lawsuits charging television networks, production companies, studios and agencies with "gray listing"—refusing to hire older talent. (In the case of some television writing jobs, "old" actually refers to the early 30's.) Last September, Doris Roberts, the septuagenarian actress who plays Ray Romano's mother on "Everybody Loves Raymond," told the Senate Special Committee on Aging that society views people her age as discardable. "My contemporaries and I are denigrated as old," she said. "Old coots, old fogies, old codgers, geezers … hags and old-timers."

Roberts was testifying about the entertainment industry, but she could have been describing almost any workplace in America. Look through the reams of age-discrimination documents, and you'll see that the biggest cases come not from Hollywood and Madison Avenue but from Old Economy sectors like auto manufacturing and retailing. (And some of the cruelest comments about old workers appear in litigation involving plumbing supplies and fiberglass sales.)

The disconnect between workers who look at themselves in the mirror and feel young and companies that look at them and

think "old-timer" has fueled much of the explosion in age-discrimination claims. But there are also some more basic social factors at work. With the graying of America, there are simply many more people eligible to be discriminated against—and to sue. The more than 70 million baby boomers now make up about half of the work force, and by next year even the youngest boomers will be 40—and therefore covered by federal age-discrimination laws. The oldest workers, who are most likely to face bias, are among the fastest-growing part of the work force. Workers over 65 increased by 20 percent in the 1990's; workers over 75 were up more than 80 percent from 1980 to 2000.

Couple these demographics with a faltering economy, and the conditions are perfect for a surge in discrimination suits. It's a typical pattern: when hard times hit, the ax falls disproportionately on older workers, who may be the most highly paid and who are often stereotyped as being less efficient. In a bad economy, with few other jobs available and retirement holdings taking a hit, fired workers are also more willing to sue.

The old face of age discrimination was the solitary worker quietly tapped on the shoulder and put out to pasture (Willy Loman, fired when the boss's son took over, left to complain, "You can't eat the orange and throw the peel away—a man is not a piece of fruit!"). These days, however, age discrimination is more often the product of broad-based company policies, like decisions to phase out entire job categories disproportionately held by older workers.

That is precisely what Harper and his fellow agents have charged Allstate with doing. At the heart of their lawsuit is the claim that Allstate executives singled out one category of workers—employee agents—because more than 90 percent of them were over 40. If Harper and his 28 fellow plaintiffs win an early procedural battle and are allowed to represent a class of 6,400 onetime employee agents, this could be the biggest case ever charging a company with age discrimination.

The suit is still in its early stages, but the agents have retained two top Washington firms, and AARP has assigned two lawyers to the case. In late 2001, the Equal Employment Opportunity Commission jumped in on the agents' side, filing its own suit charging that Allstate violated federal pension and age-discrimination laws when it forced the agents to sign away their benefits and promise not to sue in order to keep working.

The stakes are high. If the plaintiffs win, Allstate could be forced to pay hundreds of millions of dollars. But more important is what the suit could mean for older workers nationwide. Thousands—maybe millions—of older workers are discriminated against on the job every year, but many have no idea what their rights are. Age discrimination is ready for a high-profile case that serves—like Brown v. Board of Education did for race discrimination, or the Clarence Thomas-Anita Hill Senate hearings did for sexual harassment—as a lightning rod.

"I've been looking for a case like this for years," says Raymond Gregory, an employment lawyer and the author of a book on age-discrimination law. A victory in the case, he says, could generate the kind of enormous damage awards and nationwide publicity that would force corporate America to rethink its approach to age in the workplace.

ALLSTATE (THE nation's second-largest auto and home insurer and No. 57 on the Fortune 500 list) got its start in 1931 as a mail-order insurance division of Sears, Roebuck & Co. After the 1933 Chicago World's Fair, where an Allstate agent sitting at a card table in the Sears exhibit was mobbed by customers, Sears began putting agents in booths in its stores—usually under the escalator, the least valuable space on the sales floor.

In 1984, Allstate initiated the Neighborhood Office Agent program to get agents out of stores and onto Main Street. The N.O.A. program recruited agents as exclusive salesmen for Allstate's insurance products. Allstate offered lower commissions, in many cases, than the competition, and the office-expense allotments it paid—as Ron Harper learned—often did not cover an agency's costs. But what Allstate was really offering was a relationship that turned the job of insurance agent—often a lonely seat-of-the-pants existence—into the equivalent of an executive post with a major corporation. In addition to a great benefits package, Allstate's neighborhood agents would receive the best training in the industry and would be eligible for an array of old-style sales incentives—Honor Rings, Chairman Conference Awards and trips to sunny islands and European capitals.

The Neighborhood Office Agent program was initially a great success, but things began changing at Allstate in the 1990's. In an I.P.O. in '93, Sears spun off 20 percent of its Allstate stake, and two years later it sold off the rest. As Allstate began to fend for itself, its managers began rethinking the role of agents. It stopped hiring employee agents and, the plaintiffs say, began a campaign to switch the existing ones over to independent-contractor status.

Allstate dangled carrots, like bonuses for managers whose agents switched. And it wielded sticks, including tougher rules for neighborhood offices. But even as Allstate was apparently trying to prod its employee agents, it reassured them that the choice was theirs to make. "Rest easy, there is *no* plan to convert N.O.A. employee agents to … independent contractors effective 4/1/98!!!!" a December 1997 sales update promised.

The late 90's was a time of intense competition in the insurance business, and agent-oriented companies were worried. Insurgents like Geico were eliminating agents and selling directly to customers. And with the dot-com frenzy at a fever pitch, the conventional wisdom was that commerce of all kinds was moving online. The Internet's rise looked like bad news for Allstate, whose costly infrastructure of agents and offices would be a drag on earnings. Wall Street, certainly, was worried. In a booming stock market, Allstate shares plunged more than 50 percent, even as the company was furiously rebuying stock to prop it up.

In January 1999, Allstate's C.E.O., Jerry Choate, stepped down. Choate, the creator of the N.O.A. program, had worked his way up on the sales side and was well regarded by the agents. His replacement, Ed Liddy, a onetime Sears executive, lacked Choate's ties to the agents and came with a take-no-prisoners reputation. At Sears, he had helped to shutter the company's famed catalog, marveling to C.F.O. Magazine, "It's amazing how quickly you can dismantle a business that took a hundred years to build."

It was 10 months after Liddy took charge that Harper and the other employee agents were given Allstate's take-it-or-leave-it offer. Inside the "job in a box" packages handed out that day was a booklet titled "Preparing for the Future," which redefined the employment rules for employee agents. The tough new rules coincided with, and seemed designed to bolster, Allstate's widely heralded new plans to "aggressively expand the company's sales … and streamline the way the company operates."

The future that employee agents were supposed to prepare for was a grim one. As the plaintiffs see it, Allstate's motives were clear. The company was trying to cut costs by taking away their health insurance and freezing their pensions. At the same time, they say, Allstate was focused on "re-energizing" to compete against the Geicos and the dot-coms, and younger workers were the key. "We used to hear it in meetings all the time: 'We have these young people and they really go out and work,'" says Sylvia Crews-Kelly, a Tampa agent who was cut off after working 19 years, 8 months and 27 days—three months before she would have been eligible to start drawing her pension. "They said older workers just want to sit on their policies and collect commissions."

Allstate sees things differently. "There was no discrimination," insists Sue Rosborough, a lawyer for the company. "We reorganized our agency force for a lot of very good business reasons." Allstate says that its new business model cut costs by $600 million but that almost all the savings came through closing regional offices and eliminating 4,000 nonagent positions.

The "Preparing for the Future" program was never intended to cut back on the cost of agent benefits, says Barry Hutton, the executive who oversaw it. Employee agents were asked to become independent contractors, he says, to "streamline" operations. Allstate's 6,400 employee agents were part of a force of more than 15,000 agents hired under different rules at different times. There were 11 categories of agents, Hutton says, each with its own commission rates. Simplifying the categories made Allstate more efficient. "We just flat-out had to make a business decision so we could be nimble, as nimble as a large company can be," Hutton says.

What about Allstate's supposed promises that employee agents would not be terminated except for dishonesty? If these promises were made, Rosborough says, they are not legally binding on the company.

IT IS UNLIKELY that any prominent social theorist has ever put forth a vision of reform with insurance agents in the vanguard. The Allstate plaintiffs—who were highly compensated and are overwhelmingly white and male—do not look like typical victims of an unjust order. And the facts and legal issues in their suit are muddy. The animosity against older workers, if it was there, may be hard to find under all the layers of corporate cost-cutting and business strategizing.

Still, because of the number of workers affected, the prominence of the defendant, the size of the potential awards and the brazenness of Allstate's actions, this could represent the next wave in protecting the rights of older workers.

American workers are invariably surprised when they first learn, often when they have just been fired, about the concept of "employment at will." The general rule in American law is that employees hold their jobs at the whim of their bosses. Employers are free to fire workers, as the Tennessee Supreme Court explained in 1884, for "good cause, for no cause or even for cause morally wrong, without being thereby guilty of legal wrong."

Modern employment law has largely been a prolonged battle to whittle away at this doctrine. There are now a number of exceptions: workers generally can't be fired for union activity, say, or for whistle-blowing. But the largest carve-out is discrimination law. Employers may, as the Tennessee court said, fire workers for good cause or for no cause, but they cannot fire them on the basis of race, religion, sex or other prohibited factors.

Just where age fits in this list has long been unclear. It has been a kind of forgotten stepchild of the civil rights revolution. When the granddaddy of all employment-discrimination laws, Title VII of the Civil Rights Act of 1964, was adopted, there was general agreement on most of the categories. But Congress was uncertain what to do about age. The secretary of labor was asked to study age discrimination in employment and advise whether it should be covered. The secretary found that age discrimination was a real problem. At the time, about 50 percent of job listings were not open to applicants over 55, and 25 percent were closed off to those over 45. Relying on the report, Congress passed the Age Discrimination in Employment Act (A.D.E.A.).

Based on its language, which almost exactly tracks Title VII, older workers *should* be well protected. But it hasn't worked out that way. "The passage of the A.D.E.A. was the biggest victory," says Michael Lieder, a lawyer for the Allstate plaintiffs. "It's been downhill ever since."

It is almost always harder for older workers to win a bias claim than it is for the groups covered by Title VII. One of the biggest differences is the availability of an evidentiary theory known as "disparate impact." The Supreme Court has held since 1971 that plaintiffs suing under Title VII do not need to show that they were intentionally discriminated against (what the law calls "disparate treatment"); it is enough to show that a supposedly neutral policy disproportionately hurt a protected group. Once that is shown, the employer has the burden of showing that the challenged policy (a new kind of aptitude test, say, or a height requirement) is necessary for the job. Disparate impact is a powerful tool, since it is often hard for workers to prove intentional discrimination. Many of the biggest race- and sex-discrimination lawsuits could not have been won without it.

There is no reason that disparate impact shouldn't be available under the A.D.E.A., but many federal courts won't allow it. Even with intentional discrimination claims, older workers are worse off. Many judges just don't like age-discrimination lawsuits. One federal judge complained in a decision that older workers feel they can file age suits with no more evidence "than a birth certificate and a pink slip."

As a result, courts go to great lengths not to see age bias when it is obviously there. In case after case, judges excuse blatantly discriminatory comments as mere "stray remarks" and strain to find alternative reasons that older workers were fired. In one egregious case, a 56-year-old worker at a North Carolina company was fired. Two weeks before the firing, a supervisor said to him, "O'Connor, you are too damn old for this kind of work." This, a federal appeals court held, did not constitute sufficient evidence for discrimination.

Even when older workers make their case, courts are more willing to accept employers' defenses. Early in the civil rights era, it was established that a company cannot defend a race-discrimination claim by saying it acted for economic reasons. In the classic case, a restaurant that pleads "customer preference"—that it would happily hire black waitresses, but its racist customers would stop coming—still loses.

But in age cases, courts are all too willing to accept economic defenses. A company that says it laid off older workers because they were highly paid will often prevail. This can be a potent weapon for a company like Allstate, which can argue that when it pushed out all of those agents who were 40 or older, it was looking to get rid of expensive employees, not old ones.

There are many reasons that courts have been grudging about age claims. In part, judges do not see old people as a "discrete and insular minority," the classic legal formulation for a protected class. Blacks are separate and apart from the majority culture, the theory goes, but every family has old people in it, and anyone not currently in the class eventually will be. That logic ignores the fact that Congress established to its satisfaction 36 years ago that bias against older workers is real and pervasive—and passed the A.D.E.A. to do something about it.

Judges are also inclined to see pushing older workers out as part of the natural order, because they are less able, or to make room for the next generation. But stereotypes like these, about who is capable, or deserving, of employment are just what Congress was taking aim at with the A.D.E.A. There is no small contradiction in the fact that some of the worst age-discrimination law has come from Supreme Court justices, who serve for life. Lawyers for older workers have been reluctant to use the word "hypocrisy," but they have noted in their arguments that Justice Oliver Wendell Holmes stayed on the court into his 90's.

Advocates for older workers say, perhaps too hopefully, that the Supreme Court may be softening on age discrimination. They point, in particular, to a case from 2000 reinstating a jury verdict in favor of a Mississippi plumbing-products factory employee who was fired after his supervisor told him that he "must have come over on the Mayflower" and that he was "too damn old" for the job. Reversing a lower court, the Supreme Court unanimously held that the fired worker had put forth enough evidence to prove that his firing violated the A.D.E.A.

But also important, the E.E.O.C. recently signaled a willingness to challenge the court's stingy view of age discrimination. After the Supreme Court ruled in 2000 that individuals cannot sue state entities for damages under federal age-bias laws, the E.E.O.C. stepped in to represent 1,700 retired police officers, firefighters and other safety officers who charged the California Public Employees Retirement System with discriminating in benefits. In January, the retirement system agreed to pay $250 million—the largest settlement, for any kind of discrimination, in E.E.O.C. history.

RON HARPER AND his fellow plaintiffs know they have their work cut out for them. If disparate impact were available to them, they would be off to a fast start. The ratio of terminated agents who were in the protected class—more than 90 percent—is enormous by the standards of discrimination law. Under disparate impact, the burden would shift to Allstate to explain what it was up to.

As things now stand, the plaintiffs will need to come up with more proof of intentional discrimination to show that Allstate was biased against its older workers. If they can make the legal claims work, the plaintiffs say, they believe they have the sort of human stories that will put Allstate on the defensive. There are certainly plenty of plaintiffs like Harper who have stayed with the company and are struggling to stay afloat. More than 2,500 have left, and many of them describe it as if they have been fired. Gene Romero, 54, a 13-year Allstate agent in Overland Park, Kan., sold his book of business and has been unemployed ever since. He has looked for work, but the job market is weak, he says, and he hasn't found anyone who "wants to hire an old man." Michael Wilson, a lawyer for the Allstate plaintiffs, says that his clients are suffering the usual fallout of involuntary job loss—depression, divorce, alcoholism and worse. "I've had people call me and say, 'I was sitting out in my backyard with a gun in my mouth,' " he says.

Even if they don't prevail on the age-discrimination claims, they may win—as often happens in these cases—on a related claim. With sentiment running strongly against large companies that leave their retired workers in the lurch, they may do well with their challenge to the take-it-or-leave-it release.

However things work out for the Allstate plaintiffs, the case could reshape the legal landscape for older workers. Given the nation's demographic trends—and the persistence in stereotyped thinking about older people—there is every reason to believe that the age-bias complaints from television writers and teachers, bus mechanics and bankers will continue their explosive growth.

Now the law may have a chance to catch up. If the Allstate plaintiffs prevail, the case could give older workers their first true landmark case, with damage awards large enough to make corporate America recalculate the costs of discriminating.

Win or lose, advocates for older workers say, this case could be indispensable to the process of improving age-discrimination law—making it the equal of race, sex and religion. They have not given up, they say, on getting the courts to rethink the economic-defense excuse and their antipathy toward disparate impact. "We are not going to cower in front of these precedents," vows Laurie McCann, a senior AARP lawyer. "We're going to chip away to show that they're wrong."

> The Allstate plaintiffs—who were highly compensated and are overwhelmingly white and male— do not look like typical victims of an unjust order.

They also want Congress to get involved. It could amend the A.D.E.A. to bring age-discrimination rules in line with the more generous ones available under Title VII. This may seem like a uniquely inauspicious time to ask Congress to expand a civil rights law, particularly with the Republicans in control of both houses. But advocates for older workers point out that their constituents are one of the most potent voting blocs around. Politicians ignore older workers at their peril.

Harper is hoping that his dispute with Allstate rewrites the legal rules. Except for marrying his wife and rearing "two fine boys," he says, taking on Allstate is the most important thing he has ever done. "I'd be lying if I said we're not fighting for ourselves and our families," he says. "But every one of us knows that we're also carrying the ball for other people—people who will be hit by something like this in the future."

*Cohen is a lawyer and a member of the editorial board of The Times.*

# Can You Intervie for Integrity?

## Yes, and you don't need a lie detector to do it.

### By William C. Byham

After a thorough search for a new employee, one candidate has risen to the top, and he has the look of a winner. Impeccable résumé. Extensive relevant experience. Great interpersonal skills. Plenty of energy and enthusiasm. Great new ideas he's eager to set in motion.

So you hire him. And it turns out to be one of the biggest mistakes you've ever made.

That glowing individual, so impressive sitting across the conference-room table, lies to clients and misrepresents your products. He can't satisfactorily explain the irregularities in his expense reports. He backstabs co-workers and takes credit for work he didn't do. You have to let him go. But in his wake the questions remain: How were we so misled and so wrong? Why couldn't we have seen what kind of person we were *really* hiring?

Scenarios like this one are all too familiar, perhaps painfully so. But in light of the numerous examples of illegal and unethical behavior that have garnered headlines in recent months and years, managers are more interested than ever in making sure that they hire people, for positions at all organizational levels, who are trustworthy and share the organization's ethical values.

But despite their interest in doing a better job of hiring for honesty and integrity, too many managers continue to believe that their hands are tied. This is a mistake: They *can* screen for integrity and ethical behavior when selecting new employees. It might be as simple as doing background checks and checking references-steps that many organizations had tended to skip in recent years but are resurrecting. Then there is the often-overlooked yet substantial information on ethical behavior that managers can obtain during the interviewing process—by having properly trained interviewers seek examples of how candidates have handled ethical situations in the past, and by having everyone who interviews a candidate share, cross-check, and evaluate the information.

## "Doesn't Everyone Do It?"

Some people are understandably skeptical that dishonest and unethical individuals can be ferreted out simply by asking them questions about their past behavior. After all, won't a dishonest or unethical person just lie, anyway? Psychology suggests that the answer is no, they won't. People with low integrity tend to think that everybody else has the same degree or an even lower degree of integrity than they do; they readily admit to integrity lapses because they think that their behavior is normal and assume that the interviewer feels the same way.

I have seen this theory borne out many times in my own interviewing experiences and in those of others. On one occasion, I interviewed a prominent politician's administrative assistant who bragged about how she helped her boss pad his expense account. Another time, a candidate I interviewed for a sales position told me how he had obtained "gold status" on a major airline by taking needless flights—paid for out of his employer's travel budget.

## Organizations must have leaders and associates who will share and live their ethical values.

The real key to effectively interviewing for integrity is seeking multiple examples of behaviors and asking probing follow-up questions that reveal the thinking behind the behaviors described. While integrity-focused questions need be only a small part of the total interview, any ethical issues that arise must be explored fully so that the examples can be accurately evaluated and the best hiring decision reached.

...mportant to incorporate integrity questions into ...terview—and equally important to know when to ...sk those questions. Interviewers are wise to save sensitive ethical questions for late in the interview, after rapport has been developed. And, of course, as with all interview questions, once you have asked an ethical question, remember to listen and respond with empathy.

Empathy does not mean acceptance or agreement—it means understanding. You can be empathetic with a person who is telling you about an unethical behavior, without having to bend or sacrifice your own ethical standards, by reflecting the interviewee's feelings ("So you felt really good after the presentation," or "So you had second thoughts after the sales call"). And by showing empathy, you can keep the individual talking, providing other examples of behavior that will foster your understanding.

The recent bad behavior of high-profile executives has been nothing short of alarming. But it's an alarm that conscientious managers needed to hear—and to heed. Organizations must have leaders and associates who will share and live their ethical values, and extra care must be taken to ensure that these individuals are the ones who are brought into the organization—and promoted.

## The Top 11

The first step in an interviewing process to screen for honesty and integrity is for interviewers to ask the right questions. These questions need to be geared toward gathering information on past behaviors that illustrate whether a candidate's own ethical values are compatible with those of the organization.

Following is a list of questions, any of which could be incorporated into an interview to elicit examples of a candidate's past ethical behavior and to reveal insights about the candidate's honesty and integrity. While I've included 11 questions, most interview situations will dictate using only two or three such questions to obtain examples of past ethical behavior.

I've also given examples of good and questionable answers that candidates might give to these questions. The "rightness" or the "wrongness" of the answers is up to the interviewer's judgment. As such, it's important to train interviewers to follow up answers with more questions to pin down behavior and the thinking behind the behavior, to ask for additional examples, and to have a systematic integration of data so that multiple interpretations of the answers can be obtained and discussed.

**1. "We are often confronted with the dilemma of having to choose between what is right and what is best for the company. Give at least two examples of situations in which you faced this dilemma and how you handled them."**

**Good answer:** Once, we discovered a technical defect in a product after it had been shipped and used by a cli-

ent. The client did not notice the defect. We debated whether to tell the client and admit we had made a stupid error, or just let things go because the client seemed to be using the product with no problem. We decided to tell the client and replace the product at no cost.

**Questionable answer:** We discovered that our sales clerks were making errors in charging for certain combinations of products and that the errors were almost always in favor of the company. In no way were the clerks encouraged or trained to make these errors. We also learned that, with training, the errors could be eliminated, but the training would be fairly expensive. I decided not to institute the training.

**2. "How would you describe the ethics of your company? In which areas do you feel comfortable and uncomfortable with them? Why?"**

**Good answer:** My company is extremely ethical, and I've never, ever run into a situation in which I disagreed with a decision made because of ethics. In fact, we bend over backward in the treatment of our customers—such as taking back out-of-date products and providing free service past warranty, whenever there is any question about our products and services.

**Questionable answer:** I'm not sure what the ethics of our company are. People seem to do what's necessary to get the job done.

**3. "Give me an example of an ethical decision you have had to make on the job. What factors did you consider in reaching this decision?"**

**Good answer:** We had a customer return a large shipment. While technically it was in the second quarter, it would have been very easy to move the revenue hit to the third quarter. Including it in the second quarter meant that we would not meet sales expectations. To me, it was a matter of borrowing from Peter to pay Paul, and we probably wouldn't meet our expectations the next quarter. Anyway, I felt that it was better to take the bad results when you were supposed to, rather than cook the books.

**Questionable answer:** I've never really had to make a tough decision regarding ethics.

**4. "Have you ever observed someone stretching the rules at work? What did you do about it?"**

**Good answer:** One of my fellow executives took a company car to use for a weekend vacation. I spoke to him, and he agreed that it was not right and that he would not do it again.

**Questionable answer:** Everybody stretches the rules sometimes.

**5. "Have you ever had to bend the rules or exaggerate a little bit when trying to make a sale?"**

**Good answer:** My experience is that when salespeople misrepresent products and services, customers buy less from them. Having credibility with customers brings in better long-term sales. For example, when I was selling servers, we had a proprietary server and operating system. The client asked me why my machine was really worth the higher cost. I listed the advantages and disad-

## Why You Need to Read to Read Between the Lines

**W**hile interviews can uncover examples of a candidate's past unethical behavior or his lack of integrity, employers also are wise to closely scrutinize résumés. Studies find that 40 to 60 percent of résumés contain meaningful errors, such as dramatically inflated education, experience, or employment history.

These statistics and examples are hard to ignore, and demand that employers examine résumés with greater care.

Short of doing a background check before you interview an individual, there is little you can do about errors on résumés until you get into the interview. Then there are two things you *can* do.

First, look for holes, obvious or not, in the candidate's employment record and ask about those omissions.

Second, assign at least one interviewer to do a thorough review of the person's work or education record, asking questions like, "How did you get the job?" "What did you do?" "Why did you leave?" and, "How did you leave?" All dates should be verified. Often at this point an interviewee admits that perhaps the way that he presented information in the résumé is misleading: He didn't really graduate—he just attended courses; his title was sales manager but he didn't manage anybody. Often such education/job reviews are "assigned" to someone from HR and are done over the phone as part of a screening process. The interviewer covers the areas in a friendly way—"I just want to be sure that we're clear on everything so we can set you up for success if you come in for one-to-one interviews."

Sometimes dates don't line up for good reasons. For example, a candidate could show the date he received his master's degree well into the time that his résumé would indicate that he was living in another town and had a full-time job. The reason may well be that the university awards degrees only at certain times but the candidate finished his coursework for his master's degree months or even a year earlier. You should go over the dates with him and offer the chance to explain these discrepancies. Don't take action on a discrepancy without giving the candidate an opportunity to explain it.

Ultimately, recruiters and hiring managers must judge for themselves how important a particular résumé error is. But certainly the intentional deletion of critical information or inclusion of misinformation is a telling sign about what kind of person the candidate really is.

—W.C.B.

vantages, which indicated for him that the cheaper solution would work. I lost that sale but came back to win a much larger sale six months later.

**Questionable answer:** Sometimes when selling to a doctor, the doctor will state that he's heard that one of my products is effective against a certain disease. I listen and nod my head and say, "Interesting." I don't correct him even though I know that the drug is not recommended for that purpose. I'm not saying that it *does* work the way he thinks it does; I'm just not disagreeing with the doctor. You can't give advice to physicians.

**6. "Have you ever been in a situation in which you had to make something seem better than it really was?"**

**Good answer:** That's a big temptation in the high-tech field, particularly with new products. Often you know that there are errors in the program and that there are going to be some problems—what do you do? I try to be as honest as I can and give people realistic expectations.

**Questionable answer:** Our product has a very long sales cycle, and very often when we come out with a new release, it's not really done. It's "vaporware." We talk about it and sell it as if it were really done, with the expectation that by the time we make the sale and the client gets ready to have it installed, it *will* be ready. Most of the time we meet the client's deadlines, but we've had some really embarrassing situations when we didn't.

**7. "Tell me about an instance when you've had to go against company guidelines or procedures in order to get something done."**

**Good answer:** Like any manager, I move budget money around in order to get projects done with the resources that I have been allocated—for example, by reassigning people. That's what managers are expected to do. You can't precisely follow detailed budget allocations that are made six or nine months in advance.

**Questionable answer:** My wife works for one of our suppliers, and I actually buy things from her. This is technically in violation of company rules, but it doesn't hurt anything, and, frankly, it's the best product.

**8. "We've all done things that we regretted. Can you give me an example that falls into this category for you? How would you handle it differently today?"**

**Good answer:** When I first took over my job, I let seven people go without a whole lot of knowledge about their skills and contributions. Later I found that three of them were actually outstanding employees who should not have been let go. My jumping to conclusions hurt them and the company's operations. It took us several years to replace their knowledge of our equipment.

**Questionable answer:** I've never regretted anything about business. It's a game. I play the game to win.

**9. "Have you ever had anyone who worked for you do or say something that was misleading to the company or to a client? How did you handle it?"**

**Good answer:** I had a salesperson misrepresent a feature of one of our products in a presentation made to a client. I knew that the feature was important to the client. I asked the salesperson to meet again with the client to cor-

# The Art of the Ego Boost

People don't want to look bad in an interview and will very naturally put their best foot forward. An effective interviewer makes the interviewee feel at ease in giving what potentially could be negative information about himself. The interviewer does this in three ways:

- Provide a rationale for talking about poor or unethical behavior prior to asking a question. For example, "Everyone in an organization breaks the rules sometime. Can you tell me about some times when you've broken the rules?"

With the opening phrase, the interviewer is giving an excuse to the interviewee up-front to offer an example of negative behavior.

- Help the interviewee maintain self-esteem when the interviewee has offered a behavior about which she is embarrassed or uncertain (e.g., the interviewee admits she got in trouble for overstating a product's functionality). The interviewer should help the individual rationalize the behavior disclosed by saying something like, "We all make mistakes sometimes, and at least they provide an opportunity for learning" or, "That's a common mistake made by new people in

sales." Such post-confession affirmation maintains self-esteem and keeps the individual talking and providing information that will help the evaluation of ethical behavior.

- Do not take notes on negative behaviors at the time the interviewee shares the information. If the interviewer begins to write on his notepad, it is doubtful that the candidate will continue to open up or give additional, meaningful examples. Rather, the interviewer should just remember the negative behavior and later on in the interview, when the subject is more positive, write down a few notes.

—W.C.B.

rect the misrepresentation, and I made a follow-up phone call to ensure that the discussion occurred.

**Questionable answer:** I was part of a sales presentation by one of my best salespeople to a very, very big client. In the presentation, the salesperson absolutely misrepresented one of our product's features. It was an important misrepresentation because a competitor for that business had that feature. I sat through the rest of the meeting thinking about what to do but decided that I just couldn't let the misunderstanding stand. So after we left the presentation, I asked him to call the client and clarify the situation. I think he did, but I'm not sure.

**10. "There are two philosophies about regulations and policies. One is that they are to be followed to the letter; the other is that they are just guidelines. What is your opinion?"**

**Good answer:** Regulations and policies are made for important reasons. A regulation seems to me to be stronger, and I feel that I follow all regulations, such as getting reports in at a certain time and accounting for expenses in a certain way. Policies are a little bit more indefinite. They express more of a guideline and a philosophy. There are circumstances when you fall into the "gray area" when applying a policy. When I have had questions, I've checked with my boss.

**Questionable answer:** In order to get things done, you can't be held back by old-fashioned policies of your organization. You have to know what's right and do the right thing. You have to have good ethics and make decisions based on those ethics. You may have to bend the rules sometimes.

**11. "Have you ever felt guilty about receiving credit for work that was mostly completed by others? If so, how did you handle it?"**

**Good answer:** I frequently encounter this situation. By nature of being the boss, I get the credit for many of the things that my people do. I try my best to redirect that credit to them. For example, I insist that everyone who works on a proposal has her name on that proposal. We have celebrations when we win a contract at which we particularly point out the contributions of various people.

**Questionable answer:** No, I've never felt guilty. The person at the top gets credit when things go well, and he gets the blame when things go poorly. It's the nature of the job.

Interviewers should gather multiple examples from each question by employing a simple follow-up query: "Can you give me another example?" This will tell the interviewer whether the dishonest or unethical behavior was a one-time event or if there is a pattern. Also, interviewees tend to be more truthful in later examples than they are in their first example, which may be more of a PR effort.

Finally, it is vitally important for the interviewer to pin down the circumstances of the behavior so that a fair evaluation can be made. Interviewers do this by seeking the situation or task in which the behavior occurred, the actions of the individual, and the results from that action. If an interviewer doesn't have all three of these elements, it's very easy to misinterpret the response.

A candidate might relate a story in which he had to "bend the rules" on what could be put on his expense account. At first blush, this might seem like a negative behavior, but when you fully understand the circumstances—for example, "There was an opportunity to obtain some critical competitive information" and the result "that a project launch was more successful"—a different interpretation might be appropriate.

For example, when I was working as an industrial/organizational psychologist at J.C. Penney, a professional acquaintance at Sears offered to share some information on his company's selection system for management trainees. He loved to eat and drink, so I took him out for a nice lunch with wine when I flew to Chicago to meet him. He gave me two suitcases of research reports that catapulted my work ahead. I didn't have to make the same mistakes that Sears had made. The meeting and lunch were certainly worth hundreds of thousands of dollars to J.C. Penney. However, my company had a very low expense cap for taking people to lunch and refused to reimburse any alcoholic beverages. With my boss's knowledge and approval, I covered the difference elsewhere on the expense form.

Once you have uncovered examples of questionable behavior, be sure to accurately report the candidate's response to the others who have interviewed the same candidate when you meet to compare notes and arrive at a hiring decision. By obtaining multiple perspectives, you can better understand the examples' importance and check your standards before arriving at a final decision. This sharing and open discussion is a crucial step, as ethical behavior is best evaluated by a consensus decision among several knowledgeable managers.

Yes, you can interview for honesty and integrity. What's more, it's critically important that you do.

---

William C. Byham is president and CEO of Development Dimensions International Inc., an HR organization based in Pittsburgh. His last article was "Bench Strength" in February 2000.

---

# Does HR Planning Improve Business Performance?

## EXECUTIVE SUMMARY

For exceptional business performance, it's important that human resources becomes a strategic partner in the business. The authors explain how human resources planning is linked to business performance and address misconceptions about the planning process.

BY BILL MACALEER AND JONES SHANNON

For a long time, organization development pundits have maintained that improvement in business performance is directly tied to good human resources planning and closely linking this plan to strategic objectives. Most organizations strive to improve—some subtly and some with aggressive strategic plans designed to take the organization to the next level. The process to improve in specific areas is ever present within most organizations, although not always recognized as affecting overall business performance.

There are many theories, books, planning techniques, and motivational programs designed to improve performance. Executives continue to look for the ideal solution—that sure-fire, easy approach to improving performance. What most do not realize, however, is that the answer is not necessarily the latest management fad but instead comprehensive human resources planning linked to strategic objectives.

Based on decades of surveying countless businesses in all sectors of all sizes over many years, The Gallup Organization identified those factors that determine the most successful organizations from the rest. What they describe is a clear value chain that links sustainable growth and profits to engaged customers who are linked to engaged employees. Inside those organizations that have a record of sustained growth and profitability are employees who are committed to their work. It is this commitment and involvement that drives customer loyalty and engagement. In addition, Gallup found that successful organizations had great managers who were very good at selecting employees with the right strengths for the role to be filled, establishing clear performance expectations, developing employees with those strengths in mind, and creating the right motivational environment.

How do these findings relate to HR planning? The answer to this question, in large part, is determined by how the role of HR is defined by the organization. The organization must see the HR role as linked to its business strategy and that HR helps foster the culture necessary to implement that strategy effectively.

> Inside those organizations
> that have a record of sustained
> growth and profitability are employees
> who are committed to their work.

Effective human resources planning has become even more important in the highly competitive, global business environment of the 21st century. Organizations are evolving into more complex but nontraditional structures in order to be competitive and attract and retain the key individuals upon which success depends. Yet there does not seem to be a rush or increased interest in human resources planning. Often misunderstood and relegated to a task-driven, bureaucratic role, human resources is not always able to be the strategic business partner it needs to be.

**What is human resources planning?**
Human resources planning is a process intended to help guide the organization plan in any of the following general areas:
- Staffing
- Growth and development
- Leveling off and disengagement
- Replacement and re-staffing
- Job rotation and cross-functional training

- The design, implementation, and management of supporting programs such as benefits and compensation

To ensure you are developing the most effective human resources plan, your organization should review the need for having the following plans:

- Strategic business plan
- Job or role competency planning
- Manpower planning
- Training and development planning
- Career development planning and process
- Planning for and managing terminations, downsizing, and attrition

Human resources planning is not something the HR department should do on its own. So where does the responsibility for effective human resources really lie? In high performing organizations, good human resources practices are most effectively performed by line management with the human resources department providing the tools, guidance, and counseling needed for the line managers to be successful.

> Often misunderstood and relegated to a task-driven bureaucratic role, human resources is not always able to be the strategic business partner it needs to be.

While there may be any number of ways to conduct human resources planning, we find that the two most frequently used methods are standard planning and strategy-based planning.

## Standard planning

Probably the most common planning approach uses the staff size and configuration at the end of the year to project staffing levels and costs into subsequent years. Scenarios are then developed for incremental staffing and cost for new programs and projects. There are, however, drawbacks to this approach:

- It implies that all existing business activities will be continued and are as important as new strategies and plans.
- It assumes that the current business activities are the foundation for reaching the company's business goals and are being performed effectively.
- It can unnecessarily increase staff levels and not consider the specific competencies that are needed to achieve the strategic objectives.
- It will not uncover, within the organization, those who continue to want to increase the level of employees to preserve power and compensation without looking at productivity.
- It tends to institutionalize the existing planning process and systems beyond their usefulness.

- It shortcuts important communications from line and staff managers on their goals and support requirements.
- It supports an outdated concept tying compensation and recognition programs to rewarding those with the largest staffs.
- It supports the nonproductive concept that one must have sufficient staff to respond immediately to any request regardless of its importance.

## Strategy-based planning

To support the strategic business objectives of an organization, a strategy-based human resources planning process is a more effective approach. This approach is part analytical process and part creating the staffing and services based on the strategic goals, eliminating anything that does not support those goals. Here are some things to think about:

- Start by understanding the specific business priorities by department and business unit based on the overall strategic objectives.
- Understand the internal and external factors that may affect the achievement of the objectives that will ultimately impact the programs and services you will provide.
- Understand who has the responsibility and accountability for achieving each of the objectives, where they are shared, and who is to absorb the associated costs. (This will identify who your internal customers will be and what they expect.)
- Determine if alternatives for the achievement of each business objective have been developed and what impact that will have on services.
- Translate these business objectives into specific human resources programs and services.
- Determine the trade-offs in terms of resources needed and timing.
- Analyze the impact if each business objective is not achieved in terms of HR services.
- Test each priority starting with the lowest one in terms of the return versus the expenditure of time and money.
- Determine where efficiencies can be achieved.
- Determine the staffing requirements to meet the business objectives, including level of staffing required and timing; type of employees and specific competencies required; current complement versus your zero-based staffing requirements; where surpluses and gaps exist.

Every organization provides some standard human resources programs and services; some organizations offer different programs based on culture, size, and competitive needs. It is a good idea to start with a checklist of your human resources programs and initiatives. Then do some research and prepare a list of the types of human resources programs and services that are found throughout

# Turnover isn't always a PROFIT-BUSTER

Conventional business wisdom says that high voluntary turnover results in declines in productivity and profitability. However, University of Arkansas management researchers John Delery and Nina Gupta have found that this is not necessarily true.

"We found that what matters is the match. A company may choose not to invest in its people but to obtain profits in other ways," explained Delery, associate professor of management in the Walton College of Business. "That company is not really harmed by high voluntary turnover rates. But if a company chooses to obtain its profits through investment in its people, high voluntary turnover can be devastating."

In the fast food industry, for example, there is typically a high voluntary turnover rate among counter help. But if the company makes a low investment in these employees, choosing instead to make high human capital investments in managerial-level employees, it may actually enhance profitability.

Delery and Gupta, professor of management, conducted studies of voluntary turnover with Jason Shaw of the University of Kentucky. The researchers looked at voluntary turnover among core employees—those who control production processes or the direct delivery of services—in the trucking and concrete pipe manufacturing industries.

"One of the problems with some studies is that they look at all forms of turnover together," said Gupta. "But all forms of turnover don't have the same effect. Sometimes firing an employee can have a beneficial impact on productivity. We wanted to see the specific relationship between voluntary turnover and profitability and productivity."

In their studies, the researchers used pay level, benefits level, training, seniority-based pay, seniority-based layoffs, performance appraisals, and selective staffing to determine the company's investment in employees.

According to Delery, managers and educators have done a poor job in showing the financial value of people. It is said that machines depreciate and people appreciate, but no clear method exists to determine the numbers.

"Low human capital investments would always result in low productivity, no matter what the turnover rate. It is difficult to imagine that a low-skill, low-motivation work force could deliver high productivity," Delery said. "On the other hand, good financial results can be achieved by lowering human capital investments and looking to other avenues, such as technology, to yield competitive advantage. High investments in human capital can yield high returns, but only when the human capital is kept in the firm."

---

the business community. These lists will be a helpful guide during your human resources planning process.

## HR as strategic partner

In a recent survey by the Conference Board, 252 CEOs were asked to name the critical threats to their businesses and industries. The results vary by company size but "shortage of key skills," "changing technology," "regulatory compliance issues," "environment, health and safety," and "changes in competition" were among five of the top 15 concerns, with "shortage of key skills" ranked as the top concern. All of the aforementioned CEO concerns will be affected by the strategic human resources initiatives of the company.

Because the business community is moving to a knowledge-based culture, understanding the key competencies needed for your organization to be successful is critical. This should be the primary focus of human resources. An HR department must assume the role of strategic partner with the CEO and other top executives in a proactive way to ensure there is effective alignment of the overall business goals with the human resources initiatives. Human resources, in the past, has been viewed as a tactical or transactional function and often was not invited to sit at the business table. For an organization to be successful, that perception and role must change.

Human resources, as a strategic partner, will need to be involved in the business planning process, thoroughly understand the plan and be able to translate these plans into actions. This will ensure the organization has the right people with the right strengths in the right roles at the right time. It should challenge the business assumptions and plans and bring to the business table innovative ideas for how the organization can compete in the future.

Thinking outside the box, an HR department must take a leadership role, linking the business objectives to the required culture and staffing of the organization. In addition, an HR department must be asking and pressing for answers to the following questions:

- What does success look like in our organization and how can we identify and measure it? What is considered a high performing team in our company?
- Have we developed a business plan in which everyone understands their respective roles in achieving the results and buys into it?
- What do we need to deliver for the company to achieve its strategic objectives? Consider the areas of culture, recruitment, compensation, benefits, training and organizational development, and outside competition. Consider the audiences of senior management, middle management, employees, and regulatory agencies.
- What specific actions do we need to take in each area?
- What resources will be required? Are they available?
- What specific competencies are required to deliver these results? Are they currently available? How can they be developed? Are we effectively competing for knowledge-based talent? What are the competency strengths of our competitors and how can we better compete against those strengths?
- How will we address the identified competency gaps in the organization?
- To what level should we have a developed succession plan?

- How well do the team members understand the strategy and what it means to them? What can we do to enhance their understanding?
- What performance objectives do we need to establish to drive results on a group level as well as an individual level?
- How will we measure those results and how often?
- What external benchmarking will we use to measure your results against other firms?
- How will we reward employees for achieving those results?
- How will we communicate your progress and success?

In high performing organizations, the human resources department works in partnership with both line and staff managers. In these organizations, human resources professionals evolve into a strategic role and business partner, leaving the tactical responsibilities to others, whether they are within the HR department or outsourced. They challenge the status quo; they are facilitators of change and are visionaries who find alternative choices to give business partners.

> There is a common misconception that human resources planning is the same as manpower or staff planning. Not so!

## Barriers and misconceptions

Planning? Many people ask, "Do I have to?" Yet it has been demonstrated that human resources planning is an essential element of running an organization effectively and efficiently. So why are human resources planning and budgeting given so little attention compared to other elements of business planning? Considerable time is spent developing comprehensive sales, marketing, technical, financial, and other plans with often only superficial attention to the human resources implications of the business plan. There is no question that human resources planning should be closely aligned with the strategic objectives of the organization. Most human resources and business professionals understand this concept, but it is alarming how few are able to implement it. Why is this? Some possible reasons include:

- Human resources is considered a task-driven, primarily tactical function and does not have an equal seat at the business planning table.
- Human resources does not have the expertise, is unable to drive the process, and is not viewed as a strategic partner with management.
- Human resources is more focused on trying the latest management or human resources fad as a way to look good and add perceived values

rather than meeting the businesses' strategic needs.
- It is assumed that human resources will take care of planning (like finance will take care of the numbers), so discussions about HR planning are limited.
- Executives feel they have always been able to get by without detailed human resources planning and it is essentially a waste of time.
- Management believes that human resources planning limits its flexibility and ability to make decisions on a case-by-case basis during the planning year and unnecessarily ties their hands.
- The organization has always been flexible and adaptable to new situations and it is too difficult to predict what might happen and then plan for it.
- Management has never required and properly trained line managers to participate in sound human resources planning activities.

In addition to the previously mentioned potential barriers, there is a common misconception that human resources planning is the same as manpower or staffing planning. Not so! The human resources planning process must consider not only specific staff needs, but also areas such as:

- Services to be provided in support of the specific strategic objectives and the cost and timing for these services.
- Prioritization of the strategic objectives and identification of the specific services to support those objectives with cost/benefit analysis.
- Internally versus externally purchased services and costs/benefit analysis.
- The services that will be centrally provided, as well as those that will be decentralized or shared with other functions.
- Competency gaps between existing staffing and those required by the strategic plan and how those gaps will be filled.
- Training and development needs that support the strategic plan and address the competency gaps.
- Communications needs in support of specific business activities.
- Upgrades of programs, services, and equipment that will be required.
- New human resources technology introductions to the organization needed to support the business objectives.
- Where efficiencies in programs, services, and productivity could be achieved in areas that may be nice to have but do not support the strategic objectives.

- Acquisition integration issues and impact on existing resources and achievement of the strategic objectives.
- Downsizing or re-engineering issues and impact on resources.
- Succession planning and where need can be filled internally and those that will have to be filled externally.
- Compensation and benefits budget projections.
- Types of metrics to be used to evaluate performance and the costs to provide them.
- The unexpected.

To avoid the pitfalls often encountered when doing human resources planning, it is best to base your planning on the strategic objectives as opposed to the traditional projection of year-end results into the future. Yes, it takes more work, but it is an essential role that human resources must play to help the organization ensure it will achieve its objectives.

## Linking planning to performance

Several years ago, Edgar H. Schein, a social psychologist, Sloan Fellows Professor Emeritus, and senior lecturer at the Massachusetts Institute of Technology Sloan School of Management, conducted detailed research on this topic and published his findings. Schein pointed out that certain changing dynamics in the workplace increase the importance of effective human resources planning. Our own research and experience bear out his conclusions:

**Changing managerial role.** Because organizations are becoming more complex in structure and technologies and are operating in more complex economic, political, and diverse cultural environments, managers cannot safely make decisions alone. They cannot get enough information within their own head to be the integrator and decision maker. Instead, they become the managers of the decision-making process.

> To avoid the pitfalls often encountered when doing human resources planning, it is best to base your planning on the strategic objectives as opposed to the traditional projection of year-end results into the future.

**Changing social values.** Managing people has become increasingly complicated: There is a lot of emphasis on climbing the corporate ladder; people entering the workforce do not place the same value on their careers as those who went before them; and the ubiquity of dual-career families has changed work dynamics. In addition, we now recognize that growth is a lifelong process: Many issues are predictable when they appear during employees' life stages.

Schein further points out that a major problem with human resources planning and development systems is they are fragmented, incomplete, and often built on poor assumptions about both human and organizational growth. Instead, we should build upon what we know.

**Human growth occurs through continued exposure to one's environment.** To grow, individuals need both new challenges that are within the range of their abilities and knowledge about the results of their responses to the challenges.

**Organizational growth takes place through exposure to and coping with internal and external environments.** Since an organization is a complex system of individuals, knowledge, financial and informational resources, and materials, management must consider how each of those areas should be handled to achieve improved organizational effectiveness.

Why are these human resources components and plans important for improving business performance? They are intrinsically linked to each other and organizationally are one system. Many executives do not understand or treat it as one system and will make changes to parts of it without understanding the impact on the rest. A primary reason organizations fail to achieve business objectives is that the strategic goals are not fully implemented through the organization with the plans in place to ensure achievement of those goals. As often happens, employees continue to do what they have been doing with the belief that it is what the job requires. They may not understand that certain activities have become obsolete in light of the strategic goals of the organization.

Whether a start-up, emerging growth, or mature business culture, understanding the dynamics that impact the performance of your business is critical to organizations' success.

We have looked at the need for HR to be viewed as a strategic partner. We have also outlined the differences between strategy-based HR planning and the traditional planning approach and determined the value of strategy-based planning to organization performance. What has not yet been discussed is the question of measurement.

Our work and research have shown that the human resources department must develop the metrics and data to support the vital role it plays in the achievement of the business' goals.

David Becker, Mark Huselid, and Stephen Ulrich have recently addressed this issue in the book *The HR Scorecard*. The authors frame the issue as follows:

"In our experience, many HR management teams have a well-developed vision of their department's strategic value (at least from the perspective of HR), but the CEO and senior line management are at best skeptical of HR's role in the firm's success. Worse, in many firms, executives want to believe that 'people are our most important asset,' but they just can't understand how the HR function makes that vision a reality."

The authors suggest that while it is important for HR to establish itself as a strategic partner, play a key role in the development of the firm's business strategy, and translate that strategy into an HR plan, that is simply not enough. Even in those firms where HR has achieved that level of strategic acceptance, it will be subordinate to other executive functions until it is able to provide tangible evidence that what it does is directly linked to the firm's business performance.

Becker, Huselid, and Ulrich go on to note:

"In our view, the most potent action HR managers can take to ensure their strategic contribution is to develop a measurement system that convincingly showcases HR's impact on business performance. To design such a measurement system, HR managers must adopt a dramatically different perspective, one that focuses on how human resources can play a central role in implementing the firm's strategy. With a properly developed strategic HR architecture, managers throughout the firm can understand exactly how people create value and how to measure the value-creation process."

> Even in those firms where HR has achieved that level of strategic acceptance, it will be subordinate to other executive functions until it is able to provide tangible evidence that what it does is directly linked to the firm's business performance.

Just as we have found that successful firms have a value chain that links engaged employees to loyal customers that results in sustained revenue and profit growth, so too must an HR department follow this process if it is to be of strategic value on par with other executive functions. To do this, it must develop its own value chain architecture that clearly identifies and measures the relationship between what it does and engaged employee behaviors.

Becker, Huselid and Ulrich describe this as: The HR function (HR professionals with strategic competencies); the HR system (high-performance, strategically aligned policies and practices); and employee behaviors (strategically focused competencies, motivations, and associated behaviors).

In looking at the HR function, the authors point out that HR management has two essential dimensions—the technical and the strategic. The technical refers to the delivery of essential HR services such as recruiting, compensation and benefits. Strategic HR management involves delivering those services in a way that supports and enhances the firm's business strategy. The traditional transactional HR management has always focused on delivery of individual services with little regard for their strategic value.

What the authors of *The HR Scorecard* found was that organizations in which the HR system operated with a strategic focus were considered high-performance work systems, and the following actions were continuously practiced:

- Selection and promotion decisions were linked to validated competency models.
- Strategies were developed that provided timely and effective support for skills demanded by the firm's strategy implementation.
- Enacted compensation and performance management policies that attract, retain, and motivate high-performance employees.

They also surveyed 2,800 corporations and rated them according to the quality of their HR management system. The difference in business performance results between the top 10 percent and the bottom 10 percent were remarkable. Average employee turnover at the top firms was indexed at 20.8, with the bottom at 34.1; sales per employee were $617,576 against $158,101; and a market-to-book value was 11.1, to 3.6 for the bottom performers.

Does this answer our original question about HR planning and improved business performance? Yes, we believe it does, and Becker, Huselid, and Ulrich have provided not only a good theory but also compelling data.

To summarize, HR planning does enhance business performance when:

- The HR plan is strategy-based.
- HR is a credible strategic partner.
- The HR function is driven by the strategic rather than the technical.
- HR comprises professionals who have strategic competencies.
- HR sees its role as a key player in implementing the business strategy.
- HR has designed and uses a measurement system to display its influence in the achievement of the business strategy.

From *Industrial Management,* Vol. 45, No. 1, January/February 2003, pages 15–20. Reprinted with the permission of the Institute of Industrial Engineers, 3577 Parkway Lane, Suite 200, Norcross, GA 30092, 770–449–0461. Copyright © 2003 by Institute of Industrial Engineers.

# Tomorrow's
# World

A new generation of HR software should provide the tools to pursue the holy grails of productivity, performance and governance. Is your system up to date?

Carol Glover

**WITH INCREASING FOCUS ON THE MEASUREMENT** and evaluation of HR activities, technology is becoming the catalyst for changing how HR works.

Michael Howard, managing director of Frontier, says: "Self-service kiosks where staff can change their own data will grow across all sectors." In fact, Tony Price, senior sales executive at Snowdrop, says: "Over 60 per cent of our new clients are implementing web-enabled solutions currently." There are clear advantages. Marketing manager at KCS, Nicola Smith, says: "Self-service removes the danger of Chinese whispers and data distortion by layers of bureaucracy as it streamlines processes."

Organisations are even investigating biometrics to measure attendance, although sceptics still see it as a "black art". For example, staff may be resistant to identification through iris reading, fearing it damages eyes, and no HR department is going to push a measure if there are safety concerns—however unfounded. But full facial recognition—similar to a photograph—may be on its way.

Management of system "evolution"—for example, keeping up with EU employment legislation—is important to clients in any sector. Frank Beechner, CEO of Vizual, says that new technology will enable multinational, multi-lingual firms to have consistent practices across continents.

James Bennett, head of Workforce Solutions Oracle UK, who has been in the HR software business since 1986, says that performance, productivity and governance have long been HR's "holy grails" but they've never before had the tools to make it happen. "Conversations with HR departments revolve around how software can help HR improve workforce performance, productivity, and governance leading to greater shareholder value," he says. "Technology gives HR the tools to measure workforce performance and ensure that it's consistent with law and best practice."

Christopher Berry, managing director of Computers in Personnel, says: "More demands are being put on HR by the business. This automatically extends to the question of systems security, as with increased use of internet, intranets and wireless networks HR must be more IT and security savvy". HR will have to understand the technical capabilities to be able to justify "spend" to the board.

Wayne Carstensen, CEO of Arinso, believes that "people services manager" will replace the title HR manager. Arinso has confirmed a partnership contract with Shell for its SAPHR deployment. By the end of the year over two-thirds of Shell's 115,000 employees will be using the Shell People Services system that uses a single global HR IT solution across 45 countries. This is increasingly common for multinationals. Since 2001 Arinso has supported Shell in rolling out a global HR management system and 80 Arinso consultants are working with Shell HR teams in North America, Europe and Asia Pacific.

Tony Flannigan, marketing manager at ASR, says that the feel of self-service centres is important for buy-in. "For line managers and employees we've given our system an 'online banking' feel as it's not such an alien concept to people." Employee buy-in is crucial, agrees Snowdrop's Tony Price: "HR managers need to put the users first."

Eric Smart, CEO of Smart Human Logistics, says: "The web has allowed attendance to be deployed in multi-site companies more effectively. This is a great leap forward for centralised control. This goes for manufacturing or retailers with many sites. As long as they have a PC and a phone point it's as if everyone is in the same building."

# LEARNING CURVE

The learning management systems (LMS) market is entering a new phase. While value for money used to be a concern, a new generation of market-savvy buyers has led to the growth in more cost-effective products.

Buyers of the first wave of LMS often challenged the value they gained from them, says Tim Drewitt, consultant at Balance Learning. "Organisations may have features that they never use and systems that are more costly to maintain than they envisaged. Now, when contracts are up for renewal, system providers are having to work harder to convince clients of the return on investment."

However, there is a shift in this trend and observers see the LMS market entering a new phase of maturity and adoption. Donald Clark, CEO of Epic, says: "We've always believed that LMSs shouldn't be regarded as essential to e-learning, although they can be useful for large corporates." The industry predicts than only a few LMS providers will

survive. "LMSs became too big, expensive and hard to integrate and buyers were using only a fraction of their capabilities. Sociology always wins over technology—you can't make people use resources," Clark says.

Even so, the market is adapting. Matthew Borg, consultant and partner at Information Transfer, says: "We're seeing a trend towards providing extra learning resources through portals and the creation of knowledge or reference centres for ongoing learner support." Borg says clients want to integrate LMSs with existing HR systems such as self-service centres. This is important since line managers are now more involved in staff development and individuals are taking responsibility for self-learning. Web-based systems mean that people can access learning from home PCs.

One-stop-shops are the norm as customers demand service integration because implementation has

been hard. Because of these problems some larger organisations have spent a large amount on getting made-to-measure LMSs, especially since past pricing policy has often been "per employee", regardless of whether they all used the system. We have witnessed an explosion in low-to-medium cost solutions.

Jamie Johnson, business manager at DeltaNet, says: "Customers prefer a bespoke approach to managing their learning." Partial LMSs are available if organisations only want certain features.

There has also been a growth in corporate use of virtual learning environments (VLEs), originally designed for the academic community, mainly as they are cheaper. VLEs mean you can get on the learning management ladder sooner. Organisations often do their own authoring and so want tools that are compatible with their LMS, making understanding the IT architecture and engaging the IT team essential.

For example, police forces had to change how they measure ethnicity, but Cedar HR Software, which is a provider to a number of forces, could make one change to the system centrally and distribute it to all its customers, rather than having to repeat it 16 times. This dilutes the cost of system evolution or updating.

Insiders believe that the HR software market is ripe for consolidation. "We've seen several acquisitions to create

economies of scale and this trend will probably continue over the next year," Flannigan says. HR outsourcing and software supplier Northgate Information Solutions plc is buying payroll software supplier Rebus HR Group in a reverse takeover bid, doubling its own size in the process.

Whatever the future of the market, this new generation of HR managers with HR software purchasing experience is clued up and ready to champion projects.

# UNIT 3

# Creating a Productive Work Environment

## Unit Selections

## Key Points to Consider

- What are some things you might do to motivate employees, especially in a downsizing environment? What are some of the things that motivate you?

- In today's environment, do you think people should be viewed more as partners or as workers?

- What strategies could you employ to communicate more effectively with your peers or your instructor? What things can destroy effective communication? What role does correct communication play in projecting a desired image? Do you think feedback is important? In conversation? In your career?

 **Links: www.dushkin.com/online/**
These sites are annotated in the World Wide Web pages.

**Commission on the Future of Worker-Management Relations**
*http://www.dol.gov/_sec/media/reports/dunlop/dunlop.htm*

**The Downsizing of America**
*http://www.nytimes.com/specials/downsize/glance.html*

**Employee Incentives and Career Development**
*http://www.snc.edu/socsci/chair/336/group1.htm*

**Foundation for Enterprise Development**
*http://www.fed.org/aboutus/aboutus.htm*

Whenever anything is being accomplished, it is being done, I have learned, by a monomaniac with a mission.

—Peter Drucker

For years, management theorists have indicated that the basic functions of management are to plan, direct, organize, control, and staff organizations. Unfortunately, those five words only tell what the manager is to do. They do not tell the manager how to do it. Being a truly effective manager involves more than just those five tasks. It involves knowing what goals to set for the organization, pursuing those goals with more desire and determination than anyone else in the organization, communicating the goals once they have been established, and having other members of the organization adopt those goals as their own.

Motivation is one of the easiest concepts to understand, yet one of the most difficult to implement. Often the difference between successful and mediocre organizations is that the usual people in successful organizations are motivated, and the other 80 percent are also motivated. They are excited about the company, about what they do for the company, and about the company's products or services. Effective organizations build upon past successes, sometimes to the point where they can ask themselves, "Who Needs Superstars?" All of our employees are performing at very high levels. If people feel good about themselves and good about their organization, then they are probably going to do a good job. Whether it is called morale, motivation, or enthusiasm, it still amounts to the same fragile concept —simple to understand, difficult to create and build, and very easy to destroy.

In order to maintain a motivated workforce for any task, it is necessary to establish an effective reward system. A truly motivated worker will respond much more effectively to a carrot than to a stick. Turned-on workers are having their needs met and are responding to the goals and objectives of the organization. They do an outstanding job because they want to, which results in an outstanding company. "Getting Happy With the Rewards King," addresses some of the ways that management can reward employees for outstanding performance on the job.

Perhaps the single most important skill for any manager, or, for that matter, any human being, is the ability to communicate. People work on this skill throughout their education in courses such as English and speech. They attempt to improve communication through an array of methods and media, which range

from the printed word, e-mail, and television, to rumors and simple conversation. Yet managers often do not do a very good job of communicating with their employees or their customers. This is very unfortunate because ineffective communication can often negate all of the other successes that a firm has enjoyed. "The 'Write' Way to Enhance Business," tells us whether writing a business proposal, a letter to a client or customer, or a company handbook, strong writing skills are essential to instill confidence in a business. This is something that a manager must strive for if he or she wants to have people working together for a common goal. Managers, and the firms they represent, must honestly communicate their goals as well as their instructions to their employees, and this will often be in writing. If the manager does not do so, the employees will be confused and even distrustful, because they will not understand the rationale behind their instructions. If the manager is successful in honestly communicating the company's goals, ideals, and culture to the employees and is able to build the motivation and enthusiasm that are necessary to successfully accomplish those goals, then he or she has become not just a manager but a leader, and that is, indeed, rare.

Creating a positive work environment is not easy. Communicating with and motivating people, whether employees, volun-

# *Getting Happy*
## with the
# Rewards King

**Bob Nelson says praise and small rewards, not cold, hard cash, are the right way to motivate better workplace performance. Critics scoff at a "baubles and trinkets" approach, but his books sell big.**

*By Leslie Gross Klaff*

**A**s an expression of gratitude, managers at a bank in Horsham, Pennsylvania, don chef hats and aprons to flip hamburgers for employees at a "Grill Your Boss" cook-out. At a seminar-planning firm in Virginia Beach, female staff members are thanked with complimentary pedicures. Employees at a Chicago health-care company are rewarded with balloons, belly dancers, and a singer in a gorilla suit.

Why are these companies doing this? Because Bob Nelson says so.

Nelson, best-selling author of *1001 Ways to Reward Employees*, has firmly established himself as the rewards king in a field packed with hundreds of motivational speakers and writers who talk the same language. He has platoons of fans who applaud his basic premise: While money is important to employees, thoughtful recognition motivates them to perform at higher levels.

He also has critics who dismiss him as a self-promoter, arguing that giving incentives such as parties and other treats is foolish and condescending. "Rewards are, at best, a waste of time," says Boston-based Alfie Kohn, author of

the book *Punished by Rewards*. Kohn and other detractors charge Nelson with promoting simplistic, feel-good solutions to complex problems such as low morale and high turnover. "Working with employees, bringing them into decision-making, helping to design a democratic workplace takes time, talent, skill, care, and above all, courage," Kohn says. "1001 ways to manipulate people to jump through hoops" can't address those important issues—though "throwing baubles and trinkets at your employees is a hell of a lot easier."

Nelson counters by saying that the system isn't the problem. It's the personal relationships employees have with their managers that are critical to productivity and performance. Managers can't force employees to like their jobs, but they should create an environment that encourages workers to want to excel, and should provide meaningful rewards. The effectiveness of incentives has been substantiated by more than a century of research, adds Nelson, whose own credentials include a master's degree in organizational behavior from Berkeley, a Ph.D. from the Drucker Graduate School of Management at

Claremont Graduate University, and years of experience working for top executives such as management guru Ken Blanchard.

Nelson, a 46-year-old father of two who lives near San Diego, is so passionate about his work that he has trouble separating it from his personal life. At home, he and his wife, Jennifer, use his rewards philosophy in raising their two children, Daniel, 12, and Michelle, 7. Rather than badgering them about cleaning their rooms, for example, they make a real effort to give them a pat on the back for a job well done. They try to make sure the "ratio of nagging to positive encouragement" is higher on the positive end, he says.

His message is, of course, a harder sell in a soft economy, when many managers argue that employees should be happy simply to have a job. To add more credibility to his work, Nelson recently teamed up with IBM consultant Dean Spitzer to write his new book, *The 1001 Rewards & Recognition Fieldbook.* "My philosophy on rewarding and recognizing employees is to be real with employees in an up-front and sincere way," says Nelson, who earns $12,500 a day on the speaking circuit. "Managers need to think about what their employees need and what's important to them" when they design incentive programs, he says.

## Deep roots in human resources

Nelson started working in human resources and writing books right out of college. After earning a communications degree in the late 1970s at Macalester College in St. Paul, Minnesota, he got a job in human resources at a computer company and soon became known by friends as an astute job counselor. One Sunday morning he decided to write his ideas down. He was only 25 when his first book, *The Job Hunt*, was published. It sold 60,000 copies.

---

## $32 Billion Worth of Rewards at Work

There's a huge marketplace for recognition and rewards. Incentives—an area that includes travel, merchandise, trophies and plaques—is a $32 billion industry. Company spending on recognition and reward programs was nearly $27 billion in 2000. That's up from $22.8 billion four years earlier.

Of the companies that use rewards, here's what they spend:

| | |
|---|---|
| **Under $25,000:** | **49%** |
| $25,000-$50,000: | 19% |
| **$51,000-$100,000:** | **11.6%** |
| $101,000-$150,000: | 4.3% |
| **$201,000-$500,000:** | **7.2%** |
| $501,000-$1 million: | 4.3% |

*Sources:* Incentive *magazine and the 2001 Incentive Federation Study.*

---

It was in 1985 that he noticed a review of one of Blanchard's books in the *Wall Street Journal* and decided to give him a call. He landed a job interview and was hired to co-author a business textbook with Blanchard. Nelson worked there for 10 years and was vice president of product development when he left to start his own consulting company in San Diego and return to graduate school. One night his management professor at Drucker lectured on positive reinforcement and how there was little application of the theory to business. Nelson was intrigued. He decided to prove that positive reinforcement is valuable in the workplace, an idea that spawned *1001 Ways to Reward Employees.*

"I got home at midnight and told my wife that I wanted to write a book filled just with ways to praise and thank employees," Nelson says. "I didn't want to fill it with boring studies from other Ph.D.'s. I wanted to make the case through example."

The book sold 1.5 million copies. Soon after its release, speaking engagements began pouring in. Five years ago he started his own business, Nelson Motivation, Inc., in San Diego, and he has since worked with more than two-thirds of *Fortune* 500 companies. What makes Nelson stand out, says one of his industry peers, is that he offers practical help. "People need ideas" for motivating employees, says Barbara Glanz, an author and speaker on regenerating spirit in the workplace. "They don't need a lot of philosophy and theory and concept."

Nelson's ideas helped Rhonda Rhodes, vice president of human resources at Universal Orlando, replace the company's traditional recognition programs, such as raffle drawings for employees with perfect attendance, with programs that reward employees for accomplishing a variety of goals. When restaurant workers meet sales goals, they win pizza parties and their managers do their jobs for them for an afternoon. With a "Cause for Applause Card," workers who see other employees making an extra effort receive a card describing the behavior. The cards can be redeemed for prizes such as movie tickets and free meals.

Nelson encourages managers to reward employees daily. The item is less important than the action. A manager at Hewlett-Packard Co., for example, once handed an employee a banana from his lunch after the engineer solved a difficult problem, and over time the Golden Banana Award has become one of the organization's most prestigious honors. Nelson also wants managers to think beyond monetary rewards.

That's increasingly important in a weak economy. Memphis-based FedEx Express got ideas for low-cost rewards from Nelson last spring. In addition to formal recognition programs, FedEx managers reward employees by washing their cars, shoveling snow for couriers, and putting retirees' names on banners hung in warehouses. The company also holds a drawing to pick the name of an employee's child to be inscribed in large letters on the nose of each new airplane in its fleet of 330 planes. The

# Nelson's Ten Commandments of Recognition

Bob Nelson believes that today's workforce may be more motivated by a personal thank-you than a pay raise. He shares his top 10 ways (in order of priority) to motivate employees:

1. Personally thank employees for doing a good job. Thank them face-to-face, in writing, or both. Do it early, often, and sincerely.

2. Take the time to meet with and listen to employees—as much as they need or want.

3. Provide specific feedback about performance of the person, the department, and the organization.

4. Strive to create a work environment that is open, trusting, and fun. Encourage new ideas and initiative.

5. Provide information on how the company makes and loses money, upcoming products and strategies for competing in the marketplace, and how the person fits into the overall plan.

6. Involve employees in decisions, especially as those decisions affect them.

7. Provide employees with a sense of ownership in their work and work environment.

8. Recognize, reward, and promote people according to their performance; deal with low and marginal performers so that they either improve or leave.

9. Give people a chance to grow and learn new skills; show them how you can help them meet their goals within the context of the organization's goals. Create partnerships with employees.

10. Celebrate successes of the company, of the department, and of individuals. Take time for team- and morale-building meetings and activities.

Source: © Bob Nelson, Ph.D., author of *1001 Ways to Reward Employees* and *The 1001 Rewards & Recognition Fieldbook: The Complete Guide*. For more information visit www.nelson-motivation.com

winner's family is flown to Memphis for the christening of the plane.

Jack Wilkie, a vice president at 7-Eleven, Inc., hired Nelson to speak before 3,000 employees at the company's anniversary last July. "He came across as your older brother, like he was letting you in on a little secret," Wilkie says. "He had genuine humor. No corny jokes." A few weeks later, Nelson called Wilkie to check in. "He wasn't selling anything, pushing anything.... It's just a part of who he is." Nelson also welcomes his audiences to contact him, giving out his e-mail address and responding to all messages, usually about 30 a week. At his own 10-person company, he rewarded his team with a trip to Disneyland in a limousine for meeting their quarterly financial goals. For an employee who collects toy sports cars, Nelson rented him a Porsche for the day.

## The rewards debate

It's 11 a.m. at a conference hotel in Philadelphia, and Nelson has just sauntered up to the podium to speak to 300 managers about creative strategies for rewarding employees. He is dressed in a crisp suit—accented with a red-and-yellow Winnie the Pooh tie. He has no trouble getting the throng to laugh at his jokes about humdrum rewards like anniversary clocks and employee-of-the-month plaques. Usually his audiences already believe in rewarding employees. The biggest challenge is reaching philosophical opponents. Almost half of U.S. corporations with 1,000 or more employees do not use incentives, according to the 2001 Incentive Federation study.

As one of Nelson's most vocal critics, Kohn believes that rewards cannot improve performance, and points out that there is a lot of research showing that the more people are rewarded, the more they actually lose interest in the work they're doing. He contends that Nelson's approach assumes that problems occur because workers are unmotivated, when the problem is, in fact, the workplace system itself. He proposes that employers motivate their employees by making sure they like their jobs and are involved in decision-making.

Workplace consultant Carleton Kendrick views rewards such as the boss serving employees ice cream as "condescending" and "one-shot deals of happy-feel-good." Kendrick, a Boston family therapist, says workers truly want more ways to help balance work and life, not ice cream. Others say that employees would rather earn more money than receive rewards. That was the sentiment of supervisors at the Defense Supply Center in Philadelphia, which buys military supplies. Nelson recently was at the facility to give a talk and had trouble convincing some managers that money is not the top motivator even though the theory is backed by numerous studies. "You have a family, kids, two incomes—and money helps," says Gordon Ferguson, one of the managers who isn't swayed by the research.

Nelson says he agrees that the best motivation comes from within. But in reality, he points out, most jobs are not intrinsically motivating. Customer service or retail jobs, for example, can become mundane because of repetition and pressure. To get employees excited about their jobs, managers must make sure their work supports their career goals, Nelson says. If managers give meaningful rewards, employees are motivated.

For Nelson, selling his message is tougher in today's lousy economy. Some managers argue that it's too hard to measure the return on investment with rewards. According to Nelson's own Ph.D. research on the subject, managers say they don't give rewards because they don't have time, their employees didn't value previous rewards, and they're worried that employees will take advantage of them. To convince more corporate leaders of the benefits, Nelson shows the financial consequences of not rewarding employees—such as the cost of increased turnover. Most of all, he emphasizes that rewarding employees is easy and inexpensive, and almost always has a lasting impact.

"A sincere word of thanks from the right person at the right time can mean more to an employee than a raise, a formal award, or a whole wall of certificates and plaques," Nelson writes in *1001 Ways to Reward Employees*. "Part of the power of such rewards comes from the knowledge that someone took the time to notice the achievement, seek out the employee responsible, and personally deliver praise in a timely manner."

*Leslie Gross Klaff is a New Jersey-based freelance writer. To comment, e-mail editors@workforce.com.*

Reprinted with permission from *Workforce*, April 2003, pp. 47-50. © 2003 by Crain Communications, Inc. www.workforce.com

# Who Needs Superstars?

**How to do extraordinary things with ordinary people.**

## By Adrian W. Savage

Organizations are in a muddle over talent. Actually, two muddles: first because they overestimate the impact of talented people on performance, second because they have been told that there is a growing shortage of talent and must take exceptional steps to get what they can and hang onto it. These misconceptions feed off of each other—if having talented people is essential to corporate growth and supply is short, exceptional measures are clearly justified. But what if neither statement is correct?

Don't get me wrong: Talented people are valuable to any organization. But a few moments' thought will add a couple of important modifiers to this statement:

- The "war for talent" is a mirage. Over the past two or three years, some three million Americans have lost their jobs through no fault of their own. Most of these people are talented in some way; a select few are more highly talented. Far from there being a shortage of available talent, employers face a greater choice and supply than in many years.

- Even the most talented person cannot transform a messed-up,

misaligned organization into a winner. Even geniuses are human. Look at the size and complexity of today's organizations. Then look at recent history.

Remember those high-profile CEOs who were paid mega-millions because they alone could produce constant double-digit growth and transform dull, lumbering organizations into stars? How many achieved it? How many got fired for failing? How many made headlines for successes compared with those who found themselves on the wrong end of SEC and Justice Department investigations?

Organizations are groups of interlocking systems, populated by people. That's all they are. Unless the systems themselves change, the most talented and charismatic person—whether a frontline worker or top executive—will have almost no impact on what happens. Of course, those who do succeed know this. They create a group of people around them who help them change things—people who have their hands on the levers that control the organization's systems. As management guru Jim Collins found, those organizations that transform them-

selves from good to great rarely use high-profile individuals imposed on the organization. The process is driven by a group of dedicated leaders working together, most of whom have been in the organization long enough to know exactly how to make things happen, first through the systems already in place and only then by changing those systems.

### Smothered By Systems

The organization isn't the people. It's not the product. It's not the brand. It's the set of systems that links them all together. That's the bit that matters; that's what an organization is. If we don't understand and work with that, we'll usually foul up in a big way.

People in an organization think about its parts separately rather than systemically. They work on the product strategy, the marketing strategy, how they handle production, how to deal with the competition. When it comes to the people side, they think about human capital and individuals, plus administrative matters like remuneration and benefits.

It all matters. But it all *interacts.* Taking each part in isolation makes for easier thinking but falsifies the reality of the situation. It is a whole; it all works together. Of course, highly talented people make a difference, but unless the organizational structure allows them to flourish, that difference will be too small to notice.

Stars are few and far between. That's the nature of anything that is normally distributed. It's like height. There are only a handful of people over 7 feet tall, and they're probably all basketball players. People under 4 feet tall are pretty rare as well. Most of us are around the average height—some a little taller, some a little shorter, but rarely by much. Tell recruiters they must choose people 7 feet tall or taller, and you've created a shortage.

Here's the crunch point: If we bet everything on the belief that significant change and better performance can come only after we have recruited and retained this tiny number of spectacular people, we will never get there. We are giving ourselves an impossible task. And our competitors are not standing still while we waste our attention on it.

Companies look for unicorns—mythical creatures with amazing powers—because they have been told they must. Forget about it. What matters in organizational success is how well we utilize the vast bulk of ordinary people, since that is what we will always have in greatest abundance. *The organization that gets extraordinary results with ordinary people will wipe out its competition.*

## The Wrong Search

Occasionally, an organization gets lucky and finds a unicorn—but rarely does it know what to do with its new star. They harness it to drag a cart, then wonder why it doesn't handle the job up to expectation. They try to graft this alien growth onto the organization, which proves to be stronger than any individual. The star is later blamed for not changing things singlehandedly—even though the weight of the organization's systems

and tradition has ensured that is exactly what will happen.

Organizations insist that they want outstandingly creative, energetic, and innovative people. In a recent *Harvard Business Review* article, coauthors Thomas J. DeLong and Vineeta Vijayaraghavan explain why, on a gut level, companies devote such effort to drafting stars: "Most CEOs find that recruiting stars is simply more fun; for one thing, the young A players they interview often remind them of themselves at the same age. For another, their brilliance and drive are infectious; you want to spend time with them."

> Most managers want A players like they want a hole in the head.

But most managers want A players like they want a hole in the head. These people are *difficult*. They're demanding. They're clever, and they know it. They shake things up. They're unruly and tell their boss they can do her job better than she can—and they're pretty much right about that. They don't follow instructions, and they don't like being told to fit in with less able people.

Most organizations have a great deal of trouble swallowing unicorns, which is why such people usually found their own businesses or stay outside the organizational world altogether.

I once found a company that set out, deliberately, to recruit senior people who were different from those it already had. The company believed that its new superstars would transform it from being an old-fashioned, stuffy Scottish manufacturer into a sleek, modern European business. HR worked hard at the task and found outstanding people. The long-term result was no surprise: In less than five years, not one of these highly talented, *different* people remained.

### Are We Aligned?

Imagine that a general has a new and brilliant plan to defeat the enemy in battle, but he doesn't take time first to see if his troops can do it, or how they are likely to respond when given instructions that are different than they were in the past. He just goes ahead.

He doesn't see the need for that kind of intelligence—*organizational intelligence*—about the state of his own organization, his troops, and how to use them effectively. He just assumes they'll do whatever he asks. Are they properly trained? He doesn't know. Are they organized in the way most likely to support his strategy? He isn't interested. What's their morale? He hopes for the best.

Naturally, in battle, the troops become confused. The new strategy is so different and complex that they can't follow it, so they panic and fall back on doing what they've always done. They don't have the structure; they are neither ready nor aligned with the strategy.

With the organization in disarray, how much does it matter if one or two of the soldiers have more ability than the rest? If the whole regiment isn't marching alongside, no amount of bravery on the part of any one soldier will make any difference. Before we commit to action, we have to find out whether we're aligned. Does everyone know what he is supposed to be doing? Are people trained and ready? Are the resources in place the right ones? Does everyone know how to use them?

A *no* to any of these questions greatly reduces the strategy's chances of success. One reason why a superstar, once transplanted, may revert to average performance is that she couldn't take her old organization along to her new office. It was the structure in the previous job—not just her innate abilities—that enabled her brilliance.

—A.W.S

Without first changing the organizational structure, recruiting a different kind of person just increases retention problems. Given a transfusion of blood of a different type, our bodies will reject it. Why should we expect our organizations to act otherwise?

## Getting the Structure Right

If we don't give talented people work within a structure that supports them, they can't deliver their talent. Indeed, if we don't make sure that organizational systems are aligned with the people who work within them, we'll get poor performance from *everyone*, regardless of talent.

When organizations don't get the structure right, people problems linger forever. A company launches an initiative that's announced with a flourish of trumpets and drums, everyone says "wow!", and six months later nobody remembers even what it was supposed to achieve. When the next initiative is announced, it's greeted with sighs and headshakes. "Don't fret," people say. "There'll be another one along in a minute."

In this individualistic society, we have become accustomed to the media-induced cult of the star, regardless of whether the emphasis makes

any sense. Hollywood is a wonderful example: The lion's share of attention goes to the above-the-title actors, but any number of star-packed films wind up box-office bombs. It's the system that makes the film. If the film is a turkey, it takes the stars down with it.

It's the same in business. The star, whether an actor or a CEO, needs the right vehicle. Hollywood, at least, lets you have more comebacks: The "failed" CEO may make it back the first time, but the next time he resigns to "spend more time with the family" or "pursue other interests," he's history.

## Swimming in the Talent Pool

Companies *can* align themselves. It's about doing simple things consistently and finding out what the current context demands. Does every worker know what he's doing? Is everyone clear about the direction of strategy and the implications for his own actions? Is the structure suitable for carrying out the strategy?

Organizations that create alignment between the people they've got

and the strategies they want to carry out *will* get spectacular results. All they need is intelligence and the patience to get the structure aligned before they start.

The talent myth urges us to focus on the wrong things. Don't hire unicorns unless you can use them; if you can't, they'll be miserable and won't stay. Never forget that a frustrated clever worker causes more mayhem than a frustrated average worker.

The talent pool is deep, but it's filled with ordinary people. By acting as if the organization's future depends on a tiny number of unicorns, we're taking enormous risks. They don't exist in anything like the numbers needed even for a fraction of those seeking them to bring one home. It's a hopeless quest. Use your average people well, and no one need worry about unicorns.

---

*ADRIAN W. SAVAGE is president of PNA Inc., an organizational-intelligence consultancy based in Irvine, Calif., and author of* A Spark From Heaven? The Place of Potential in Organizational and Individual Development.

---

# The "Write" Way to Enhance Business

**Whether writing a business proposal, a letter to a client or customer, or a company handbook, strong writing skills are essential to instill confidence in a business.**

*Dawn Josephson*

In today's business world, writing skills have taken a backseat to other seemingly more important corporate development activities. Most business executives would rather attend a seminar on negotiation strategies or marketing tactics rather than learn the proper usage of "that" or "which" in a sentence. What they fail to realize, however, is that good writing skills are just as important to their future success as is their ability to locate prospects and close deals. Without good writing skills, your printed documents may very well undermine the professional image you work so hard to achieve.

The fact is that prospects, clients, and even the media judge businesses based on the written documents put out to the world. Sales letters riddled with errors, advertising copy that is boring, and media announcements that ramble on for pages send a message of carelessness, uncreativity, and possibly incapable of delivering quality work. People want to do business only with those individuals they perceive as knowledgeable and competent. Writing is the perfect opportunity to showcase professionalism and win the deal.

## Tricks of the trade

It doesn't take a professional editor or journalist to write effectively. In fact, there are a number of self-editing techniques professional writers use to catch embarrassing errors that could cost them the job. Use these guidelines as a way to proofread your own writing so you can make all your printed materials reflect the professionalism you display in every other business activity.

1. Re-read your work out loud. After a document is written, most people re-read it to themselves to scan for errors. While this is certainly a good start, it should not be the sole means of proofreading. After scanning the document silently, read it out loud and really listen to the words you're saying. Does your tongue stumble over a block of words? Do certain phrases sound funny or out of place? Is a sentence so long that you're gasping for breath by the time you reach the period? Do your own words put you to sleep? All these are signs that a section of the document needs some tweaking.

When you read a document to yourself, you're relying on only your eyes to catch writing errors. However, when you read a document out loud, you're activating your sense of hearing and forcing your brain to concentrate on each individual word rather than visual cluster. Now you not only see missing commas, incorrect words, or subject-verb disagreements, but you can also hear when something sounds out of place. When you hear—as well as see—what you're writing, you can catch more errors and produce a written document that holds the reader's attention.

2. Don't rely on [spell] check. The spell check feature on your computer is both a blessing and a hindrance to writing success. While spell check can locate and correct blatantly misspelled words, it can't catch those words that are spelled correctly but used incorrectly. You know the words: right/write, meet/meat, you're/your, there/their/they're, no/know, plus a host of others. Such words, called homonyms, are often immune to computerized spell check features and can single-handedly undermine your writing skills.

As you re-read your document, both silently and out loud, pay special attention to known homonyms and read out your contractions. So if the text reads, "Please know which word *you're* supposed to use," proofread it as "Please know which word *you are* supposed to use." This way, you'll be able to catch those instances when you write, "You're writing skills are impeccable," but really mean "Your writing skills are impeccable."

3. Start from the end. The more you read something, the more your brain begins to memorize it. If you re-read a document over and over, you eventually get to the point where your brain knows what's coming next, so your eyes go into scan mode. While you think you're really reading the document closely, your brain is only picking up key words and drawing on memory to fill in the blanks. So even though your fiftieth read-through confirms that the document is error-free, your reader (who has never seen the document before) will quickly spot careless errors you scanned right over.

When you feel that you've read your document too many times and can't get past scan mode, mix things up for your brain. Read the last sentence of your document first just to check for things like sentence structure, grammar, spelling, etc. Then read the sentence above the last and do the same. Pull sentences out of the text at random and check for errors. By treating each sentence as a stand alone unit rather than as part of a flowing document, your brain will perk up and not be anticipating the next memorized line.

You'll catch more errors when you look at the individual elements of your document instead of focusing on the overall content.

4. Go to the experts. You may have a dictionary on your office bookshelf and perhaps even a thesaurus. But do you have a good grammar guide? Anyone who produces written documents can quickly improve his or her writing simply by referring to a grammar guide for writing tips.

Your local bookstore has many grammar guides available. Browse through a few to determine which one adequately addresses your particular writing challenges. Some guides focus specifically on grammar issues, while others pay particular attention to matters of writing tone and style. Some target fiction writers or journalists, while others angle their topics to business writing. Choose a guide you're comfortable with, refer to it often, and watch your writing improve.

## Better writing now

Competition in business is fierce these days. Don't let a misspelled word or incorrect sentence kill the deal. Practice the tricks of self-editing so every written document you produce showcases your knowledge, competence and professionalism. Before you know it, your prospects and clients will be unable to resist your written messages, and your company's profits will soar.

---

Dawn Josephson is the president and founder of Cameo Publications, an editorial and publishing services firm. She helps professional speakers, authors, and business leaders transform their ideas into written materials that entertain and inform audiences worldwide. For more information e-mail Dawn@CameoPublications.com.

# *In Praise* *of* Boundaries

## A Conversation with Miss Manners

BUSINESS ENVIRONMENTS have become much less formal than they once were. The dark suits and ties of the 1960s have been replaced with polo shirts, chinos, and loafers. Everyone is on a first name basis, and the boss's door is always open. An army of consultants and HR officers make it their business to transform the workplace into a less forbidding setting, often using informal off-sites or games to break down social barriers between colleagues.

This informality originated with the American democratic belief that everyone is equally valuable, and it has taken hold throughout the business world as America's global presence and MBA-style education has spread. Yet informality in the workplace is becoming more common for another reason. Informal environments, many organizational experts argue, are more open and trusting. And with the freedom to "be themselves" workers are more comfortable and more creative. From that perspective, it's easy to characterize etiquette and formality as European vices that America's immigrant forebears did well to leave behind.

The irony is that many of the most successful challenges to American business have come from countries and companies that champion etiquette in the workplace. Company life in Japan, for example, is governed by intricate rules that often appear stilted to the outsider. Just think of the elaborate rituals of business card exchange, where the act of presenting and receiving cards reflects different levels of respect. While the famously hierarchical structure of Japanese society may not be fertile ground for the rags-to-riches stories in which America delights, it is Japanese-style work practices that have arguably played the greatest role in empowering the American worker. And Japan is not the only country to successfully combine business performance with etiquette. China, too, places a premium on formal manners, as do the Germans, who get down to first names at work only after using five honorifics.

So has the American workplace become too informal for its own good? To gain some insight into this question, HBR senior editor Diane L. Coutu visited etiquette writer and syndicated columnist Judith Martin in Washington, DC. Raised there and in foreign capitals, Martin, known to millions of Americans as Miss Manners, has been writing about etiquette for more than 25 years. During that time, she has published ten books on the subject, including best sellers such as *Miss Manners' Guide to Excruciatingly Correct Behavior* and *Miss Manners' Guide to Rearing Perfect Children*, as well as the recently published *Star-Spangled Manners: In Which Miss Manners Defends American Etiquette (For a Change)*.

In the following interview, edited for clarity and length, Martin makes a compelling case that business needs more etiquette, not less. Without some formality in social intercourse, she argues, human interactions end up being governed by laws, which are too blunt to guide people through the nuances of personal – or professional – behavior.

**Erasmus wrote about etiquette. So did Thomas Jefferson. What is so riveting about the subject?**

It is the basic question of civilization: How we should treat one another? Erasmus was a relative latecomer; Socrates was asking such questions long before. When you study philosophy, history, or anthropology, you come to understand that all societies develop formal rules – sometimes complicated ones – around basic human experiences such as eating and dying.

Yet there seems to be something in us that rebels against form and etiquette. Every 200 years or so, an anti-manners movement surfaces in which leaders urge us to be ourselves – whatever that means – and break free of the shackles of form and tradition. The basic idea behind these movements seems to be that we should return to some state of nature that existed before etiquette. But to assume that etiquette is an invention of advanced civilizations is absurd. The more primitive a society, the more precise its etiquette. Cannibalistic tribes, for example, have created elaborate rituals around their feasts. More fundamentally, it is false to argue that artificiality is unnatural and bad. Indeed, the whole point of etiquette is precisely its artificiality, which helps us deal with the extremes of human emotion by expressing them in a way that others can tolerate.

*It's taken us half a century to realize that when you remove everybody's inhibitions, you create more problems than you solve.*

We have recently come out of one such naturalistic phase, which was characterized by a strong denial of the rituals surrounding death. We had gotten used to hearing things like, "Why go to the funeral? He's dead and won't care. He would have wanted me to go to my tennis game and enjoy myself." That kind of thinking ended on September 11, 2001. The sacrifices made by America's firefighters and police officers and the losses suffered by the victims' families brought back a respect for people's lives and deaths. People suddenly started wearing black to funerals again.

**Is etiquette in trouble at the workplace?**

It is, partly because of that naturalism. An inevitable and unfortunate part of the "I want to be me" movement has been the idea that there is no distinction between your business life and your personal life. People treat colleagues as friends and family – often to disastrous

effect. Sexual harassment is a prime example. If you flirt with somebody at a party, that person can't have you arrested. But if you flirt at the office, it could cost you your job. Well, flirting at work has always been unmannerly. The distance of formality should make it obvious that office flirtation is wrong. But because people don't care about etiquette anymore, we have to use the law to make them obey. That is not trivial for the people involved. An exposed office flirt was once just a cad. Now someone who misunderstands the limits of office friendship could become a criminal with a record. The problem with many of today's workplace issues is that they are too subtle and nuanced for the law, which is a very heavy-handed instrument. But if people don't obey the rules of etiquette, we have no choice but to use the law.

Unfortunately, the pseudofriendliness, personal e-mails, and office collections for the umpteenth bridal or baby shower have destroyed the sense of boundaries that characterizes professional behavior. If we hope to reassure our customers that we are indeed professional, we need to be aware of those boundaries. But in our relationships with colleagues, we also need to acknowledge that we are often too distant from our coworkers to be able to resolve problems on a personal level. At home, if your stereo is too loud, your partner feels free to say, "Honey, will you turn that thing down? It's driving me crazy." And you will know him well enough to answer, "Oh, I'm sorry. I didn't realize you were trying to read." But at work, if the person in the next cubicle is being loud, you can't really solve the problem with that sort of exchange, because the worker in the next cube is not a friend of yours. That's where office etiquette comes in. Setting formal limits to behavior reduces the chance of conflict from the outset. Rules decree whether or not you can play music or take personal calls in open space. We need such limits to keep people from upsetting one another unnecessarily.

Interestingly, the kind of professional demeanor I am arguing for is found in people who are having an affair in the workplace and don't want anybody to know about it. They often keep that formal aloofness.

**You talk a lot about setting boundaries. But Jack Welch often spoke about making General Electric boundaryless. Do you think he was wrong?**

Yes. My views are the exact opposite of Mr. Welch's. I want formality back so we can all regain some dignity. Besides, employees were never taken in by all that talk about informality. On one hand, the boss was firing people; on the other, he was saying, "Oh, we're just like family." And employees thought, "Oh no we're not!" Now, I know some executives believe that informality will help put more flexibility and truth into the system. But I am one of those people who believes that we have quite enough honesty in the world, and I'm not looking for more. Oddly, in today's social realm, honesty seems to trump every other moral value. Truth has become so overblown in situations of criminal wrongdoing that people will say, "Well, I don't mind that he did this or that, but then he lied about it"–as if the lie were the worst part, which it is not. I'm not recommending lying, but I am saying that you have to judge a lie within the context of other values. And whether you are in a business or a social setting, it is not valuable to go around all the time spewing your own truths, which are often mere opinions. Of course, there are times when honesty is terribly important, and certainly in a fact-gathering situation in an organization, honesty is critical. But let's face it: It isn't etiquette that keeps people from telling the truth to the boss, it's the fear of losing their job. We all know what the boss likes. If he's the kind of person who wants you to tell him what's going on, then you're going to keep him well informed. But if he hired you as a yes-man, then it isn't etiquette that will hold you back from getting the facts across. After all, there are polite ways for employees to raise issues. You don't necessarily have to say, "I think you're stealing." Instead you might say, "We're having a little trouble. The office supplies keep disappearing."

**Let's look at some specific issues. Is talking about money ever vulgar in a business situation?**

The business world deals in money, so it is certainly not vulgar to discuss it. True, at one time there were fewer women in the workplace, and men would never let women pay for business lunches. So I would have all these women asking, "How do I pay a business bill? Should I go to the restaurant and pay the bill before he sees it?" Things have improved a bit since then; today's women feel free to pay for meals. But we still have a long way to go. Research shows that women feel they can't ask the boss for a raise. But talking about money at work is only vulgar if it gets too personal. Asking the boss for a raise is not the same as asking her how much she paid for her dress.

I think bosses need to spend more time talking about money with their employees, not less. There is still this ridiculous charade that goes on between bosses and their employees at Christmas. Even big-name executives will ask me, "So what do I get my assistant for Christmas?" And I'll say, "How should I know? And how should you know? You probably shouldn't be so close to your assistant that you know her taste in perfume. Give her a bonus instead." Presents such as clothing and perfume are highly symbolic and, hence, inappropriate. If you work for me and I give you a bigger desk, that's office symbolism, so that's fine. But if I buy you a coat, I've crossed the boundaries of appropriateness. A good boss keeps things professional, showing approval with money, not presents. So instead of buying a Thanksgiving turkey for each employee—even for the vegetarians—he gives them a bonus.

## Does entertaining have a place in business?

Business entertaining is an oxymoron. Asking people to labor without pay isn't fair. Worse, it cuts into their personal lives. I originally came to this conclusion by observing the social lives of diplomats here in Washington. Entertaining in Washington is usually very high-level, very interesting. People get so used to it that they often want to retire here after they finish their careers. The ironic thing is that after they retire, they feel terribly cut off. But why should things be any different? Well, when they were using their country's money or their com-

pany's money, they were in a very desirable position. They weren't being loved for who they were. Once they lost that power and influence, they were no longer so appealing. The unfortunate part is that these diplomats and senior executives often give up the opportunity to have real friends. You don't have time to make friends if you're out socializing every night with pseudo-friends. And on a smaller scale, the same is true in business offices. It is a terrific imposition for a business to ask people to give up their weekends and their evenings for unpaid work. I get these pathetic letters from 70-year-old retired executives who say, "I worked for 40 years in this office, and everybody loved me, They gave me this huge party when I left. And now nobody calls me. What happened?" What happened, I say, is that your colleagues aren't your friends–and they never were.

## So you also disapprove of business retreats?

Absolutely. I sincerely hope that we're seeing the end of retreats. This personalization of business relationships is misguided. For one thing, it's expensive to have people climb poles or shoot at one another with paint guns. But the more depressing thing is that it's taken us half a century to realize that when you remove everybody's inhibitions, you create more problems than you solve. Regrettably, the whole retreat thing started with touchy-feely consultants who believed that if we all loved one another, then good behavior would follow. Whatever made anyone believe that? Think about it: People marry because they love each other, and good behavior doesn't necessarily follow. People love their children, and good behavior doesn't necessarily follow. Love is no guarantee, and we certainly don't love everybody in our business environment. At the height of this retreat business, I was president of the board at my children's school. One gentleman kept proposing a retreat until finally I said, "You know my dear sir, you and I disagree on every possible issue within this school. But I give you the benefit of the doubt because I assume your good intentions, and I don't know you that well. Do you want to remove all

doubt?" That was the end of that. But I tell people who find themselves sitting around a campfire with coworkers, forced to reveal something personal about themselves, to limit their comments to something like, "I was fat and shy as a kid"– because that's charming. Or, "I didn't like my freckles." Whatever you do, don't reveal too much. You will come to regret it.

> When someone asked me how to be rude to his mother-in-law without getting caught, I replied that the only way to do that is by being extremely polite.

## You've written that etiquette condemns all rudeness. Is there no place for rudeness?

We all secretly recognize that being rude to a superior has a bit of reckless glamour to it. It at least does not violate the principle of noblesse oblige, whereby the powerful are expected to carry a heavier burden than the rest of us. But etiquette does not bar polite people from self-defense or let rude people walk all over them. When someone asked me how to be rude to his mother-in-law without getting caught, I replied that the only way to do that is by being extremely polite. The same is true in business: If you want to be rude to a customer or to someone on the board, the only way to do it – and get away with it–is to be extremely polite. By withdrawing into cold formality, you are telling the other person that you are not willing to deal with him in the same way that you would deal with someone of goodwill. This sort of polite withdrawal can take many forms, from exclusion from a luncheon invitation right up to the ultimate act of shunning. And while shunning is unpleasant, even devastating for the one shunned, it does not constitute rude behavior.

## Let's step back a bit. Who makes all these rules on etiquette?

In most cases, we don't know. The rules are just handed down to us, often by people who try to imbue them with meaning they may never have had. For instance, people will tell you that men are always supposed to walk on the outside of the sidewalk because in the olden days the gutters were full of sewage and people walking on the inside were protected from it. There's no evidence for that. In Europe, where those "olden days" took place, men today always walk to the left of women regardless of which side the gutter is on. And so it is with most rules of etiquette: When you examine them, you find that any logical meaning imputed to them is retroactive. We do things this way because this is the way we do them. Of course, everybody inherits the rules a little differently, and the rules do change over time to adjust to social, philosophical, and technological shifts.

In the few cases where we can correctly determine the provenance of a rule, we are usually surprised by what we learn. Some rules are actually the creation of opportunistic businessmen. Let me give you an example. In the mid-nineteenth century, a number of silver mines were built during the Industrial Revolution that suddenly put silver at the disposal of people who had hardly ever seen it. And because eating rituals are so closely tied to human identity, people got very interested in silver tableware. At the same time, a lot of new money was being created, and these newly wealthy people wanted a patina of respectability. This created an enormous opportunity for silverware companies, which started making specialty items – like terrapin forks and marrow scoops – that they convinced their new customers were essential to civilized living. The marketing tactics these companies employed have had a lasting impact: Even today, now that these items have disappeared from use, people still claim to worry about which fork to use first. (It's the one on the far left.)

### How do you learn the rules?

The particular conventions of each society have to be memorized. But the basic principle behind etiquette is thinking from the other person's point of view, and you have to train for that in childhood. For a child, empathy is a counterintuitive lesson that must be taught and

retaught from an early age. This doesn't mean that a well-mannered child will naturally grow up to be empathetic. Maybe she will; maybe she won't. But she will at least learn to behave as if she is, which will make her socially acceptable.

I can't stress strongly enough the importance of child rearing. When I look at my mail, it's clear that the number one problem facing American society today is greed. My mailbox is full of questions from the perpetrators and the victims of greed – from a bride who is angry about receiving a present that wasn't on her registry to outright begging from friends for contributions to a vacation or college fund. I don't blame the business world for this problem. Since the mid-twentieth century, this country has been ruled by the idea that manners are bad for children because they inhibit them. Well of course they do–if we're lucky. That's the idea. Etiquette is supposed to inhibit the instinct to act on our offensive impulses. That's what civilization is all about.

---

*Since the mid-twentieth century, this country has been ruled by the idea that manners are bad for children because they inhibit them. Well of course they do – if we're lucky.*

---

That said, it's important not to confuse learning etiquette with learning morals. Good manners may have a moral base, but they are not a moral system. The rationale is pragmatic. I take your feelings into consideration because I want you to take mine into consideration. If I am in business, I want you to trust me, because if you don't, then you're not going to do business with me. If you are a businessperson trying to outmaneuver somebody, then you benefit greatly from understanding the other person's point of view, even if you're not going to accommodate that person. Indeed, there are many well-mannered villains who can sweet-talk people into anything.

**A final question: As America goes global, other countries fear that we will bring our culture and manners with us. What is so bad about American etiquette?**

One problem we have is that other societies learn American manners through movies and television. But movies enact conflict; conflict is at the heart of drama. So learning American manners from American films is like learning traffic rules from watching car chases. In reality, we don't allow speeding on our streets. We don't allow people to career down the road the wrong way, knock over a fruit stand, and jump over a bridge. But if you watched American movies, you would think we did. To be fair to Hollywood, if they had to produce well-behaved movies, people would be bored senseless. And in truth, we don't lack manners – we just have a lot of rude people, as does every country. The Japanese, for instance, who have a very complicated code of etiquette, are having trouble getting their children to follow the rules. The British have horrendous problems with bad manners at all levels of society, from soccer hooligans to the royal family.

---

*Learning American manners from American films is like learning traffic rules from watching car chases.*

---

In our case, many violations of etiquette are actually exaggerations of our virtues. Our loudness, for example, reflects our friendliness. Or take the American tendency toward casual dress. In more-hierarchical societies, leaders had to create sumptuary laws to prevent people from getting too competitive about their appearance and clothing. In England, they introduced a tax on wig powder to discourage the conspicuous consumption of the upper classes. By contrast, the principle in America is that we have no class distinctions, so everyone can wear the same type of clothing. Of course, it is possible to have too much of a good thing, and our anti-hierarchical instincts have also eroded some very legitimate hierarchies within society among young and old, boss and employee. That erosion has repercussions that more-traditional societies can't stomach.

It is important to distinguish between the theory and the practice of etiquette. America has – in theory – the best code of manners the world has ever seen. That's because it is based on respect for the individual, regardless of his or her origin. Good manners in America are about helping strangers. They're also about judging people on their qualities rather than on their backgrounds. These are principles that were deliberately worked out by our founding fathers to assure the dignity of the individual and to keep society nonhierarchical. Is this theory true in practice? Of course not; it's a work in progress. But let us not forget that every day, more and more people wake up to the fact that they do not have to be limited by the circumstances of their birth. What's so bad about spreading that?

# Fear *of* Feedback

by Jay M. Jackman and Myra H. Strober

*If you're nervous about asking the boss how you're doing, you're not alone. Getting the guidance you need requires recognizing your fears, countering them with adaptive techniques, and gathering comments before your annual review.*

Nobody likes performance reviews. Subordinates are terrified they'll hear nothing but criticism. Bosses, for their part, think their direct reports will respond to even the mildest criticism with stonewalling, anger, or tears. The result? Everyone keeps quiet and says as little as possible. That's unfortunate, because most people need help figuring out how they can improve their performance and advance their careers.

This fear of feedback doesn't come into play just during annual reviews. At least half the executives with whom we've worked *never* ask for feedback. Many expect the worst: heated arguments, impossible demands, or even threats of dismissal. So rather than seek feedback, people avoid the truth and instead continue to try to guess what their bosses think.

Fears and assumptions about feedback often manifest themselves in psychologically maladaptive behaviors such as procrastination, denial, brooding, jealousy, and self-sabotage. But there's hope. Those who learn to adapt to feedback can free themselves from old patterns. They can learn to acknowledge negative emotions, constructively reframe fear and criticism, develop realistic goals, create support systems, and reward themselves for achievements along the way.

We'll look closely at a four-step process for doing just that. But before we turn to that process, let's explore why so many people are afraid to hear how they're doing.

## Fear Itself

Obviously, some managers have excellent relationships with their bosses. They receive feedback on a regular basis and act on it in ways that improve their performance as well as their prospects for promotion. Sadly, however, such executives are in the minority. In most companies, feedback typically comes via cursory annual performance reviews, during which managers learn little beyond the amount of a forthcoming raise.

People avoid feedback because they hate being criticized, plain and simple. Psychologists have a lot of theories about why people are so sensitive to hearing about their own imperfections. One is that they associate feedback with the critical comments received in their younger years from parents and teachers. Whatever the cause of our discomfort, most of us have to train ourselves to seek feedback and listen carefully when we hear it. Absent that training, the very threat of critical feedback often leads us to practice destructive, maladaptive behaviors that negatively affect not only our work but the overall health of our organizations. The following are some examples of those behaviors.

**Procrastination.** We procrastinate—usually consciously—when we feel helpless about a situation and are anxious, embarrassed, or otherwise dissatisfied with it. Procrastination commonly contains an element of hostility or anger.

> Adapting to feedback is critical for managers
> who find themselves in jobs, companies,
> and industries undergoing frequent transitions.

Consider how Joe, a highly accomplished computer scientist in a large technology company, responded to his frustration over not being promoted. (As with all the examples in this article, people's names have been changed.) Although everyone in the company respected his technical competence, he sensed something was wrong. Instead of seriously assessing his performance and asking for feedback, he became preoccupied with inessential details of his projects, played computer solitaire, and consistently failed to meet project deadlines. When

Joe asked about his chances for advancement in his annual review, his boss singled out Joe's repeated failure to finish projects on time or to seek formal extensions when he knew work would be late. In fact, Joe's continued procrastination became a serious performance issue that cost him a promotion.

**Denial.** We're in denial when we're unable or unwilling to face reality or fail to acknowledge the implications of our situations. Denial is most often an unconscious response.

Angela, a midlevel manager in a consulting firm, drifted into a state of denial when a hoped-for promotion never materialized. Her superiors told her that she hadn't performed as well as they'd expected. Specifically, they told her she'd requested too much time off to spend with her children, she hadn't sufficiently researched a certain industry, she hadn't met her yearly quota of bringing in ten new clients, and so on. Every time she tried to correct these problems, her male superiors put her off with a new series of excuses and challenges. The fact was, they had no intention of promoting her because they were deeply sexist. Accepting that fact would have required Angela to leave, but she chose instead to live in denial. Rather than recognize she was at a dead end, she did nothing about her situation and remained miserable in her job.

**Brooding.** Brooding is a powerful emotional response, taking the form of morbid preoccupation and a sense of foreboding. Faced with situations they feel they can't master, brooders lapse into passivity, paralysis, and isolation.

Adrian, a training manager, brooded when his boss set forth several stretch goals for him. Believing the goals to be unrealistic, Adrian concluded that he couldn't meet them. Rather than talk with his boss about this, he became desperately unhappy and withdrew from his colleagues. They in turn saw his withdrawal as a snub and began to ignore him. The more they avoided him, the more he brooded. By the end of six months, Adrian's brooding created a self-fulfilling prophecy; because he had met none of his goals, his new projects were assigned to someone else, and his job was in jeopardy.

**Jealousy.** Comparing ourselves with others is a normal behavior, but it becomes maladaptive when it is based on suspicion, rivalry, envy, or possessiveness. Jealous people may overidealize others whom they perceive to be more talented, competent, and intelligent; in so doing, they debilitate themselves.

Leslie, a talented vice president of a public relations firm, fell into the jealousy trap when her boss noted during a meeting that one of her colleagues had prepared a truly excellent report for a client. Leslie began comparing herself with her colleague, listening carefully to the boss's remarks during meetings and noting his smiles and nods as he spoke. Feeling that she could never rise to her colleague's level, Leslie lost all enthusiasm for her work. Instead of seeking a reality check with her boss, she allowed the green-eyed monster to consume her; ultimately, she quit her job.

**Self-Sabotage.** Examples of self-sabotage, usually an unconscious behavior, are all too common. Even national leaders such as Bill Clinton and Trent Lott have hoisted themselves on their own petards.

Workplaces are full of people who unconsciously undercut themselves. Take, for example, the story of Nancy, a young associate who found herself unable to deal with more than two projects at once. During her review, Nancy resented her boss's feedback that she needed to improve her ability to multitask. But instead of initiating further discussion with him about the remark, she "accidentally" made a nasty comment about him one day within his earshot. As a result, he began looking for ways to get rid of her. When she was eventually fired, her innermost feelings of unworthiness were validated.

These and other maladaptive behaviors are part of a vicious cycle we have seen at play in too many organizations. Indeed, it's not uncommon for employees, faced with negative feedback, to rain private maledictions upon their supervisors. No wonder, then, that supervisors are reluctant to give feedback. But when employees' imagined and real fears go unchecked, the work environment becomes dysfunctional, if not downright poisonous.

## Learning to Adapt

Adapting to feedback—which inevitably asks people to change, sometimes significantly—is critical for managers who find themselves in jobs, companies, and industries undergoing frequent transitions. Of course, adaptation is easier said than done, for resistance to change is endemic in human beings. But while most people feel they can't control the negative emotions that are aroused by change, this is not the case. It is possible—and necessary—to think positively about change. Using the following adaptive techniques, you can alter how you respond to feedback and to the changes it demands.

**Recognize your emotions and responses.** Understanding that you are experiencing fear ("I'm afraid my boss will fire me") and that you are exhibiting a maladaptive response to that fear ("I'll just stay out of his way and keep my mouth shut") are the critical initial steps toward adaptive change. They require ruthless self-honesty and a little detective work, both of which will go a long way toward helping you undo years of disguising your feelings. It's important to understand, too, that a particular maladaptive behavior does not necessarily tell you what emotion underlies it: You may be procrastinating out of anger, frustration, sadness, or other feelings. But persevering in the detective work is important, for the payoff is high. Having named the emotion and response, you can then act—just as someone who fears flying chooses to board a plane anyway. With practice, it gradually becomes easier to respond differently, even though the fear, anger, or sadness may remain.

## Reframe Your Thinking

Almost everyone dreads performance reviews, which typically take place once a year. But how you respond to the boss's feedback—and how often you request it—will largely affect your performance and chances for career advancement. We've found that getting beyond that sense of dread involves recognizing and naming the emotions and behaviors that are preventing you from initiating feedback discussions. Once you determine those emotional and behavioral barriers, it's a matter of reframing your thoughts and moving toward more adaptive behavior. Below are some examples of how you might turn negative emotions into more positive, productive thoughts.

| Possible Negative Emotion | Maladaptive Response | Reframing Statement |
| --- | --- | --- |
| Anger (I'm mad at my boss because he won't talk to me directly.) | Acting out (stomping around, complaining, being irritable, yelling at subordinates or family) | It's up to me to get the feedback I need. |
| Anxiety (I don't know what will happen.) | Brooding (withdrawal, nail biting) Avoiding I'm too busy to ask for feedback.) | Finding out can open up new opportunities for me. |
| Fear of confrontation (I don't want to do this.) | Denial, procrastination, self-sabotage (canceling meetings with boss) | Taking the initiative puts me in charge and gives me some power. |
| Fear of reprisal (if I speak up, will I get a pink slip?) | Denial (I don't need any feedback. I'm doing just fine.) | I really need to know honestly how I'm doing. |
| Hurt (Why did he say I wasn't trying hard enough?) | Irritability, jealousy of others (silence, plotting to get even) | I can still pay attention to what he said even though I feel hurt. |
| Defensiveness (I'm better than she says.) | Acting out by not supporting the boss (You can bet I'm not going to her stupid meeting.) | Being defensive keeps me from hearing what she has to say. |
| Sadness (I thought he liked me!) | Brooding, withdrawal (being quieter than usual, feeling demotivated) | How I'm doing in my job isn't about whether I'm liked. |
| Fear of change (How will I ever do all that he wants me to do?) | Denial (keep doing things the same way as before) | I *must* change to keep my job. I need to run the marathon one mile at a time. |
| Ambivalence (Should I stay or should I go?) | Procrastination, passivity (waiting for somebody else to solve the problem) | What really serves my interests best? Nobody is as interested in my well-being as I am. *I* need to take some action now. |
| Resignation (I have to leave!) | Resistance to change (It's just too hard to look for another job. It's not really so bad here.) | I'll be much happier working somewhere else. |

Maria, a midlevel manager with whom we worked, is a good example of someone who learned to name her emotions and act despite them. Maria was several months overdue on performance reviews for the three people who reported to her. When we suggested that she was procrastinating, we asked her how she felt when she thought about doing the reviews. After some reflection, she said she was extremely resentful that her boss had not yet completed her own performance evaluation; she recognized that her procrastination was an expression of her anger toward him. We helped her realize that she could act despite her anger. Accordingly, Maria completed the performance evaluations for her subordinates and, in so doing, felt as if a huge weight had been lifted from her shoulders. Once she had completed the reviews, she noticed that her relationships with her three subordinates quickly improved, and her boss responded by finishing Maria's performance review.

We should note that Maria's procrastination was not an entrenched habit, so it was relatively easy to fix. Employees who start procrastinating in response to negative emotions early in their work lives won't change that habit quickly—but they can eventually.

**Get support.** Identifying your emotions is sometimes difficult, and feedback that requires change can leave you feeling inhibited and ashamed. For these reasons, it's critical to ask for help from trusted friends who will listen, encourage, and offer suggestions. Asking for support is often hard, because most corporate cultures expect managers to be self-reliant. Nevertheless, it's nearly impossible to make significant change without such encouragement. Support can come in many forms, but it should begin with at least two people—including, say, a spouse, a minister or spiritual counselor, a former mentor, an old high school classmate—with whom you feel emotionally safe. Ideally, one of these people should have some business experience. It may also help to enlist the assistance of an outside consultant or executive coach.

**Reframe the feedback.** Another adaptive technique, reframing, allows you to reconstruct the feedback process to your advantage. Specifically, this involves putting the prospect of asking for or reacting to feedback in a positive light so that negative emotions and responses lose their grip.

> Divide up the large task of dealing with feedback into manageable, measurable chunks, and set realistic time frames for each one.

Take the example of Gary, a junior sales manager for a large manufacturing company. Gary's boss told him that he wasn't sociable enough with customers and prospects. The criticism stung, and Gary could have responded with denial or brooding. Indeed, his first response was to interpret the feedback as shallow. Eventually, though, Gary was able to reframe what he'd heard, first by grudgingly acknowledging it. ("He's right, I'm not very sociable. I tested as an introvert on the Myers-Briggs, and I've always been uncomfortable with small talk.") Then Gary reframed the feedback. Instead of seeing it as painful, he recognized that he could use it to help his career. Avoiding possible maladaptive responses, he was able to ask himself several important questions: "How critical is sociability to my position? How much do I want to keep this job? How much am I willing to change to become more sociable?" In responding, Gary realized two things: that sociability was indeed critical to success in sales and that he wasn't willing to learn to be more sociable. He requested a transfer and moved to a new position where he became much more successful.

**Break up the task.** Yet another adaptive technique is to divide up the large task of dealing with feedback into manageable, measurable chunks, and set realistic time frames for each one. Although more than two areas of behavior may need to be modified, it's our experience that most people can't change more than one or two at a time. Taking small steps and meeting discrete goals reduces your chances of being overwhelmed and makes change much more likely.

Jane, for example, received feedback indicating that the quality of her work was excellent but that her public presentations were boring. A quiet and reserved person, Jane could have felt overwhelmed by what she perceived as the subtext of this criticism: that she was a lousy public speaker and that she'd better transform herself from a wallflower into a writer and actress. Instead, she adapted by breaking down the challenge of "interesting presentations" into its constituent parts (solid and well-constructed content; a commanding delivery; an understanding of the audience; and so on). Then she undertook to teach herself to present more effectively by observing several effective speakers and taking an introductory course in public speaking.

It was important for Jane to start with the easiest task—in this case, observing good speakers. She noted their gestures, the organization of their speeches, their intonation, timing, use of humor, and so forth. Once she felt she understood what good speaking entailed, she was ready to take the introductory speaking course. These endeavors allowed her to improve her presentations. Though she didn't transform herself into a mesmerizing orator, she did learn to command the attention and respect of an audience.

**Use incentives.** Pat yourself on the back as you make adaptive changes. That may seem like unusual advice, given that feedback situations can rouse us to self-punishment and few of us are in the habit of congratulating ourselves. Nevertheless, nowhere is it written that the feedback process must be a wholly negative experience. Just as a salary raise or a bonus provides incentive to improve performance, rewarding yourself whenever you take an important step in the process will help you to persevere in your efforts. The incentive should be commensurate with the achievement. For example, an appropriate reward for completing a self-assessment might be an uninterrupted afternoon watching ESPN or, for a meeting with the boss, a fine dinner out.

## Getting the Feedback You Need

Once you've begun to adapt your responses and behavior, it's time to start seeking regular feedback from your boss rather than wait for the annual performance review to come around. The proactive feedback process we recommend consists of four manageable steps: self-assessment, external feedback, absorbing the feedback, and taking action toward change. The story of Bob, a vice president of human resources, illustrates how one executive used the four-step process to take charge of his work life.

When we first met Bob, he had been on the job for three years and felt he was in a feedback vacuum. Once a year, toward the end of December, Harry—the gruff, evasive CEO to whom he reported—would call Bob in, tell him what a fine job he had been doing, announce his salary for the following year, and give him a small bonus. But this year, Bob had been dealing with thorny issues—including complaints from senior female executives about unfair compensation—and needed some real feedback. Bob wondered how Harry viewed his work. Were there aspects of Bob's performance that Harry wasn't happy with? Did Harry intend to retain Bob in his current position?

**Self-Assessment.** We encouraged Bob to begin by assessing his own performance. Self-assessment can be a tough assignment, particularly if one has never received useful feedback to begin with. The first task in self-assessment was for Bob to determine which elements of his job were most important. The second was to recall informal feedback he had received from coworkers, subordinates, and customers—not only words, but facial expressions, body language, and silences.

> Feedback conversations with colleagues can often serve as a form of dress rehearsal for the real thing.

Bob took several weeks to do his self-assessment. Once we helped him realize that he was procrastinating with the assessment, he enlisted a support system—his wife and an old college buddy—who encouraged him to finish his tally of recollections. At the end of the process, he recognized that he had received a good deal of positive informal feedback from many of the people with whom he interacted. But he also realized that he was too eager to please and needed to be more assertive in expressing his opinions. We helped him reframe these uncomfortable insights so that he could see them as areas for potential growth.

**External Feedback.** The next phase of the proactive process—asking for feedback—is generally a two-part task: The first involves speaking to a few trusted colleagues to collect information that supports or revises your self-assessment. The second involves directly asking your boss for feedback. Gathering feedback from trusted colleagues shouldn't be confused with 360-degree feedback, which culls a wide variety of perspectives, including those from people who may not know you well. By speaking confidentially with people you genuinely trust, you can keep some of the fear associated with feedback at bay. Trusted colleagues can also help you identify your own emotional and possibly maladaptive responses to criticism, which is particularly beneficial prior to your meeting with your superior. Additionally, feedback conversations with colleagues can often serve as a form of dress rehearsal for the real thing. Sometimes, colleagues

point out areas that warrant immediate attention; when they do, it's wise to make those changes before meeting with the boss. On the other hand, if you think you can't trust any of your colleagues, you should bypass such feedback conversations and move directly to setting up a meeting with your boss.

Bob asked for feedback from two trusted colleagues, Sheila and Paul, at meetings that he specifically scheduled for this purpose. He requested both positive and negative feedback and specific examples of areas in which he did well and in which he needed to improve. He listened intently to their comments, interrupting only for clarification. Both told him that he analyzed problems carefully and interacted well with employees. Yet Sheila noted that at particularly busy times of the year, Bob seemed to have difficulty setting his priorities, and Paul pointed out that Bob needed to be more assertive. Armed with his colleagues' feedback, Bob had a clearer notion of his strengths and weaknesses. He realized that some of his difficulties in setting priorities were owing to unclear direction from Harry, and he made a note to raise the matter with him.

The next step in external feedback—the actual meeting with your boss—requires delicate handling, particularly since the request may come as a surprise to him or her. In setting up the meeting, it's important to assure your boss that criticisms and suggestions will be heard, appreciated, and positively acted on. It's vital, too, to set the agenda for the meeting, letting your superior know that you have three or four questions based on your self-assessment and feedback from others. During the meeting, ask for specific examples and suggestions for change while remaining physically and emotionally neutral about the feedback you hear. Watch carefully not only for specific content but also for body language and tone, since feedback can be indirect as well as direct. When the meeting concludes, thank your boss and indicate that you will get back to her with a plan of action after you've had time to absorb what you've heard. Remember, too, that you can terminate the meeting if it becomes counterproductive (for example, if your boss responds to any of your questions with anger).u

During his feedback meeting with Harry, Bob inquired about his work priorities. Harry told him that the company's financial situation looked precarious and that Bob should focus on locating and implementing a less costly health benefit plan. Harry warned Bob that a new plan would surely anger some employees, and because of that, Bob needed to develop a tougher skin to withstand the inevitable criticism.

As Bob learned, feedback meetings can provide more than just a performance assessment; they can also offer some other important and unexpected insights. Bob had been so immersed in HR issues that he had never noted that Harry had been otherwise preoccupied with the company's financial problems.

**Absorbing the Feedback.** Upon hearing critical feedback, you may well experience the negative emotions and maladaptive responses we described earlier. It's important to keep your reactions private until you can replace them with adaptive responses that lead to an appropriate plan of action.

Bob, for example, realized he felt irritated and vaguely hurt at the suggestion that he needed to toughen up. He brooded for a while but then reframed these feelings by recognizing that the negative feedback was as much a commentary on Harry's preoccupations as it was on Bob's performance. Bob didn't use the reframing to negate Harry's feedback; he accepted that he needed to be more assertive and hard-nosed in dealing with employees' issues.

**Taking Action.** The last phase of the proactive feedback process involves coming to conclusions about, and acting on, the information you've received. Bob, for example, chose to focus on two action strategies: implementing a less costly health care plan—which included preparing himself to tolerate employee complaints—and quietly looking for new employment, since he now understood that the company's future was uncertain. Both of these decisions made Bob uncomfortable, for they evoked his fear of change. But having developed his adaptive responses, he no longer felt trapped by fear. In the months following, he implemented the new health benefits plan without taking his employees' criticism personally. He also kept an eye on the company's financials and reconnected with his professional network in case it became clear the organization was starting to founder.

## The Rewards of Adaptation

Organizations profit when executives seek feedback and are able to deal well with criticism. As executives begin to ask how they are doing relative to management's priorities, their work becomes better aligned with organizational goals. Moreover, as an increasing number of executives in an organization learn to ask for feedback, they begin to transform a feedback-averse environment into a more honest and open one, in turn improving performance throughout the organization.

Equally important, using the adaptive techniques we've mentioned can have a positive effect on executive's private lives. When they free themselves from knee-jerk behaviors in response to emotions, they often find that relationships with family and friends improve. Indeed, they sometimes discover that rather than fear feedback, they look forward to leveraging it.

*Jay M. Jackman is a psychiatrist and human resources consultant in Stanford, California. He can be reached at jayj@stanfordalumni.org. Myra H. Strober is a labor economist and professor at Stanford University's School of Education, and by courtesy at the Stanford Graduate School of Business. She is also a human resources consultant and can be reached at myras@stanford.edu.*

# UNIT 4
# Developing Effective Human Resources

## Unit Selections

## Key Points to Consider

- Organizations spend a great deal of money on training and development. Why do many organizations feel it is necessary to provide courses in-house? Why do other organizations spend money on outside programs? Why might the training programs of some firms be inadequate, even though a great deal of money is spent on them? What are some of the new techniques being used in corporate education? What are some of the questions organizations should be asking of their training and development operations?

- What are your career plans, and how do you plan to implement them? How has career development changed over the years? Do you think you are likely to have a number of careers in the future? What do you think will be the impact of the internet? What do you think about the outsourcing of domestic jobs to lesser developed countries? What do you think you can do to prevent your job from being outsourced?

- Do you think the concept of diversity is a good idea? Why or why not? How should diversity be attained? What are some of the problems with diversity?

 **Links: www.dushkin.com/online/**
These sites are annotated in the World Wide Web pages.

**Employment Interviews**
*http://www.snc.edu/socsci/chair/336/group3.htm*

**Feminist Majority Foundation**
*http://www.feminist.org*

**How to Do an Employee Appraisal**
*http://www.visitorinfo.com/gallery/howapp.htm*

Every organization needs to develop its employees. This is accomplished through a number of activities, including formal corporate training, career development, and performance appraisal. Just as the society and the economy will continue to change, so will the human resource needs of organizations. Individuals and their employers must work together to achieve the effective use of human resources. They must plan together to make the maximum use of their abilities so as to meet the challenge of the changing environment in which they live.

American industry spends approximately the same amount of money each year on training and developing employees as is spent by all colleges and universities combined. It also trains roughly the same number of people as there are students in traditional post-secondary education. Corporate programs are often very elaborate and can involve months or even years of training. In fact, corporate training and development programs have been recognized by academia for their quality and excellence. The American Council for Education has a program designed to evaluate and make recommendations concerning corporate and government training programs for college credit. Corporations, themselves, have entered into the business of granting degrees that are recognized by regional accrediting agencies. For example, McDonald's grants an associate's degree from "Hamburger U." General Motors Institute (now Kettering University) offers the oldest formalized corporate sponsored/related degree-granting program in the United States, awarding a bachelor's in industrial management; and a Ph.D program in policy analysis is available from the Rand Corporation. American industry is in the business of educating and training employees, not only as a simple introduction and orientation to the corporation, but as a continual and constant enterprise of lifelong learning so that both firms and employees can meet the challenges of an increasingly competitive world. Meeting these challenges depends on knowledge, not on sweat, and relies on the ability to adapt to and adopt technological, social, and economic changes faster than competitors do. But, for training to be truly effective and beneficial for the organization, management must be able to set priorities that will be effective and appropriate for the firm. Corporations must also take advantage of the latest in instructional technology, recognizing the value of performance simulations, and address the problem of employees who do not respond well to the new methods of instruction as discussed in "What To Do About E-dropouts."

There is an important difference between jobs and careers. Everyone who works, whether self-employed or employed by someone else, does a job. Although a career is made up of a series of jobs and positions over an individual's working life, it is more than that. It is a sense of direction, a purpose, and a knowledge of where one is going in one's professional life. Careers are shaped by individuals through the decisions they make concerning their own lives, not by organizations. It is the individual who must ultimately take the responsibility for what happens in his or her career. Organizations offer opportunities for advancement and they fund training and development based on their own self-interest, not solely on workers' interests. Accordingly, the employee must understand that the responsibility for career development ultimately rests with him- or herself. In today's world of short job tenure, people will frequently change jobs and they

must be prepared to do so at a moments notice. Jobs are being lost, but they are also being created. A "Competitive Global Job Market Strains Employees," to be more proactive in preparing for a possible identity shift in their careers. They must continue to learn and remain competitive or become a kind of commodity worker whose skills will be employed by the lowest bidder.

One of the ways that organizations can assist in the career development of their employees is to engage in appropriate and effective performance appraisals. This process benefits both the employee and the employer. From the employer's perspective, it allows the organization to fine-tune the performance of the individual and to take appropriate action when the performance does not meet an acceptable standard. From the employee's perspective, appraisal allows the individual to evaluate his or her situation in the organization. Appraisal will indicate, in formal ways, how the individual is viewed by the organization. It is, for the employee, an opportunity to gauge the future.

One of the pressing issues today is diversity. The American, and for that matter, the global workforce is made up of many different people with many different backgrounds. All of them have a wide degree of potential, none of which is based on race, creed, gender, or ethnic origin. It is very dangerous for any organization to ignore any potential labor pool whose talent can be used in a competitive environment, especially if that talent can be used competitively against the organization. Organizations that ignore diversity do so at their peril. The next Henry Ford, Bill Gates, or Warren Buffett could come from anywhere, and given today's world it is far less likely to be a white male than twenty or thirty years ago.

To ignore the development potential of the employees of any organization is to court disaster —not only for the organization, but for the employee. People who have stopped developing themselves are cheating themselves and their employers. Both will be vulnerable to changes brought on by increased competition, but the workers will be the ones who join the statistics of the unemployed.

# What to Do About E-Dropouts

## What if it's not the e-learning but the e-learner?

By Allison Rossett and Lisa Schafer

There is a lot of literature about e-learning, but little attention on the e-learner. That's ironic, because the success of e-learning depends on good choices by the learners.

A frequently touted benefit of e-learning is that it shifts control from the bureaucracy and instructor to the learner. Should learning and performance professionals be enthusiastic about that movement? The answer rests, in large part, on what e-learners will do with their opportunity. Much depends on their eagerness and ability to learn independently and online.

Let's start by looking at learners' eagerness. Will they *choose* e-learning? Will they do what needs to be done diligently, on their own? Will they use the rich resources provided online? Or head for the refrigerator? Will they return online repeatedly to review models, reflect on exercises, take tests, practice on cases, refer to tools, search out examples, and contribute to communities?

An internal study in a large government agency found little enthusiasm for e-learning among employees. A 2001 ASTD/Masie Center study reported grim participation statistics, with only 69 percent of employees electing to begin compulsory online courses and 32 percent starting voluntary courses. Even organizations with a financial interest in the success of e-learning are admitting lukewarm acceptance within their ranks. Karen Frankola, e-learning solutions manager for NYU Online, reported in 2001 that Sun Microsystems's studies found that only 25 percent of its employees completed online self-study courses. Study after study has found that despite organizations' good intentions, e-learning initiatives are failing to capture and sustain the interest of learners.

"Many students given control over their own learning choose to terminate the experience before mastering the training task," says Ken Brown, a University of Iowa assistant professor specializing in business management and psychology.

Such lack of interest and dismal completion rates from employees would appear to point to a problem with the courseware or its implementation. Accordingly, those aspects receive the most attention and finger pointing. For some e-learning experts, it's a cut-and-dry argument: Learners don't complete e-learning because they're not engaged. But what if the courseware is sound? What if the problem isn't with e-learning but with the e-learner?

The fact is that many employees don't know how to be effective self-learners. They're just not aware of or in control of independent learning strategies. Though many learners can establish goals, assess progress, earmark time, and exert continuous effort to work-related projects, when it comes to e-learning they're more likely to go for a cup of coffee.

What is the problem? Are e-learners just plain ornery? Are they angling to return to the comforting embrace of instructors?

We see no plot afoot. Instead, we see unprepared people with habits cultivated in classrooms dominated by instructors. It should be no surprise that learners often experience confusion and failure when they go it alone online.

Because so many learners resist e-learning, should we abandon all hope, wash the whiteboards, and return to the classrooms? Of course not. What we must do is recognize the threats to e-learners' success and take steps to build their enthusiasm and strengthen their commitment to e-learning. Our focus here will be on two critical links: the e-learning and e-learners.

## E-levating the e-learning

It's essential that we focus first on the learning programs. They have the greatest potential to influence whether e-learners succeed or fail. Here's what you can do to ensure a successful program.

**Provide meaningful content.** E-learners crave content that helps them work better and faster. For example, PeopleSoft sales consultants want to understand new product features to prepare outstanding client presentations. Customer service representatives at Sprint want to know how to order an international toll-free number for a new account. For John Speicher, a systems engineer at Cisco Systems, it's simple: "I'm more likely to pay attention when I know it's going to affect a client in an hour."

Content must be ruled by the priorities of users, not the passions of subject matter experts. Talk to the potential audience. Provide what they say they need. Frame resources in light of learners' questions, concerns, and priorities. And whenever possible, lead them directly to an example of how to handle a particularly troublesome problem.

# The fact is that many employees don't know how to be effective self-learners.

During development and prototyping, test the content with potential users. Ask if the program will help today, tomorrow, and two months from now. Make certain that the e-learning transcends the obvious. As one e-learner remarks, she often finds herself "waiting for the good part." Her patience is the exception; most learners won't wait.

**Provide *my* content.** Although meaningful content is good, tailored content is better. Land's End is an excellent example. Parkas, boots, flannel shirts, turtlenecks, and monogramming—the content is there, as is the information to support it. But the company takes it a step further. It tries to match its products to customers by creating an online model, or avatar, that is unique to you. Weight? Height? Hair? Body shape? Land's End even lets you craft a model that is more or less "mature." (You get to decide what that means.) Land's End then recommends clothing. How will you look in that jacket? Those pajamas? The online experience is tailored to your needs.

E-learning must move in that direction—offering choices about tone, path, practice, and community. E-learning should be able to adapt to a learner's style, consider his or her successes, and then offer an experience with more of the elements that appeal and fewer that baffle.

Julia Manson, a product consultant with PeopleSoft, says, "Forget the fluffy background and flowery language. Talk to us like adults." Another e-learner might want detailed background information, elaboration, and support. Though an in-class instructor is limited to only one approach, e-learning has the potential to fulfill multiple approaches. Designers should tailor courses for a range of learning preferences, but a program can't do that without involvement from participants. They have to know what they need and acknowledge the difficulties, for example, in converting legacy materials to the Web. They have to be honest about their weight when Land's End asks them to type in a number.

In another example, at the IRS online experiences are matched to the tasks confronting its HR and training professionals. (Tasks were determined through a needs assessment.) Those professionals were asked such questions as what kept them up at night as the organization moved towards more reliance on technology for learning. **GO TO "IRS Goes E," May *T+D*.**

## Provide opportunities for action

A course's design should encourage e-learners to seek, try, decide, compare, and commune.

**Seek.** One broadband provider's TV ad shows a man who has surfed the Web to the point of reaching "the end of the Internet." What can we, as instructors, do to harness that kind of curiosity into an engaging learning experience? A possible solution is the inclusion of inquiry-oriented activities such as a WebQuest, which engages learners by encouraging them to seek out resources on the Internet.

**Try.** The essence of action is nudging the learner to *do* something. E-learning for tech-related fields often uses the "try" action. For example, Element K requires e-learners to use the Feather option in a Photoshop course or expects Windows administrators to modify the startup process as part of the course. With other types of content, an e-learner can try his or her hand at interactive quizzes or games. The Nobel e-museum includes a game with practice identifying blood types www.nobel.se/medicine/educational/landsteiner/index.html. Land's End online encourages shoppers to try before they buy.

**Decide.** Chinos or jeans? Take the quiz or skip to the explanation? Presenting the e-learner with choices parallels realities in the workplace. Do I recommend investment in that bond or this equity? What would the ethical action be in this circumstance? E-learners constantly face such decisions at work. Excluding the decision-making process from a course wastes a valuable learning opportunity. Indecision is an obstacle to progress; decision is a call to action.

**Compare and commune.** The ability to identify what you know and what you don't know is critical to the success of independent learning. At the First Things Fast Website www.jbp.com/legacy/rossett/rossett.html, training professionals have the opportunity to compose their own responses to skeptical, disinterested, or resistant customers. They then compare their approaches with a model effort.

For PeopleSoft's Manson, real-time collaboration brings the training to life: "When people ask questions, you say, 'Oh, yeah, that's what I was thinking, too.'"

Communing goes beyond asynchronous discussion forums to include virtual classrooms, electronic brown-bag discussions, and instant messaging. "Participants don't realize how much they learn from each other," says Jean Ezell, HR business partner at Bank One.

## Structure experiences for success

E-learners fail when they face online content for which they're unprepared or from an interface or a structure that confuses or confounds.

**Focus content.** To keep e-learners away from ending an online session, guide them into appropriate choices and avoid placing them in situations in which their confidence will be dashed. It's important to provide prerequisite information and to help online learners decide whether they're qualified for the experience. For example, basic math facts must be mastered before long division.

It's also useful to provide a roadmap. Barnes and Noble University www.barnesandnobleuniversity.com details course descriptions, including prerequisites and the intended audience. IBM provides roadmaps for its PC Institute learners to steer them to content that's suitable for their needs and skills. For knowledgeable e-learners, IBM recommends the use of job aids, or reference sheets, in lieu of a course.

**Detail outcomes.** Whether users need to perform statistical calculations in Excel or want to make sure they've included the required elements on a food nutrition label, represent the outcomes and related challenges in ways that e-learners can use to count themselves in or out of the online experience.

## Presenting the e-learner with choices parallels realities in the workplace.

**Interface.** The interface must show learners where they are, where they've been, what's to come, and what needs to be done to achieve success. Cisco's Speicher requires online mechanics that are as easy as "hit play and go." That can be done by providing an intuitive structure: organizers, headings, summaries, and overviews that orient the e-learner. Most tax software does that well.

It's also important to guide the learner's choices. Mike Williams, in *Handbook of Research for Educational Communications and Technologies*, says that learners with control over their instruction often make poor choices. On the other hand, e-learners remain fond of the choices that pepper many e-learning environments. Our challenge: finding a proper balance between choice and direction. Bradford Bell and Steve Kozlowski, in an article for *Personnel Psychology*, suggest adaptive guidance. Adaptive guidance uses technology to check progress and provide recommendations, also offering model routes and approaches to decide how, what, and where to study.

## Touch minds and hearts

Successful online experiences not only challenge the mind, they also touch the heart. Try these strategies to encourage enthusiasm and transfer:

**Communicate the why.** Show why all new employees need background on company products. Tell why it's important that a salesperson know how to avoid computer viruses. E-learners left wondering why will click the close box.

**Frame the experience in authentic ways.** Specific problems, war stories, and vivid examples are suitable for framing. For example, to convey the importance of avoiding computer viruses, you can depict an employee that unknowingly receives a computer virus, sends an infected email to all customers in her address book, and is then mercilessly and understandably chewed out.

**Use characters with challenges and priorities similar to the e-learner's.** IBM's Basic Blue features other new supervisors as they grapple with the growth and challenges natural to their new position.

**Inoculate e-learners against the obstacles to come.** When training managers are about to set up a new merit increase program, run through the challenges they'll face from employees. Detail the nature of likely concerns, and suggest honest and substantive ways to counter workers' objections.

**Reiterate the content through job aids, ongoing discussion forums, and coaching.** Providing detailed information during the e-learning process is all well and good, but it's useless if it can't be accessed later. Make sure employees can get to needed information or help when back on the job.

## When e-learners commit to e-learning

Learners can take advantage of e-learning by talking to themselves. Enhancing awareness of the learning process, also known as metacognition, is the foundation of successful independent learning.

Here are some questions e-learners should ask themselves:

**Am I able and willing?** Learners must feel comfortable with the basics, such as using the Internet, as well as the intangibles, such as why they're taking the course, whether they're certain about how it affects their career, or if they're interested in learning more about the topic at hand.

**Am I inclined to try something new?** Many e-learners have expressed preference for the familiarity of the classroom. An independent learner recognizes that but is willing to give online approaches a try. Bank One's Ezell encourages others to be open to e-learning. "Don't be intimidated, you can't break it," she says.

**Am I honest with myself?** Learners need to be honest about their strengths and weaknesses related to learning independently. Jumping in head first and hoping for the best is a good way to end up discouraged. They should consider whether they have the background knowledge to be successful, whether they can track their progress, and whether they have enough time to complete a course. Sarah Ryan-Roberts, an e-learner in the online San Diego State University Educational Technology masters program, says that honest self-assessment ultimately influenced her choice about programs. "I need the structure of a formal program," she says. Without clear expectations and deadlines, she knew she would fall behind and quickly become overwhelmed. Likewise, Cisco's Speicher prefers programs that let him see the instructor and experience nonverbal cues, even when those messages are delivered online.

**Am I responsible?** As adults, it's likely that we're all reasonably responsible, but we're not all responsible learners. Do you set goals and use time-management skills? Do you take responsibility for your learning and for your participation in team activities and online communities? Do you deliver what is expected and promised? Do you provide prompt feedback to teammates? Those are questions to consider when approaching e-learning. Suzanne Moore, another online learner in the San Diego State University program, suggests, "Read your syllabus thoroughly at the beginning of the semester and map out your time and deadlines." She found it necessary to go online two to three times a week to stay on top of her course.

**Am I anticipatory?** Look around the bend and imagine what might hinder your progress. Top-priority projects and family crises often lurk just out of sight. Successful e-learners anticipate distractions.

## E-learners should prepare for e-learning just as they would for the classroom.

Cisco's Speicher sums it up this way: "You don't have people contained, and you can't control the distractions—coffee, phone, and such. With e-learning, you don't go through the same transition like you do when you go into a classroom." He suggests that e-learners prepare for e-learning just as they would for the classroom: Turn off the telephone or forward calls, use the restroom, dispense the coffee, and dispense with the chit-chat. Many organizations have produced environmental cues, such as yellow tape and signs on top of computers, to warn colleagues that employees are participating in online learning.

## Talk to management

Just as e-learners profit from looking inward, they'll benefit from talking to their managers about any proposed online learning. It wouldn't hurt any e-learner to pose these questions before taking an e-learning course:

**What is your perception of the relationship between this online experience, my career, and our unit goals?** Learners should understand the relationship of those resources to current and future trends and priorities. It's best to know in advance whether the topic is germane to company goals, relates to performance appraisals, or is important to advancing one's career path.

**What kind of support is available?** When learners falter, it's helpful for them to know what resources are available, such as coaches or support from their manager. In addition, learners should know whether employers will provide time at work for e-learning or recognition for contributing to online communities and online knowledge bases.

**What choices exist?** Learners should ask management which learning paths and online resources have been most fruitful. A little investigation of other units will help learners discover recommended combinations of face-to-face activities and online resources, or which strategies boosted success.

**Does e-learning work?** It's helpful to hear the e-learning success stories, but pay particular attention to e-learning failures. Learning from others' mistakes is a painless way to get the most out of any e-learning.

## Click or quit

E-learning critics point to flabby programs, an ambivalent audience, and high cost. But e-learners are the crucial link in e-learning success. When people go online to learn, they often make bad choices, including a propensity to become e-dropouts. Ecstasy about e-learning and references to anytime, anywhere often turn off busy people who say, "Not now, perhaps later."

There are tangible strategies to increase the likelihood that people will participate, persist, and learn. First, strengthen your e-learning programs for the people who stand to benefit most. It's a reasonable place to start taking advantage of technology for learning and support.

**Allison Rossett,** *professor of educational technology at San Diego State University, is the editor of the ASTD E-Learning Handbook and co-author of* Beyond the Podium: Delivering Training and Performance to a Digital World. *Rossett received ASTD's 2002 award for Workplace Learning and Performance; arossett@mail.sdsu.edu.*

**Lisa Schafer** *is a founder of Collet and Schafer, a firm that improves clients' organizational performance through the application of technology. Schafer is currently pursuing her MA in educational technology at San Diego State University; lhschafer@colletandschafer.com.*

# Who's Next?

Creating a formal program for developing new leaders can pay huge dividends, but many firms aren't reaping those rewards

## Susan J. Wells

What would you do if all of the senior managers in your company departed unexpectedly tomorrow? Would the firm be thrown into a leadership crisis? Or would there be a group of successors ready to take the helm?

Bill Moore, vice president of organizational development at K. Hovnanian Enterprises Inc. in Red Bank, N.J., one of the nation's largest homebuilders, asked those questions of his company's CEO and senior management team last year. He got very few reassuring answers.

But, by asking the question, Moore did get the attention and the action he wanted. Within several months, the CEO endorsed a wide-ranging succession plan that all six top executives committed to push throughout the $2.6-billion company.

Under the year-old plan, successor candidates have been identified for group, region, division and area presidents companywide. At least 50 leader candidates have been tapped, and the company is confident that nearly half of them will be ready to move into senior management within one to two years, Moore says. (For more on K. Hovnanian's succession planning program, see "Case Study: A Growing Business Needs More Managers.")

While the successful efforts to groom leaders at K. Hovnanian are inspiring, they represent the exception, rather than the rule. Studies show that many organizations are not acting on the critical need to develop management talent.

Consider these recent findings:

• Only 29 percent of 428 HR professionals polled this year have implemented succession planning or replacement charts. Nearly a third say their organizations aren't doing anything to prepare for the impending wave of retiring older workers and the impact those departures will have on the workforce, according to the "Older Workers Survey," conducted by the Society for Human Resource Management of Alexandria, Va., with the National Older Worker Career Center of Arlington, Va., and the Committee for Economic Development of Washington, D.C.

• Of 200 HR professionals polled between February and June of this year by DBM, an HR consulting firm based in New York, 94 percent say their organizations have not adequately prepared younger workers to step into senior leadership positions.

Most companies are realizing only now that their sole competitive edge is the bench strength of current and future leaders, says Bobbie Little, senior vice president of global leadership and learning for DBM. As a result, many have no formal succession planning program in place.

## Companies that consistently use a formal process to help workers advance also are consistently high-performing firms.

That is troubling because there is evidence that succession planning can pay dividends in many ways, and not just for high-potential employees. By identifying the abilities and qualities needed to move up, and by communicating these to the workforce at large, employers may help to boost retention and corporate performance across the board.

In fact, according to a study of more than 100 companies by Hewitt Associates, an HR consulting firm in Lincolnshire, Ill., the companies that consistently use a formal process to help workers advance also are consistently high-performing firms, as measured by total shareholder return.

## Formal Plans Are Best

Experts agree that formal succession management planning—except in the smallest of organizations—is vital.

The absence of a formal plan denies employers two critical levers for building great talent, says Mare Effron, global leader of the leadership consulting group at Hewitt Associates. Without formal plans in place, "you can't proactively have leaders develop the skills they need to assume the next level of responsibility, because you don't know what roles you might move them into," he says. And, "you can't communicate to leaders what their potential future is in the organization, giving the appearance that you either don't care or aren't strategic enough to know."

The Hewitt study found that only 55 percent of firms consistently used a formal approach to identify high-potential leaders, Effron says. However, all of the firms in the top quartile of total shareholder return consistently used such an approach.

"We are often asked by smaller firms: 'Do I really need all these processes in place? I only have 500 people or 1,500 people.' Our answer is that the fundamental rules apply no matter the size of your organization; it's simply much easier in a smaller organization," Effron says.

For example, when a *Fortune* 100 company gathers its succession planning data each year, it might take months and involve thousands of hours of HR investment, he says. "In a smaller company, you can do this around the conference table in an afternoon, but the basic steps still need to be in place for it to be successful."

However, management succession plans at most companies aren't as well-established as they should be, concludes a study based on responses from 908 directors from 209 boards of *Fortune* 1,000 companies conducted last fall by executive search firm Korn/Ferry International in New York. Directors say having a "formal management succession process in place" is one of the most important factors in good corporate governance, but only 64 percent have a management succession committee or process—and only 50 percent believe they're effective, the study found.

## Common Traps

Why don't more companies have successful succession management programs? Experts say such programs often fall prey to several common traps.

For example, among companies that actually commit to a succession plan, few follow through with the rigorous implementation required. In fact, 70 percent of succession plans fail due to execution errors, according to a 2002 report, "Succession Planning for Results," from business research firm Cutting Edge Information in Durham, N.C.

**'This is a startling change from those heady days when corporate America deluded itself into thinking it could predict an individual's career path.'**

Lack of executive-level support is another challenge to a successful program, says Bill Byham, co-author of *Grow Your Own Leaders* (Financial Times Prentice-Hall, 2002) and CEO of Development Dimensions International Inc. (DDI), an HR consulting firm in Bridgeville, Pa. "Succession management has to be a senior management program" driven by all senior leaders, he says.

Moore, whose program at K. Hovnanian Enterprises Inc. has been so successful, agrees that top-level commitment is vital. "To assure the success of the succession planning process, you must have 100 percent support and buy-in of the CEO," he says. "He or she must be the driver of your entire process."

However, buy-in from the top alone is not enough. Effron says an over-designed process can be the death knell for succession management programs.

"This is normally a 'textbook' design that incorporates every possible bell and whistle into the process," he says. "Many times this means lots of forms, too many criteria for evaluating potential, extensive training on the process and a high time demand on the manager."

Managers perceive this as simply more bureaucracy, he says, and participate only grudgingly—even if the CEO supports the process.

"When we see succession planning work, it's integrated into the yearly performance review process, so that managers are evaluating current year performance and future years' potential—succession likelihood—at the same time," he says.

## HR's Role

As demands for leadership development grow—due to changing market conditions, corporate growth or the impending retirements of large numbers of baby boomers—HR's role becomes increasingly important. While consultants and practitioners disagree about the best level of HR involvement, most succession management efforts evolve and grow from HR's urging.

And while HR needs to guide the process, it also needs to involve others. Hewitt's Effron says HR should:

- **Co-design the process with the line**. Ideally, succession planning shouldn't emerge from HR alone. A design team of HR and line leaders should co-design the process, with HR bringing examples and content knowledge to the table, and the line serving as the "voice of the customer." The team should test, measure and analyze feedback before rolling out the plan across the organization, he says.

- **Manage the infrastructure**. HR must keep, track and report data to support the process. HR can also track the success of placements, provide updates on depth levels in the organization and analyze diversity.

- **Be an active voice in the process**. Leadership development staff or HR must speak up in succession planning meetings as an equally knowledgeable, equally authoritative participant.

"Succession management must be spearheaded by HR—it is the only logical choice," says George Cauble Jr., SPHR, director of human resources for Henrico County, Va., which has a workforce of nearly 4,000.

Faced with rising numbers of employees eligible for retirement and dwindling numbers of younger employees to replace them, Cauble two years ago led the implementation of a succession plan that created an organizational culture of learning and development at all levels. The plan also created a structured de-

## Filling Soon-to-be-Empty Jobs

Henrico County, Va., recently took a close look at its workforce and saw two demographic trends on a collision course: Its upper managers were becoming eligible to retire in record numbers and a decreasing number of younger employees were available to grow into higher-level positions.

Younger employees (40 and under) made up just 44 percent of the workforce in 2000, compared to 66 percent in 1983. What's more, an HR analysis forecast that 29 percent of upper-level managers would be eligible for full retirement and 78 percent for reduced-benefit retirement by 2005, says George Cauble Jr., SPHR, director of HR.

Those statistics spurred Cauble to develop a two-phase succession-management program: Phase 1 teaches supervisors how to guide employees through an individualized professional development process. Phase 2 helps upper-level managers create strategies for developing subordinate managers.

### 'We decided to attempt to involve and develop as many people as possible in our organization'

"After much research, we decided to attempt to involve and develop as many people as possible in our organization—while the typical model is to only select and develop the few," Cauble says. "Our approach created an environment where leadership development was truly a high priority and has become a part of our workplace culture."

The county's HR department won an award from the Society for Human Resource Management's Richmond chapter for its succession management work last year. Also, over the last 17 consecutive years, the department has grabbed an unprecedented 34 National Association of Counties Achievement Awards.

To roll out its program, the county held eight information sessions over four months and offered managers a half-day training session on how to lead developmental conversations with employees, analyze employee assessment tools and supervise employee development.

Some managers below the department head level didn't want to participate because they didn't plan to move up. "To counter this, we made it clear that development was important for the current job just as much as it was for prospective higher-level jobs," Cauble says.

The county now boasts near 100 percent participation, he says.

—Susan J. Wells

velopmental process for upper managers and provided practical tools for advancement.

Cauble and his staff conducted information sessions for all department heads, deputy county managers and assistant department heads. The group identified key leadership positions, and HR followed up with additional training on implementation.

The results have been "spectacular," Cauble says. For the fiscal year that ended in June 2003, the county filled 57 percent of all openings internally through promotions and career advancements, including seven upper management posts. (For more information about the county's program, see "Case Study: Filling Soon-to-be-Empty Jobs," left.)

## Finding the Unsung Heroes

Where do companies start to identify employees who should be targeted for advancement? DDI's Byham advocates forming what he has dubbed "acceleration pools."

Much like a championship athletic team that first finds the best available players and then decides where to put them in the lineup, this strategy pulls candidates from a wide range of leadership levels.

"Given sufficient resources and attention, an acceleration pool provides the leverage to both respond to the immediate talent gap and grow outstanding talent for the future," he says. "This is a startling change from those heady days when corporate America deluded itself into thinking it could predict an individual's career path."

Candidates chosen for their basic skills are developed through training and job experiences to maximize their potential contributions to the organization at large, rather than to a specific position, Byham says.

"Companies like this better than 'high-potential pools' because that term implies that people not in the pool don't have high potential," he says. Rather, an acceleration pool indicates that a worker's growth is being accelerated, not that others lack potential.

With its Leadership Potential Index, DDI rates an individual's potential by measuring four core factors and gauging strengths in each:

- **Leadership promise**. Has a motivation to lead, brings out the best in people and exemplifies authenticity.
- **Personal development orientation**. Is receptive to feedback and has learning agility.
- **Balance of values and results**. Fits the culture and has a passion for results.
- **Master of complexity**. Practices adaptability and conceptual thinking and navigates ambiguity.

### 'If employers truly seek to develop their leaders, criteria for advancement must be made clear.'

## To Tell or Not to Tell

The question of whether or not to tell high-performing workers they've been tapped for executive grooming is a subject of continuing debate.

There are advantages and disadvantages to each choice, says William J. Rothwell, professor in charge of workforce education and development at Pennsylvania State University's University Park campus and author of *Effective Succession Planning* (Amacom, 2000).

# A Growing Business Needs More Managers

For K. Hovnanian Enterprises Inc., developing a surefire succession plan is key to filling its fast-growing homebuilding empire with a crop of next-generation leaders.

"We initiated our program to make sure we have leaders in place to grow our company," says Bill Moore, vice president of organizational development. Its growth needs are great: *Fortune* magazine recently named the Red Bank, N.J.-based company as the nation's 15th fastest-growing company. It has acquired seven other home-building companies in the last three years.

The company formed a succession planning committee that includes the chief executive officer, chief operating officer, chief financial officer, vice president of HR, senior vice president of corporate operations and Moore. This panel selects and approves candidates and tracks their progress throughout a one- or two-year employee development program.

## Candidates who completed the program and were promoted have been 100% successful.

Before the committee reviews candidates, members gather data on each—including feedback from 12 to 14 direct reports, colleagues and senior managers. This confidential e-mail survey is designed to assess leadership ability.

Next, the panel examines the candidate's employment history and experience for technical and managerial skills. The goal: To discover and fill any gaps in work history.

The committee lays out this information in a two-page spreadsheet and assigns grades ranging from 1.0 to 5.0. Any grade of 3.9 or below requires an individualized training plan.

After the committee accepts a candidate's nomination, Moore and the candidate home in on any necessary training or coaching and map out an action plan. Candidates must spend 10 percent to 20 percent of their work time on this personal development plan.

Next, Moore says, the committee places each candidate into one of three categories indicating readiness to move up: ready in two years, ready in one year or ready now.

The succession plan has netted measurable results, Moore says. Internal candidates who completed the program and were promoted have been 100 percent successful, compared to executives hired from the outside, whose success rate is closer to 50 percent, he says.

—Susan J. Wells

An advantage to not telling is that employers keep their options open. "As business conditions change, managers may feel that a different kind of person is needed to fill a key vacancy or do the work," Rothwell says. The key disadvantage: "Superstars may leave the organization because they don't see a future for themselves."

By contrast, when top performers are told they are being considered for advancement, they are more likely to stay because they see a possible future for themselves, says Rothwell. The key disadvantages to sharing such information are that star workers may stop performing because they believe a promotion is "in the bag" or that managers may inadvertently commit themselves to an oral contract to promote the worker.

Rothwell predicts that more companies will be forced to tell promising leadership candidates about their selection as a retention strategy. However, companies must consider how to do that.

"The telling must be done in a legally defensible way," says Rothwell. "Managers need coaching from HR and from the legal department." For example, managers "must, above all, avoid promising anything in a blanket way to mollify an otherwise outstanding performer so as to retain him or her," Rothwell says.

There are two potential legal risks here: First, employment-at-will laws in most states give employers the freedom to dismiss an employee at any time for virtually any reason. Employers should not surrender that right with direct promises, he says.

Second, employers need to avoid making any implied promises that could unintentionally create a job contract.

Bottom line: A succession program should never pledge job security or guarantee promotions; it merely indicates that a worker's potential has been noted.

## Keeping Secrets

The potential drawbacks of communicating succession planning status have prompted many companies to keep the process secretive, says Tom McKinnon, executive consultant at Novations/J. Howard & Associates, a diversity consulting and training company in Boston.

A recent Novations/J. Howard survey showed that 37.5 percent of companies tell executives they have been targeted for potential advancement, while 45.8 percent do not. Only 16.7 percent of employers polled make the criteria for inclusion known throughout the organization.

Such corporate secrecy has its down side, McKinnon says.

"If employers truly seek to develop their leaders, criteria for advancement must be made clear," he says. "If employers don't define the criteria or help people develop the skills, the only ones who will get promoted will be those who remind leaders of themselves."

The Hewitt study of 100 companies showed that 64 percent of high-performing employers tell employees of their status as up-and-coming leaders—and that 75 percent of these companies also tell employees when they're no longer considered for advancement.

Effron says deciding whether to tell has generated more discussion than any other finding in the study.

"While higher-performing companies tell their best talent that they are high potential and the benefits of that status, there's more to this than just the conversation," he says. "At the companies that tell, most of them are very committed to having a great working environment for all employees. They don't want a two-class system to emerge because certain people will get some extra attention, so they start with the fundamental premise that everyone is treated well and everyone will know where they stand regarding performance."

Knowing where you stand on the performance curve and what you need to do to be considered leadership material helps prohibit retention problems, Effron says. Clear communication about status and future in the organization is important.

"Also, the companies that are best at this also tell high potentials what this status doesn't mean. It doesn't mean that you're going to be CEO next year. It doesn't mean you permanently have this designation," he says. "It likely means you'll have increased burden placed on you to prove the potential you have."

Because smart companies are also confident they've accurately assessed potential, there's little danger of having to revisit the conversation.

In the end, succession work is never done, notes DBM's Little. The good news: You can see results from a succession plan in the first year.

"You know your program is working when line managers take ownership over from human resources and senior managers are driving the process regularly and consistently," she says.

---

SUSAN J. WELLS IS A BUSINESS JOURNALIST BASED IN THE WASHINGTON, D.C., AREA WITH 18 YEARS OF EXPERIENCE COVERING BUSINESS NEWS AND WORKFORCE ISSUES.

# Competitive Global Job Market Strains Employees

BY FRED MAIDMENT

Over the past several years, the U.S. economy has been coming out of a recession that has been marked by very slow job growth. The recovery has been very slow because of several events, including 9/11, the dot-com bubble burst and corporate scandals.

While the job creation is always a trailing indicator in any economic recovery, this time around job creation seems to be particularly slow to emerge.

The growth of new jobs in January was only 112,000 when 300,000 or more would have been the more historic expectation at this stage in the recovery. December was a mere 1,000, statistically insignificant for an economy the size of the United States. February added only 21,000 jobs and November contributed 57,000.

This adds up to fewer than 200,000 new jobs over four months, a number that during any previous recovery would have been considered alarmingly low for a single month.

## Why does job growth lag behind?

During the initial stages of a recovery, organizations tend not to hire new employees as business picks up. Rather, they add overtime until they are forced to hire employees because the work has reached the point where it has created a demand for more labor. That is why hiring new workers after an economic downturn is always a lagging economic indicator. In today's world of international trade, the question is really not whether or when employers will hire new workers, but where they will hire the workers.

## Where are the new jobs?

Multinational corporations have learned that their employees outside the United States can do much of the work currently being done by workers who get a much higher wage in America. So when additional work needs to be done—and much of the work is not place specific and can be done by employees in almost any location—there is no particular reason to hire American workers. Jobs that in previous recoveries may have been filled in the United States may now be filled abroad.

Not only can large multinational firms take advantage of lower-paid employees overseas, but smaller firms may also participate in this through "third-party providers," a technique that is often used in information technology.

**To get the highest possible pay for one's labor, it is necessary to do things that are in high demand, but are scarce.**

Today's headlines are filled with stories of firms sending jobs outside the United States to locations where they can pay the workers less money to do the same job.

Often, foreign employees are brought to the United States and are trained by the people they are replacing in the jobs. The American workers are told they are lucky to have a job while they are training these foreigners. They are sometimes given the carrot of a separation package when they are eventually let go and the possibility of being considered for a transfer in the unlikely event of an opening occurring elsewhere in the company.

## The job as a commodity:

A commodity is something that is undifferentiated and easily replaced. Scarcity of something, coupled with a high demand, means that it will not become a commodity and can demand a high price in the marketplace.

Agricultural labor became a commodity and easily replaced by machines. This does not mean that growing food was exported from the United States, but the jobs were replaced by machinery. Manufacturing jobs were either exported or replaced by machinery during the industrial revolution. In the United States, today fewer people produce many more goods than they produced in the past, to say nothing of the goods that are imported into the country representing jobs that were once in the United Stares.

Today, service-sector jobs are leaving the United Stares for less-expensive locations due to advances in technology and communication. The people who are taking these jobs are often well educated and fully capable of performing them. Fifteen years ago, programming in Java was a unique skill. Today, there are millions of people worldwide who know how to program in Java. People who know how to program in Java are a commodity, and as such they are unable to demand a premium price for their services. Buyers of the services of people who know how to program in Java will naturally look for the best deal, the lowest price to pay for those services. If that means having the programming done in India and restructuring the operations in the United States, then so be it.

American programmers have allowed their skills to become a commodity. Even if an American programmer is the very best Java programmer in the world, how much better is that programmer than one who is very good in India and fully capable of doing the job? Is the American programmer worth the difference?

## Don't become a commodity:

In the global marketplace a key to success is to not allow oneself or ones skills to become a commodity. To get the highest possible pay for one's labor, it is necessary to do things that are in high demand, but are scarce. For years, educators and corporate executives have talked about the need for lifelong learning. It is now clear that the responsibility for that lifelong learning is with the employee, not the organization.

The employee may find him or herself restructured out of his or her job at almost any time through no fault of their own, only because their job can be done for less money by someone else, someplace else. In other words, because their skills, their jobs and they have become a commodity.

The employee has to be prepared and take responsibility for their continued education and development. Only in this way can the employee avoid becoming a commodity in an increasingly competitive, global job market and the possibility of the thankless task of training one's own replacement to take their job with them to another, less costly location.

---

*Fred Maidment is associate professor of management at Ancell School of Business, Western Connecticut State University.*

---

# 7 Habits of SPECTACULARLY Unsuccessful Executives

It's not easy to become as disastrous a boss as Dennis Kozlowski, Jean-Marie Messier, or Jill Barad—but you can, if you work at it. And here's the best part: Each of the qualities that you need to be a spectacular failure is widely admired in today's business world.

BY SYDNEY FINKELSTEIN

The past few years have witnessed some admirable business successes—and some exceptional failures. Among the companies that have hit hard times are a few of the most storied names in business—think Arthur Andersen, Rubbermaid and Schwinn Bicycle—as well as a collection of former high flyers—think, Enron, Tyco and WorldCom. Behind each of these failures stands a towering figure, a CEO or business leader who will long be remembered for being spectacularly unsuccessful.

The truth is, it takes some special personal qualities to be spectacularly unsuccessful. I'm talking about people who took world-renowned business operations and made them almost worthless. People who destroyed billions of dollars of value. People whose destructive capacities go far beyond the scope of ordinary human beings.

What's amazing is not that such people exist, or even that they rise to positions of authority. What's remarkable is that the personal qualities that make this magnitude of destruction possible are regularly found in conjunction with genuinely admirable qualities. It makes sense: Hardly anyone gets a chance to destroy so much value without demonstrating the potential for creating it. Most of the great destroyers of value are people of unusual intelligence and talent. They show personal magnetism and often inspire others. They are the leaders who appear on the covers of *Fortune* and *Forbes*.

Yet when it comes to the crunch, these people fail—and fail monumentally. The list of leaders who have failed spectacularly isn't a list of people who merely weren't up for the job. It's a list of people who had a special gift for taking what could have been a modest failure and turning it into a gigantic one. (See "Big-Time Failures.")

What's the secret of their destructive powers? Seven habits characterize spectacularly unsuccessful people. Nearly all of the leaders who preside over major business failures exhibit four or five of these habits. The truly gifted ones exhibit all seven. But here's what's really remarkable: Each of these seven habits represents a quality that is widely admired in the business world. Business not only tolerates the qualities that make these leaders spectacularly unsuccessful; business celebrates them.

Here, then, are seven habits of spectacularly unsuccessful people. Study them. Learn to recognize them. These habits are most destructive when a CEO exhibits them, but any manager who has these habits can do terrible harm—including you.

## #1 They see themselves and their companies as dominating their environment.

This first habit may be the most insidious, since it appears to be highly desirable. Shouldn't a CEO be ambitious? Shouldn't the company try to dominate its business environment, shape the future of its markets, and set the pace within them?

The answer to all of these questions is yes—but there's a catch. Successful leaders try to shape the future precisely because they know that they *can't* dominate the environment. They know that no matter how successful they've been in the past, they're at the mercy of changing circumstances. Leaders who think that they and their companies dominate their environment tend to forget this. They vastly overestimate the extent to which they actually control events and vastly underestimate the role of chance and circumstance in their success.

CEOs who fall prey to this belief suffer from the illusion of personal preeminence: Like certain film directors, they see themselves as the auteurs of their companies. As far as they're concerned, everyone else in the company is there to carry out their personal conception of what the company should be. CEOs who do, in fact, exhibit a degree of business genius tend to think that it's transferable from business to business. Samsung's CEO Kun-Hee Lee was so successful with electronics that he thought he could repeat this success with automobiles. He invested $5 billion in an already oversaturated auto market. Why? There was no business case. Lee simply loved cars and had always wanted to be in the auto business.

One symptom of leaders who suffer from the illusion of personal preeminence: They tend to see people as instruments to be used, as materials to be molded, or as audiences for their performances. Just as frequently, they tend to believe that their companies are central to suppliers and customers. Rather than looking to satisfy customer needs, CEOs who believe that they run preeminent companies act as if their customers were the lucky ones. And that is a prescription for a spectacular failure.

# #2 They identify so completely with the company that there is no clear boundary between their personal interests and their corporation's interests.

Like the first habit, this one seems innocuous, perhaps even beneficial. We want business leaders to be completely committed to their companies. We want their interests to be tightly joined. But when you examine spectacular failures, you find that failed executives weren't identifying too little with the company, but rather too much. Instead of treating companies as enterprises that they need to nurture, spectacular failures treat them as extensions of themselves. They start to have a "private empire" mentality. They begin to behave as if they own their companies, and they begin to act as if they have the right to do anything they want with them.

CEOs who succumb to this mentality often use their companies to carry out personal ambitions. Once they launch a project, such leaders often invest in it with no sense of proportion or restraint, because they feel that betting on the project is betting on themselves. They take big risks with other people's money, not because it's other people's money, but because they are treating it as their own money and they happen to be big risk takers.

The most slippery slope of all for these executives is their tendency to use corporate funds for personal reasons. CEOs who have been on the job for a long time or who have overseen a period of rapid growth may come to feel that they've made so much money for the company that the expenditures they make on themselves, even if extravagant, are trivial by comparison. This twisted logic seems to have been one of the factors that shaped the behavior of Dennis Kozlowski of Tyco. His pride in his company and his pride in his own extravagance weren't in conflict. They seem, in fact, to have reinforced each other—which is why he could sound so sincere making speeches about ethics while using corporate funds for personal purposes. Being CEO of a sizable corporation today is probably the closest thing to being king of your own country—and that's a dangerous, and sometimes self-destructive, title to assume.

# #3 They think they have all the answers.

Here's the image of executive competence that we've been taught to admire for decades: a dynamic leader, making a dozen decisions a minute, dealing with many crises simultaneously, and taking only seconds to size up situations that have stumped everyone else for days.

The problem with this picture is that it's a fraud. Leaders who are invariably crisp and decisive tend to settle issues so quickly that they have no opportunity to grasp the ramifications. Worse, because these leaders need to feel that they have all the answers, they have no way to learn *new* answers. Their instinct, whenever something truly important is at stake, is to allow no uncertainty—even when uncertainty is appropriate.

One of the special pleasures of having all the answers is the performance that executives can give, where they summon underlings and make a point of making snap decisions. CEO Wolfgang Schmitt of Rubbermaid was fond of demonstrating his ability to sort out difficult issues in a flash. A former colleague remembers that under Schmitt, "the joke went, 'Wolf knows everything about everything.' In one discussion, where we were talking about a particularly complex acquisition we made in Europe, Wolf, without hearing different points of view, just said, 'Well, this is what we are going to do.' " But that kind of arrogance has real consequences. Rubbermaid went from being *Fortune*'s most admired company in America in 1993 to being acquired by the conglomerate Newell a few years later.

# #4 They ruthlessly eliminate anyone who isn't 100% behind them.

CEOs who think that their job is to instill a belief in their vision also think that it is their job to get everyone to buy into it. Anyone who doesn't rally to the cause is undermining the vision. Hesitant managers have a choice: Get with the plan, or leave.

The problem with this approach is that it's both unnecessary and destructive. CEOs don't need to have everyone endorse their vision without reservation to have it carried out successfully. In fact, by eliminating all dissenting and contrasting viewpoints, destructive CEOs cut themselves off from their best chance of seeing and correcting problems as they arise. Sometimes CEOs who seek to stifle dissent only drive it underground. Once this happens, the entire organization grinds to a halt—regardless of whether the CEOs were right or wrong in their judgments.

Executives who have presided over major business disasters have regularly removed or ousted anyone likely to take a critical or contrasting position. General Motors' Roger Smith was especially successful at getting rid of any executives or board members who happened to see things differently than he did—sometimes by having them fired, but often by sending them to distant outposts where they could have no influence on what happened at headquarters. At Mattel, Jill Barad removed her senior lieutenants in short order if she thought they harbored serious reservations about the way that she was running things. Schmitt created such a threatening atmosphere at

# Big-Time Failures

Welcome to the CEO Hall of Shame. Here are six leaders who were spectacularly unsuccessful, the habits that help explain their particular failures, descriptions of the craters they left, and executive summaries of their core (in) competencies.

### William Smithburg
### Quaker Oats

**Habits:** 3, 4, 6, 7
**Failure:** Acquired Snapple for $1.7 billion in 1994 and wound up having to unload Snapple just three years later for a paltry $300 million.
**Diagnosis:** Missed numerous warning signs during the due-diligence process; never really knew what made the Snapple brand successful; assumed that he and his colleagues at Quaker knew Snapple better than Snapple knew Snapple.

### Dennis Kozlowski
### Tyco

**Habits:** 1, 2, 3, 5, 6, 7
**Failure:** Company lost almost 90% of its market value in less than a year.
**Diagnosis:** Took the company on an acquisition binge, which brought it straight up, then straight down; led Tyco during its era of questionable accounting and expenditures; was accused of spending company funds for personal use.

### George Shaheen
### Webvan

**Habits:** 1, 3, 5, 6, 7
**Failure:** Gave up millions to take a CEO job in a company that ended up losing billions.
**Diagnosis:** Adopted a business plan that was flawed; hired to bring credibility but ended up as chief operating officer fighting fires; cheerleader for first-mover advantage that never came.

### Jean-Marie Messier
### Vivendi Universal

**Habits:** 1, 2, 3, 5, 6
**Failure:** His hubris cost shareholders billions of dollars.
**Diagnosis:** Transformed company from water utility to media giant but didn't stop to consider how to make money in the process; spent a lot of time blaming others for what went wrong; let the trappings of leadership dominate him.

### Jill Barad
### Mattel

**Habits:** 4, 5, 7
**Failure:** Branding genius, promoted to top job, decimated earnings and morale.
**Diagnosis:** Vastly overpaid for Learning Company acquisition and then let its failure dominate her tenure; consistently missed earnings estimates but kept promising that next quarter would be better; her intransigence drove away most of her top lieutenants.

### Samuel Waksal
### ImClone

**Habits:** 2, 3, 5, 6, 7
**Failure:** Fast-and-loose stewardship of company ate up 80% of its market cap, with continuing earnings restatements.
**Diagnosis:** Played the industry like a hustler, hyping the cancer drug Erbitux until he and the company lost credibility; reveled in his celebrity while ImClone foundered; copped a plea on a variety of insider-trading charges.

## #5 They are consummate spokespersons, obsessed with the company image.

You know these CEOs: high-profile executives who are constantly in the public eye. They spend a lot of time giving speeches, appearing on television, and being interviewed by journalists. They regularly perform with remarkable charisma and aplomb. Their public persona inspires confidence among employees, potential new recruits, the public at large, and, especially, investors.

The problem is that amid all the media frenzy and accolades, these leaders' management efforts become shallow and ineffective. Instead of actually accomplishing things, they often settle for the *appearance* of accomplishing things. In extreme cases, they can no longer tell the difference: A meeting where they give a good performance seems as valuable as a meeting where something actually gets done.

Behind these media darlings is a simple fact of executive life: CEOs don't achieve a high level of media attention without devoting themselves assiduously to public relations. Samuel Waksal, the former CEO of ImClone who pleaded guilty to insider-trading charges, was a master at drumming up media interest in his company's cancer drug Erbitux.

Consumed as they are by their public-relations efforts, these CEOs often leave the mundane details of their business affairs to others. Tyco's Kozlowski sometimes intervened in remarkably minor matters but left most of the company's day-to-day operations unsupervised. When CEOs are obsessed with their image, they have little time for operational details.

As a final negative twist, when CEOs make the company's image their top priority, they tend to encourage financial-reporting practices that promote that image. In other words, instead of treating their financial accounts as a control tool, they treat them as a public-relations tool. The creative accounting that is practiced by such executives as Enron's Jeffrey Skilling or Tyco's Kozlowski is as much or more an attempt to promote the company's image as it is to deceive the public: In their eyes, everything that the company does is public relations.

## #6 They underestimate obstacles.

Part of the allure of being a CEO is the opportunity to espouse a vision. What happens next is predictable: CEOs become so enamored with their vision of what they want to achieve that they overlook or underestimate the difficulty of actually getting there. And when it turns out that certain obstacles that they casually waved aside are more troublesome than they anticipated, these CEOs have a habit of plunging full steam into the abyss. For example, when Webvan's existing operations were racking up huge losses, CEO George Shaheen was busy expanding those operations at an awesome rate. While Tyco was struggling to maintain profitability in many of its divisions, Kozlowski responded to every setback by simply increasing the pace of his acquisitions—earning himself the nickname "Deal-a-Month Dennis."

Rubbermaid that firings were often unnecessary. When new executives who had been brought in to effect change realized that they'd get no support from the CEO, many of them left almost as fast as they'd come on board. Eventually, these CEOs had everyone on their staff completely behind them. But where they were headed was toward disaster. And no one was left to warn them.

Why don't CEOs in this situation reevaluate their course of action, or at least hold back for a while until it becomes clearer whether their policies will work? Some feel an enormous need to be right in every important decision they make, partly for the same reason that they think they are responsible for their company's success. If they admit to being fallible, their position as CEO seems highly precarious. Their employees, business journalists, and the investment community all want the company to be run by someone with the almost-magical ability to get things right. Once a CEO admits that he or she made the wrong call on an important issue, there will always be people who say that that CEO wasn't up for the job.

All of these unrealistic expectations make it exceedingly hard for a CEO to pull back from any chosen course of action. What's more, if the only option available to you is to keep going in the same direction, then your response to an obstacle can only be to push that much harder. That's why leaders at Iridium and Motorola kept investing billions of dollars to launch satellites even after it had become apparent that land-based cell phones were a better alternative. After each succeeding round of investment, it becomes more difficult to change direction.

It's almost impossible for the person in charge to recognize when an escalating commitment is getting out of hand. Most leaders want recognition for their determination and for their persistence. Take the case of Quaker Oats' acquisition of Snapple in 1994. Quaker's CEO, William Smithburg, paid $1.7 billion for Snapple, assuming mistakenly that the drink would be another smash hit like Gatorade—and without analyzing the real differences between the products. When Snapple started to tank, Smithburg stood his ground, publicly stating that he would never give up on Snapple because, as he put it, "I've never run away from a challenge, and I'm not running away from this one." In 1997, Quaker sold Snapple for a paltry $300 million.

We're all taught to admire courage in the face of adversity. In the case of Quaker's acquisition of Snapple, however, the longer that Smithburg held fast to his resolve, the more damage was done, both to Snapple and to its parent company.

# #7 They stubbornly rely on what worked for them in the past.

Many CEOs on their way to becoming spectacularly unsuccessful accelerate their company's decline by reverting to what they regard as tried-and-true methods. In their desire to make the most of what they regard as their core strengths, they cling to a static business model. They insist on providing a product to a market that no longer exists, or they fail to consider innovations in areas other than those that made the company successful in the past. Instead of considering a range of options that fit new circumstances, they use their own careers as the only point of reference and do the things that made them successful in the past. When Jill Barad was trying to promote educational software for Mattel, she used the promotional techniques that had been effective for her when she was promoting Barbie dolls—despite the fact that software is not distributed or consumed the way that dolls are.

Frequently, CEOs who fall prey to this habit owe their careers to some "defining moment"—a critical decision or policy choice that resulted in their most notable success. It's usually the one thing that they're most known for, the thing that gets them all of their subsequent jobs, the thing that makes them special. The problem is that after people have had the experience of that defining moment, they tend to let themselves be defined by it for the rest of their careers. And if they become the CEO of a large company, they allow their defining moment to define the company as well. The sad irony is that CEOs who get caught in an endless repetition of their defining moment fail not because they can't learn. They fail because they learned one particular lesson all too well.

---

**Sydney Finkelstein** is the Steven Roth Professor of Management at the Tuck School at Dartmouth College. Read about his book on the Web (www.whysmartexecutivesfail.com). From *Why Smart Executives Fail*, by Sydney Finkelstein. Copyright © Sydney Finkelstein, 2003. Reprinted by arrangement with Portfolio, a member of Penguin Group (USA) Inc.

---

Diversity

# Equality's
## Latest
# Frontier

**More companies are knocking down barriers pertaining to employees with nontraditional gender identities—and for good business reasons.**

By Diane Cadrain

How do you go to work every day with a personal secret that threatens to burn its way through your corporate uniform? With "a lot of trepidation," says American Airlines pilot Bobbi Galarza, who started life as Robert.

Galarza is a 55-year-old former Vietnam combat veteran who grew up in a very religious home and was chastised for being attracted to feminine things. He cultivated a macho veneer—joined the Marines, took up skydiving, got involved in so-called manly activities. But inside, Galarza says, he was troubled by a current of confusion, which was diagnosed in the mid-1980s as gender dysphoria.

In 1996 Galarza accepted his orientation and over the following year became comfortable being referred to as "she." In 2001 Galarza "came out" at work. In the male-dominated world of airline pilots, Galarza's action took more than a little courage.

But the process was smoother than Galarza may have expected because his employer—for business reasons—had already developed a nondiscrimination policy for employees who may have nontraditional sexual identities.

"A friend knew I was terrified," Galarza says. "Through him, I found Jack Wing, an HR manager in our Tulsa office. Jack told me American valued me as an employee, and helped me come up with a plan to approach my boss. We did it in a letter. After my boss finished reading, he looked up at me and said, 'How can I help?'"

American's Dallas flight office accepted Galarza's choice and offered to let the accomplished pilot continue flying or work elsewhere in the company. Galarza had risen in the ranks to become a check airman, a pilot who evaluates other pilots' performance and serves as an instructor.

Galarza decided to return to the position of line pilot at American but identify as a woman. Galarza had to obtain a Federal Aviation Administration waiver for hormone use and, under agency rules, has to have a psychiatric evaluation every six months. The company helped with applications for a change of gender identity on government documents. Galarza decided to inform co-workers of the gender identity change via e-mail and got more than 200 responses—all but two expressing support.

## Attitudes About Ambiguity

Gender identity refers to a person's self-described gender—whether male, female or somewhere in between—regardless of whether the person's appearance is male or female, according to "Transgender 101: An Introduction to Issues Surrounding Gender Identity and Expression," an article on the web site of the Human Rights Campaign (HRC). The Washington, D.C.-based advocacy group focuses on gay, lesbian, bisexual and transgender (GLBT) issues. The article's author, Jennie Smith, editorial coordinator of the HRC's web site, writes: "Some people say they have felt trapped in the wrong body for as long as they can remember and, at an early age, redefine their gender. Others don't come out until middle age, and still others don't realize or aren't able to be honest with themselves until they are seniors."

Although employers generally embrace the concept of racial equality and include women in the ranks of upper management, many are still uncertain how to treat employees with ambiguous sexual identities.

## The Top Tier

Following are the companies that received 100 percent ratings in the Human Rights Campaign's Corporate Equality Index, which ranks 319 survey-respondent companies from 100 percent to zero on the basis of their nondiscrimination policies regarding sexual orientation and gender identity or expression:

    Aetna
    American Airlines[*]
    Apple Computer
    Avaya
    Capital One Financial
    Eastman Kodak
    IBM[*]
    Intel
    J.P. Morgan Chase
    Lucent Technologies
    NCR
    Nike[*]
    Pacific Gas and Electric
    Replacements Ltd.[*]
    Worldspan
    Xerox

[*]Companies that are among the Human Rights Campaign's 15 national corporate sponsors.

That's only human nature—it's disturbing for people when they can't figure out if a particular person is a man or a woman. "Nature loves variety. People hate it," says Amy Bloom, a psychotherapist and author whose recent book, *Normal,* explores the lives of those whose gender is variegated rather than monochromatic. "People respond to displays of sexual androgyny out of fear and anxiety," she says.

Nonetheless, employers increasingly are adopting nondiscrimination policies pertaining to GLBT workers, who generally have no legal protection from being fired if they express a nontraditional gender identity on the job.

In 2001, the latest year for which statistics are available, the HRC identified about 2,000 companies, colleges and government bodies with written nondiscrimination policies covering sexual orientation, up 17 percent from the previous year. Nearly 300 were *Fortune* 500 companies. "The closer a company is to the top of the *Fortune* 500 list, the more likely it is to have such a policy," according to a 2001 HRC report, *The State of the Workplace.*

## The Business Equation

More and more companies are deciding that it makes business sense to attract and retain the best employees regardless of how they identify their gender. Consider what happened after the HRC last year released its Corporate Equality Index, awarding perfect scores to more than a dozen companies—among them American Airlines—for their nondiscrimination policies regarding sexual orientation and gender identity or expression. (See "The HRC's Yardstick" and "The Top Tier,".) When aerospace giant Lockheed Martin and the Cracker Barrel restaurant chain found themselves at the bottom of the list, they worked their way to higher rankings by adopting nondiscrimination policies regarding sexual orientation.

"Quite candidly," says Lockheed Martin spokesman Tom Jurkowsky, adopting the policy "was a business decision." He explains: "The aerospace industry needs to hire and retain tens of thousands of employees over a relatively short period of time. The people who are the 'engines' of the industry are aging and retiring."

Establishing a GLBT policy is also a competitive move, says Dennis Liberson, executive vice president for HR at Capital One Financial, a consumer lending company based in Falls Church, Va. "The way we win is by being better than other companies. And we win when our people are better than everyone else's. We ask what we can do to attract the best talent. It's a very business-focused approach."

Nondiscrimination policies for GLBT workers offer morale benefits as well, says Suellen Roth, vice president of global policy and diversity at Avaya, a communications systems provider based in Basking Ridge, N.J. "People who are comfortable and who feel included are more effective as employees—more creative and committed. That helps the company attract and retain top talent and reach more markets."

Moreover, a company can benefit from becoming known for its nondiscrimination policies toward GLBT employees. Bob Witeck of Witeck-Combs Communications in Washington, D.C., says about seven of every 10 gays are brand-loyal to companies that publicize progressive GLBT policies. Estimates of the GLBT consumer market range widely—from $456 billion to $532 billion last year, for example—and are based on the belief that the country's GLBT population is 6 percent to 7 percent of the total adult population.

## The Three Main Ingredients

Companies at the forefront in establishing GLBT nondiscrimination policies share several characteristics: commitment at the top, advocacy from the bottom up—and HR in the middle to craft the approach.

Support for diversity at Avaya comes from Don Peterson, president and CEO, who recognizes its competitive value, says Roth. The company's nondiscrimination statement addresses not only sexual orientation but also gender identity, characteristics and expressions.

## The HRC's Yardstick

The Human Rights Campaign (HRC), which rates companies on their policies regarding workers with nontraditional gender identities, is a Washington, D.C., group that works "to ensure that gay, lesbian, bisexual and transgender [GLBT] Americans can be open, honest and safe at home, at work and in the community."

The group's Corporate Equality Index ranks 319 survey-respondent companies from 100 percent to zero on the basis of whether they:

- Have written nondiscrimination policies covering sexual orientation and gender identity and/or expression.
- Offer health insurance coverage to employees' same-sex domestic partners.
- Officially recognize and support a GLBT employee resource group or council or have a company policy that gives employee groups equal standing regardless of sexual orientation and gender identity.
- Offer diversity training that includes sexual orientation and/or gender expression in the workplace.
- Engage in respectful, appropriate marketing to the GLBT community and/or provide support through a corporate foundation or otherwise to GLBT or AIDS-related organizations or events.
- Refrain from corporate actions that would undermine the goal of equal rights for GLBT people.

The index "drew media attention to the nonperformers," says Kim Mills, HRC's education director, and it "is doing what we intended it to do, inspiring people to make… changes" in policies toward GLBT employees. "Within hours of its publication, we got calls from companies about how to better their scores."

---

IBM, based in Armonk, N.Y., has had nondiscrimination policies regarding race, color and religion for 50 years. Sexual orientation was added in 1984. Last year gender identity and expression were included in the company's nondiscrimination policy—an action driven by upper management, specifically by Ted Childs, IBM's vice president of global workforce diversity.

In many companies, even those with strong support from upper management, the push for GLBT nondiscrimination policies has come from below. Kara Choquette, a spokeswoman for Xerox, headquartered in Stamford, Conn., says a caucus group took the issue to the company's HR team, and caucus member Jim Lesko, vice president for e-business and web operations, carried the idea to senior managers, including CEO Anne Mulcahy.

At American Airlines, the GLBT policy had input from within the company's ranks but initially was an attempt to recover from a misstep. In 1993 the airline, part of Forth Worth-based AMR Corp., drew criticism in news accounts for perceived insensitivity in its treatment of passengers with HIV and AIDS. That prompted American to undertake marketing outreach to GLBT travelers.

In turn, an employee resource group called GLEAM (Gay, Lesbian, Transgender, Bisexual Employees at AMR) decided to make sure that internal corporate policies matched the external marketing campaign. "It kind of rings hollow if the company says, 'We value GLBT customers as flyers but not as employees,'" says corporate spokesman Tim Kincaid. American is now the official airline of national GLBT groups.

### HR's Crucial Connection

In companies with strong GLBT policies, HR managers typically have played a critical part: benchmarking, gathering pertinent information for formulating the policy, showing how the policy would be consistent with the company's strategic purposes, drafting it and implementing it. "Obviously, HR controls what goes into the policies," says Capital One's Liberson.

> ## 'People who are comfortable and who feel included are more effective as employees— more creative and committed.'

HR also can expect to be a key source of help for employees seeking to come out at work. Airline captain Galarza found a sympathetic HR manager. "He was totally supportive and understanding, and it's been that way all the way through," Galarza says. "HR really drove the process, from setting the tone of the corporate response to helping me document my identity change."

Galarza also cites the support of Sue Oliver, American's vice president for human resources, who had directed that gender identity be added to AMR's employment policies.

American spokesman Kincaid says HR "listened to GLEAM when it brought out the gender identity issue" and "let the company know that employees were in transition, or cared about someone who is. We decided that it would be good to have a policy of treating them with respect. We looked around at other airlines and saw they weren't doing much."

At Xerox, the entire HR leadership team, including HR Director Patricia Nazemetz, got involved in benchmarking, brainstorming issues, taking the idea to senior management, drafting it and communicating it to employees, says Choquette. "Xerox has an HR representative assigned to every business group within the company. When we were studying this issue, HR did benchmarking, examining the practices of other companies, and figuring out issues that may arise and how to deal with them."

Developing the GLBT policy at IBM "was a very collaborative process," says Childs. "We worked with people in the legal office and throughout the company to make sure it was phrased properly. It was a long and thoughtful operation that took several months."

## Reaching Employees

All the best GLBT policymaking by HR and other core company groups would matter little, of course, if their work failed to reach employees. Virtually all companies with diversity policies communicate them on their company intranets and through other channels. At Avaya, for example, the policy appeared on an electronic employee guide, in e-learning courses stressing the company's cultural mores and behavior expectations, and in internal communication about various GLBT issues.

Xerox has stated its GLBT policy in many internal communications, including an HR-oriented "What's New" section on the company's internal web site and an annual e-mail asking all employees to read the diversity statement and acknowledge that Xerox won't tolerate harassment of any kind.

Communications are especially important because of the sensitivity many people have to this particular diversity issue.

"There will always be people who, as a result of previous learning, will bring with them preconceived biases or notions," says Avaya's diversity executive Roth. "We provide them opportunities to learn about the culture we're fostering here. We can't change people's beliefs, but we make a strong effort to say, 'When you're in the workplace, we expect you to behave in a manner consistent with our cultural expectations.'"

IBM corporate spokesman Jim Sinocchi says: "We took out the religious aspects of the issue—the idea that gay people are 'choosing not to do right by God's law.'" IBM's response: "We're not mandating your religious beliefs. We're talking about fairness in the workplace and the marketplace. We're giving people the opportunity to work in environments that will show their talents."

Says psychotherapist Bloom: "What people are objecting to is, in fact, nature. People's reactions are natural, too. A great many people like to imagine nature as a sweet, simple voice: tulips in spring, Vermont's leaves falling in autumn. But nature is more like Aretha Franklin: vast, magnificent, capricious, occasionally hilarious and infinitely varied."

---

DIANE CADRAIN IS AN ATTORNEY AND HAS BEEN COVERING WORKPLACE LEGAL ISSUES FOR 20 YEARS. SHE IS LEGISLATIVE AFFAIRS DIRECTOR OF THE HUMAN RESOURCE ASSOCIATION OF CENTRAL CONNECTICUT.

---

From *HR Magazine,* March 2003, pp. 64-68. © 2003 by Society for Human Resource Management, Alexandria, VA. Reprinted by permission.

# Limits To Diversity?

**Few today would argue that diversity is not a good thing,
but are we making claims for it that it cannot support?**

### by Melissa Master

**D**iversity is an intimidating subject to take on. Just mention the word and most people have the same knee-jerk reaction that they would to, say, world peace: "Oh, yes, I support that. *Everyone* is in favor of diversity." And to their credit, most people really do see benefit in having a diverse organization: increased innovation, connection to a wider customer base, better community relations.

If it's difficult to quantify diversity's contributions—well, it's difficult to quantify the effectiveness of many things, such as training, that are undoubtedly a boon for companies. And then, less discussed but still present, there's a small, nagging fear among skeptics of any color: If I so much as question diversity's benefit to the organization, will I be perceived as racist? Sexist? Hopelessly backward?

For many people, the easy thing to do is smile widely, nod enthusiastically, and climb on the bandwagon. But Thomas Kochan had to go and make things complicated.

Kochan, a professor of management at MIT's Sloan School of Management, is the coordinator of a study sponsored by the Diversity Research Network, which is composed of Business Opportunities for Leadership Diversity, a group of CEOs and HR professionals; the Society for Human Resource Management Foundation; and the Alfred P. Sloan Foundation. The study sent researchers from top business schools into four companies, all widely acclaimed for their diversity initiatives, to quantify the connection between diversity and performance.

The purpose of the study was to find evidence supporting the sponsors' view that "a more diverse workforce will increase organizational effectiveness." It's a lofty goal, and it's clear from the researchers' analysis of their results that they really did want to offer the conclusive proof that the Network was looking for.

The trouble was, they couldn't.

## What Happened?

The researchers' first challenge was convincing companies to participate in the study; they approached more than 20 *Fortune* 500 companies before finding the four that agreed. Part of the problem was a simple matter of logistics, since the study would require collecting large amounts of data. "In some companies, the diversity advocates lacked sufficient influence or support to convince line managers to spend the time required," says Katerina Bezrukova, a Wharton professor and researcher for the study. "Another problem is that this type of research raises politically and emotionally charged issues, as well as legal concerns. Managers can be very reluctant to share their experiences or data, given the potential for litigation."

In the end, the four companies that participated were identified only as a large information-processing firm; a financial-services firm; another information-processing firm; and a large retail company. The measures of performance that the researchers used varied somewhat from company to company, as did the results. The overall conclusion, however, was striking: "There is no reason to believe diversity will naturally translate into better or worse results."

Keep in mind that these were not companies in which diversity initiatives were limited to inspirational posters and cultural-cuisine days. One had had active women's and minority resource groups for over 15 years; another had a company-wide diversity council and had integrated diversity goals into every aspect of business growth; another had received several national awards for its diversity program.

So what did the researchers find within these paragons? In the large information-processing firm, for example, researchers Bezrukova and Karen Jehn, another Wharton professor, looked at two measures of success within teams: average performance-appraisal ratings and the average bonuses of team members. They also looked at how well the teams worked together, based on the company's own measures, such as commitment, group spirit, innovation, and exploring new perspectives. They found that race or gender diversity within teams had no effect on those team members' performance appraisals or bonuses, and that while gender diversity in teams actually did improve how the teams functioned together, racial diversity inhibited the teams' functions.

At the financial-services firm, Harvard Business School professors Robin

Ely and David Thomas looked at the company's retail branches and examined how diversity within the branches affected six measures: revenue from new sales, revenue from growing the customer portfolio, revenue from growing the business portfolio, customer satisfaction, number of qualified referrals to bank services, and sales productivity.

Their results? Gender diversity had no effect on any of those performance measures; racial diversity was positively associated only with growth in branches' business portfolios.

Results from the large retail company undermine that part of diversity's business case that says it's important for your employees to look like your customer base. Researchers looked at sales for the company—a national chain with retail stores in every major U.S. market—and found that communities with more whites, blacks, Hispanics, or Asians did not buy more from stores with similar employees. They found "no consistent evidence that most customers care whether the salespeople who serve them are of the same race or gender," though they did concede that those elements might be more important in sectors with closer and longer-standing relationships between customers and service providers.

"Basically, our research shows that the simplistic 'business case' for diversity of the past does not work," Bezrukova says. "There is no strong evidence to support that race or gender diversity will automatically create better—or worse—effects."

## Right Idea, Wrong Reason

In their analysis of the results, the researchers look well beyond the numbers and conclude that corporate diversity efforts do in fact deserve support—but that only well-managed support pays off. Kochan counsels that "one has to manage diversity very consciously and very creatively to produce the potential positive results that it offers. That means focusing on communication, leadership, and conflict resolution—the very nuts and bolts of group behavior. We have to focus training efforts around actual skills and behaviors, not attitudes and sensitivity issues."

Harvard Business School's David Thomas suggests that before you can even proceed to managing diverse groups, you must first look at why you've chosen to embrace the cause. He points out that there are three perspectives that a company can bring to diversity. In the first, which he calls the discrimination-and-fairness approach, a company will try to increase its level of demographic diversity in order to show—to employees, customers, or whomever else is looking—that the organization is not discriminatory. In this case, he says, the company generally brings in a range of people but ends up ignoring and homogenizing their differences and then being baffled by the cultural conflicts that arise.

**Corporate diversity efforts do deserve support—but only well-managed support pays off.**

The second perspective, which he calls the access-and-legitimacy perspective, contains elements of the traditional business case for diversity; it involves looking at your customer base or available labor market and working to make your employee population demographically representative of those groups. However, this perspective has its downsides as well. "A major problem often emerges with people who were brought in because they were representative of, let's say, a particular customer base," Thomas says. "For example, when a Hispanic person who is a super bank manager in a Hispanic area puts his hat in the ring for several banks that aren't in Latino communities, he's often told, 'Well, you're not really qualified—you don't really have experience with this broader market.' And he'll feel resentful, because he feels like he's of value only as long as he's talking to another person who looks like him or shares a language with him. Nobody's looking at the fact that he's also a stellar banker."

The third perspective—and the one that Thomas advocates—is the integration-and-learning perspective, in which companies truly believe that the "insights, skills, and experiences" that employees have developed as a part of their cultural identity are valuable to the firm and can contribute to business growth. The branches he studied that emphasized this approach, he

points out, performed better than those whose motivation for embracing diversity was one of the other two perspectives.

Apparently, doing the right thing for the wrong reasons can be worse than not doing the right thing at all.

## The Difficult Question

The study has garnered mixed reactions from diversity practitioners. "The consultants and academics who reviewed the study were very positive," Bezrukova says. "We haven't heard much from corporate executives, but we expect less optimistic reactions from them. Some of our findings diverge from the popular rhetoric, and this may cause some disappointment."

That indeed seems to be the case for those who feel that diversity is often under attack, despite the researchers' best intentions. "Why do we have to keep proving that this is an airtight business case?" asks Deborah Dagit, executive director of diversity and work environment for Merck. "They put the burden of proof on diversity having to prove that it makes a difference. Why put all that effort into trying to prove the opposite?"

That burden is particularly heavy since diversity's contributions are so difficult to measure; many companies take an approach similar to Dagit's. She explains, "We anecdotally believe that diversity leads to innovation, but we haven't done a research study of that nature."

That's a common theme in conversations with diversity practitioners, and it's a sticky question: If companies don't have metrics in place that tie diversity to performance, how do they justify their spending on diversity initiatives? Is diversity the sacred cow that no one is willing to touch?

## Telling the Stories

But if hard numbers are in short supply, the anecdotal evidence is unlimited—and, in many cases, quite convincing. Just ask Emilio Egea, vice president of human resources at Prudential Financial. For him, diversity goes far beyond different faces in the employee cafeteria. One of his best examples of how diversity benefits Prudential occurred during the company's IPO in December 2001, when he asked what the company was doing with firms in the underwriting community owned by women and people of color. The end result of his query was that 27 percent of Prudential's underwriters were minority-owned firms; the Williams Capital Group, which has been one of *Black Enterprise's* top investment banks for the last several years, was at the senior co-manager level for the first time.

**If hard numbers are in short supply, the anecdotal evidence is unlimited.**

"That's the kind of thing that typically people in the business community wouldn't think of as an implication of diversity," Egea says. "But all of a sudden, they're seeing the connections, and I think everybody benefits. Our people benefit because as they start building authentic relationships with people who are different, the lightbulb goes off relative to tapping the creativity of the resources we have at the company."

May Snowden, chief diversity officer at Eastman Kodak Co., agrees that diversity has implications far beyond those that are usually discussed. She offers the example of mergers and acquisitions, noting, "Guess what? That's bringing two different types of cultures together. That's diversity. Most mergers and acquisitions don't live up to expectations because they have not addressed the diversity between the two companies and how they're going to work together and engage those issues."

For other companies, customers are a key consideration in making diversity a part of the business. That's the case for Deloitte & Touche. Redia Anderson, national principal for the company's diversity and inclusion initiative, explains, "We quite often get requests for our diversity and inclusion information when we're proposing on a particular client's work. We know it's been a key factor in several of our client wins because they have come back and said to us, 'We like the way you've come to the table with a very diverse team.'" For Anderson, a diverse team goes beyond visible diversity, such as race and gender; Deloitte & Touche takes a wide approach to diversity, taking elements such as education, thinking style, previous employment,

and industry specialization into account when putting together a picture of a diverse workforce. "Where we have visible diversity and where we can match the client, we always try and do it, but sometimes that's not possible," Anderson says. "But we always try and make sure that we have the diversity of thought and perspective."

For most companies, though, the most pressing diversity issues still center around employees, and that's where companies really focus their efforts. There are a number of plausible reasons to do so, but the most convincing is always, of course, the bottom line. Simply put, increasing retention reduces costs; for Deloitte & Touche, for example, a 1 percent reduction in turnover translates to a savings of $22 million. That's a major reason for the consultancy to monitor what Anderson calls the "turnover gap"—i.e., the gap in turnover rates between women and men, or between minority and white employees.

For Williams Co., a pipeline engineering and construction firm based in Tulsa, Okla., eliminating problems related to diversity is essential because the company has enough other problems to worry about: In the last three years, Williams has reduced its workforce from 26,000 people to just 4,000. Companies less committed to diversity might have used these problems as an excuse to back off from diversity initiatives, but Williams sees diversity as a key element of its recovery and future growth, linking it—anecdotally—to retention of talent, acquisition of talent, and increasing efficiency and effectiveness. Eric Watson, the company's executive director of diversity and workforce capability, explains, "The critical business case for us is maintaining productivity throughout all the change. We still have to be able to get the job done, working through that muck and mire, which requires that we know each other and understand each other better. Diversity helps us do that."

## The Inevitable Initiative

Does all of that evidence add up to a strong case for diversity? A better question might be: Does it matter? Simple demographics show that the diverse workplace is a corporate reality, one with which American companies are coping with varying degrees of success. The most important finding of the Diversity Research Network's study was not that diverse teams do not have an automatic advantage—it was that diverse teams, managed correctly, *could* have certain advantages. It's the companies that recognize this that will succeed as the United States grows ever more diverse.

"Most companies have accepted diversity as a good thing to do on a good day, but I don't think they feel that it is something they have to do in order to have a good day," says Harvard Business School's Thomas. "Companies will have to get there, or we will be living in a much more fractured society than we live in today."

Of course, societal needs have traditionally held little weight when it comes down to the bottom line. In the case of diversity, however, that may be changing—as indicated by corporations' rush to publicly reaffirm their commitment in the wake of the Supreme Court's recent split decision on affirmative action at the University of Michigan.

"The companies that are serious about cultural transformation often have leaders who first and foremost *believe* diversity is the right thing to do. It burns in their bellies," says William Guillory, founder of consultancy Innovations International. "It's a moral violation of their ethics as a human being to come to work every day and preside over an organization where they know systemic discrimination occurs."

No other corporate initiative inspires such personal emotion or has such sweeping societal implications. And that, in the end, may really be what makes diversity different.

*Melissa Master is assistant managing editor of* Across the Board. *She wrote "How Much Should a CEO Make?", the Nov/Dec 2002 cover story.*

---

# The draw of diversity

## Companies are quick to tout diverse staffing. But that doesn't guarantee a bottom-line boost.

By Stacy A. Teicher

It's almost a corporate mantra: Diversity is good for business. Many companies recruit with that mantra in mind. They devote meetings to it and tout it in ads. But does a workforce with a mix of races, genders, and cultures really make a difference to the bottom line?

Not as automatically as those glossy ads suggest. At least that's the conclusion of a recent study that looked at four companies with diverse staffs.

Overall, racial and gender diversity did not have any resounding impact—positive or negative, the researchers found. At one company, store branches where employees were as diverse as their customers did not outperform the others. In some instances, racial diversity seemed to hinder teamwork.

But the study's key conclusion: For businesses to make diversity a real asset, they have to know a lot more about how to manage it well. It's an idea that's starting to push companies to move beyond feel-good messages.

"When you look at it strategically, there's very little science attached to it," says Luke Visconti, cofounder of DiversityInc magazine. "[Diversity] as a management subject is in its infancy."

Measuring diversity's impact isn't easy, and it's not just a matter of dollars and cents, diversity experts say. But the challenge is to figure out how best to use the varied perspectives that people bring to the office.

"Our concern is that some consultants are still focused on diversity awareness and

[changing attitudes] ... but that puts people in a defensive posture," says Thomas Kochan, professor of MIT's Sloan School of Management in Cambridge, Mass., and lead author of the report from a group of independent scholars. "You can get more positive results from diverse groups if you provide the skills to help people learn from each other's background—communication skills, conflict and negotiation skills, drawing out the strengths of different people."

Commissioned by a group that advocates for diversity—the BOLD Initiative (Business Opportunities for Leadership Development)—the five-year study tested many diversity theories.

Since the report was published in the Human Resource Management Journal earlier this year, at least one large company has responded by shifting its whole diversity approach, says Beatrice Fitzpatrick, president of BOLD.

Rather than continue with diversity-awareness training that dwells on people's feelings, it plans to help managers tap into diverse work groups to increase productivity, Ms. Fitzpatrick says of the company, which did not want to be identified.

## Achieving the right mix

Some workplaces are still trying to recruit a more diverse staff. Others may look like a rainbow but have an undercurrent of cynicism because employees equate diversity with "annually being held hostage for

a seminar," Mr. Visconti says. But where there's a top-down commitment to diversity, it's becoming much more intertwined with other aspects of employee development and accountability.

The term some consultants use is "inclusion"—creating an environment in which people feel valued as individuals.

"Here in the US, we like to pretend to be all the same ... so we list five or six criteria that mean you are professional—generally based on the values of white males ... in their 40s or 50s," says Elmer Dixon, vice president of Executive Diversity Services in Seattle. In trying to conform, "people lose parts of who they are, and you're not getting the most out of them."

The skills people need to develop to change that "are typically referred to as soft skills," Mr. Dixon says with a laugh, "but I think they're hard."

After offering training, some companies tie managers' bonuses to demonstrating these skills and meeting other diversity goals. If you want to show better business outcomes, they argue, make it something that is tied to individuals' own bottom lines.

## Ford's success

Consumer-products companies are leading the way in making a business case for diversity, experts say, because they can see the potential for hundreds of millions of dollars in lost market share if they aren't able to reach out to the fastest-growing

# The dangers of 'guerrilla bias' and how to tackle subtle stereotypes

By the time she realized that a hidden bias had crept in, it was too late. The human-resources director of a Beverly Hills hotel was interviewing a woman for sales director, and everything about her seemed perfect—until it came up that she was from Japan. Suddenly, images of shy and soft-spoken women took over.

A competing hotel snapped up the candidate—who's as outgoing as they come—and has been doing brisk convention business ever since.

Many people sheepishly confess such stories to Sondra Thiederman, a longtime consultant and the author of "Making Diversity Work: 7 Steps for Defeating Bias in the Workplace."

Biases happen in all directions, she says. An African-American man being interviewed by a white Southern manager might sabotage himself by assuming he won't get fair consideration.

"This isn't just a bad white guy thing," Ms. Thiederman says. "I put responsibility for fixing it on everybody."

But how to fix it? Here's a condensed version of her advice:

• Recognize your biases. Over the course of a few weeks, watch the first thought that pops into your mind when you see skin color, hear an accent, or meet someone in a wheelchair.

• Prioritize which biases to address based on what will be most likely to interfere with work. Do you hold members of certain groups to lower standards because you think they can't handle criticism? That's what Thiederman calls a "guerrilla bias," because it comes under the guise of being nice.

• Dissect your biases. Where did you learn them? Do you know many people from a group you stereotype, or are you judging based on one encounter?

• Identify what you have in common with people in groups you hold a bias toward. Maybe it's a similar work ethic, religious values, or emotions.

• Practice shoving biased thoughts aside as soon as they come up. The steps above drain the power from biases, Thiederman says, and help you make a habit of stopping them before they do damage.

—Stacy A. Teicher

---

groups of consumers. Estimates of the buying power of African-Americans, Asian-Americans, and US Latinos range from $750 billion to $1.3 trillion a year.

That's not to suggest that only Latinos can market to Latinos, Visconti says, but if you have a staff where people from minority groups are encouraged to speak up about viewpoints that differ from the mainstream, it can improve the "cultural competency" of everyone on the staff.

In 2002, Ford Motor Company encouraged its employee-resource groups (organized by racial background or other commonalities) to reach out to friends and neighbors with discount offers for Ford autos. They brought in $100 million worth of business, according to DiversityInc, which granted Ford the No. 1 spot on its list of Top 50 companies for diversity this year.

"Supplier diversity" is another area Ford emphasizes. The company spent more than $3 billion last year with businesses owned by women and minority men. And to create jobs and wealth that it hopes will translate back into auto purchases, Ford moved a company that builds motor-home parts from Mexico to inner-city Detroit.

Because major companies like Ford pay attention to the diversity of their suppliers, there's a strong spillover effect. "I'm getting more inquiries [from businesses] that are not retail oriented ... [but] they're getting challenged by their potential clients to advance their diversity," says Michael Hyter, president of Novations/J. Howard & Associates, a management consulting firm in Boston.

That may help explain why the recent economic downturn led companies to cut diversity training budgets only 15 percent, compared with 30 percent cuts for other training, according to a Novations report.

## Value of change

Even companies recognized for their devotion to diversity know they have a long way to go toward changing the subtle biases in their culture.

"Senior leaders who have seen the value of diversity see it as a long-term strategy," says Laura Liswood, senior adviser to Goldman Sachs on diversity issues and a fellow at the University of Maryland's business school. "They want to be in the Top 100 workplaces that are good for women or for minorities; they know that to get the best and brightest [employees], they're going to have to do that."

When Shirley Harrison was promoted in 1992 to vice president in charge of diversity at Altria, the parent company of Philip Morris and Kraft, she found that senior executives wanted to put diversity into the parameters of a one- or three-year plan. She persuaded them to see it as a lifetime plan.

"I was looking for the [senior team] to define for me, early on, what was their legacy: If their children worked [here], what did they want to leave behind [so they] would be able to see a culture that supported diversity," she says.

Everyone from vice presidents to mailroom clerks have partnered with the diversity staff to conduct relevant training sessions, Ms. Harrison says. That helps people see the link between diversity and business, instead of resenting diversity training as something imposed by an outside consultant.

"What's neat is when leaders of any color, or white males in middle management, will share their story of how they corrected an issue on their own," Harrison says. "I hear about those things all the time."

At times, other business goals trump diversity, but Harrison has learned not to take it personally. When her company divested itself of Entenmann's baked goods, it took a big bite out of the number of Hispanic employees.

"I could have been bummed out," she says. Instead, she urged the company to boost its recruitment efforts and she helped organize a focus group for current Hispanic employees to share ideas for new products and marketing.

# UNIT 5

# Implementing Compensation, Benefits, and Workplace Safety

## Unit Selections

## Key Points to Consider

• Companies are involved in worldwide competition, often with foreign organizations with much lower wage rates. What should management do to meet this competition? What do workers need to do to meet this competition?

• When companies merge, what do you see as some of the problems that could happen from an HR perspective?

• How would you implement a merit/incentive program in a staff department such as research and development or data processing? In a line department such as sales or production?

• What strategies should employers implement to control the rising costs of benefits while still getting the maximum value for their employees? How would you address the health care crisis for an organization? A benefit not to be forgotten is Social Security, which is again a major issue. How would you suggest fixing it? Should it be privatized? Partially privatized?

• One of the problems facing American industry is an increase in violence. What can be done about it? What would you do about stress on the job?

 **Links: www.dushkin.com/online/**
These sites are annotated in the World Wide Web pages.

**BenefitsLink: The National Employee Benefits Web Site**
  *http://www.benefitslink.com/index.php*
**Executive Pay Watch**
  *http://www.aflcio.org/corporateamerica/paywatch/*
**Social Security Administration**
  *http://www.ssa.gov*
**WorkPlace Injury and Illness Statistics**
  *http://www.osha.gov/oshstats/work.html*

Money makes the world go around…the world go around!

—From "Money" in the musical *Cabaret*

Individuals are usually paid what others perceive their work to be worth. This situation is not necessarily morally correct. In fact, it does not even have to be logical, but it is a reality. Police officers and college instructors are often underpaid. They have difficult jobs, requiring highly specialized training, but these jobs do not pay well. Other professions pay better, and many illegal activities pay better than law enforcement and college teaching.

When a company is trying to determine the salary of individuals, two markets must be considered. The first is the internal structure of the firm, including the wages that the company pays for comparable jobs. If the organization brings a new employee on board, it must be careful not to set a pay rate for that individual that is inconsistent with those of other employees who are doing the same or similar jobs. The second market is the external market for employees. Salary information is available from many sources, including professional associations and the federal government. Of course, both current and prospective employees, as well as organizations, can easily gain access to this information. To ignore this information and justify pay rates only in terms of internal structure is to tempt fate. The company's top producers are the ones in whom the competition is the most interested, and no organization can afford a mass exodus of its top talent. Organizations must ask themselves how they can achieve "Top Pay for Best Performance."

One recent development in the area of compensation is a return to the concept of pay for performance. Many firms are looking for ways to directly reward their top performers. As a result, the idea of merit pay has gained wide acceptance in both industry and government. Pay for performance has been used in industry for a long time, most commonly in the sales and marketing area, where employees have historically worked on commission plans based on their sales productivity. Organizations are constantly looking at these types of programs as may be seen in, "Ten Steps to Designing an Effective Incentive Program." Theoretically, merit pay and other types of pay for performance are effective, but they can easily be abused, and they are often difficult to administer because measuring performance accurately is difficult. Sales and production have numbers that are easily obtained, but research and development is a different situation. How does a firm measure the effectiveness of research and development for a particular year when such projects can often take several years for results to be achieved?

One issue that has evolved over the past several years is the question of pay for top executives as seen in "Executive Compensation: Are Some Paid Too Much?" During times of economic recession, most workers are asked to make sacrifices in the form of reduced raises, pay cuts, cuts in benefits, other compensation reductions, or layoffs. Many of these sacrifices have not been applied to top management. Indeed, the compensation for top management has increased substantially during the past several years. Are chief executives overpaid, and if so, how did they get that way and who should set their pay?

The fastest-growing aspect of employee compensation is benefits. Benefits are expensive to any firm, representing an ever-increasing burden to employers. As a result, many firms are reducing benefits and attempting to find more effective ways to spend their benefit dollars, as discussed in "The Battle Over Benefits" and "The Cutting Edge of Benefits Cost Control." Also, the needs of the employees are changing. As our society ages, there is greater interest in health benefits and pensions, and less interest in maternity benefits. Another facet of the issue is that employees are seeking greater benefits in lieu of salary increases, because the benefits, with some exceptions, are not usually taxed.

Health and safety are also major concerns of employers and employees. The workplace has become more violent as workers act out against their employers for unfairness—whether real or imagined. Some firms have had to address the anger of employees and other problems as seen in "The Most Effective Tool Against Workplace Violence." The problems facing companies may even extend beyond the workplace and "Employers May Face Liability When Domestic Violence Comes to Work." Today, issues concerning safety and health in the workplace include AIDS, burnout, and substance abuse. These issues reflect not only changing social conditions but also a greater awareness of the threats presented by unsafe working conditions. An attempt to address some of these issues has been to practice what is essentially preventive medicine with wellness initiatives. While there was initially some doubt about their effectiveness, the results are now in, and wellness programs do work.

All in all, salaries, wages, and benefits represent a major expense, a time-consuming management task for most firms, and health and safety requirements are a potential area of significant loss, in terms of both dollars and lost production.

Compensation & Benefits Agenda

# Plastic Paychecks

Employers cut expenses by shifting from paper paychecks to payroll debit cards.

By Elayne Robertson Demby

The Dallas city government doesn't issue paychecks anymore. All 13,000 city employees are paid by electronic means—either through the familiar arrangement of direct deposit to a bank account or by the newer method of deposit to a personal account set up by the employer and accessed by the employee with a debit card.

In its effort to shift employees away from costly paper paychecks, Dallas has joined the ranks of employers ranging from giants—Sears, Office Depot, Chicago's public school system—to small firms with a few hundred on the payroll. Like many employers, Dallas seeks to cut payroll costs by steering paycheck employees to a cheaper, faster—and perhaps safer—way to convert their earnings to cash.

> The principal risk for employees in being paid by debit card is that a misplaced or stolen card might be drained of its balance before its loss is reported.

The decision to have all employees paid by electronic means effective this past March will save the city about $150,000 annually in check-distribution costs and will free up human resource staff time as well, says Drew Corn, a financial services manager for the city. Distributing paper checks "was very labor-intensive" for HR, he says. Although nearly 90 percent of Dallas' city employees are paid via direct deposit, "our overriding goal is to get 100 percent," says Corn. "But we understand that not everybody can get a bank account," he adds.

And that's where debit cards play a role.

Payroll debit cards can be particularly useful for employees who don't have bank accounts. These so-called unbanked workers include members of the 12 million or more U.S. households in which no one has a bank account—an estimate by Visa U.S.A. They also include others, such as teenagers with part-time jobs but with no bank accounts yet.

For example, Cutting Edge Pizza LLC, a Hartford, Conn., company that operates Little Caesars franchises in six states, has "a lot of high school kids and younger workers," says Rita

Viviano, human resource director. Most don't have bank accounts, and some lack identification because they don't have driver's licenses. They like getting paid via debit card, she says, because then they can "go to the mall and spend it."

All payroll debit cards can be used in automated teller machines (ATMs), and some cards are accepted by retailers. Generally the cards can be used only with a personal identification number (PIN), but cards that are branded with the Visa or MasterCard logo can be used without a PIN.

A major plus of a payroll debit card for unbanked workers is the ability to get cash without resorting to check-cashing services, which charge up to 6 percent of the face value of a paycheck, according to the San Antonio-based American Payroll Association, an organization of payroll professionals. Some check-cashing fees may be even higher. Any debit card fees paid by the employee are almost certain to be lower than check-cashing fees, and funds are available immediately on payday anywhere in the world.

Moreover, some say, tapping a payroll debit card for cash may sometimes be safer than cashing a check. Some Dallas city employees, for example, have been robbed after leaving check-cashing services, says Corn.

The principal risk for employees in being paid by debit card is that a misplaced or stolen card that's usable without a PIN might be drained of its balance before its loss is reported. But debit card providers generally don't hold consumers liable for such losses.

## The Matter of Fees

Debit cards are "less expensive than paper checks" for employers—even when some card fees are paid by the employer, says James Medlock, a senior director of education at the payroll association.

Video retailer Movie Gallery, based in Dothan, Ala., does not pass on monthly fees to employees and permits two free ATM withdrawals per pay period—and still is saving about $160,000 per year since initiating an electronic payment program that includes debit cards. Movie Gallery's savings result from eliminating overnight mailing charges to get checks to its 14,000 employees in 43 states and Canada.

Similarly, the city of Dallas is saving almost the same amount while it splits fees with employees, paying the monthly maintenance cost for each debit card account and letting employees withdraw funds twice per pay period from ATMs without charge.

Paychex Inc., a payroll and benefits services company in Rochester, N.Y., that offers the Paychex Access Visa card, charges a $3 monthly maintenance fee and $1.50 for each ATM transaction in addition to any fee charged by the ATM. There are no fees when the card is used to make a purchase.

Paychex's fees are much lower than what employees would pay to cash their checks at a check-cashing service, says Diane Rambo, vice president of human resource services. For example, a worker who cashed four $100 paychecks a month and paid a 6 percent fee each time would spend $24. But the fees for getting cash four times in one month from a debit card would total $9.

That assessment is echoed by Viviano at Cutting Edge Pizza. The company started offering the Paychex card last July, and about 85 of its 700 employees now use it.

The company picks up none of the fees. Employees are charged $2 a month to maintain the card and $1.50 for each ATM transaction.

## Pay Stubs and Persuasion

Whether to absorb debit card fees or pass them on to employees is just one of several decisions a company must make in considering whether to offer such an option. Debit cards' features and fees differ from vendor to vendor, says Medlock. "Each one does it differently, and a company should research to find the best one for it."

Generally, accounts for debit cards belong to the company that establishes them, while the funds belong to the employee, says Medlock. Each account set up with a bank is federally insured up to $100,000, just as other bank accounts are. If an employee with a payroll debit card account leaves the company, Medlock explains, the account remains open until the funds are withdrawn. He notes, however, that most states require that unclaimed wages pass to the state after one year, so a former employee who neglects to withdraw all funds risks forfeiting them.

Paychex works with Bank One to set up accounts for employees. If the employee leaves the company, Paychex terminates the account and sends the employee a check for the balance.

Methods of providing pay stubs also vary. Employees using a Paychex system receive a paycheck-like form stamped "nonnegotiable" (the net pay is already in the employee's account) plus a pay stub showing deductions and other information.

Even when pay stubs are mailed, their distribution costs are far below those of paychecks, which require special paper and

often are sent overnight. Some companies e-mail stubs to branch offices for managers to print out and distribute. Others, like Movie Gallery, enable individual employees to download and print their own stubs at work. In addition, employees with payroll debit cards typically receive monthly statements of their account activity.

Although such details about debit cards may vary, some things are not negotiable. For example, many states require that employees be given at least one no-fee means of getting cash for their earnings. A paper paycheck meets that requirement, Medlock notes, even if the employee pays a fee to a check cashing service. Employers usually provide one or two free cash withdrawals per month to employees paid via debit cards.

Moreover, in most states, private employers cannot force current employees to change the method by which they're paid, though generally a company can make electronic payment a condition for employment for new employees. (Although Texas prohibits private employers from requiring employees to make a switch, the city of Dallas concluded, with the support of its legal counsel, that as a public employer it was not subject to the prohibition and thus could require that all employees be paid electronically, says financial manager Corn.)

## Selling the Future

Payroll debit cards and direct deposit are just the latest chapters in the ongoing evolution of payroll practices, says Medlock. "Forty or 50 years ago people were paid in cash. Then paper checks became the dominant form of payment in the 1970s. Now employers are moving to a paperless system."

But getting employees to go along with the trend can be a hard sell, says Paychex's Rambo. Jim Pongonis, vice president of human resources at Movie Gallery, says: "One of the biggest problems I had was education. People don't like change."

At Movie Gallery, the move from paper to electronic payment is being made with a twist. Since October, all employees are paid via debit card unless they opt for a check or direct deposit. "We're trying to get to a paperless payroll," says Pongonis. Debit cards help toward that goal because the vast majority of Movie Gallery's part-time employees do not have checking accounts. Moreover, in New Hampshire, Virginia and West Virginia, states that let employers mandate a means of payment, all Movie Gallery employees are required to pick an electronic method.

Pongonis advises HR professionals considering debit cards to advertise their advantages for employees far in advance of putting them in place. One reason the switchover has gone smoothly in Dallas, says financial services manager Corn, is that the debit card concept was unveiled—and promotion began—a year before electronic payment became mandatory, prompting many employees to sign on long before the deadline.

ELAYNE ROBERTSON DEMBY IS A FREELANCE BUSINESS WRITER IN WESTON, CONN.

# Merging Compensation Strategies

HR's efforts to integrate compensation strategies and practices are a key component of successful mergers and acquisitions.

By Susan J. Wells

**I**n today's whirlwind of mergers and acquisitions (M&As), everyday HR issues such as employee compensation may get blown aside as countless financial and legal priorities take center stage. However, recent research suggests that HR could play a greater role in successful M&As, and, the earlier HR gets involved, the better.

Depending on the circumstances of the deal—and the compensation policies of the merging companies—HR may be called on to splice disparate payment plans into a program that fits the new organization, or HR may have to discard the original plans and then create a program from scratch that complements the merged entities. Either way, old and new employees will be concerned about what is happening with their pay, so HR also must develop an effective communications plan to inform and reassure them.

More organizations—and HR professionals—are likely to face this challenge as the economy improves. A handful of industry-changing newsmakers drove the market last year, but M&As among mid-size companies also saw increased activity in 2003, according to FactSet Mergerstat LLC, a global mergers and acquisitions research firm in Santa Monica, Calif. The company's data predicts M&A volume will continue to rise this year. (See "Big Deals.")

Behind the headlines that such corporate marriages generate are rough tactical

and strategic waters that HR and compensation professionals must navigate. The journey is by no means simple, but the destination is worthy: the union of two sets of employees and pay structures that can ultimately influence the success of the merger and its return on investment (ROI).

## Too Little, Too Late

The more capable an HR department is, the greater the chances of M&A success, studies show. Yet too many employers involve their HR professionals too little—or too late—in the M&A process.

The most common responsibility given to HR during M&As is to provide ad hoc advice to senior managers, rather than carrying out a structured and formal role, according to a 2003 survey of 132 senior executives worldwide by professional services firm Towers Perrin of Stamford, Conn., called "The Role of Human Capital in M&A, 2003." (See "Most Common HR Responsibilities in M&As." Also, see the online version of this article for a link to the study.)

And a 2001 survey of more than 440 HR professionals conducted jointly by Towers Perrin and the Society for Human Resource Management (SHRM) Foundation found that HR involvement in the critical early stages of M&As is uneven. This study, "How the Human Resource Function Adds Value During Mergers & Acqui-

| Most Common HR Responsibilities in M&As | |
|---|---|
| **Responsibility** | **\* Percentage of respondents** |
| Ad hoc advice to senior management on HR issues | 59 |
| Identifying and retaining key talent in merged group | 47 |
| Due diligence on compensation/benefit plans of prospective firms | 45 |
| Delivering cost savings through downsizing of duplicate functions | 35 |
| Managing communications to the whole company on M&A activities | 34 |
| Designing new post-deal reward programs | 30 |
| Performing due diligence on the culture of prospect firms | 27 |
| Helping to define the new business strategy | 18 |

\* Respondents could choose more than one criteria.

Source: "The Role of Human Capital in M&A, 2003," a Towers Perrin survey.

sitions," formed the basis of a book, *Making Mergers Work: The Strategic Role of People* (SHRM Foundation, 2002).

**'We are firmly committed to the philosophy of tying employees' rewards to the same yardstick that our shareholders have.'**

# Big Deals

U.S. companies conducted $528 billion in mergers and acquisitions (M&As) last year, a 13 percent jump from 2002, according to FactSet Mergerstat LLC, a global mergers and acquisitions research firm in Santa Monica, Calif. That growth marked the first year-over-year upturn since 2000.

Among the tip megadeals were:

- Bank of America's $47.8 billion agreement to buy FleetBoston Financial Corp.
- The St. Paul Cos. Inc. acquisition of Travelers Property Casualty Corp. for $16 billion.
- Anthem Inc.'s $14.8 billion purchase of Wellpoint Health Networks, Inc.
- Manulife Financial Corp.'s deal to buy John Hancock Financial Services Inc. for $10.7 billion.

But it wasn't just the titans that spurred M&A escalation. Deals worth $50 million to $90 million chalked up a 12 percent hike in 2003 over 2002, according to FactSet Mergerstat data.

The boom is likely to continue this year. A survey conducted in December 2003 by Thomson Financial in New York and the Association for Corporate Growth in Glenview, Ill., found that 85 percent of 1,301 business executives from companies of all sizes—those with annual revenues of less than $5 million to those with revenues of $500 million or more—think the M&A environment will improve this year, and 90 percent of those polled expect the number of deals to rise.

In addition, HR's involvement often comes too late in the merger process. Of the four stages in the life of M&A deals—pre-deal, due diligence, integration and implementation—HR tends to have a big role only in the later stages. However, research suggests that by getting more involved during the pre-deal and due diligence processes, HR can better carry out the vital functions it performs, such as:

- Reviewing the target company's compensation policies to compare organizational philosophy and cultural fit.
- Educating financial and operating executives about possible risks and costs.
- Mapping job descriptions at the target company.

## Merging Old Plans

The importance of giving HR an early role in mergers was borne out when Church & Dwight Co. Inc., a Princeton, N.J.-based manufacturer of household and personal care products, acquired in 2001 the consumer-goods business of Carter-Wallace, a Cranbury, N.J., manufacturer of consumer and pharmaceutical products.

Church & Dwight's acquisition of Carter-Wallace added significant product lines and manufacturing capability. The $739 million purchase, in partnership with a New York-based private eq-

uity group, Kelso & Co., also doubled Church & Dwight's employee population. As a result, HR had to migrate the new employees into Church & Dwight's original compensation plan.

The target company's employees brought knowledge and experience in areas where Church & Dwight was lacking, says Jim Levine, director of HR and compensation at Church & Dwight. However, combining the staffs raised some difficult employee compensation issues: Carter-Wallace paid high base salaries and bonuses with few long-term incentives, whereas Church & Dwight's compensation packages placed much more of an emphasis on long-term incentives.

Employees at Carter-Wallace who were not on a bonus plan had few transition issues: In general, these positions also were not eligible for bonuses at Church & Dwight, Levine says. "On average these people tended to be paid more than their counterparts at Church & Dwight, but not significantly so, and issues could be addressed through the normal merit review process."

There were, however, significant concerns for highly paid employees, as Carter-Wallace relied on base salary and short-term incentives, while Church & Dwight uses those programs as well as stock options.

Eventually, "Church & Dwight made the decision to maintain our pay system and transition Carter-Wallace employees

to it," Levine says. "We are firmly committed to the philosophy of tying employees' rewards to the same yardstick that our shareholders have. The process that we used was to develop a number of possible transition scenarios, review employees' compensation on an individual basis, and then use the appropriate transition plan based upon each employee's unique circumstances—current base pay against our salary range and extent of short-term incentives."

Church & Dwight achieved the business goals it set when the deal was made, Levine says.

"Compensation issues and our ability to retain employees were vitally important—and they became a significant consideration in the language of the deal itself and in the ultimate success of the transaction," he says.

Harmonizing the pay systems of merging companies is a complex and difficult process. But it's also an opportunity for HR to create new and improved systems, which in turn can dramatically affect both the culture of the new firm and retention success.

"Acquisitions are an opportunity to do things you haven't done before," says Dave Kompare, senior consultant in the corporate restructuring and change department of Hewitt Associates LLC, an HR consulting firm in Lincolnshire, Ill. "It's a good time to rethink your overall strategy in terms of competitive compensation."

# Managing Compensation Differences

Whether it's a merger of equals in which a high-level compensation committee will determine and guide compensation policy for the new entity, or an acquisition in which a smaller company or start-up's employees may be governed by a larger firm's policies, there are five common compensation issues that HR must tackle in any M&A situation, says Stephanie Penner, senior compensation consultant in the Philadelphia office of Mercer Human Resource Consulting LLC. They were:

1. **Understanding why the deal was done.** Knowing the business strategy and objectives—both short-and long-term—behind the decision will determine the level of compensation integration you can expect.

2. **Setting a competitive compensation strategy for the merged organization.** For example, a company with only 10 grade levels will have to integrate the acquired company's 23 grade levels. And the companies may have very different methods for determining merit increases, as well as short- and long-term incentives.

3. **Deciding which programs and common language need to be redesigned or redefined, such as job titles and pay bands.** The responsibilities of a "manager" in one company, for example, can be very different in another.

4. **Determining costs once programs and practices are redesigned.**

5. **Applying an appropriate transition plan to put new elements in place.** This involves easing transitions and uncertainties, communicating the changes to employees and altering HR systems to handle the new policies.

Barring any legal pacts to the contrary, companies usually have the freedom to make changes to many elements of the total compensation package, which comprises base salary, short-term incentives (such as an annual bonus or profit-sharing), long-term incentives (such as stock options), benefits and other perks.

## Starting from Scratch

Sometimes, the compensation policies of the merging companies are so different that the best approach is to throw them out and start over. "It's unbelievable how frequently you have two companies come together with so many similarities but [with] totally different compensation plans," says Stephanie Penner, senior compensation consultant in the Philadelphia office of Mercer Human Resource Consulting LLC.

For example, when two then-Baby Bells—Bell Atlantic Corp. and Nynex Corp.—announced their $23 billion merger in 1996, HR and other executives determined that the uniting organizations' pay plans were so distinct that the best solution was to start over.

To start the process, a team of compensation professionals, HR and company executives took a complete inventory of the two companies' compensation policies, including executive management and general salary struc-

tures, job titles, performance evaluations and incentives.

The goal was to determine guiding principles, says Catherine Beck, director of compensation policy in the Arlington, Va., office of Verizon Communications, the telecommunications giant created from Bell Atlantic's 2000 merger with GTE Corp. Beck was manager of compensation planning at Bell Atlantic then. During both mergers she was merger project manager for general management compensation.

What the team found was a very different set of salary structures and incentive measures, Beck says. The sheer magnitude of the differences called for a large-scale change.

"There was no way to reasonably map employees to a combined salary structure given the difference in the number of pay grades. And one company used a team approach to incentives, while the other used an individual approach," Beck says. "So we essentially decided to throw everything out in favor of a completely new compensation system—a soup-to-nuts revamp."

Completed in 1997, the mega-merger encompassed some 30,000 management employees—and also a team of union workers who came on board with existing collective bargaining agreements in place. Integrating the new compensation plan took about a year, Beck says.

The evaluation and rollout process was repeated just a few years later when

Bell Atlantic announced its merger with GTE in 1998—a deal that involved about 60,000 management employees and made Verizon the second-largest telecommunications firm behind AT&T. But this time, there were many more shared similarities between the two companies' compensation plans. "The level of change wasn't as huge as before, and, overall, it was a smoother transition," Beck says.

Once the policy decision has been made, the administrative complexities of implementation can be enormous. For example, in the Bell Atlantic-GTE merger, the broad parameters of the sign-on bonus policy were established early, but it took six to eight months to incorporate and finalize that policy because two separate payroll systems had to be integrated and there were other administrative process delays.

> **'Communication is often the most important part of a merger, yet it often falls between the cracks.'**

"You can't underestimate how long it takes and how complex it can be," Beck says of the integration and implementation process. "There are so many things that are touched by compensation matters."

## Communicating the Changes

Whether you merge compensation plans or create a new one, big changes are in store for employees. To ease their uncertainty and fear, and to squash rumors, consultants and HR professionals agree that a prompt, straightforward communications strategy is critical.

The problem: Information may be limited, because—even after an announcement—the sharing of certain data is restricted for antitrust reasons or until due diligence is completed.

"After an M&A announcement, there's often concern, fear and trepidation among employees, customers and the public, too," says Ravin Jesuthasan, principal and practice leader of rewards and performance management consulting in the Chicago office of Towers Perrin. "Communication is often the most important part of a merger, yet it often falls between the cracks."

Insecurity over compensation issues such as earnings and benefits can negatively affect morale and productivity. As a result, companies experience a loss of momentum that may be difficult and time-consuming to recoup.

"It's important to manage the messaging right away," agrees Mercer's Penner. "If you don't form the message, it will be formed for you." That can fuel the disruptive rumor mill, she says.

When Church & Dwight acquired Carter-Wallace, the company tailored specific communications to all employees based on their current compensation and how their transition would be handled.

"We communicated with employees as soon as we were able to," Levine notes. "We began with presentations at the various facilities conducted by the CEO and head of HR." This was followed by written communications in the form of questions and answers, and more local and specific meetings conducted by functional vice presidents.

The goal was to show employees that everyone was focused on the success of the merged companies, Levine says.

"Historically, the big mistake is for companies to say 'we don't know' or 'we haven't made any decisions yet,'" says Hewitt's Kompare. "The worst thing is to say nothing. Whatever decisions you do know, tell them as soon as possible. For those you don't know, describe the factors involved in the decisionmaking and give employees a best estimate for having an answer."

Once the deal closes and compensation plans are completed, decide how best to present them to employees, says Penner. "Many companies use a combination of approaches to get the word out," she says. "The important thing is to have a consistent response."

Commonly used tools include town hall-type meetings, one-on-one meetings, site presentations and training, written or web-based question-and-answer explanations and newsletters.

Communicating compensation changes to Bell Atlantic and Nynex employees involved face-to-face meetings and training sessions, personal letters and periodic newsletters describing the policies, Beck says.

Yahoo! Inc. in Sunnyvale, Calif., uses several communications vehicles during acquisitions, says Libby Sartain, SPHR, senior vice president of HR and chief people Yahoo. During 2003, the Internet services company acquired Inktomi Corp. of Foster City, Calif., and Overture Services Inc. of Pasadena, Calif.—both providers of web search services.

"Pre-close, we would provide answers to [frequently asked questions] to the company" being acquired, Sartain says. "This information would be general and not detail-oriented. Our objective would

be to let the new employees know we are concerned about their well-being and to say, 'We know there will be issues, and we are working on those and will have answers at the appropriate time.'"

After a deal closes, Yahoo! provides letters to employees that explain their new role and any compensation changes, Sartain says. In addition, the company also holds meetings for all employees to outline basic compensation information, she says.

"We also hold meetings with managers to explain the Yahoo! compensation philosophy and our guidelines," she says. Compensation and reward guidelines are posted on the intranet.

Paying attention to communications during such times of change can pay off in better acceptance of the terms associated with pay, according to a recent survey of employee sentiment. Employees tend to believe their company's pay policy is fair if HR professionals fully explain compensation packages to them, according to a 2003 survey, "SHRM/CNNfn Job Satisfaction Series: Job Compensation and Pay Survey Report," conducted jointly by SHRM and CNNfn, the financial network of the CNN News Group in New York, and released in February.

Nearly half of the employees who were dissatisfied with the communications explaining how their pay was determined also reported dissatisfaction with their total compensation package. Conversely, when employees understand how compensation is determined, they tend to be happier with their pay and jobs overall, the survey concluded.

---

SUSAN J. WELLS IS A BUSINESS JOURNALIST BASED IN THE WASHINGTON, D.C., AREA WITH 18 YEARS OF EXPERIENCE COVERING BUSINESS NEWS AND WORKFORCE ISSUES.

# Top **Pay for** Best
# **Performance**

In a sluggish economy, compensation system gets new focus
by rewarding star performers more than the rest of the pack.

*By Steve Bates*

Like many companies, fiber optic cable manufacturer Corning Inc. is struggling financially. Sales are way down. Its stock price recently dipped to just over $1—about 1 percent of its value three years ago. Executives have slashed more than 16,000 jobs in two years and have frozen salaries for everyone who's left.

But while the Corning, N.Y.-based company hasn't had a profitable quarter since early 2001, next month it will give bonuses to employees who met their goals this year.

Why reward employees for a disastrous year?

The answer, says Corning, is that rewarding good workers is the best way to increase productivity and to secure dominance in its potentially lucrative market. The bonuses will likely be very small this year. But the payments will fulfill a promise to the workforce that better employee performance results in better compensation.

Forward-thinking companies are using the sluggish economy "as a time to capture market share, to do things that aren't common" in their industry to gain competitive advantage, adds Thomas B. Wilson, president of Maynard, Mass.-based Wilson Group consultants, a firm specializing in consulting on performance-based total reward systems.

In fact, compensation experts argue that paying for performance is more important in a down economy than in boom times. The reason is that companies typically have a smaller pot of money to allocate for compensation during a slowdown. So, instead of giving everyone an equal but minimal increase to their base pay, some organizations are dishing out salary increases, bonuses or both in varying amounts, with the most going to the best performers or to the most essential employees. In some cases, poor performers get little or nothing above their base pay.

"For the first time, companies truly have to differentiate" among their workers in a visible, dramatic way, says John M. Bremen, national compensation practice leader for consulting firm Watson Wyatt Worldwide in Chicago.

Compensation experts urge companies to take this opportunity to move farther from a system that relies heavily on across-the-board merit increases to one that focuses on rewarding top performers substantially more than the rest of the field. Companies need a compensation system that catches a top performer's attention and sends a signal to a poor performing employee. To do this, the system must differentiate between the two.

"We can't think of a better time in the last 20 years to talk about this," says Peter LeBlanc, senior vice president of Sibson Consulting in Raleigh, N.C. "It's a major opportunity for companies now."

The devil is in the details, however. Executing such a system can be treacherous.

## Seizing the Opportunity

Performance can be assessed based on individual or team contribution, on business unit results or on corporate profit or share price. It can be rewarded through traditional salary adjustments but also through variable pay techniques such as one-time or recurring bonuses.

Surveys show that about two-thirds of U.S. companies have some sort of variable pay, and about 10 percent of all compensation is variable.

Rewarding "top-performing employees" does not mean rewarding solely high-level employees. Organizations are using performance pay for middle managers, professionals and hourly workers, determined not to let the depressed business climate lead to a depressed workforce.

## Goalsharing at Corning

Rewarding employees for meeting important goals—whether or not the company is raking in lots of money—is the heart of the "goalsharing" program at Corning Inc. in Corning, N.Y. Started in the early 1990s, the variable pay plan can give each U.S.-based Corning employee an annual bonus of up to 10 percent of salary.

Employees helped develop the system, which is reviewed and adjusted annually at the business unit level by committees that include workers, managers and union representatives.

One-fourth of the bonus is based on earnings per share of company stock for the preceding year. The rest of the payment depends on how well the worker has met job performance goals established for his or her business unit over the year.

"One of the basic premises of goalsharing is that every employee would have line of sight" to the corporate goal, says Larr Lukefahr, Corning's manager of variable pay programs. Individual performance standards "are set with the idea that each employee can somehow contribute to meeting that goal."

"Everybody must improve from where they ended up last year," says Hang Jonas, the corporation's manager of organizational effectiveness. But in addition, "everybody has an equal chance of success." It's not always easy to set goals that satisfy the interests of the employee and the company, Lukefahr and Jonas note. A research scientist "might say 10 failures is a success. How do you measure 10 failures and pay someone for 10 failures?" asks Lukefahr.

And it's not always easy to explain handing out bonus checks when the company is losing money. "I've had a lot of people look at me like I'm crazy because where they're coming from is profit sharing," notes Jonas. Corning has a portfolio of businesses, some of which are in the black, which helps support bonuses for all eligible workers.

"I envisioned that there would be good times and bad times," Jonas says. "We want it to fairly reflect how we're doing as a company in good times and bad."

Adds Lukefahr: "Our employees are very aware of goalsharing and how goalsharing works." In Lukefahr's seven years at Corning, he says, "I've never heard anybody question goalsharing."

—Steve Bates

"It's not an economic issue. You need performance whether it's a good economy or a bad economy," says Ed Lawler, an author, professor and director of the Center for Effective Organizations at the Marshall School of Business in Los Angeles.

Paying top pay for best performance is a marked shift from just a few years ago. Many firms established generous but somewhat haphazard pay systems when the economy was hot in the 1990s. "We were just throwing money at talent," says Jay Schuster of consulting firm Schuster-Zingheim and Associates in Los Angeles.

> Giving all of an organization's workers an annual merit salary increase of about 4 percent 'is a joke. The after-tax difference is a Starbucks coffee.'

Today, "companies are being much more careful about who gets incentive pay," says Bremen. In some organizations, "we're seeing fewer people getting variable pay. Those who are getting it are getting more than they did before."

Some experts say this increased use of performance pay could mark the end of an era of entitlement in employee compensation. The bedrock of that era has been a merit pay system predicated on lifetime employment with steadily rising, virtually equal wages for all workers in a grade or job category.

The shift from a manufacturing economy to a knowledge-based economy, a more mobile workforce and the economic downturn have changed the way people look at pay, experts say.

"People used to fear the day that merit increases went below 10 percent, then 5 percent. We're now dealing with numbers so small that it is difficult to differentiate" between the best and worst performers with traditional salary adjustments, says Bremen.

Research shows that "you need [a] 7 percent or 8 percent [compensation increase] just to catch anybody's attention," says Robert Heneman, a professor of management and HR at Ohio State University. Anything below that is welcome but doesn't lead to significantly greater effort on the part of the employee to drive business results.

In fact, giving all of an organization's workers an annual merit salary increase of about 4 percent "is a joke," says Wilson. "The after-tax difference is a Starbucks coffee."

For many years, agrees LeBlanc, "we have been guilty in corporate America of spreading it evenly like peanut butter. Why do we put a merit increase in base pay?" he asks. "It ceases to be base pay. We've handcuffed ourselves and lost our imagination."

Brad Hill, senior consultant with the Hay Group in Chicago, offers the following example to illustrate the difference creativity in compensation can make: Consider a firm that gives each worker a 5 percent salary increase each year for 10 years. Instead, reduce that raise to 3.5 percent per year. Because the firm is not compounding the

# Reward the Best, Prod the Rest

One of the criticisms of compensation systems is that they fail to adequately distinguish between the best and worst performers.

Another criticism is that some compensation systems don't take full advantage of bonus pay and focus instead on increasing base pay—a strategy that can compound payroll obligations over time and limit an organization's options for rewarding its best employees.

The following example demonstrates how the combination of these two factors can affect an organization's ability to compensate top performers. In this example, Companies

A, B and C each have 1,000 employees. Each company has 100 below-average performers, 800 average performers and 100 top performers. Further, each company spends essentially the same amount in salary and bonuses over a five-year period.

However, that's where the similarities end. As the numbers below demonstrate, each company rewards its top employees very differently over time. (Editor's note: The numbers in the following charts have been rounded.)

*—Patrick Mirza and Adrienne Fox*

## Company A

- Offers poor performers a salary increase of 3 percent.
- Offers average performers a salary increase of 4 percent.
- Offers top performers a salary increase of 5 percent.
- Offers no bonus.

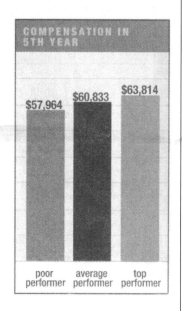

COMPENSATION IN 5TH YEAR

|  | YEAR | POOR PERFORMERS | AVERAGE PERFORMERS | TOP PERFORMERS |
|---|---|---|---|---|
| Starting salary |  | $50,000 | $50,000 | $50,000 |
| plus merit increase | 1998 | $51,500 | $52,000 | $52,500 |
| 0% bonus |  | $0 | $0 | $0 |
| salary plus merit increase | 1999 | $53,045 | $54,080 | $55,125 |
| 0% bonus |  | $0 | $0 | $0 |
| salary plus merit increase | 2000 | $54,636 | $56,243 | $57,881 |
| 0% bonus |  | $0 | $0 | $0 |
| salary plus merit increase | 2001 | $56,275 | $58,493 | $60,775 |
| 0% bonus |  | $0 | $0 | $0 |
| salary plus merit increase | 2002 | $57,964 | $60,833 | $63,814 |
| 0% bonus |  | $0 | $0 | $0 |
| **TOTAL FIVE-YEAR COMPENSATION BUDGET** | | | **$218,670,632** | |

larger raises year after year, it can give each employee an annual bonus of 7.2 percent of salary in addition to the 3.5 percent raises—for the same total outlay over the decade.

Now take it another step: With the same overall compensation budget, reward your top performers significantly more with higher salary increases and larger bonuses while giving your average and poor performers lower salary increases and bonuses—or no bonus at all. For a detailed example of how this can be achieved with nearly the same compensation outlay, see the sidebar "Reward the Best, Prod the Rest."

## Hard to Understand, Execute

Paying for performance does more than deliver the best financial rewards to the best workers. When done right, it sends a vital message about the organization's priorities and values, experts say. "Compensation is really one of the main communication vehicles between companies and employees. Companies forget this," says Bremen.

Indeed, it seems top performers aren't getting the right message. A recent survey by Watson Wyatt reported that fewer than 40 percent of top-performing employees believe that they receive "moderately or significantly better pay raises, annual bonuses or total pay than do employees with average performance." The same survey found that companies providing variable pay to their best workers are 68 percent more likely than other firms to report outstanding financial performance.

## Company B

- Offers poor performers a salary increase of 2 percent.
- Offers average performers a salary increase of 4 percent.
- Offers top performers a salary increase of 6 percent.
- Offers a bonus of 4 percent of salary to all employees.

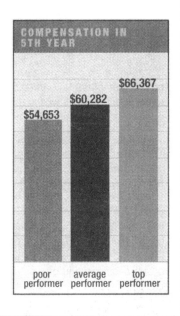

| | YEAR | POOR PERFORMERS | AVERAGE PERFORMERS | TOP PERFORMERS |
|---|---|---|---|---|
| Starting salary | | $50,000 | $50,000 | $50,000 |
| plus merit increase | 1998 | $50,500 | $51,500 | $52,500 |
| 0% bonus | | $2,020 | $2,060 | $2,100 |
| salary plus merit increase | 1999 | $51,005 | $53,045 | $55,125 |
| 0% bonus | | $2,040 | $2,122 | $2,205 |
| salary plus merit increase | 2000 | $51,515 | $54,636 | $57,881 |
| 0% bonus | | $2,061 | $2,185 | $2,315 |
| salary plus merit increase | 2001 | $52,030 | $56,275 | $60,775 |
| 0% bonus | | $2,081 | $2,251 | $2,431 |
| salary plus merit increase | 2002 | $52,551 | $57,964 | $63,814 |
| 0% bonus | | 2,102 | $2,319 | $2,553 |

**TOTAL FIVE-YEAR COMPENSATION BUDGET    $284,446,276**

## Company C

- Offers poor performers a salary increase of 2 percent and no annual bonus
- Offers average performers a salary increase of 4 percent and an annual bonus of 3 percent.
- Offers top perfromers a salary increase of 6 percent and an annual bonus of 7 percent.

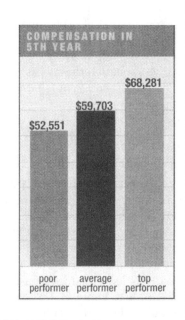

| | YEAR | POOR PERFORMERS | AVERAGE PERFORMERS | TOP PERFORMERS |
|---|---|---|---|---|
| Starting salary | | $50,000 | $50,000 | $50,000 |
| plus merit increase | 1998 | $50,500 | $51,500 | $52,500 |
| 0% bonus | | $0 | $1,545 | $3,675 |
| salary plus merit increase | 1999 | $51,005 | $53,045 | $55,125 |
| 0% bonus | | $0 | $1,591 | $3,859 |
| salary plus merit increase | 2000 | $51,515 | $54,636 | $57,881 |
| 0% bonus | | $0 | $1,639 | $4,052 |
| salary plus merit increase | 2001 | $52,030 | $56,275 | $60,775 |
| 0% bonus | | $0 | $1,688 | $4,254 |
| salary plus merit increase | 2002 | $52,551 | $57,964 | $63,814 |
| 0% bonus | | $0 | $1,739 | $4,467 |

**TOTAL FIVE-YEAR COMPENSATION BUDGET    $282,098,796**

According to Russell Miller, a principal with Washington, D.C.-based Mercer Human Resource Consulting, a well-crafted performance pay system establishes a pact with workers that says, in effect, "We're going to hold you accountable, and we're going to reward you." Employees will share in the fruits of business success, but they also will share the risk of belt-tightening. It's both carrot and stick.

"That's a major leap," adds Miller.

But few companies get it right. While traditional merit pay is designed to reward workers for past performance, performance pay attempts to motivate future behavior, which is less tangible. Therefore, performance pay is not well understood or well executed by many firms, say academics and consultants. "Even the financial people aren't recognizing the potential," says Hill.

---

# When to Tinker or Start Over

Compensation experts say that roughly one-third of performance pay plans fail. Some don't get set up properly, and some don't work as well in a poor economy as in a strong one. Even the best pay systems need regular check-ups.

Murray Hill, N.J.-based telecommunications giant Lucent Technologies had a sales compensation system that provided huge payouts to top sales people in the boom days of the 1990s. However, by mid-2001, Lucent's market had collapsed so precipitously that sales compensation was way out of line with revenues coming in the door. Lucent stopped the pay plan in its tracks. Officials discovered that there were several different sales compensation systems in the corporation and came up with a single plan that they explained in group sessions and one-on-one meetings to gain employee buy-in.

Often, even in non-sales performance pay plans, "at some point it's better to start over. You can say: 'We didn't get it right' or 'it ran its course,'" says Ed Lawler, an author, professor and director of the Center for Effective Organizations at the Marshall School of Business in Los Angeles.

But don't tweak the system too often. "It's something that should be used consistently," says Allan G. Bateson, SPHR, senior consultant with Runzheimer International in Baltimore and a member of the Compensation and Benefits Committee of the Society for Human Resource Management. "There's a problem for employees when an organization switches back and forth."

"You have to be committed to change for a number of years," notes Russell Miller, a principal with Washington, D.C.-based Mercer Human Resource Consulting. "It's always going to be difficult to set up a plan that is viable for every [economic] scenario," he states. An organization should be satisfied "as long as it works nine out of 10 years."

The biggest red flag indicating a failing performance pay system is usually fairly obvious. "If you're paying out the money and not seeing the results," then it's not working, says Monica Barron, a senior analyst at AMR Research, a Boston-based business consulting firm.

The goal is to establish a system that makes sense in bad economic times as well as good ones, and not to undermine it by rewarding employees who have not produced.

---

One reason HR professionals and line managers might be hesitant to use performance pay to its full potential is that taking money away from one individual or group of workers to fatten the checks of another can be disruptive or demoralizing. People talk, and they often know who gets the big payout.

> And while changing any pay system is risky, 'the biggest risk is mediocrity' if a company fails to reward its top employees adequately.

But Monica Barron, a senior analyst at AMR Research, a Boston-based business consulting firm, argues: "It's OK for people to know that. You should make your best performers role models and say to the others: 'Here's what you can do to get one of these checks.'"

Ken Abosch, talent business leader of consulting firm Hewitt Associates in Lincolnshire, Ill., agrees. "Maybe there's a fear [in HR] that employee satisfaction will be cut. We're trying to improve performance," not satisfaction, through performance pay, he says. "Sometimes we need a healthy dose of tough love."

And while changing any pay system is risky, says Miller, "the biggest risk is mediocrity" if a company fails to reward its top employees adequately. "Your stars are going to look elsewhere, and your average and below-average employees will say 'I'm going to stick around.'"

Another hurdle to establishing performance pay is determining what a company wants to achieve through its compensation plan. "One of the symptoms of a poor performing company is the inability to set goals effectively," states Bremen. "A compensation system cannot resolve inadequate goals setting; it actually makes it worse."

In addition, the corporate culture has to accept this kind of reward/risk system. "First you have to build a culture of high performance," says David Balkin, chair of management at the University of Colorado at Boulder. "Pay works best when it follows other changes that have already been made in the culture. It legitimizes; it's the final cementing of that change."

"The variable pay risk should be commensurate with an individual's ability to impact results," adds Bremen, and workers should see clearly how they can accomplish what's asked of them.

Education and communication are critical to this process. "You need basic communication about what you're trying to do and how the employee can help you get there," says Barron.

Employees who are knowledgeable about a performance pay plan not only show better individual performance but also can explain it to their colleagues, notes Hill. "You need to identify disciples in every element of the organization to talk up the program."

Hill favors involving employees in the design of a performance pay system, albeit with some guidance from managers and perhaps a consultant. "I've been very impressed" by plans that employees help develop. "About half the time the plan they come up with is the plan I would have come up with."

Employee participation was crucial to the development and success of the incentive pay plan created at Corning. Called "goalsharing," the system establishes specific performance standards for workers in each business unit. These are re-evaluated annually, and payments are made annually to employees who meet their goals. (See box, "Goalsharing at Corning")

Goalsharing is not the same as "gainsharing" where employees typically get a set percentage of business unit or corporate profits in addition to base pay. In addition, individuals, small teams and large teams in gainsharing programs can earn variable pay increases based on their contribution to business success.

## Emphasis on Measurement

Perhaps the greatest challenge in establishing and using performance pay systems is identifying and quantifying the job performance factors that can be linked directly and meaningfully to the organization's goals. It's all about measurement.

> 'This is without a doubt the most incredible opportunity in a decade for the profession to demonstrate its value.'

"A company's culture becomes formed around how you measure," explains Miller. "You've got to make sure that what you measure is what you want.

"It's not easy," he adds.

Establishing performance pay systems has been easiest in organizations or units where job performance and results are easiest to see and quantify, such as in sales. "It has been a very sales-oriented concept," says Mike Lieberman, vice president of marketing at compensation software and services firm Synygy in Conshohocken, Pa. Today, his clients' managers in non-sales departments "are seeing some similar advantages."

"There is a lot of traction in organizations that face the customer and where there are quantifiable metrics," adds Barron. For example, in a customer relations call center, managers can record the number and length of calls handled by each worker or each group of workers and can survey customer satisfaction levels. Those results can factor directly into call center employees' compensation.

Schuster suggests creating a list of the critical skills needed in good times and bad times. "Identify the people who are market leaders in those skills," he says. "It could be people in the hourly ranks."

Such an approach "might sound harsh" to other employees, says Schuster, but these are harsh times.

"There is no magic formula for how organizations go about using variable pay effectively," says Abosch. Each organization has to look objectively at its financial goals and at the employee behaviors that drive the desired results. Each has to identify a few measures—some experts say no more than three to five—that the worker and line manager and other managers can agree on as crucial to linking individual performance and business success.

## The Role of HR

In some organizations, HR departments are integrally involved in proposing, designing and implementing performance pay systems. But even where HR is not at the forefront of such efforts, it still can play a role.

Sibson's LeBlanc views performance pay as "the best opportunity for HR departments to take a good look at what they're doing and to challenge the entitlement mentality." In doing so, says LeBlanc, "HR should educate and up-skill the manager first."

To do this, HR can help managers "give people the information they need to see themselves and understand what they need to do," says Wilson. "HR can be the catalyst for managers who want to do something different."

Compensation is of critical importance to the viability of a business. HR departments are "essentially managing the biggest cost center that most organizations have," says Schuster. "This is without a doubt the most incredible opportunity in a decade for the profession to demonstrate its value and create a whole new generation of HR professionals."

---

*Steve Bates is senior writer for* HR Magazine.

# Ten Steps to Designing an Effective Incentive Program

*Bruce Bolger*

It seems obvious that having motivated employees, channel partners (retailers or other distributors), and vendors can provide a competitive edge, yet surprisingly few organizations put a strategic emphasis on motivation. Those business leaders who do focus on motivation tend to do so out of faith, because the vast business, media, and academic community has paid comparatively little attention to the issues specifically related to motivating customers to buy, channel partners to produce, and all sales, service, and operations employees to work with maximum commitment toward achieving organizational goals.

The lack of business focus on motivation is demonstrated by the fact that few organizations have any one person responsible for motivating customers, employees, channel partners, and vendors. Is it the CEO, or head of human resources, sales, or marketing? Is that function written into anyone's job description? Is anyone measured by how well he or she motivates? The fact is that numerous people in an organization face the issue of motivation, often using their own approaches with little linkage to other organizational efforts. The HR department may have one approach for management and rank-and-file workers, while the sales department handles sales and channel-partner motivation, and marketing tackles customer motivation. "The Interaction Between Marketing & Human Resources and Employee Measurement & Incentives," a study conducted at the end of 2003 by the Forum for People Performance Management at Northwestern University, found that a large gulf existed between the motivational efforts of HR on the one side and sales and marketing on the other.

Based on the department from which the plan emanates, the need, or the audience, organizations use many different types of strategies to motivate people. These can include benefits, workplace environment, training, meetings, newsletters, compensation, recognition, and, in many cases, incentive programs. Maximizing overall motivation clearly involves a careful integration of these many factors.

Motivation clearly has an impact on performance, but it alone cannot guarantee success. A group of employees in a hamburger chain may love their work and provide great service, but motivation cannot replace the business lost if a nearby factory shuts down. What sets incentive programs apart from other motivation strategies is the ability to link the campaign to measurable, desirable actions or outcomes, such as increased effort by salespeople or increased customer loyalty due to better customer service. The specific objective of an incentive program is to drive measurable performance improvement.

Another element unique to the issue of motivation is the potential benefit of better integrating external motivation of consumers and internal motivation of employees, as well as specific tactics, such as meetings, print communications, and promotions. This integration, which focuses activities on the targeted audiences and desired behaviors and not the interests of tactical managers defending their budgets, requires a level of alignment that may not be present at many large companies today. Very few organizations have in place a management structure that clearly bridges internal and external audiences and the internal departments that serve them.

*Business planners traditionally have often placed too much emphasis on incentives and not enough on the other elements that can affect performance.*

The process of motivating people to improve performance can involve a variety of tactics, but all have in common the goal to produce a measurable action or outcome in the target audience. So the focus starts on the audience, by asking who do we want to motivate, and then proceeds to what are we asking them to do, how will we help them succeed, and how will we measure success and reward people in order to reenergize them for the new challenges beyond?

## WHAT IS AN INCENTIVE PROGRAM?

The lack of focus on motivation has created a fuzzy world of nomenclature related to incentive programs and other recognition and consumer promotion programs. Definitions and terms vary depending on the industry, audience, and individual businesspeople; these terms include *sales contents, recognition, rewards, tangible rewards, premiums*, and *dealer loaders*. Incentive programs comprise internal or external marketing campaigns designed to promote specific actions on the part of a specific audience to produce measurable outcomes through the integrated use of motivational strategies, including awards, communication, involvement, feedback, and recognition.

Actions promoted by incentive programs can include:

- Make more sales calls.
- Put up displays.
- Buy more of a product.
- Attend an event.

Outcomes can include:

- Increased sales,
- Expanded productivity,
- Improved quality, or
- Improved cycle times (how long it takes to get something done).

When referring to incentive programs, businesspeople and media often use the term *incentives*, as if the strategy focuses primarily on giving something to someone for doing something. This may be the case, but unless the campaign addresses the other issues related to increasing motivation, the program likely will fail. Business planners traditionally have often placed too much emphasis on incentives and not enough on the other elements that can affect performance.

## WHAT MOTIVATES?

Because the issue of motivation stretches across an organization's entire audience, the answer depends on the audience: sales force, operations employees, administration or research, channel partners, or consumers. To simplify the answer, we'll break this into internal and external audiences.

## INTERNAL AUDIENCES

Despite the lack of research and attention paid to the relationship between motivation and business performance, over the years numerous researchers have looked at different aspects of the issue. A study conducted in 2003 by the International Society of Performance Improvement, entitled "Incentives, Motivation, and Workplace Performance," provides an excellent summary of what is known on the subject. Commissioned by the SITE Foundation, a not-for-profit research foundation focused on incentive research, the study was undertaken to provide a comprehensive review of past academic research as well as provide a snapshot of current business practices via both a broad-based and in-depth survey of U.S. organizations. The study of current organizations found several elements critical to achieving performance improvement through motivation.

*Incentive programs should instill a feeling of importance, because everyone's job counts when it comes to improving performance.*

- *Emotion.* The study found that the workplace mood has a fundamental impact on performance. How employees feel about their jobs, work environment, and company directly affects their level of service and productivity. Further support for this hypothesis comes from a 2002 survey of U.S. workers,

entitled "2002 Motivation for Excellence," which found that 85 percent of employees see a link between their level of motivation and the quality and quantity of their work. When properly designed, incentive programs have a positive, measurable impact on the emotional state of participants.

- *Communication.* The data support the existence of a direct link between performance and the degree to which participants understand the desired goals and steps they can take to help get there. Incentive programs should foster a greater understanding of organizational goals and how each participant's actions can contribute to overall success.
- *Buy-in.* The study found that performance thrives when employees feel engaged in the goal. Incentive-program proponents specifically use the campaign development process to foster engagement by involving employees in the design process.
- *Feasibility.* The study found that programs rewarding individuals based on their own achievement, rather than rewarding a predetermined number in so-called tournament or closed-ended programs, provide much better results.
- *Work utility.* The research confirms the intuitive link between work satisfaction and sense of purpose. Incentive programs should instill a feeling of importance, because everyone's job counts when it comes to improving performance.
- *Employee capability.* People quickly become discouraged if they want something but lack the skills to get it; motivation goes hand-in-hand with a participant's sense of ability. So every incentive program should include training that complements the actions requested by the program.

Analysis and feedback provide the method for utilizing the invaluable information that comes from directing people toward specific goals. What happens, or does not happen, provides a road map for better results in the future, no matter what the outcome.

## EXTERNAL MOTIVATION

Recently, much more research has been conducted regarding the understanding of customer behavior. Although much debate continues on many granular issues, a solid basis of evidence suggests the following key factors can come into play, depending on the audience and individuals. Curiously, many of these external marketing elements relate to internal audiences.

- *Availability.* Do consumers even know the product or service exists, and is it easy to find it? Availability could be a function of willingness of channel partners to carry a product, which in turn could be determined by how they are treated by sales or other employees.

*What customers say to employees may be one of the most overlooked areas of business intelligence in helping organizations better understand what they can do to please.*

- *Function.* Does the product or service fill a big enough need and do what it says it will do? Function can be a product of innovation that comes from a committed employee base looking for new ways to please the customer.

- *Value*. Is the price paid comparable to similar products in the market? Value can also be viewed in terms of productivity and the efficiency of internal employees.

- *Emotion*. Many people respond to what they perceive to be fun, exciting, and hip, and want to feel valued and recognized. Marketing strategies that address emotion often require the involvement of employees or channel partners.

- *Convenience*. Is the product relatively easy to buy and use with a minimum of problems? Convenience can suffer greatly when internal employees have little interest in customer satisfaction or understanding of what they can do to foster it.

- *Identification*. Can customers or prospects emotionally identify with the "brand," and do they feel comfortable interacting with the company's people or image? Many organizations spend millions to build a brand through advertising, only to have it thwarted by employees who interact with customers but whose attitudes can't always be covered up by a uniform, dress code standards, and one-week intensive training programs.

- *Communication*. Do customers and external channel partners understand your latest products, services, and value propositions? Communication is a two-way street, with marketers advertising and marketing to external customers, who in turn communicate to the internal employees they encounter on a day-to-day basis. What customers say to employees may be one of the most overlooked areas of business intelligence in helping organizations better understand what they can do to please.

- *Integrity*. If there is a problem, how does the company handle it? Many marketing departments overlook the extent to which the internal audience—employees, salespeople, and channel partners—can influence these outcomes.

When properly constructed, consumer incentive programs get a better response if they address both external and internal audiences.

## THE LINKAGE TO PERFORMANCE

Companies do many things to motivate employees, but incentive programs are designed to drive specific actions that lead to increased performance.

In addition, incentive programs are among the very few business strategies whose cost varies according to the outcome. Whether your organization uses benefits, meetings, newsletters, advertising, promotions, recognition, training, or many other related strategies, your cost will likely be the same no matter what the outcome. With properly designed incentive programs, your cost will have a direct correlation to results, meaning that, under ideal circumstances, you pay more if your program succeeds, and much less if it doesn't.

The design steps will show how to direct motivational energy toward the achievement of specific, measurable goals. Also, performance measures are described that your organization can use to determine the specific value derived from an incentive program.

## STEPS TO DESIGNING A PROGRAM

The following overview covers the basic elements of incentive program design, no matter what the audience.

### 1. Design a Strategic Plan

The overall strategy of an incentive program is to perform a specific action to obtain a specific result. Your incentive program should address specific objectives with a specific strategy and tactics so that you have measurable results. The strategic plan should read like a business plan, outlining all of the elements covered below, along with the items that produce a return on investment.

### 2. Identify the Audience

Before you can do anything to set up an incentive program, you need to pinpoint the audience(s) that can drive the desired performance. Often, including more target groups can have a greater impact than you might think. For instance, customer service people might have a direct bearing on the efforts of your salespeople to increase sales. Retail personnel at a retail outlet might have a direct impact on whether or not customers see the point-of-sale displays that outlet agreed to put up. Employees in the shipping department might play just as much a role in helping you meet customer production deadlines as those in the assembly operation. No matter what department you're in, you can benefit by looking at all of the people who can affect your goals.

*Your incentive program should address specific objectives with a specific strategy and tactics so that you have measurable results.*

When identifying your audience, don't forget to take into account the anecdotal but useful 20-60-20 rule: 20 percent of your best performers will probably continue to perform no matter what you do, because they already perform under the current circumstances. Another 60 percent can go either way. The final 20 percent probably won't budge no matter what you do.

### 3. Conduct Appropriate Fact Finding

This process lies at the root of identifying what actions will yield the desired results. You need to find out how motivation can drive the behaviors your objectives require and what obstacles potentially stand in the way. This step often includes employee involvement programs or focus groups with consumers to determine what your targeted audience can do (or not do) to help you achieve your goal. This step helps you make sure your program addresses whatever hidden factors might stop people from doing the things you need them to do. The output of this process provides the basis for developing your program structure by confirming the specific actions required by the specific audience that can lead to the specific results.

*Many programs overlook the value of integrating communications with incentive program design.*

## 4. Create the Program Structure

Think of this step as the blueprint for your strategy. It spells out precisely what people have to do to reach their goal—how the organization will assist them, how people will be rewarded and recognized, and how you will measure the return on investment. There are essentially two types of incentive program structures underlying almost any type of program:

- Open-ended programs enable anyone to win based on his or her own actions and, therefore, give participants the greatest potential control over their success. The research confirms that these programs generally have greater motivational value because they offer accessibility to the broadest possible audience.

- Closed-ended programs have a predetermined number of winners. They have the benefit of letting you offer a larger, more impressive award with a fixed, predictable budget, but research clearly shows that they often discourage a large portion of participants who quickly count themselves out of the running.

Many companies use closed-ended programs in conjunction with open-ended programs as a means of fostering loyalty among top performers by making them feel valued and appreciated.

## 5. Integrate Communications

Many programs overlook the value of integrating communications with incentive program design. The incentives used in conjunction with the program help draw attention to company communications, and company communications help direct people toward the behaviors and training tools that can help them succeed. Communication can take the form of imprinted promotional products delivered with training; announcements; standings reports showing how well partners or teams are performing; meetings, including local, regional, national, or international; newsletters (print or e-mail); personal letters; brochures; and more.

## 6. Select Rewards

Award selection depends largely on your objectives. If the goal is to compensate employees for work they accomplish year after year, cash is clearly the currency of choice. But if the goal is to recognize people for special behavior that may not be rewarded in subsequent years and to foster communications, alignment, etc., then it may pay to use noncash awards that won't become confused as compensation and, therefore, expected year after year.

So, the question becomes, How do noncash awards compare with cash rewards when the goals include rewarding exceptional behavior, enhancing communications, and better aligning employee actions with external marketing promises? In a survey of incentive-award users released in September 2003, the majority of users surveyed believe that merchandise and travel awards get remembered longer and are more promotable than cash and that cash awards have the least residual value. These findings support the use of noncash awards when the goal involves getting attention and deriving derivative value in terms of focus and commitment levels. If memorability has no place in your recognition strategy, cash may be a better solution.

Both common sense and research support the theory that presentation is as important as the award itself, because people respond best to genuine appreciation for their efforts.

## 7. Develop a Budget

Several rules of thumb help guide incentive planners to more measurable, cost-effective programs. First, set up your program so that your fixed costs consist primarily of strategic planning, communications, training, and tracking and administration and that your rewards and recognition are based on incremental performance generated by participants, customers, channel partners, or employees. Return-on-investment measures below can help you determine how much to payout in awards, but companies generally budget top awards to equal about 3 percent to 5 percent of a recipient's annual earnings to get attention. Under this scenario, only about 20 percent of the program's budget has a fixed cost; the rest varies based on performance improvement.

Open-ended programs can be more difficult to budget, because how much you spend depends on how much individuals or groups perform, which no one can accurately predict. On the other hand, your budget only goes up if your results go up; and if your program is structured correctly, you won't pay nearly as much for your program if results fall short. Most other marketing options have a fixed cost no matter what the outcome. Closed-ended programs are easy to budget, because you set the predetermined number of winners, but that also may mean you'll pay full freight for your program even if you don't achieve your objectives.

*Both common sense and research support the theory that presentation is as important as the award itself, because people respond best to genuine appreciation for their efforts.*

## 8. Develop Measures

In the early 1990s, the American Productivity and Quality Center created the Master Measurement Model for the SITE Foundation in order to guide planners toward the development of measurable programs. The model has the following elements.

1. Determine the processes to be measured in a numeric way. Measures could include unit sales, dollar sales, repeat customers, defect percentage, customer satisfaction scores, cycle times, etc.
2. Decide on two to three related processes or outcomes to be measured, and make sure that you measure related issues, such as sales, sales presentations conducted, repeat business or number of repairs per day, timeliness of repair report submission, or number of suggestions made to repair the update manual.
3. Create a basis for comparison. What is the rate of unit sales, dollar sales, repeat customers, defects, customer satisfaction, or cycle times to which your program's performance will be compared?
4. Translate the numerical goal into a unit of measure that can easily be tallied against a previous, comparable period.
5. Weight that measure based on how important it is to the overall program objective. A sales incentive campaign might weight the goals as follows: 50 percent for sales; 25 percent for sales presentations; and 25 percent for repeat customers. (See **Exhibit 1**.)

### Performance Feedback Report

| | Base Data | New Data | New Base | Weight | Result |
|---|---|---|---|---|---|
| Measure A | 12.11 | 12.52 | 103.44 | .50 | 51.7 |

(This indicates an improvement in performance of 3.4 percent, translating into a unit measure of 51.7.)

### Benefit Report for Field Service Reps

| | Base Data | New Data | Improvement | $ per Unit | Benefit |
|---|---|---|---|---|---|
| Measure A | 14.32 | 15.17 | .85 | $50K/1 | $42.5K |

(By multiplying the unit improvement by the estimated benefit per unit, you arrive at an estimate of the benefits derived from your program.)

Source: *The Master Measurement Model of Employee Performance, created for the SITE Foundation by the American Productivity and Quality Center.*

### *Exhibit 1. Performance Feedback Report and Benefit Report for Field Service Reps*

## 9. Track Results

Tracking and administration of incentive-program design ironically can create some of the biggest challenges and opportunities. The challenges relate to the practical issues of collecting and sharing data. Fortunately, the Internet, intranets, and enterprise software or customer relationship applications have made this task much easier, and administration is now further supported via the proliferation of online incentive technology. Some of the available online incentive technology has easily customizable functions enabling you to set up the type of measurement and award allocation features outlined under step 8.

The most important elements of tracking and administration include:

- Implementing the program business plan according to the time line;
- Having an up-to-date database of each participant;
- Setting up a simple system for collecting and reporting data;
- Sending out all standing and other reports on schedule;
- Making sure all awards get distributed on schedule;
- Running tracking reports to determine award redemptions and costs;
- Calculating results and return on investment as indicated above;
- Feeding back market or other knowledge obtained from the program.

One of the key benefits of an incentive program is the ability to collect valuable data not only about results, but also about the processes necessary for success. Often, an incentive program helps collect useful data you might not ordinarily get unless people (especially channel partners) have an incentive to do so.

## 10. Analyze Results and Solicit Feedback

Your program might have both quantitative and qualitative measures of success. Quantitative measures are reflected in the actual results; qualitative measures might come from some other indices, such as results from employee or customer surveys, customer or employee turnover rates, revenue or other productivity measures per employee, etc. These qualitative results can represent byproducts with an additional value to the organization over that achieved through the actual results.

During the analysis and feedback phase, you want to look at your program results against your business plan and attempt to isolate any outside factors that could have affected performance, either accounted for or unaccounted for in your plan. Review actual results and whatever qualitative information you gleaned so that you can prepare a recommendations report for any future programs.

This process can include a per-participant review to see whether any patterns have emerged about group or individual performance that could provide ideas for improvement in the future.

If you have used both results and process measures, you have powerful tools to determine the precise impact of your incentive program. If the results went up, but the processes being measured went down in quantity or quality, then you can assume that the results had little to do with the program. If, on the other hand, the processes showed improvement but results went down, you can conclude that some outside circumstance other than motivation or work effectiveness contributed to the outcome. Also, if you can continue to track data following the end of the formal program, you can continue to monitor what happens to results and process measures to see what happens without the incentive program.

Many companies that use incentive programs do so in the belief that there's almost always a value to promoting important behaviors and that the use of rewards helps sustain commitment to positive behaviors over time.

---

***Bruce Bolger*** *is a founder of the Forum for People Performance Management and Measurement in the Department of Integrated Marketing Communications at the Medill School at Northwestern University. He is also managing director of the Incentive Performance Center, a not-for-profit organization dedicated to improving the effectiveness of incentive programs, and president of Selling Communications Inc. (Irvington, New York), a target marketing, media, and technology company. He is also author of* Principles of Incentive Program Design *(Association of Incentive Marketing, 2004), from which this article has been adapted.*

---

# Executive Compensation: Are Some Paid Too Much?

**Fred Maidment**

During the 1990s, the pay of chief executive officers (CEOs) of major corporations grew almost exponentially. Highly respected business publications complained loudly that many CEOs seemed to be making large amounts in compensation, with little or no correlation between their performance and their pay. Despite a 16 percent decline in the average pay of CEOs in 2001, as calculated by *Business Week* using Standard & Poors EXECUCOMP, almost certainly caused at least in part by a general decline in the stock market, Lawrence J. Ellison, the CEO of Oracle Corporation, set a new record for annual executive earnings with $706.1 million in long-term compensation. *Business Week* was quick to point out that the method it used to calculate compensation was not perfect and that stock options, the primary source of much executive compensation, have been poorly handled in the past, but it expressed hope that in 2002 these options have been more accurately accounted for. Ellison also may have been the biggest loser in 2001, according to *Business Week*. If Oracle's stock had not declined by over half during 2001, he would have made over $2 billion dollars more than the $706.1 million he was awarded. Stated simply, if Oracle's stock had not declined, Ellison would have received close to $3 billion for his services during 2001.

As it was, Ellison was paid nearly $2 million a day, or slightly more than $80,000 for every hour of every day, more than twice the annual per capita income in the United States in 2000. Put another way, if someone had an income of $100,000 per year, a little less than three times the annual per capita income in the U.S., and had started work in 5000 B.C., the absolute earliest date generally accepted as the beginning of recorded history, he or she would not have been paid as much, to date, as Ellison was paid in 2001.

It is only fair to mention that Ellison was not the only very well-paid CEO or other executive in American business in 2001. The top-paid CEOs and other executives in 2001, as reported in *Business Week*, are shown in Tables 1 and 2.

It also should be noted that some of the executives were in the last year of their tenure with these organiza-

## TABLE 1. The 20 Top-Paid Chief Executive Officers in 2001

| Executive (Company) | Compensation (in millions of U.S. dollars) |
|---|---|
| Lawrence Ellison (Oracle) | $706.1 |
| Jozef Straus (JDS Uniphase) | 150.8 |
| Howard Solomon (Forest Laboratories) | 148.5 |
| Richard Fairbank (Capital One Financial) | 142.2 |
| Louis Gerstner (IBM) | 127.4 |
| Charles Wang (Computer Associates Inc.) | 119.1 |
| Richard Fuld, Jr. (Lehman Brothers) | 105.2 |
| James McDonald (Scientific Atlanta) | 86.8 |
| Steve Jobs (Apple Computer) | 84.0 |
| Timothy Koogle (Yahoo!) | 64.6 |
| Tony White (Applied Biosystems Group) | 61.9 |
| David Rickey (Applied Micro Circuits) | 59.5 |
| John Gifford (Maxim Integrated Products) | 58.0 |
| Paul Folino (Emulex) | 56.2 |
| Douglas Daft (Coca Cola) | 55.0 |
| Geoffrey Bible (Philip Morris) | 49.9 |
| Michael Devlin (Rational Software) | 47.3 |
| Bruce Karatz (KB Home) | 44.4 |
| Sanford Weill (Citicorp) | 42.6 |
| Micky Arison (Carnival) | 40.5 |

tions. Some of the compensation packages therefore might be looked on as a kind of retirement bonus given to

## TABLE 2. The 10 Top-Paid Non-CEO Executives in 2001

| Executive (Company) | Compensation (in millions of U.S. dollars) |
| --- | --- |
| Stephen Case (AOL Time Warner) | $128.3 |
| Gregory Doucherty (JDS Uniphase) | 121.4 |
| Donald Scifres (JDS Uniphase) | 94.4 |
| Gregory Zeman (CDW Computer Centers) | 90.1 |
| Nigel Morris (Capital One Financial) | 89.5 |
| Jeffrey Henley (Oracle) | 86.5 |
| M. Zita Cobb (JDS Uniphase) | 69.5 |
| Robert Herbolt (Microsoft) | 68.2 |
| Robert Pittman (AOL Time Warner) | 67.6 |
| Jeffrey Raikes (Microsoft) | 58.0 |

## TABLE 3. The 24 Countries With the Lowest GDP in 2000 in Descending Order

| Country | GDP (in millions of U.S. dollars) |
| --- | --- |
| St. Lucia | $701 |
| Antigua | 665 |
| French Guiana | 641 |
| Djibouti | 553 |
| Cape Verde | 535 |
| Bhutan | 478 |
| Maldives | 435 |
| Gambia | 419 |
| Trinidad and Tobago | 403 |
| Grenada | 390 |
| Afghanistan | 387 |
| Solomon Islands | 365 |
| St. Vincent and the Grenadines | 343 |
| St. Kitts | 314 |
| Dominica | 298 |
| Guinea-Bissau | 225 |
| Western Samoa | 215 |
| Vanuatu | 213 |
| Chad | 161 |
| Tonga | 141 |
| Anguilla | 68 |
| Kiribati | 46 |
| Nauru | 32 |
| Tuvalu | 6 |

a chief executive officer for a job well done. On the other hand, certain of these names appear on this list nearly every year. Although Mr. Ellison of Oracle may have set a new record for a single year's compensation, and was on the list in 2000, he certainly is not the leader in career compensation. That honor is more or less shared by two executives, Sanford Weill of Citigroup, number 19 on the 2001 list, and Michael Eisner of Disney. Both of these individuals have received over $1 billion during their careers with their respective organizations. Charles Wang of Computer Associates International, also on the 2001 list, whose record of $655.4 million for a single year's compensation in 1999 was broken by Ellison, is also in the running for the title of best-paid employee during his or her career.

Some would say that these executives make more than the gross domestic product of certain small countries. Well, if so, which countries? Table 3 shows a list from *International Marketing Data and Statistics, 2001* of the 24 countries whose gross domestic product for 2000 (the last year for which data was available) was less than Ellison's compensation for 2001.

CEOs and other executives are the hired help, a fact that they probably do not wish to contemplate or frequently discuss. They are there to represent the interests of the stockholders and also must consider the interests of other stakeholders including employees, customers, suppliers, and the society as a whole. Lawrence J. Ellison of Oracle Corporation received in compensation, in 2001, more than any other employee in the history of the world during a single year, while the price of Oracle stock declined sharply, by well over half. *Business Week* calculated that Ellison was the worst-performing CEO in terms of pay for performance over the three-year period from 1999 to 2001. The best-performing CEO, as calculated by *Business Week* for the same period, was B. Wayne Hughes of Public Storage, who made a total of $300,000 for the same three-year period, about what Ellison made during a single day at the office before lunch.

Fred Maidment is Associate Professor of Management at the Ancell School of Western Connecticut State University.

From *Journal of Pension Planning and Compliance*, Winter 2003, pp. 56-59. © 2003 by Aspen Publishers, Inc.

# Employers May Face Liability When Domestic Violence Comes to Work

STACEY PASTEL DOUGAN

On August 27, 1999, a Pennsylvania woman named Mary* was beaten by her husband. Afterwards, she called the police and obtained an order of protection. During the days that followed, Mary's husband continued to show up at the retail store where she worked. On August 30, 1999, her husband returned to the store and asked one of Mary's managers when she was coming to work that evening. He came back later that night and shot Mary in the head before turning the gun on himself.

Mary miraculously survived and sued her employer, claiming it was negligent in failing to call police when her husband arrived at the store; failing to have adequate security; and failing to implement and enforce a domestic violence policy for abused employees. Specifically, the suit alleges that the employer knew that the employee had been abused by her husband days before the shooting and also knew that the employee had obtained a court order requiring her husband to stay away from her. Yet, the lawsuit contends, the employer failed to take reasonable steps to provide the employee a safe place to work.[1]

This true story speaks volumes about the liability employers can face when domestic violence spills into the workplace. Tragedies like this are not uncommon. Even more common, however, are the less dramatic impacts of domestic violence.

Domestic violence does not remain "domestic" by staying at home when its victims go to work. An estimated 13,000 acts of domestic violence are committed in the workplace every year and homicide is the leading cause of death for women on the job. This violence poses a threat not only to the victim, but also threatens the safety and well-being of co-workers and customers. Even when domestic violence does not spill over into the workplace, its effects are enormous.[2]

- Businesses pay an estimated $3 to $5 billion annually in medical expenses associated with domestic violence.
- Firms forfeit another $100 million a year in lost wages, absenteeism, and reduced productivity.
- One study found that 96 percent of employees who were victims of domestic violence reported some form of workplace problem as a direct result of emotional or physical abuse.
- Seventy-eight percent of human resource professionals polled by *Personnel Journal* said that domestic violence is a workplace issue.

It is estimated that 25 percent of the most acute workplace problems—absenteeism, increased insurance costs, high turnover, and reduced productivity—stem directly from domestic violence. All of these problems, of course, can have a tremendous effect on the operation and bottom line of a business.

- Forty-seven percent of senior executives polled said that domestic violence has a harmful effect on the company's productivity.
- Ninety-four percent of corporate security directors surveyed rank domestic violence as a high security problem at their company.
- A large majority of employee assistance program (EAP) providers surveyed have dealt with specific partner-abuse scenarios in the past year, including an employee with a restraining order (83 percent) or an employee being stalked at work by a current or former partner (71 percent).

These facts and figures show what we now know to be true: Domestic violence is an issue that no employer can afford to ignore. With nearly one out of every three women reporting physical abuse by an intimate partner at some point in her lifetime,[3] it is a certainty that domestic violence is affecting the workplace in many companies.

> ...it is essential to establish and train a domestic violence response team to provide the front-line response to employees who choose to disclose their situations.

In addition to the exorbitant costs associated with domestic violence, employers face the specter of legal liability for failing to respond appropriately to this issue. In addition to traditional statutory and common law remedies, in the past three years alone more than 45 states and locales have enacted legislation or have adopted executive orders designed to create protections for victims of domestic violence.[4] In addition, the Victims' Economic Security and Safety Act—which would require private employers to make certain accommodations for employed victims of domestic violence—is currently pending before Congress.

These new laws are predicated on the understanding that the workplace is often a prime place for domestic violence to occur because the worksite may be the only place where the perpetrator can gain access to the victim. Moreover, perpetrators often deliberately abuse their victims during the workday because the perpetrators know that their victims fear losing their jobs if their employers realize what is happening. Employers who are unaware of the various laws governing their conduct in this area may face exposure to legal liability under the following laws:

- Occupational safety and health laws require employers to maintain a safe workplace.
- The Americans with Disabilities Act or state disabilities laws that may require job accommo-

dation of a victim of domestic violence who is or becomes mentally or physically disabled.
- Family and medical leave laws may require employers to grant leave to employers who are coping with serious health conditions resulting from domestic violence situations.
- Victim assistance laws may prohibit employers from taking adverse job actions against women who disclose their situation or who take time off from their jobs to deal with domestic violence-related issues.
- Victim assistance laws may require employers to grant periods of unpaid leave for employees to attend court appearances and medical appointments for themselves and/or their children.
- Antidiscrimination laws prohibit employers from discriminating against employees on the basis of their actual or perceived status as victims of domestic violence.
- Insurance legislation prohibits discriminating against victims of domestic violence in determining eligibility for, benefits under, and/or the cost of health, life, disability, auto, or homeowner's insurance.
- Unemployment compensation insurance laws may classify domestic violence as "good cause," and exclude domestic violence situations from "misconduct."

## WHAT EMPLOYERS CAN DO

Taking a proactive approach to domestic violence should include designing and implementing a specific policy covering domestic violence in the workplace. A domestic violence policy can stand alone or be integrated as an essential element of a general policy on violence in the workplace. It is vital to understand, however, that while the two policies may be addressed in tandem, issues related to domestic violence, because of its prevalence in and impact on the workplace, demand a specific analysis and implementation process.

The policy should focus on providing information and referrals to employees who are victims of domestic violence and should address issues related to the need for time off, security, and performance problems. It should also articulate an explicit zero-tolerance policy toward using the employer's time or resources to perpetrate domestic violence. Such an approach allows the employer to create a safer and more supportive environment while reducing its exposure to liability.

Before rolling out the policy, however, it is essential to establish and train a domestic violence response team to provide the front-line response to employees who choose to disclose their situations.

Once the policy is disclosed, the employer must provide training to supervisors, managers, and employees on the dynamics and impact of domestic violence. It is important to emphasize that domestic violence policies are not designed to place the employer or its response team members in the position of counselors or advocates. Rather, they are designed to mitigate the effects of domestic violence in the workplace by providing victims with a link to community resources that serve those functions. Thus, the employer's partnership with a local domestic violence agency is essential to carrying out the policy's central mission of providing information and referrals to employees. It also ensures that the employer becomes the link to resources rather than the resource itself.

As evidenced by the proliferation of protective legislation in this area, employers must act with extreme caution in ensuring that their responses to the effects of domestic violence in the workplace do not inadvertently violate federal, state, or local laws. The employer is tasked with applying its policies in a manner that does not discriminate against the victim on a prohibited basis and that fosters a safe work environment.

## NOTES

*Not her real name.

1. *See* Civil Action 01-CV-4277, U.S.D.C., E.D., Pa. (filed August 22, 2001).
2. *See* http://endabuse.org/programs/workplace/.
3. The Commonwealth Fund, *Health Concerns Across a Woman's Lifespan: 1998 Survey of Women's Health,* May 1999.
4. *See* generally www.nowldef.org/html/issues/work/ Factsheet Page.htm. Regarding insurance discrimination, see www.end abuse.org/statereport/list.php3.

**Stacey Pastel Dougan, Esq.,** is the assistant general counsel and a shareholder of Greenberg Traurig LLP. She is also the founder and former director of the Greenberg Traurig/Florida Coalition Against Domestic Violence Alliance for Battered Women. You can contact her at 305-579-0500, e-mail at dougans@gtlaw.com, or visit the firm's Web site at www.gtlaw.com. *The views expressed are solely those of the author and should not be attributed to the author's firm or its clients.*

From *Employee Benefit Plan Review,* February 2003, pp. 9-10. © 2003 by Aspen Publishers, Inc. Reprinted by permission.

SAFETY

# The Most Effective Tool Against Workplace Violence

You may consider training to be a function that's designed to enhance job skills, productivity, efficiency, and employee growth. While it certainly is all those things, it is also a valuable tool for protecting your employees from workplace violence.

Recent research by *HRfocus* publisher IOMA bears this out. The *2002 Security Management & Salary Survey* found that:

1. Companies that provide training to supervisors and employees in workplace-violence awareness are cutting their incidence rate for employee-on-employee violence.

2. With the incidences of violence between employees and non-employees growing, so is the need to train workers on how to handle disputes with outsiders.

## TRAINING AS PREVENTION

As reported by the 300 respondents to the IOMA survey, supervisor training seems to lead directly to reductions in employee-on-employee violence. Among the organizations that train supervisors to identify and address troubled workers, 20.2% reduced the number of violent incidents between employees. Only 17.9% of companies that don't conduct such training have been able to cut these incidents.

Providing workplace-violence training to all employees as opposed to just supervisors seems to make an even bigger difference: 21.9% of companies that do so reduced employee-on-employee violence, compared to 15.7% of companies that don't provide such training.

Devising a violence-prevention policy is the best place to start, even before training. Organizations with a written policy addressing workplace violence were 25% more likely to reduce violent incidents between workers in the past year than companies without such policies.

Some but not all experts see drugs as a contributing factor in workplace violence. *A significant finding:* Of employers that conduct drug testing, 23.3% reported reductions in incidents of violence between employees

compared to only 15.8% of companies that do no such testing.

*Other notable findings:*
- More than 20% of companies in the survey admitted that they have no written policy.
- Close to 40% provide no training on the subject.
- Almost half (48%) say they drug-test all employees.
- The failure of almost 10% of companies currently to track incidents of workplace violence makes it more difficult to target solutions to the workers most at risk. (For additional benchmarks, see the table, "Workplace Violence Prevention Programs, 2002, by Company Size.")

## VIOLENCE FROM OUTSIDERS

More responding companies report that violence between employees and non-employees is growing than report that it's decreasing. While the difference is minimal—just 20—the huge cost associated with this category of worker injury makes it a problem companies can't afford to ignore. (For additional data, see the figure, "Trends in Workplace Violence, 2001 vs. 2000.") Organizations need to acknowledge this problem and to include non-employees in their prevention strategies. While the majority of organizations cited "no change," in some areas the problem is growing: Twice as many retailers reported an increase in violent incidents as reported a decrease.

When it comes to violence from non-employees, how employees handle themselves can make the difference between gunshots and a peaceful resolution. *Case in point:* On May 31, 2002, at the Top Valu Market in Long Beach, Calif., a man with a gun opened fire, killing two customers and wounding four others, before being fatally shot by police. *What prompted this tragedy?* According to news reports, the shooting spree was the result of escalating hostility over the store clerk's refusal to cash the shooter's check.

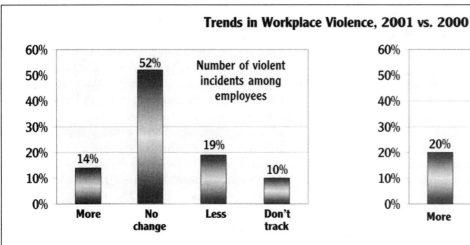

**Trends in Workplace Violence, 2001 vs. 2000**

Number of violent incidents among employees

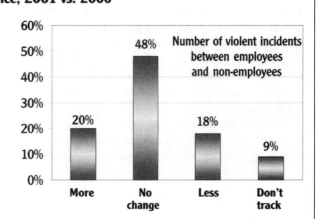

Number of violent incidents between employees and non-employees

Percentages do not add up to 100% because of some non-responses.

(Source: IOMA)

## Workplace Violence Prevention Programs*, 2002, by Company Size

| | Number of Employees | | | | | |
| --- | --- | --- | --- | --- | --- | --- |
| | 1 to 99 | 100 to 499 | 500 to 999 | 1,000 to 2,999 | 3,000 or More | All |
| Has a written workplace violence policy | 71% | 74% | 83% | 81% | 76% | 77% |
| Gives training to supervisors on how to handle workplace violence and spot troubled employees | 50 | 56 | 67 | 66 | 73 | 67 |
| Provides workplace violence awareness training to all employees | 54 | 57 | 70 | 59 | 57 | 59 |

*Based on responses from 320 companies. Industry of resondent companies: health care (23%); manufacturing (14%); retail (13%); financial/insurance/real estate (11%); education (6%); service/consulting (2%); non-profit (1%); other (26%); no response (3%).
(Source: IOMA)

This incident is not atypical of violent workplace events involving visitors, clients, or customers. Client frustration contributes significantly to the frequency of threats and attacks against employees, according to research published in *Security Journal* ("Addressing Staff Safety at High Risk Social Assistance Offices," Spring 2002, *SJ*, Perpetuity Press, +44 (0) 116-221-7778; www.perpetuitypress.co.uk). Safety efforts must look beyond specific controls, according to the study's author, Stephen Schneider, a research consultant and professor in crime prevention (Ryerson Polytechnic University, Toronto; srschneider@rogers.com).

"Increasing the safety of staff ... must also address the causal factors that give rise to these threats," he says.

### DEVELOP AN ACTION PLAN

What can you do to prevent violence in the workplace—besides providing better service and understanding that customer disputes can put employees at greater risk?

Panic alarms and timely emergency response teams can help, but perhaps your best prevention tools are the employees. You must see that workers who deal with frustrated or angry clients have the skills to resolve the situations peacefully, according to a report from the National Institutes for Occupational Safety & Health (NIOSH; www.cdc.gov/ niosh).

Although the NIOSH report ("Violence-Occupational Hazards in Hospitals," publication number 2002-101; April 2002) focuses on threats facing hospital workers, it identifies several risk factors that apply to employees in many industries. *The research shows that training is critical for employees who:*

- Have to manage crowds.
- Work directly with volatile people, especially individuals who are occasionally under the influence of drugs or alcohol.
- Deal personally with individuals who experience long waits for service.
- Deal with individuals in uncomfortable environmental conditions, such as heat, extreme cold, overcrowding, and so on.

- Must take away individuals' "rights," such as smoking.
- Restrict the movement of individuals, such as telling them where they cannot go.

Companies should develop policies for preventing and managing crises with potentially violent visitors or customers, and should train workers in recognizing and managing assaults, resolving conflicts, and maintaining hazard awareness.

*One idea:* Integrate safety training into customer service or regular job training. Some organizations teach employees how to handle potentially violent situations at the same time they teach sales or customer service skills. *NIOSH recommends that employees in high-risk environments receive training in:*

- **How to look for signals that indicate the potential for violence by:**
1. Noting verbal expressions of anger or frustration.
2. Spotting threatening gestures or other body language that suggest anger.
3. Recognizing indications of drug or alcohol use.
4. Looking for the presence of weapons or objects that individuals might use as weapons.
- **How to maintain behavior that helps defuse anger by:**
1. Exhibiting a calm, caring attitude.
2. Not matching threats.
3. Not giving orders.
4. Acknowledging the person's feelings (e.g., "I know you have been waiting a long time").
5. Avoiding any behavior that individuals may interpret as aggressive (e.g., moving rapidly, getting too close, touching, speaking loudly).
- **How to reduce the risk of getting in a violent situation by:**
1. Evaluating each situation for potential violence when entering a room or relating to a client, visitor, or customer.
2. Remaining vigilant throughout the encounter, looking for signals of escalating frustration.
3. Never isolating themselves with a potentially violent person.
4. Being aware of the path a potentially violent person will have to take to exit the environment and never standing between that person and the exit.
- **How to protect themselves from uncontrollable situations by:**
1. Knowing when to remove themselves from the situation.
2. Knowing the organization's procedures for calling for help.
3. Reporting any troubling incidents to safety and security staff, so they can accurately match safety controls against the risk.

---

From *HRfocus*, February 2003, pp. 11-14. © 2003 by IOMA (the Institute of Management & Administration), Editor, Sue Sandler, 212/244-0360, http://www.ioma.com. Reprinted by permission.

# The Battle Over Benefits

The **COST OF HEALTH CARE** is strangling companies, **PROMPTING STRIKES** and leaving an increasing number of Americans **WITHOUT ANY COVERAGE AT ALL**. Some companies are coping, but experts fear that a **SICK SYSTEM** will have to come close to collapse before there is reform.

## By Sheila Anne Feeney

FROM JANITORS IN NEW ENGLAND and autoworkers in the nation's heartland to grocery workers, bus mechanics and sheriff's deputies on the West Coast, union picketers are focusing renewed attention on the health-care crisis in America. At a time when health-care costs are rising faster than the rate of inflation and employers are aggressively revamping benefit options, the sight of cashiers and butchers fighting for health benefits is the latest, most arresting example of the mounting discontent and anger surrounding the subject of who pays what for health insurance.

In Southern California, the story isn't only about the 70,000 grocery-store workers battling attempts by supermarket employers to curtail medical benefits, says Kate Bronfenbrenner, director of labor education research at Cornell University. It's also about the customers who honored picket lines last month. "The unions are fighting for health benefits for everyone," Bronfenbrenner says. "They set the standard, and the public is sympathetic."

The recent strikes are symptomatic of the pressure that skyrocketing health-care costs place on all employers—public and private, union and non-union—and on labor and employee relations, says Joe Martingale, national leader for health-care strategy at Watson Wyatt Worldwide's New York office. "Unless we do something to resolve the health-care crisis, there won't be any winner in a strike like this," he says. "We have two choices. We can ask government to take over health care, which is not realistic. Or we can solve the problem from the bottom up: We all will have to be more involved in health care as powerful consumers."

Throughout the country, employers are persistently trying to reduce double-digit cost increases by making changes to their health-care plans, modifications that are shifting more of the expense to employees—from raising premiums for family members to offering greater choices of medical care. Employers, employees, health professionals and government officials are all questioning the old ways of providing health coverage, and racking their brains for new solutions. While there is little agreement on how to lower health-care costs, developing shrewder consumers is fast becoming the mantra of the times.

Some companies, like Sears, Roebuck & Co., are moving away from fixed-dollar co-payments to programs that require workers to pay a percentage of each medical bill. Sears also has reduced the number of HMOs it offers to employees, from 53 to 35 in 2003. Five years ago the company offered more than 200 HMOs, says company spokesman Stanley Aldis. Procter & Gamble Co. has increased co-payments from $12 to $15 for primary-care physicians, and from $15 to $25 for specialists, says company spokeswoman Vicky Mayer. Some prescription drugs that had been covered at 70 percent are now covered at 50 percent. Many other companies also are making it far more expensive to buy brand-name and designer drugs than generics. And a few are providing company-operated clinics that treat employees and their families.

In September, the Kaiser Family Foundation and Health Research and Educational Trust announced that health-care premiums rose 13.9 percent this year—the steepest increase in 13 years and the third consecutive year of hefty increases. Workers are paying 48 percent more than they did three years ago. There are indications, however, that rate hikes may begin moderating. Hewitt Associates is projecting a 12.6 percent increase for employers in 2004.

While some say the solution lies in nothing less than a national health plan and universal coverage, others, such as Larry Akey, director of communications for the Health Insurance Association of America, counter that such a major overhaul "risks disrupting the system and making it worse than it is."

## WHAT COMPANIES ARE DOING

Most employers are responding to cost increases in one of two ways, says Gary Kushner, president and CEO of Kushner & Co., a Portage, Michigan, benefits consulting firm. "One is a continuation of the status quo: year by year making plan-design tweaks and passing costs on to employees." Another trend is the now familiar option of "consumer-driven" health-care plans that give employees an annual cash allowance to spend on medical care. A survey by the American Management Association this year showed that 8 percent of respondents offered such a plan to their workers, among them Aon Corp., Medtronic Inc. and Raytheon. Another 40 percent were considering implementing similar models within the next six years.

Companies also are demonstrating far more interest in health-care appraisals and promoting group exercise and lifestyle improvements to curb disease, notes Lee Exton, vice president of The Segal Company in Glendale, California. No one disputes that comprehensive disease management improves outcomes and quality of life for patients, but "there is a lot of conflicting research as to whether it saves money," says Alwyn Cassil, spokeswoman for the Center for Studying Health System Change.

Dan Conroy, human resources manager for Nexen Group Inc., a manufacturer of brakes and clutches, last year began offering a consumer driven plan to the 150 employees of his Vadnais Heights, Minnesota, firm. "We didn't save a dime the first year," Conroy says. But this year when Nexen re-enrolled, the company paid 7 percent less. He says that most of the savings "came from [lower] reinsurance fees, but our utilization fees were also lower."

Overnight, Nexen's employees began calling free health-advice lines instead of running to the doctor, and they pushed their providers for generic drugs. "This is the only ray of light I've seen in terms of continuing to provide health insurance to employees. I'm surprised that people don't just go running and sprinting to this kind of plan," Conroy says.

"All the major carriers spent two years explaining why this model wouldn't work, and now they're offering it," adds Chris Delaney, a marketing vice president for Definity Health, a Minneapolis firm that was among the first to offer consumer-directed health-care plans in 2000. Delaney says that about a million people are enrolled in similar plans nationwide. Definity covers 320,000 of them.

Critics say that the plans are unproven, that they often present stopgap coverage problems and unfairly penalize workers who have several dependents with costly chronic conditions and health problems. They also say that, just as for-profit HMOs can be successful in tamping down costs for the first few years, there is a clear limit as to how much can be pared without compromising care.

## A UNIVERSAL SYSTEM: SAS

SAS, a billion-dollar-a-year private software company headquartered in Cary, North Carolina, has a lavish campus fitness facility plus a medical center with a staff of 55, including three family-practice physicians, 11 nurse practitioners and a part-time psychologist. "This is family practice in practice," says Gale Adcock, corporate health services manager. "Everyone would be in favor of universal health insurance if they had an SAS plan." While employees can use the SAS self-funded indemnity insurance to see outside doctors, 50 percent use the SAS health-care center for primary care and 90 percent make use of it each year. Last year, 7,500 employees and dependents used the center for things like pregnancy tests and flu shots, and for treatment of diseases ranging from bronchitis to diabetes.

Virtually every visit, procedure, shot and test at the medical center is free. Adcock, who points out that SAS hasn't had a losing year or a layoff or a turnover rate above 5 percent, says that the clinic actually contributes to the bottom line by saving the firm money in recruitment, replacement and time. SAS calculates that administering health care on-site saves about $500,000 in "hard" costs and another $500,000 in "soft" costs, such as employee time spent driving to outside doctors. By having health care that is exceedingly accessible (the center is open 12 hours a day and the average wait is five minutes), employees are more motivated to address incipient health conditions before they have a chance to become acute and costly.

*The immensity and seeming hopelessness of the health-care crisis have driven some executives to conclude that nothing less than a wholesale overhaul of the system is in order.*

Supplementing insurance with on-site primary care makes the most sense for self-funded companies with a workforce of at least 300 people, Adcock says. "If you want to do primary care for 200 people, this is not an effective way to deliver it. But we didn't start out as a Lexus; we began as a Volkswagen. We began in 1984 with just one nurse practitioner."

## A TOTAL OVERHAUL: RSD TRANSPORTATION

The immensity and seeming hopelessness of the health-care crisis have driven some executives to conclude that nothing less than a wholesale overhaul of the system is in order. Scott Perrault, controller for RSD Transportation Inc., in White River Junction, Vermont, is thinking that national health care may be the only answer. When Dr. Deborah Richter, a family-practice physician who is past president of Physicians for a National Health Program, asked for a meeting, he listened to her. She said that a 5.8 percent employer payroll tax and 2.9 percent employee payroll tax could whittle his overall costs from $500,000 to $700,000 a year down to a guaranteed $472,000. (Richter's numbers were to implement a single-payer system in Vermont. Other funding schemes for a national single-payer system typically require a 7 percent employer payroll tax, or involve taxing personal income.)

"I was very surprised by her numbers," Perrault says. "We'd have a lot more profit" under such a system if the percentages stayed stable, he notes.

RSD subjects prospective employees to pre-employment physicals, covers physicals and many preventive services at 100 percent and offers wellness programs. It also ratcheted up deductibles and co-pays, pitted insurers against each other to achieve the most economical package and still found costs bubbling up 5 to 10 percent a year. "There's only so much an organization can bear," Perrault says. "Where does it end?" He says that he can't even calculate the drain of all the executive hours spent on looking for ways to contain health-care costs. "I would love to be out of the health-care business."

Uwe Reinhardt, an internationally known health economist and the James Madison Professor of Political Economy at Princeton University, says that a Canadian-style health-care system would be cheaper for corporations for several reasons. Overhead costs would be dramatically diminished, he says, care would be distributed more rationally and effectively, and risks would be borne more equitably. But Reinhardt, who supports such a system financed by personal income taxes, says that most CEOs and chief executives eschew the idea because they preside over large personal fortunes that they prize more than increasing their companies' profits. He adds that employers like the fact that U.S. workers are tied to their jobs by the threat of losing health care for themselves and their families.

Not all corporations would benefit equally from a nationalized system. Under Richter's scheme, which would be financed by payroll taxes, "IBM would save a fortune," she says. Smaller firms that provide coverage would also save, but not as much. Companies that do not now provide benefits would face increased costs because they would be forced to ante up their fair share.

# INFORMED BUT DEMANDING: STANFORD

Stanford University has an unusually literate, intelligent workforce of 11,000 employees and 3,000 retirees who comprehend how individual health habits and consumer practices influence rising costs and enthusiastically participate in wellness programs. "The downside is that they do a lot of reading, hear all about the latest things, and they ask for it," says Sue Cunningham, Stanford's benefits program manager. The average Stanford employee is 48, which means that many are at an age when they are more likely to encounter costly illnesses and operations.

For 2003, the average health-care cost per employee was $5,873, and $3,919 per retiree on a Stanford plan involving Medicare supplementation. The total tab for medical, mental and drug benefits is projected to be $53 million for 2003. This year, the university began mining data from its claims to find out where cost increases were originating. "We're carving out our prescription drug plan so we can have all the claims in one place. We chose Express Scripts because they have very good data possibilities. All the drugs are priced at a negotiated rate.

We had a pharmacist do the negotiating." If a generic drug is available, the employee has no option but to take it. "That's built into the plan."

Cunningham would like to see the U.S. government follow the lead of other industrialized nations by imposing price controls on the pharmaceutical industry. Yet most of the increases she confronts come from fee increases for provider visits and hospitalizations. Stanford creates incentives to corral costs by paying the premiums for employees who choose the cheapest HMO option among its five plan offerings. California HMOs tend to be better than many offered elsewhere in the country and are not reviled there. "Here, the physician groups do utilization management and decide if an MRI is needed or not—not the carriers," Cunningham says. As a result, only 19 percent of Stanford employees enroll in the pricey PPO product.

Before lasting solutions to the health-care crisis can be found, experts say, it's essential for companies to understand where the costs are coming from. In a 2001 to 2002 study, PricewaterhouseCoopers found that fraud and abuse made up only 5 percent of the 13.7 percent rise in health-care costs for the previous year. Litigation and risk management represented another 7 percent of that increase. Heightened consumer demand and the cost of implementing government mandates and regulations were each responsible for 15 percent of the increases. The biggest drivers of increased costs were rising provider expenses, which made up 18 percent of the surge, and ever pricier drugs, medical devices and medical advances, which were blamed for 22 percent of higher costs. An analysis in the August 21 *New England Journal of Medicine* reports that administration costs accounted for 31 percent of all health-care expenditures in the United States, an average of $1,059 per capita.

In the coming months and years, it's unlikely that employers will be able to swing their way off the ropes alone. Still, Akey is hardly a lone voice when he says: "Employer-sponsored health insurance is a fact of life in America." Maybe so, but consumers will have to be move involved in cost cutting, Martingale notes. "That's what shows promise," the national health-care strategist says. "There is hope. But tensions between employers and employees will continue. Nobody's happy. If companies can't pay for benefits, and employees can't afford them, where's the money going to come from?"

---

SHEILA ANNE FEENEY *is a freelance writer who lives in New York, NY. To comment e-mail editors@workforce.com.*

From *Workforce Management,* November 2003, pages 29-32. Copyright © 2003 by Crain Communications. Reprinted by permission.

# The Cutting Edge of
# Benefit Cost Control

**Benefit costs are ripping a hole in the bottom line, and many employers don't see a way out.
But some executives are finding that they can cut, cost-share, and renegotiate their way to significant savings.**

*By Fay Hansen*

Robert B. Catell, chairman and CEO of KeySpan Corporation, the largest distributor of natural gas in the Northeast, closed out 2002 with an announcement that no CEO wants to make: Rising expenses from employee benefits will shave 20 to 30 cents off earnings of $2.86 per share that had been expected for 2003. Something has to be done.

With 12,000 mostly long-tenured employees spread over several states and organized into different unions, the Brooklyn-based company is short on cost-cutting options. The CEO'S aim traditionally has been to keep cost increases in line with the general rate of inflation. "In the past, this was a reasonable goal," says Elaine Weinstein, senior vice president of human resources. "However, given the escalating cost of health care, this is now a very aggressive target." In 2002, KeySpan's benefit costs rose 13 percent. For 2003, "our stretch goal is to keep the increase at 7 to 10 percent. If I achieve 7 percent, I'll be a hero."

---

**"We negotiate very aggressively with our health-benefit carriers, and because of the pressures they face, we have been able to extract some concessions."**

Elaine Weinstein, Senior VP of Human Resources, KeySpan Corp.

---

Weinstein faces the same deadly combination of rising pension contributions and runaway health-benefit costs that now preoccupies human resources executives at other top companies. Employers absorbed health-benefit cost increases averaging 15 to 20 percent in 2002 and budgeted for increases averaging 15 percent this year. Many must also ante up huge pension contributions forced by poor investment returns. "Equities have tanked, so our cash contribution is up dramatically," she says. "Our as-

sumption is that equity markets will remain flat for 2003, and all HR planning is based on that assumption." Watson Wyatt Worldwide reports that 30 percent of companies were forced to make cash contributions to their pension plans in 2002; 65 percent will have to do so this year.

With little or no revenue growth to cover these additional expenses, rising benefit costs are ripping a hole in the bottom line. Human resources executives are on notice from top management to contain or cut costs—now. Depending on the degree of economic pressure, the composition of the workforce, and conditions in the local labor market, executives are pursuing different objectives and strategies. Some are cutting benefits and slicing salary budgets to offset rising costs. Others are turning to aggressive vendor management to achieve cost reductions without cuts or greater employee cost-sharing. In all cases, successful cost control hinges on well-defined objectives, careful workforce analysis, and a holistic approach to the problem.

## Long-term, incremental change

Given KeySpan's workforce composition, Weinstein's goal of simply holding costs constant is daunting. Hemmed in by heavy contractual obligations and extremely low employee turnover, she focuses on long-term, incremental changes in both retirement and health-care benefits, and begins laying the groundwork before cost increases hit crisis proportions. "HR is extremely tough these days," she says, "and controlling costs is difficult, but my job is easier because my CEO and my company are very employee-sensitive, and I have tremendous access to and dialogue with top management."

Weinstein has the information and leverage she needs to make major changes because she sits on the company's

# Maytag: Solutions Found in Consolidation, Redesign, and Automation

**M**aytag Corporation executive vice president and CFO Steven H. Wood told analysts in November 2002 that the company had pulled $135 million out of cash flow for pension contributions in 2002 and would pay an additional $160 million in pension contributions plus higher retiree medical expenses in 2003. The Newton, Iowa, appliance manufacturer also faced increased health-benefit costs for its 21,000 employees worldwide. "There are union health plans that we cannot change, but we have reduced the number of plan offerings for salaried employees," says Tracy Sears, director of benefits programs. The company consolidated offerings in 2002 and estimates savings of $2 million for 2003. "Before we consolidated, we had 81 plans across the organization supplied by 50 different vendors," she says. "Now we're dealing with 12 vendors, so we will be able to reduce costs through economies of scale. Also, we're no longer offering an HMO option, so employees do not have first-dollar coverage.

The company is also addressing pension costs. Effective July 1, 2003, new hires will be offered a cash-balance plan and will not be eligible for retiree medical coverage. Current employees will be offered a choice between their current retirement plan and a cash-balance plan, and must meet new eligibility criteria for retiree medical coverage.

Maytag will shave almost $1 million off 2003 benefit costs with a new automated enrollment system from ProAct Technologies that went live in October 2002. Before automation, Maytag administered enrollment with staff at 12 regional offices. Five regional benefits administrators now perform the same functions. "Using an online system also frees up time for the regional benefits staff to communicate to each location the benefit costs for the site and a comparison to a company norm," Sears says. "Top management was behind the changes to support the head-count reduction and also felt there was a need to automate."

*—FH*

executive committee. "When I came into the company seven years ago and saw that there was no cash-balance plan, for example, I said to the committee, 'Let me show you some best practices and what we can do for new hires.' I drove the pension issue." She launched a cash-balance plan for managers in 2000 and for some unions in 2001 and 2002.

Of all the issues related to benefit cost increases at major companies, pension funding is now the most expensive and the most intractable. KeySpan's new cash-balance plan will cut the company's annual pension costs by 30 percent for each new hire, but moving existing employees into the new plan is a slow process. "Two-thirds of our employees are unionized, so we attempt to negotiate the cash-balance plan as various contracts come up, but our defined-benefit plan is still very dominant," Weinstein says. Cash-balance plans help control costs because final retirement benefits are not predetermined, as is the case in traditional defined-benefit plans. Benefits are based solely on the amount that accumulates in each employee's account from annual employer contributions, which are usually a percentage of salary, plus earned interest.

With a viable solution in place in the area of pensions, she is focusing on health-benefit costs. "We negotiate very aggressively with our health-benefit carriers, and because of the pressures they face, we have been able to extract some concessions," she says. The company is also inching up employee contributions for both union and nonunion workers. Management employees now contribute 23 percent of their premiums, up from 20 percent in 2002. KeySpan also adopted a three-tier design for its prescription program and eliminated multiple vendors to reduce administrative costs. A new mandatory mail-order program for recurring prescriptions has saved the company $1 million.

KeySpan's limited ability to find sufficient immediate savings in benefit costs has forced it to take a holistic, total-compensation approach to cost control. In February 2003, KeySpan froze all merit increases for 12 months for managerial employees and for 24 months for executives. "This has been traumatic for our company" Weinstein says. "The decision came from the top, and the impact starts at the top."

For some cost issues, top management approaches Weinstein with questions, and she does the research and provides the information that the executive committee needs. "Then we discuss it and vote on it," she says. In other cases, she initiates proposals for change. "There's a lot of verbal noise about HR being a business partner, but you must bring to the table a knowledge of the business or you can't possibly play a partnership role. If you can't do that, then all the talk is just garbage. I understand the business, which is why I can take an aggressive approach to defining the problems and proposing solutions."

## Deep cuts without layoffs

Human resources also took an aggressive approach at CUNA Mutual Group, which provides financial services to credit unions and their members. Vice president of compensation Teri Edman spent the better part of three months handling 80 percent of the analysis, design, and approval process to cut $23.2 million from the company's compensation and benefit costs for 2003. Like Weinstein, Edman operates in relatively tight spaces. Half of the company's 5,000 employees are at corporate headquarters in Madison, Wisconsin, two-thirds of them union-

# IGT: When Salary Cuts Are Not an Option

International Game Technology, a supplier of slot machines and other gaming devices based in Reno, Nevada, has been hit by double-digit health-benefit cost increases for its 4,000 employees. The message was clear, says Randy Kirner, vice president of human resources. "Either we make significant interventions to manage costs, or suffer cost increases outpacing our corporate revenue and earnings growth. Our dilemma on the employee side was equally compelling. We are an employee-oriented company and felt it was unfair to shift costs to employees to minimize corporate responsibilities. Cutting benefits was also distasteful." Cutting salaries or wages was "absolutely not an option," Kirner says. IGT is a growing company operating in one of the tightest labor markets in the country. Unemployment in Reno is a mere 3.2 percent.

Kirner turned to aggressive vendor management and new plan designs to control costs without cuts in wages or benefits or increased cost-sharing. "We engaged our broker, ABD Insurance and Financial Services, and other key stakeholders," he says. The result was a top-to-bottom re-evaluation of administration and design based on a careful analysis of utilization and options. The firm consolidated two company health plans into one PPO, which enabled it to submit RFPs to third-party administrators. "We determined we wanted to look at vendors offering catastrophic and large-case management, disease management, maternity management, and elec-

tronic access for the company, providers, and employees," Kirner says. The company chose a vendor on the basis of these needs and anticipates saving more than $1 million.

IGT also moved pharmacy management out of its PPO and into a separate company, which resulted in first-year savings of $300,000. In the process, the company identified an opportunity to change its delivery of specialty drugs, for additional savings of $25,000 a year. It also outsourced its COBRA/ HIPAA services, saving more than $25,000, and self-insured its vision plan. In conjunction with a new HRMS implementation, IGT tapped a data clearinghouse to improve benefit-billing accuracy.

IGT renegotiated its employee assistance program as well as short- and long-term disability and AD&D contracts for additional savings, and gained new features such as direct claim services and travel assistance. Finally, the company outsourced flexible spending account management, which increased service levels for employees while reducing internal costs. Kirner spent a great deal of time on the vendor and design overhaul. "The process was detailed and involved many, many sessions and decision points," he says, "but the projected savings will ease cost pressures." IGT carefully communicated the changes to employees. "Overall, employees were prepared for the changes and felt that the company had done its homework," he says.

---

ized. The company wanted cost improvements without significant staff reductions.

"Both our revenues and expenses have been dramatically affected by the economy, and the majority of our controllable expenses are staff-driven," Edman says. Human resources developed proposals for the changes; top management discussed them over a two-month period and gave final approval. Edman took a total-compensation approach. A substantial $15 million in savings will come from the elimination of the 2003 salary-increase budget, with no merit or across-the board increases for any employee group. The company also eliminated the annual holiday gift—$300 per employee—for both 2002 and 2003.

An additional $8.2 million in savings will come from health-care and vacation-benefit changes based on careful market analysis. "We targeted benefit plans in which we were over market and obtained feedback from our employees about what types of changes were most acceptable to them," Edman says. To minimize the impact on recruitment and retention, "we modeled the cost savings of various alternatives and compared the proposed changes to market-competitive data and to our own experience in recruiting."

Although many employers have eliminated HMO plans, which now register the highest cost increases of all plan types, CUNA Mutual kept its HMO but added co-

pays for office visits. It also joined the significant employer shift to a three-tier prescription plan, increased drug co-pays, and obtained new networks for its medical-indemnity and dental plans. Edman anticipates saving $3 million from the combined health-benefit changes.

The company will save $5.2 million from a new vacation-buyback program. "We had a very generous carry-over provision that allowed employees to accumulate up to two years' worth of vacation earnings," Edman says. "This unused vacation had grown to an expense liability of $24 million. We needed to decrease this expense, but because of our workload, we could not afford to have employees taking larger than normal amounts of vacation." Under the new program, employees can elect to give up earning new vacation for 2003, and in exchange can sell for cash an equal number of days from their carryover. They also commit to using an equal number of days from their carryover for time off this year.

CUNA Mutual carefully communicated the reasons for the changes to employees. "We illustrated the negative trend in our revenues and expenses over the past few years and our projections for 2003 and beyond," Edman says. "We explained the environmental economic factors that are beyond our control, and demonstrated our need to take action now to protect our future." The company has not experienced higher turnover or a drop in benefit enrollments because of the cost-reduction measures, but

# Random Cuts Can Endanger Performance

Jane Paradiso, practice leader for workforce planning at Watson Wyatt Worldwide, offers this cautionary message: "Before you begin cutting benefits, take a step back. HR executives tend to be reactive and often don't have the metrics needed to look strategically at what is best for the organization."

Cutting benefits without clear objectives and consideration of the impact on employees can undermine performance. Any changes in benefit plans should be part of workforce planning, which entails analyzing the demographics for employees and their dependents, identifying the most important positions, and calculating turnover and replacement costs. "With this information in hand, you can create an ROI model to determine which cuts make sense and what savings can be anticipated," she says. "This is an unemotional analysis that looks at costs and the level of risk involved."

Paradiso advises executives to look at the problem holistically and scientifically, and aim for a package of solutions—a combination of cutting some benefits and adding others—that is attuned to the needs of the organization, particularly in terms of retaining key people. "Otherwise, you'll be left with a company of lower performers, and any cost savings derived from benefit cuts will be lost," she says.

Effectively communicating the changes to employees is absolutely critical. "Make it honest, and make sure employees understand why the cuts are necessary." She advises against asking employees for input on possible benefit cuts. "This approach frequently backfires," Paradise says. "If you find that you cannot act on their recommendations, which is often the case, then you are in a difficult situation. It's best for executives to make the decisions about cuts on the basis of business needs and objectives. This is their job and what they get paid for."

Edman continues to monitor employee reaction. "We stay in touch with our employees through various feedback methods, including electronic communications, departmental meetings, staff forums with the CEO, and culture surveys."

KeySpan provides comprehensive information to its employees about its benefit changes. "Our communica-tion strategy is a cascading model," Weinstein says. "After the executive committee approves the changes, we first present them to the officers, who then present the information and explanations to their employee groups." For the presentations, KeySpan uses a program called "Straight Talk," which scripts the communications delivered by officers. The scripts for benefit changes are "a way to assist employees in managing their expectations about employee contribution increases and to explain why changes are necessary," she says. An employee-benefits newsletter, the company's intranet, and open-enrollment packages also explain benefit changes in detail. "By the time employees receive the open-enrollment packages, they have already heard the message three or four times."

Working in relatively restricted environments and with specific mandates to control costs without jeopardizing employee relations, Weinstein and Edman have found substantial long-term savings. KeySpan and CUNA Mutual are among a growing number of employers that are adjusting total compensation to address the crisis in benefit costs. Benefit cost increases have outpaced wage and salary cost increases for the past three years and will continue to do so for the foreseeable future. Almost one-fourth of employers have decreased or are considering decreasing 2003 salary-increase budgets to offset rising health-care and pension costs, according to a survey by Mercer Human Resource Consulting. The holistic approach to cost-cutting at KeySpan and CUNA Mutual erases the line commonly drawn between salary and benefits budgets and allows executives full range of movement to tackle rising costs.

Most companies have already picked all the low-hanging fruit among benefit cost-cutting options without achieving sufficient results. Many continue to approach cost-cutting on an ad hoc basis, without careful analysis of which cuts will yield the greatest long-term savings with the lowest impact on business objectives. Executives at companies with focused strategies can push their costs into more acceptable territory, secure support from top management, and minimize the impact on employees.

*Fay Hansen is a business and finance writer based in Cresskill, New Jersey. To comment, e-mail editors@workforce.com.*

# UNIT 6

# Fostering Employee/ Management Relationships

## Unit Selections

## Key Points to Consider

- Unions have a special exemption under the anti-trust laws. Do you think this is fair? Why or why not? Are the laws being fairly administered?

- Taking disciplinary action is often one of the most difficult and unpleasant activities that a manager must do. If you were a manager, how would you take disciplinary action? If you were the employee being disciplined, what would you do? What would you do about executives who have committed fraud? What do you think about the Enron scandal? What about the role Arthur Andersen played in the scandal?

- What are some of the advantages of hiring temporary employees? How would you feel about being one? For over a year?

- Should managers be concerned about ethics? Why or why not? Do you think that unethical behavior can be economically justified?

 **Links: www.dushkin.com/online/**
These sites are annotated in the World Wide Web pages.

**Fair Measures: Legal Training for Managers**
*http://www.fairmeasures.com/asklawyer/archive/*

The American labor movement has a long history dating back to the start of the Industrial Revolution. That history has been marked by turmoil and violence, as workers sought to press their demands on business owners, whether represented by managers or entrepreneurs. The American labor movement exists because working conditions, pay, and benefits were very poor during the early years of the Industrial Revolution in both the United States and the rest of the world. It should be remembered that the American labor movement is only a small part of a broader, worldwide labor movement that includes most Western European societies. The working conditions under which the first American industrial workers labored would be unacceptable today. Child labor was common. There are documented instances of 6- and 7-year-old children, chained to machines for 12 hours a day, 6 days a week, who threw themselves into the machines—choosing death over life in the dehumanized and mechanized existence of the early factory. Conditions in some factories in the North prior to the Civil War were so infamous that Southern congressmen used them as a justification for the institution of slavery. Slaves sometimes lived in better conditions than the factory workers of New England and many other Northern states.

Unions exist because workers sought a better working environment and a better standard of living. Companies often took advantage of employees, and the government sided with management and the owners, frequently quelling strikes and other forms of labor protest initiated by the workers. Such incidents as the Pullman Strike, the Hay-Market Square Riot, and the Homestead Strike exemplify the struggle of the American labor movement to achieve recognition and success in the attempt to improve the lives of all workers, whether unionized or not. The victories of labor have been hard fought and hard won. But, labor has not been without blemish in the struggle for worker's rights. The Marion County Turkey-Shoot, in Southern Illinois, probably the most violent day in American labor history, involved coal miners deliberately chasing and killing strikebreakers from the mines.

During the past hundred years, the fortunes of the American labor movement have varied, and now their fortunes may be taking an even deeper downward turn, with attempts at unionization even more difficult as seen in "The Barbed Wire Straitjacket."

Unions have been able to achieve their gains through the mechanism of collective bargaining. The individual has very little bargaining power when compared to a company, especially huge companies such as General Motors or General Electric. Collective bargaining allows workers to pool their collective resources and power to bargain with the corporation on a more equal footing. Unfortunately for the unions, many of the industries in which they are strongest are in decline. New leadership is necessary if the American labor movement is to survive and rebound in the next century and if it is to serve as a useful organ of society.

A union's ultimate weapon in contract negotiations, the strike, represents a complete breakdown of discipline from management's perspective. Disciplinary situations are almost always unpleasant and today they can often lead to court cases, with all of the attendant legal questions and problems. A key to effective

disciplinary action is documentation of employees' actions and the steps that were taken to correct them. "The ABC's of Employee Discipline" are outlined in the article of that name. Management needs to implement procedures and policies to assure employees are treated fairly and equitably in the workplace.

The American labor movement has come a long way since the first strike by printers in Philadelphia in 1786. The journey, while difficult, has led to greater justice in the workplace and an increased standard of living for the nation as a whole. Unions have experienced both declines and increases in membership, but they have endured as a powerful social, political, and economic force. Whether or not they will again successfully "reinvent" themselves and adapt to a changing environment is a major question.

During the past fifteen years, primarily as a result of the dislocations in the job market, temporary workers became available to organizations. There are certain advantages to this situation for the employer, but perhaps not so for the employee, as discussed in "Temporary Worker, Permanent Loser."

There is also the issue of ethics. How companies treat their employees and their customers is going to be of increasing concern in the future. Ethical behavior will be at a premium, and managers know that it will be part of the job of "Big Companies to Teach Business Ethics to Employees." Unfortunately, some managers of organizations will always make the economic/legal calculation that doing something that is illegal or unethical at best will benefit them, if not their shareholders, customers, and/ or employees. "Accounting for Corporate Behavior" will always be a problem no matter what the laws may be or the enforcement of those laws. Someone will always try to get away with some sort of illegal, unethical, or dishonest gain. Flawed human nature will always play a role.

# The Barbed Wire Straitjacket

## By David Bacon

In 1981, when President Ronald Reagan replaced thousands of air traffic controllers and threw their leaders in jail, the permanent replacement of strikers became a normal aspect of U.S. labor relations. Strikes became far riskier for workers than they'd been at any time since the turn of the century.

Labor relations are now undergoing a similar, equally profound change. West coast dockers have compared the new terrain they faced in bargaining their recent contract to negotiations in a barbed wire straitjacket. Although their union and the world's largest shipping companies reached agreement on a new pact in late November, the circumstances overshadowing the talks were a clear warning to the rest of labor throughout the country.

A new attitude towards unions under the Bush administration is changing that terrain. Threats and legal intervention by the Federal government essentially made job action by longshore workers, intended to pressure their employers to arrive at an equitable settlement, as risky as the air traffic controllers strike a generation ago.

"Given what we went through over the last six months, including the lockout of workers in every port, and then the invocation of the Taft-Hartley Act, we're glad we were able to reach an agreement at all," explained Steve Stallone, communications director for the International Longshore and Warehouse Union (ILWU). "So the fact that we were able to make progress on all three issues important to us was a big achievement."

In December, representatives of the local unions that work the docks from San Diego to Canada met for four days, and after intense discussion, recommended by a 92.4 percent margin that ILWU members ratify the package in January (results were still not known at the time this article is written).

Other voices in the union, however, were critical. "A labor contract is much more than benefits," said San Francisco longshoreman Jack Heyman. "The truth is that labor can not negotiate a good contract with a Taft-Hartley gun pointed at its head.... We, longshore workers, should reject this contract and send our negotiating committee back, this time to negotiate with some muscle by lining up concrete support in the U.S. and internationally."

Longshore workers went into negotiations last June with three goals, according to Stallone.

- They wanted to preserve their healthcare benefits in the face of demands by the Pacific Maritime Association that they pay part of skyrocketing costs
- They wanted increases in their pensions

- They wanted to ensure that employer proposals to implement new technology wouldn't result in the loss of jobs

The new agreement preserves longshore workers' health benefits with no copayment by workers, at an estimated present cost to employers of $220 million annually. By the end of the six-year agreement, that cost is estimated to rise to $500 million. The pension settlement will increase benefits by 60 percent over the same period.

But both provisions came at a cost. The PMA will implement a new system for tracking container movement using scanners and other computer-aided devices, replacing the system under which longshore clerks manually entered information into the shippers' database. That will eventually eliminate about 400 jobs, out of a total clerk workforce on the west coast of 1,200. No clerk will actually lose his or her job, since the contract guarantees 40 hours of work a week for the career of every current member. But in the future, the number of jobs covered will be reduced. In return, the union was able to win jurisdiction over jobs planning the movement of containers on trains and in yards on the waterfront. Those jobs were previously outsourced.

The objective of the employers was to keep workers using the new technology out of the union entirely.

Workers in these categories also included vessel planners, who tell the cranes where to put containers on the ships, and clerical workers in company offices. A few hundred of them have already joined the ILWU in many ports, attracted by its high wage rates. To make up for the potential job loss among the clerks, the union sought to include them in all ports by extending its jurisdiction. Now it will have to organize them.

"There are problems with the settlement, as you might expect from any contract negotiated under the gun of Taft-Hartley," Stallone noted. "The wage differential between the highest- and lowest-paid increased, which we've always fought against." In addition, there is now a new differential between the wages of drivers in the huge container cranes and those operating cranes used to load and unload bulk cargo.

The six-year agreement is also unusual. Unions normally seek to limit contracts to two or three years, since inflation can spiral out of control, taking large chunks out of paychecks. Other changes involving automation and technology can be difficult to resolve under agreements that don't foresee them. The ILWU agreed to the long term in order to space the large pension increase out over a number of years. The expiration of the agreement in 2008 also means that the union might avoid renegotiating it under Bush, even if he's reelected in 2004.

The bargaining strategy of the Pacific Maritime Association rested on removing the union's ability to exert pressure during negotiations to protect wages and conditions on the docks. With the Bush administration in office, now was the time, employers believed, to take their best shot.

Before negotiations began in June, the shippers and some of their biggest customers, including the Gap, Target, Mattel, and Home Depot, organized the West Coast Waterfront Coalition. Together, they held secret meetings with a Bush administration task force headed by White House advisor Carlos Bonilla. Once negoti-

ations began, Homeland Secretary Tom Ridge, and representatives of the Department of Labor, phoned ILWU President Jim Spinosa, warning him that the Administration would view any strike or interruption of work on the docks as a threat to national security. They threatened to invoke the Taft-Hartley Act, to use the military to replace striking workers, to place the waterfront under the Railway Labor Act (making a strike virtually illegal), and removing the union's ability to negotiate a single labor agreement covering all ports on the coast.

The ILWU avoided being provoked into a strike, but finally, at the peak shipping season, employers locked out their own workers. As a pretext, the PMA accused the union of organizing an alleged work slowdown. According to the *Journal of Commerce*, however, 30 percent more cargo was crossing the docks than last year—the greatest volume in history. The speedup on the docks was so intense that the accident rate shot up, costing the lives of five longshore workers in 2002. When the union told its members to work at a safe speed, the PMA called it a slowdown.

Once the dockers were locked out, employers then demanded Bush invoke Taft-Hartley. The Administration's legal brief before Judge Alsup voiced a startling new philosophy, elaborated by Defense Secretary Donald Rumsfeld. He held that all commercial cargo could be considered important to the military, not just specifically goods intended for military use abroad. Any stoppage on the docks, therefore, was a threat to national security.

Instead of defining a threat to national security in terms of vital life-dependent services, this use of national security defines it as economic. Any strike halting the continued operation of an industry or a large profitable enterprise could be defined as such a threat and made illegal.

PMA based its strategy on this philosophy. Long before negotia-

tions even started, it sponsored a steady media drumbeat announcing that a waterfront strike would send the economy into a tailspin. One study made in April predicted losses of $1-2 billion a day. The study was made by a Lancaster, Pennsylvania management consultant firm, Martin Associates, and paid for by the PMA. During the lockout, those figures were often quoted in the press as a measurement of actual losses, not predicted ones.

After U.S. District Court Judge William Alsup invoked Taft-Hartley, using those numbers as a justification, Patrick Anderson of the Anderson Economic Group made another study. He was only able to document actual losses of $1.67 billion, or $140 million a day. The higher figure, he said, was "closer to the economic impact of sinking the ships than delaying them." By then, however, the original figures had already justified Federal action.

At the beginning of October, the men and women of the docks went back to work, after having been locked out for 12 days. They returned, not voluntarily, as they had offered to do from the beginning, but under the Federal injunction won by the shipping corporations. Bargaining continued for another month, therefore, under the Taft-Hartley Act's 80-day "cooling off" period.

On the surface, it seems incomprehensible why the association would need a Federal order to open the gates of the closed terminals. After all, they'd shut them themselves and could have opened them at any time. But the resumption of work was never really the issue. Instead, the PMA wanted two things. It wanted a guarantee that dockers would be forced to continue unloading ships through the peak shipping season, when goods traveling from the sweatshops of the eastern Pacific rim are en route to stores for the Christmas rush. It wanted to make the union so vulnerable that it would be unable to put any pressure on employers during negotiations.

After work resumed, the PMA continued to accuse the union of slowing the pace as a means of threatening to invoke further Federal intervention. "The ILWU is playing games with the U.S. economy, and inflicting economic pain and hardship on scores of companies and their employees," said Joe Miniace, PMA director. Longshore wages were never the primary issue. The hourly rate on the docks, prior to the new contract, ranged from $27.68 to $33.48—about the same as a plumber or electrician. These are good wages in terms of the U.S. industrial average, but the shipping companies never claimed poverty, and are making large profits.

At the root of the dispute was the PMA's decision to try to end an arrangement that successfully allowed the introduction of advanced technology onto the docks for the last 40 years. In 1960, the union agreed that employers could introduce the first container cranes, the giant machines that now move cargo containers on and off the huge ships built specially to carry them. Even though this change cost the jobs of tens of thousands of west coast dockers, the union agreed that so long as its members did the new jobs technology produced, it would not try to stop it.

Over the coming two decades, the companies want to automate shipping far beyond the use of automated scanners and tracking devices. In their vision of the future, cranes and dockside machines will eventually be operated by remote control, perhaps by people miles away from the wharves. That day, however, is further in the future than the expiration of the present contract. The definitive battle to determine whether the philosophical framework of the 1960 agreement still holds—technology for jobs—was not fought to a conclusion this time around.

What did surface, however, was the new interventionist attitude of the Bush administration, justified in the name of national security. While a contract is in place, the new Republican-dominated Congress could still implement the threats made by Bush when negotiations started. One possible move might place the union under the Railway Labor Act, eliminating its right to strike. Even under Clinton, with Democrats in control of the Senate, Congress placed Federal Express under the RLA, effectively ending efforts by its workers to organize. A Republican Congress might also break up the ILWU's coastwide contract into separate agreements in every port, making strikes pointless, since employers would be able to ship goods to working ports while workers struck in others.

Agreeing to a six-year contract was designed to forestall that possibility. "We think it will help avoid legislation coming after us," said Stallone. "By showing labor stability on waterfront, we're hoping that problem won't resurface after Congress convenes in January."

But the Bush administration, which also used back-to-work orders against employees at Northwest and United Airlines last year, has established a precedent. Interruptions of economic activity, this new doctrine says, are a threat to national security. As a result, other workers may see the Federal government intervene forcefully on their employer's side.

David Bacon is a freelance writer and photographer.

# the abc's of employee discipline

By William Cottringer, Ph.D.

In any business or industry, it is important to establish high standards of performance and conduct. From time to time supervisors are required to discipline employees in order to enforce the expected work standard.

Carrying out employee discipline can have a major impact on the company and on individual employee's lives. It is critical to take the appropriate action in being fair and considering all the relevant facts.

By following this simple ABC system for disciplining employees, you will be successful in assuring a good work performance standard and helping your company meet its business goals by providing quality products or services in whatever industry you are part of.

## ACT

A common mistake supervisors make is to not take appropriate preventative action to catch a work problem in the making, when the employee can still be "rescued." Problems such as chronic lateness, poor performance, lack of teamwork and negative attitudes can not be corrected without immediate action from the beginning. Two months later is too late. All disciplinary actions should be proceeded by a clear communication of expectations and prompt feedback when those expectations are not being met.

Of course, some work rule violations are non-negotiable and once all the facts are collected. immediate ac-

tion must be taken—which is usually termination. This is true in cases such as theft, serious insubordination, substance abuse, serious safety violations, verbal abuse of clients, taking company secrets and other behaviors that are unlawful, jeopardize the safety and welfare of employees or put the business in serious risk.

In other situations, an employee may need to be suspended or removed from the site until a proper investigation can be conducted.

Cases such as these may involve suspected theft reported by a client, a sexual harassment complaint, a work accident or other conduct that might put the company business or other employees in jeopardy.

Other violations should follow a system of progressive discipline, in which the least harsh corrective action is implemented first and then harsher ones to follow. The object is to get the employee's attention before the performance problem becomes a chronic habit. Be fair, consider all relevant facts and then act. Act first by providing prompt and clear feedback about the specifics of the problem, explain why the problem can't continue, communicate the desired expectation and set the consequences for continued failure. Then make sure you follow up.

Employee discipline is an essential part of effective management. There are good reasons to act including:

- To change problem behavior
- To maintain performance standards

- To meet business goals
- To protect rights and due process
- To identify any unclear procedures
- To correct wrong workplace conditions

## BE FAIR

Employee discipline has to be carried out in a consistent and fair manner or otherwise it may do more harm than good. Before you decide to discipline an employee over a work rule violation, ask a few key questions:

- Does the employee understand exactly what is expected and is he or she able to do the job?
- Are there any performance barriers or other legitimate problems that need to be removed?
- Is the violation strictly willful misconduct or intentional poor performance?
- Have personality issues been separated from performance ones?
- Is the rule or policy reasonable and necessary for the safe, legal and productive operation of the company?
- Has the rule or policy been properly communicated and distributed to all employees? Are all employees aware of the rule and do they really

understand it? Has there been adequate training?

- Has the rule been consistently enforced in the past?
- Have other employees been disciplined for the same offense throughout the company?
- Has there been a thorough, prompt and unbiased investigation conducted?
- Have all witnesses been contacted who can help prove or disprove the violation?
- How condemning is the evidence? Who is most credible and why?
- What needs to be done that will balance the needs of the individual employee and the good of the over all organization?

You may want to create your own checklist of questions to ask in order to help you remain objective and fair. As a supervisor you are required to avoid doing anything that might be perceived as being inconsistent and unfair. One mistake in the area can be costly.

# CONSIDER THE FACTS

Another common mistake supervisors make is to arrive at a judgment of guilt and plan the punishment before taking the time to do a thorough investigation. It is imperative to get at all the relevant facts. Sometimes the last bit of evidence that is most likely to be missed can change the entire direction of a case. Below are several questions you should ask in order to determine the most appropriate disciplinary action to take, once you have completed a good investigation to verify the offense.

- How condemning is all the evidence? How serious was this offense? What were the actual consequences? What was the intention? How deliberate was it?
- What kind of prior record does the employee have?
- Are there any mitigating or aggravating circumstances of the violation?
- What is the attitude of the employee toward the violation?

- What is the likelihood of the employee changing for the better?
- What has been the practice in the past with similar violations?
- Will the disciplinary action or lack of it adversely effect the company operation?
- Are the intended disciplinary measures appropriate for the offense, all things being considered?

Be proactive in preventing minor performance and conduct issues before they become serious problems.

Take the time to be fair, consider all relevant facts and then act appropriately to carry out a system of employee discipline that will encourage all employees to help the company achieve its goals.

WILLIAM COTTRINGER, Ph.D., is a business consultant, sport psychologist and college teacher in St. Louis, Missouri. He is the author of *You Can Have Your Cheese & Eat It Too*, published by Executive Excellence. He can be reached at 1(618) 288-4956 or ckurtdoc@charter.net.

From *Supervision,* Vol. 64, No. 4, April 2003, pages 5, 7. Copyright © 2003 by National Research Bureau, 320 Valley Street, Burlington, Iowa 52601. Reprinted by permission.

# Three Strikes, You're Out:
# HOW TO PLAY FAIR AT FIRING

## by Claire Sykes

It's one of the toughest things you'll ever do as owner or manager of your business. But when you've had it with your receptionist's tardiness or you catch your stock person stealing, it's time to terminate. Make sure you do it right. Be precise with your decision, prepared with written documentation, and professional when you break the news.

Terminate fairly, and prevent further harm to your company. A fired, angry employee might bad-mouth you and/or seek litigation. For the least disruption to your business, put careful thought and preparation into the firing process.

### TO FIRE OR NOT TO FIRE
The decision to terminate, however, may not be your wisest choice. Dave Allison, president of Allison & Associates, a business training company in Duluth, Minn., suggests instead of forcing the employee to leave, leave it to him whether he'll change or quit. "Calmly confront the employee with the specific problem behavior," such as too many customer complaints or personal phone calls. "Objectively describe his behavior, don't interpret it, so the person has no

room to argue," states Allison. "Tell him your concerns about his behavior, and ask how he feels about that. Then give him one chance and a couple of days."

If the employee changes his behavior, great; if he opts to quit, there's no lawsuit. And what if he does neither? "Write a statement to that effect, and ask the employee to sign it," continues Allison. "If he refuses, get a witness to hear him say that. At this point, you'll have to fire him, but at least you're completely, and most likely legally, justified."

This approach takes practice and requires the employer to be in control enough to let the employee control his own destiny, something many business owners may find difficult. If you're one of them, consider other alternatives to firing. Provide the employee with more training or counseling, or place him in a different position or department. Consider giving the person more than one chance to change and prove himself.

Scottsdale, Arizona-based business advisor Richard S. Deems, Ph.D., president of WorkLife Design and author of *I Have to Fire Someone!*

(American Media Publishing), says, "Some companies spend lots of time and energy to make sure the employee has every chance; others give just a couple of warnings. Whatever your approach, be consistent throughout all departments."

Be clear with at least one valid reason to fire, citing company policy for support. Before you make your decision to terminate, be prepared to legally defend it. "Anyone can sue for anything, and the burden of proof is on the employer," says Anita Gorino, SPHR (Senior Professional in Human Resources), president of Creative Resources in Thousand Oaks, Calif.

### GET READY
Once you're set on firing an employee, prepare yourself for the termination meeting with the following points in mind:
- Keep it private. Tell only the employee's supervisor of your plans to terminate, so the person doesn't hear about it from the rumor mill.
- Have documented warnings ready. The employee should already be familiar with these from previous meetings with you or his

# WHAT IF?

Most termination meetings go smoothly, without incident. But even the most prepared and experienced business owner may encounter a difficult situation while breaking the bad news.

## WHAT IF THE EMPLOYEE...

### ... STARTS CRYING?

Just pause and give room to cry. "But if the tears don't stop in a reasonable amount of time, gently encourage continuation of the meeting," says Gorino.

### ... GETS ANGRY?

If the employee starts yelling loudly, open your office door so others don't think you're hurting him. Then escort the person out of the building.

### ... DOESN'T SAY ANYTHING?

"Don't push him," says Gorino. "Give the employee written documentation of the firing, see him to the door, and invite him to call you later to discuss it."

### ... WON'T LEAVE THE BUILDING?

Don't physically grab him yourself—that's fuel for a lawsuit. Instead, call a security guard or the police to show the employee out.

### ... THREATENS OR DISPLAYS VIOLENCE?

Don't attempt to resolve the situation on your own. Have your fingers poised to dial 911, and be ready to get out of there.

supervisor in attempts to change his behavior.

- Prepare the exit letter. State the reason(s) for firing, the dates of employment, and any continuing benefits.
- Cut the final paycheck. Pay the person through the date of the termination meeting, and prepare to hand the check to him then.
- Choose the right time. Early in the week is best, so the person can immediately look for another job, says Gorino.
- Choose and prepare the right place. Make it private, and remove anything in the room that could be used as a weapon.

## WHEN IT'S TIME TO SAY GOODBYE

When you're well prepared, you can present the bad news with authority and grace—and stay out of court. So, when the meeting time comes:

- Don't do it alone. It takes two to fire fairly, one to control the meeting and the other to witness it.
- Be prompt. Call the employee in for the meeting as soon as possible to avoid any tension or added stress.
- Be brief. Keep the meeting short to discourage emotional buildup and the employee's attempt to negotiate for alternatives.
- Stay calm. Remain in a controlled state of mind so you don't say something you might regret.
- Get to the point. Start with a description of the person's offense(s) and a history of the chances you've given him, and then break the news.
- Focus on the behavior. Emphasize that your decision is based on the person's actions, not on who he is as a person.
- Put an end to it. Express your decision as final, and be prepared to repeat yourself if the employee tries to refute you.

- Say goodbye for good. The sooner the person leaves, the better, so you don't invite any inappropriate behavior.

## AFTERWARDS

If you want to position yourself as an employer of choice, continues Deems, "There's no better way to do it than by treating your employees well, even once you've fired them. They'll be more likely to speak well of your company. Employers forget this connection."

Indeed, your job isn't over just because the fired staff member has shut the door for good on your company. After the termination meeting:

- Write up a summary. Document the meeting date and details, and file it away in case of a lawsuit.
- Inform the staff discreetly. Only you or a supervisor should tell coworkers the employee has been fired.
- Give minimal information to prospective employers. Provide only dates of employment at your company.
- Provide post-employment assistance. Offer to help the employee rewrite his resume, or hand him a list of job counselors.

## A LEARNING EXPERIENCE

Do all you can to avoid firing someone, short of hanging on to an unsatisfactory employee just because you don't want to do the deed. Remember, it's all part of your job as owner or manager of your business. Sure, it's never easy, but when there's no other choice—fire away! View the loss as an opportunity to learn how to make better hiring decisions and prevent firing someone else in the future.

Claire Sykes (claire@sykeswrites.com) is a freelance writer living in Portland, Ore.

From *Office Solutions,* March/April 2003, pp. 23-24. © 2003 by Claire Sykes. Reprinted with permission of the author.

**My Turn**

# Temporary Worker, Permanent Loser?

## I can deal with the low pay and lackluster love life.
## But please, don't ask me if I'm having fun yet.

### BY MICHAEL RYBICKI

ONE DAY I WAS TALKING WITH ONE OF my fellow temporary employees when he let it drop that he merely uses temping to supplement the income from his private business. So I asked him how he employs himself. Turns out he pet-sits on the weekends.

That gives you a good idea where temps stand on the vocational food chain—scooping poop starts to look like ambition. I'm a grown man with a bachelor's degree, and I am a temp. A staffing solution. A job gypsy. One of those shiftless mercenaries your company calls in when a menial task can't be put off any longer. If there are data to be entered, files to be filed or bulk to be mailed, I'm your man. And like a certain bug-eyed comedian, I am respect-deprived.

Nobody likes temps, and it's not out of jealousy. On the infrequent occasion that I land an interview for a permanent job, my temping background is openly regarded with suspicion. Employers assume that I am by nature capricious and disloyal. You'd think, on grounds of economic principle—temps keep wages low and profits high—that I'd engender more reverence. I'm "flexible." Isn't that what they want?

Granted, when it comes to reliability, temps aren't exactly Chevy trucks. Sure, there may be some who have used the company phone to call foreign countries. And yes, I was on the clock when I downloaded those pictures. I just don't see how this separates me from regular employees. Just because I don't work in the same building every day doesn't mean I can't wait to swipe all the glue sticks or go out to lunch and never come back.

My permanent co-workers (henceforth, "perms") treat me much better. Many apologize for the work their company assigns, assuming it to be the most degrading task I've ever undertaken, when in reality it's par for the course. The only bad thing perms do—and I've yet to meet a perm who doesn't do this—is ask me if I'm "having fun yet" as I work. Indeed, the question is posed several times a day, eventually supplanting all conventional greetings. I am at a loss for a response. I am clearly not having fun, nor is any fun pending.

---

**ALL TIED UP: Agencies have rigid dress codes, yet send you to assignments so menial they barely require pants.**

---

The fine folks running the temp agency don't refer to us as "temps," preferring instead to use an array of patronizing euphemisms like "field agent" or "representative." My personal favorite is "talent." As in "We match the best talent with the best job." Talent? Well, if lacking marketable skills is a talent, then yeah, we're a pretty gifted bunch. For some reason, temp-firm people find it necessary to weave an intricate fantasy wherein something they call our "skill set" undergoes meticulous examination, our career goals are thoroughly assessed by a panel of experts and a fulfilling, rewarding position tailor-made to fit our dreams and ambitions materializes.

They also pressure us relentlessly to brown-nose the clients, since goody-goody temps make for better business. Makes sense, but unfortunately no tangible benefits exist for those who do the brown-nosing. If I take the initiative and ask for extra work, the client might never switch temp companies, but I'm stuck doing more work! Would they mind if I took the initiative and asked for extra pay? I have to pull teeth to get my weekly pittance as it is. Temps are required to get a supervisor's signature confirming that we did, in fact,

show up. Woe be the temp who discovers on Friday afternoon that everyone resembling a supervisor has gone home for the weekend. Half the time my time sheet is signed by the janitor. Any other line of work, it's a given that you get paid for your labor. In temping, they make you beg.

It gets better. Many agencies have rigid dress codes and then send you to assignments so menial they barely require pants. Do I really need to be in top hat and tails to make binders all day? Meanwhile, the employees I'm supposed to be dazzling with my sartorial splendor are milling about in leotards and bathrobes, asking me why I dressed up.

It goes without saying that temps have no health coverage, no vacations and go to sleep not knowing if they'll have a job in the morning. And you can forget about meeting women. If you're a temporary employee, you're a temporary eunuch, too. Pet-sitters get more action.

For all the derision temps endure, every one of us—you, me, the pet-sitters and even the agency consultants—is in the same boat. We are wage slaves with far fewer rights than the corporations we make up. We get fired if the economy doesn't grow fast enough, and we have no political party to represent our interests. Aren't we all "temps"? Isn't all employment fleeting and transitory? The chairman of the Federal Reserve openly proclaimed that controlling labor costs is paramount to the nation's financial health, and the key to that is worker insecurity. Remember, it ain't the temps' financial health he's talking about, and it's probably not yours, either.

---

*RYBICKI lives in Salem, Mass.*

# Big Companies Teach Business Ethics to Employees

By Harold Brubaker
The Philadelphia Inquirer Knight Ridder/Tribune Business News

Mar. 26—With corporate America's image battered by high-profile scandals, many companies are beefing up programs that train directors, executives and other employees in ethics and legal compliance.

The challenge for big companies is figuring out how to reach tens of thousands of employees scattered around the world in a way that does not break the bank.

DuPont Co. in Wilmington, Rohm & Haas Co. in Philadelphia, and Unisys Corp. in Blue Bell are among the companies that have been training employees on ethics and legal issues for years but have started using online services to reach deeper into their organizations.

"Companies are finding it an effective way to train a far-flung workforce," said Steve Voien, director of services at Business for Social Responsibility, a San Francisco nonprofit group.

In a study of a dozen big global companies completed this month, Business for Social Responsibility found that 11 were conducting online training on business ethics, compared with none four years ago.

The corporate scandals involving Enron Corp., WorldCom Inc., Tyco International Ltd., and others have made it easier for ethics and legal-compliance officers to get their message across to employees.

"We can say: 'See, this was important!'" said Marjorie Doyle, associate general counsel and chief compliance counsel at DuPont. "They pay more attention now."

Advocates of online training said it allowed companies to spread a consistent message far and wide in a variety of languages.

"For a company like Rohm & Haas with employees all around the world, it's an invaluable service," said Dennis Wilson, assistant corporate secretary and senior counsel at the Center City specialty-chemical company, which provides online training in a dozen languages, including German, French, Spanish, Korean, Portuguese and Japanese.

Online training is most effective for nuts-and-bolts compliance issues, such as following the rules on testing a new pharmaceutical. That kind of training shows employees: "If you do this, you go to jail," said Stuart Gilman, president of the nonprofit Ethics Resource Center in Washington.

But Gilman and others said ethics training—which is a matter of exploring gray areas—required face-to-face dialogue. These include issues involving conflicts of interest in hiring, gift-giving, or even the expectation of bribes in some countries.

Cigna Corp., Rohm & Haas, and Unisys said they used both online and classroom training. Doyle, at DuPont, said the company held "Law Day" on specific topics and in June held its first "Ethics Day" for employees.

Rohm & Haas started a classroom training program in 2001 with presentations about the company's code of business conduct. The program reached 10,000 of its 18,000 employees. An additional 3,000 were trained by video. The rest of the workforce went through the training last year.

Employees at Rohm & Haas have to go through the training every 24 months, Wilson said. The online program is primarily for supplemental legal training, said Karl Stauss, the company's compliance coordinator.

Business is booming for companies that offer such online services. LRN, a Los Angeles company whose clients include Rohm & Haas and DuPont, has logged $100 million in contracts for online training since 1998—more than half of it in the last 12 months, said Dov Seidman, chief executive officer.

Midi Interactive Multimedia Inc., in Princeton, has been providing legal-compliance and ethics training for 12 years. Its first customer was the former GE Aerospace in King of Prussia. Midi chief executive Jack Noon said his company had doubled its business in the last two years. Lockheed Martin Corp., which now owns those King of Prussia operations, is still a Midi customer. Unisys also uses Midi.

Some corporate ethics and legal-compliance programs are rooted in the 1992 Federal Sentencing Guidelines, which established that an effective program must contain specific elements. A company must have an individual in charge of ethics, written standards of conduct, employee training on the code document, and a hotline for whistleblowers.

But there are skeptics about corporate ethics programs. The programs often have more to do with managing reputations than deep-rooted values, said William S. Laufer, an associate professor of legal studies and sociology at the Wharton School of the University of Pennsylvania.

"In many firms, business ethics is less about leadership and corporate culture than preventive law," he said.

Still, corporate scandals and new laws have encouraged change. Many companies are taking a close look at their ethics and compliance programs because of the federal Sarbanes-Oxley Act of 2002 and ethics rules proposed by the New York Stock Exchange.

"Some people are ethically healthy and don't need it," said Jeff Kaplan, a New Jersey lawyer who helps companies develop compliance training programs. "Some people are ethically unhealthy, and it won't matter. For a lot of people in the middle, having that will help them make the right decision at a critical moment."

Online training programs range from general ethics overviews to illustrations of when a person could be jailed under the Foreign Corrupt Practices Act for paying a bribe to a foreign official.

High-end presentations feature streaming video. At the low end, employees click their way through textbook-like tutorials. Participants must pass a quiz at the end to get a certificate.

A key to the success of any training program is its memorability, said Kaplan, an adviser to Midi who is a member of Stier, Anderson & Malone L.L.C. in Skillman, N.J.

"Nobody is asked to commit a crime 10 minutes after training. It's usually six months or a year later. The question is: Will it be in your mind?"

---

**A GLOSSARY:**

- **Business ethics:** An aim to ensure that a company's employees conduct business responsibly.
- **Corporate compliance:** Adhering to federal, state and local laws and regulations.
- **Corporate responsibility:** Fulfilling obligations to a company's stakeholders—employees, customers, investors, vendors, and communities where it operates.
- **Social responsibility:** Specific community concerns, such as charitable activities, environmental preservation, and providing jobs for residents.

Source: International Business Ethics Institute

---

# Accounting for Corporate Behavior

## John A. Weinberg

The year 2002 was one of great tumult for the American corporation. As the year began, news of accounting irregularities at energy giant Enron was unfolding at a rapid pace. These revelations would ultimately lead to the demise of that firm and its auditor Arthur Andersen. But Enron was not an isolated case, as other accounting scandals soon followed at WorldCom and Global Crossing in the telecommunications industry and at other prominent companies in different sectors. In July of 2002, Forbes.com published a "corporate scandal sheet" listing some twenty companies that were under investigation by the Securities and Exchange Commission (SEC) or other government authority.[1] Of these cases, the vast majority involved misreporting of corporate earnings.

These allegations certainly created the appearance of a general phenomenon in corporate finance, and the resulting loss of confidence in financial reporting practices arguably contributed to the weakness of markets for corporate securities. The fact that many of the problems were surfacing in industries that had been at the center of the new economy euphoria of the late 1990s contributed to the sense of malaise by shaking investor confidence in the economy's fundamental prospects. In most of the recent cases, the discovery of accounting improprieties was accompanied by a spectacular decline of high-flying stocks and, in a number of cases, criminal charges against corporate executives. Consequently, the state of corporate governance and accounting became the dominant business news story of the year.

To some observers, the recent events confirm a sense that the stock market boom of the 1990s was artificial—a "bubble" backed solely by unrealistic expectations with no grounding in economic fundamentals. According to this view, investors' bloated expectations were nourished by the fictitious performance results reported by some firms. In the aftermath of these events, Congress enacted a new law known as the Sarbanes-Oxley Act to reform corporate accounting practices and the corporate governance tools that are intended to ensure sound financial reporting.

The attention received by the various scandals and the legislative response might easily create the impression that a fundamental flaw developed in the American system of corporate governance and finance during the late 1990s. It *does* appear that the sheer number of cases in which companies have been forced to make significant restatements of their accounts, largely as the result of SEC action, has risen in recent years. Beginning in 1998 with large earnings restatements by such companies as Sunbeam and Waste Management and with a heightened commitment by the SEC, under then chairman Arthur Levitt, to police misleading statements of earnings, the number of cases rose significantly above the dozen or so per year that was common in the 1980s.[2] While the frequency and magnitude of recent cases seem to be greater than in the past, accounting scandals are not new. Episodes of fraudulent accounting have occurred repeatedly in the history of U.S. financial markets.

In the aftermath of the stock market crash of 1929, public attention and congressional investigation led to allegations of unsavory practices by some financial market participants during the preceding boom. This activity led directly to the creation of the Securities and Exchange Commission in 1934. One of the founding principles of this agency was that "companies publicly offering securities... must tell the public the truth about their businesses."[3] The creation of the SEC, however, did not eliminate the problem, and scandals associated with dubious accounting remained a feature of the financial landscape. In 1987 a number of associations for accounting and finance professionals organized a National Commission on Fraudulent Financial Reporting. The commission studied cases from the

This article first appeared in the Bank's 2002 Annual Report. It benefited from conversations with a number of the author's colleagues in the Research Department and from careful and critical readings by Tom Humphrey, Jeff Lacker, Ned Prescott, John Walter, and Alice Felmlee. The views expressed herein are the author's and not necessarily those of the Federal Reserve System.

1980s and characterized the typical case as involving a relatively small company with weak internal controls. Although incidents of fraud were often triggered by a financial strain or sudden downturn in a company's real performance, the companies involved were usually from industries that had been experiencing relatively rapid growth. So while the size of companies involved in recent cases may be atypical, the occurrence of scandals in high-growth firms fits the established pattern.

Does fraudulent financial reporting represent the Achilles' heel of U.S. corporate finance? This essay addresses such questions by examining the problem of financial reporting in the context of the fundamental problem of corporate governance. Broadly stated, that fundamental problem is the need for a large group of corporate outsiders (shareholders) to be able to control the incentives of a small group of corporate insiders (management). At the heart of this problem lies a basic and inescapable asymmetry: insiders are much better informed about the opportunities and performance of a business than are any outsiders. This asymmetry presents a challenge that the modern corporation seeks to address in the mechanisms it uses to measure performance and reward managers.

While the tools of corporate governance can limit the effects of the incentive problem inherent in the corporate form, they cannot eliminate it. Ultimately, there are times when shareholders just have to trust that management is acting in their best interest and realize that their trust will sometimes be violated. Still, management has a powerful interest in earning and preserving the trust of investors. With trust comes an enhanced willingness of investors to provide funds, resulting in reduced funding costs for the business. That is, the behavior of corporate insiders is disciplined by their desire or need to raise funds in financial markets. This discipline favors efficient corporate governance arrangements.

As discussed in the next section, there are a variety of tools that a corporation might use to control managerial discretion, ranging from the makeup and role of the board of directors to the firm's relationship with its external auditor. To say that such tools are applied efficiently is to say that managers will adopt a tool as long as its benefit outweighs its cost. In the absence of government intervention, the forces of competition among self-interested market participants (both insiders and outsiders) will tend to lead to an efficient set of governance tools. It bears repeating, though, that these tools do not eliminate the fundamental problem of corporate governance. The observation of apparent failures, such as the accounting scandals of 2002, is not inconsistent, however, with a generally well-functioning market for corporate finance. Still, such episodes often provoke a political response, as occurred during the Great Depression and again in 2002 with the Sarbanes-Oxley Act. Through these interventions, the government has assumed a role in managing the relationship between shareholders and management.

The final sections of the essay consider the role of a government authority in setting and enforcing rules. After reviewing the functions of the SEC, discussion turns to the Sarbanes-Oxley Act, the provisions of which can be classified into two broad categories. Parts of the act attempt to improve corporate behavior by mandating certain aspects of the design of the audit committee or the relationship between the firm and its external auditor. The discussion in this essay suggests that there is reason to doubt that such provisions, by themselves, can do much to reduce fraud. Other parts of the act deal more with enforcement and the penalties for infractions. These provisions are more likely to have a direct effect on incentives. An open question is whether this effect is desirable. Since reducing fraud is costly, it is unlikely that reducing it to zero would be cost effective from society's point of view. Further, it is unrealistic to expect the new law to bring about a substantial reduction in instances of fraud without an increase in the resources allocated to enforcement. Given that it is in the interest of corporate stakeholders to devise mechanisms that respond efficiently to the fundamental problem of corporate governance, one might doubt that the gains from government intervention will be worth the costs necessary to bring about significant changes in behavior.

# 1. THE NATURE OF THE MODERN CORPORATION

In the modern American corporation, ownership is typically spread widely over many individuals and institutions. As a result, owners as a group cannot effectively manage a business, a task that would require significant coordination and consensus-building. Instead, owners delegate management responsibilities to a hired professional. To be sure, professional managers usually hold some equity in the firms they run. Still, it is common for a manager's ownership stake to be small relative both to the company's total outstanding equity and to the manager's own total wealth.[4]

This description of the modern corporation featuring a separation between widely dispersed ownership and professional management is typically associated with the work of Adolf Berle and Gardiner Means. In their landmark study, *The Modern Corporation and Private Property*, Berle and Means identified the emerging corporate form as a cause for concern. For them, the separation of ownership and control heralded the rise of a managerial class, wielding great economic power but answerable only to itself. Large numbers of widely dispersed shareholders could not possibly exert effective control over management. Berle and Means' main concern was the growing concentration of economic power in a few hands and the coincident decline in the competitiveness of markets. At the heart of this problem was what they saw as the impossibility of absentee owners disciplining management.

Without adequate control by shareholders in the Berle and Means view, managers would be free to pursue endeavors that serve their own interests at shareholders' expense. Such actions might include making investments and acquisitions whose main effect would be to expand management's "empire." Managers might also use company resources to provide themselves with desirable perks, such as large and luxurious corporate facilities. These actions could result in the destruction of shareholder wealth and an overall decline in efficiency in the allocation of productive resources.

The experience of the last seventy years and the work of a number of writers on the law and economics of corporate governance have suggested that the modern corporation is perhaps not as ominous a development as imagined by Berle and Means. A field of financial economics has developed that studies the mechanisms available to shareholders for exerting some influence over management's decisions.[5] These tools represent the response of governance arrangements to the forces of supply and demand. That is, managers implement a governance mechanism when they perceive that its benefits exceed its costs. The use of these tools, however, cannot eliminate the fundamental asymmetry between managers and owners. Even under the best possible arrangement, corporate insiders will be better informed than outsiders.

The most obvious mechanism for affecting an executive's behavior is the compensation arrangement between the firm and the executive. This tool, however, is also the most subject to problems arising from the separation of ownership and control. Just as it would be difficult for owners to coordinate in directly running the firm, so it is difficult for them to coordinate employment contract negotiations with managers. In practice, this task falls to the board of directors, who, while intended to represent owners, are often essentially controlled by management. In terms of this relationship, management can benefit by creating a strong and independent board. This move signals to owners that management is seeking to constrain its own discretion. Ultimately, however, shareholders face the same challenge in assessing the board's independence as they do in evaluating management's behavior. The close contact the board has with management makes its independence hard to guarantee.

Another source of control available to owners comes from the legal protections provided by corporate law. Shareholders can bring lawsuits against management for certain types of misbehavior, including fraud and self-dealing, by which a manager unjustly enriches himself through transactions with the firm. Loans from the corporation to an executive at preferential interest rates can be an example of self-dealing. Of course use of the courts to discipline management also requires coordination among the widespread group of shareholders. In such cases, coordination can be facilitated by class-action lawsuits, where a number of shareholders come together as the plaintiff. Beyond suing management for specific actions of fraud or theft, however, shareholders' legal rights are limited by a general presumption in the law that management is best positioned to take actions in the firm's best business interest.[6] For instance, if management chooses between two possible investment projects, dissatisfied shareholders would find it very difficult to make a case that management's choice was driven by self-interest as opposed to shareholder value. So, while legal recourse can be an important tool for policing certain types of managerial malfeasance, such recourse cannot serve to constrain the broad discretion that management enjoys in running the business.

Notice that this discussion of tools for controlling managers' behavior has referred repeatedly to the coordination problem facing widely dispersed shareholders. Clearly, the severity of this problem depends on the degree of dispersion. The more concentrated the ownership, the more likely it is that large shareholders will take an active role in negotiating contracts and monitoring the behavior of management. Concentrated ownership comes at a cost, though. For an investor to hold a large share of a large firm requires a substantial commitment of wealth without the benefits of risk diversification. Alternatively, many investors can pool their funds into institutions that own large blocks of stock in corporations. This arrangement does not solve the corporate governance problem of controlling incentives; however, it simply shifts the problem to that of governing the shareholding institutions.

In spite of the burden it places on shareholders, concentrated ownership has won favor as an approach to corporate governance in some settings. In some developed economies, banks hold large shares of equity in firms and also participate more actively in their governance than do financial institutions in the United States. In this country, leveraged buyouts emerged in the 1980s as a technique for taking over companies. In a leveraged buyout, ownership becomes concentrated as an individual or group acquires the firm's equity, financed through the issuance of debt. Some see the leveraged buyout wave as a means of forcing businesses to dispose of excess capacity or reverse unsuccessful acquisitions.[7] In most cases, these transactions resulted in a temporary concentration of ownership, since subsequent sales of equity eventually led back to more dispersed ownership. It seems that, at least in the legal and financial environment of the United States, the benefits of diversification associated with less concentrated ownership are great enough to make firms and their shareholders willing to face the related governance challenges.[8] Still, there is considerable variation in the concentration of ownership among large U.S. corporations, leading some observers to conclude that this feature of modern corporations responds to the relative costs and benefits.[9]

A leveraged buyout is a special type of takeover, an additional tool for controlling managers' incentives. If a firm is badly managed, another firm can acquire it, installing new management and improving its use of resources so as to increase profits. The market for corporate control, the market in which mergers and acquisitions take place, serves two purposes in corporate governance.[10] First, as just noted, it is sometimes the easiest means by which ineffective managers can be replaced. Second, the threat of replacement can help give managers an incentive to behave well. Takeovers, however, can be costly transactions and may not be worth the effort unless the potential improvement in a firm's performance is substantial.

The threat of a takeover introduces the idea that a manager's current behavior could bring about personal costs in the future. Similarly, a manager may have an interest in building and maintaining a reputation for effectively serving shareholders' interest. Such a reputation could enhance the manager's set of future professional opportunities. While reputation can be a powerful incentive device, like other tools, it is not perfect. There will always be *some* circumstances in which a manager will find it in his best interest to take advantage of his good reputation for a short-run gain, even though he realizes that his reputation will suffer in the long run. For example, a manager might "milk" his reputation by issuing misleading reports on the company's performance in order to meet targets needed for additional compensation.

The imperfections of reputation as a disciplining tool are due to the nature of the corporate governance problem and the relationship between ownership and management. Any tools shareholders have to control management's incentives are limited by a basic informational advantage that management enjoys. Because management has superior information about the firm's opportunities, prospects, and performance, shareholders can never be perfectly certain in their evaluation of management's actions and behavior.

## 2. CORPORATE GOVERNANCE AS AN AGENCY PROBLEM

At the heart of issues related to corporate governance lies what economists call an agency (or principal-agent) problem. Such a problem often arises when two parties enter into a contractual relationship, like that of employer-employee or borrower-lender. The defining characteristic of an agency problem is that one party, the principal, cannot directly control or prescribe the actions of the other party, the agent. Usually, this lack of control results from the agent having superior information about the endeavor that is of mutual interest to both parties. In the employer-employee relationship, this information gap is often related to the completion of daily tasks. Unable to monitor all of their employees' habits, bosses base workers' salaries on performance to induce those workers to put appropriate effort into their work.[11] Another common example of an agency problem includes insurance relationships. In auto insurance, for instance, the insurer cannot directly monitor the car owner's driving habits, which directly affect the probability of a claim being filed. Typical features of insurance contracts such as deductibles serve to enhance the owner's incentive to exercise care.

In interpreting corporate governance as an agency problem, it is common to identify top corporate management as the agent and owners as the principal. While both management and ownership are typically composed of a number

of individuals, the basic tensions that arise in an agency relationship can be seen quite clearly if one thinks of each of the opposing parties as a single individual. In this hypothetical relationship, an owner (the principal) hires a manager (the agent) to run a business. The owner is not actively involved in the affairs of the firm and, therefore, is not as well-informed as the manager about the opportunities available to the firm. Also, it may not be practical for the owner to monitor the manager's every action. Accordingly, the control that the owner exerts over the manager is primarily indirect. Since the owner can expect the manager to take actions that maximize his own return, the owner can try to structure the compensation policy so that the manager does well when the business does well. This policy could be supplemented by a mutual understanding of conditions under which the manager's employment might be terminated.

The agency perspective is certainly consistent with a significant part of compensation for corporate executives being contingent on firm performance. Equity grants to executives and equity options are common examples of performance-based compensation. Besides direct compensation, principals have a number of other tools available to affect agents' incentives. As discussed earlier, the tools available to shareholders include termination of top executives' employment, the possibility of a hostile takeover, and the right to sue executive management for certain types of misbehavior. Like direct compensation policy, all of these tools involve consequences for management that depend on corporate performance. Hence, the effective use of such tools requires that principals be able to assess agents' performance.

In the usual formulation of an agency problem, the agent takes an action that affects the business's profits, and the principal pays the agent an amount that depends on the level of those profits. This procedure presumes that the principal is able to assess the firm's profits. But the very same features of a modern corporation that make it difficult for principals (shareholders) to monitor actions taken by agents (corporate management) also create an asymmetry in the ability of shareholders and managers to track the firm's performance. Since owners cannot directly observe all of the firm's expenses and sales revenues, they must rely to some extent on the manager's reports about such measures of performance. As discussed in the next section, the problem of corporate governance is a compound agency problem: shareholders suffer from both an inability to directly control management's actions and an inability to easily obtain information necessary to assess management's performance.

The characterization of corporate governance as an agency problem might lead one to doubt the ability of market forces to achieve efficient outcomes in this setting. But an agency problem is not a source of market failure. Rather, agents' and principals' unequal access to relevant information is simply a condition of the economic environment. In this environment, participants will evaluate contractual arrangements taking into account the effects on the incentives for all parties involved. An individual or a firm that can devise a contract with improved incentive effects will have an advantage in attracting other participants. In this way, market forces will tend to lead to efficient contracts. Accordingly, the economic view of corporate governance is that firms will seek executive compensation policies and other governance mechanisms that provide the best possible incentive for management to work in shareholders' best interest. The ultimate governance structure chosen does not eliminate the agency problem but is a rational, best response to that problem, balancing the costs and benefits of managerial discretion.

## 3. ACCOUNTING FOR CORPORATE PERFORMANCE

All of the tools intended to influence the incentives and behavior of managers require that outsiders be able to assess when the firm is performing well and when it is performing poorly. If the manager's compensation is tied to the corporation's stock price, then investors, whose behavior determines the stock price, must be able to make inferences about the firm's true performance and prospects from the information available. If management's discipline comes from the threat of a takeover, then potential acquirers must also be able to make such assessments.

The challenge for effective market discipline (whether in the capital market or in the market for corporate control) is in getting information held by corporate insiders out into the open. As a general matter, insiders have an interest in providing the market with reliable information. If by doing so they can reduce the uncertainty associated with investing in their firm, then they can reduce the firm's cost of capital. But it's not enough for a manager to simply say, "I'm going to release reliable financial information about my business on an annual (or quarterly or other interval) basis." The believability of such a statement is limited because there will always be some circumstances in which a manager can benefit in the short term by not being fully transparent.

The difficulty in securing reliable information may be most apparent when a manager's compensation is directly tied to accounting-based performance measures. Since these measures are generated inside the firm, essentially by the same group of people whose decisions are driving the business's performance, the opportunity for manipulation is present. Certainly, accounting standards set by professional organizations can limit the discretion available to corporate insiders. A great deal of discretion remains, however. The academic accounting literature refers to such manipulation of current performance measures as "earnings management."

An alternative to executive compensation that depends on current performance as reported by the firm is compensation that depends on the market's perception of current performance. That is, compensation can be tied to the behavior of the firm's stock price. In this way, rather than depending on self-reported numbers, executives' rewards depend on investors' collective evaluation of the firm's per-

formance. Compensation schemes based on this type of investor evaluation include plans that award bonuses based on stock price performance as well as those that offer direct grants of equity or equity options to managers.

Unfortunately, tying compensation to stock price performance hardly eliminates a manager's incentive to manipulate accounting numbers. If accounting numbers are generally believed by investors to provide reliable information about a company's performance, then those investors' trading behavior will cause stock prices to respond to accounting reports. This responsiveness could create an incentive for managers to manipulate accounting numbers in order to boost stock prices. Note, however, that if investors viewed earnings management and other forms of accounting manipulation as pervasive, they would tend to ignore reported numbers. In this case, stock prices would be unresponsive to accounting numbers, and managers would have little reason to manipulate reports (although they would also have little incentive to exert any effort or resources to creating accurate reports). The fact that we do observe cases of manipulation suggests that investors do not ignore accounting numbers, as they would if they expected all reports to be misleading. That is, the prevailing environment appears to be one in which serious instances of fraud are occasional rather than pervasive.

In summary, the design of a system of rewards for a corporation's top executives has two conflicting goals. To give executives an incentive to take actions that maximize shareholder value, compensation needs to be sensitive to the firm's performance. But the measurement of performance is subject to manipulation by the firm's management, and the incentive for such manipulation grows with the sensitivity of rewards to measured performance. This tension limits the ability of compensation plans to effectively manage executives' incentives.[12]

Are there tools that a corporation can use to lessen the possibility of manipulated reporting and thereby improve the incentive structure for corporate executives? One possible tool is an external check on a firm's reported performance. A primary source for this check in public corporations is an external auditor. By becoming familiar with a client and its performance, an auditor can get a sense for the appropriateness of the choices made by the firm in preparing its reports. Of course, every case of fraudulent financial reporting by corporations, including those in the last year, involves the failure of an external auditor to detect or disclose problems. Clearly, an external audit is not a failsafe protection against misreporting. A significant part of the Sarbanes-Oxley legislation was therefore devoted to improving the incentives of accounting firms in their role as external auditors.

An external audit is limited in its ability to prevent fraudulent reporting. First, many observers argue that an auditor's role is limited to certifying that a client's financial statements were prepared in accordance with professional accounting standards. Making this determination does not automatically enable an auditor to identify fraud. Others counter that an auditor's knowledge of a client's operations makes the auditor better positioned than other outsiders to assess the veracity of the client's reports. In this view, audit effectiveness in deterring fraud is as much a matter of willingness as ability.

One aspect of auditors' incentives that has received a great deal of attention is the degree to which the auditor's interests are independent of the interests of the client's management.[13] Some observers argue that the objectivity of large accounting firms when serving as external auditors is compromised by a desire to gain and retain lucrative consulting relationships with those clients. Even before the events of 2002, momentum was growing for the idea of separating the audit and consulting businesses into separate firms. Although the Sarbanes-Oxley Act did not require such a separation, some audit firms have taken the step of spinning off their consulting businesses. This step, however, does not guarantee auditor independence. Ultimately, an auditor works for its client, and there are always strong market forces driving a service provider to give the client what the client wants. If the client is willing to pay more for an audit that overlooks some questionable numbers than the (expected) costs to the auditor for providing such an audit, then that demand will likely be met. In general, a client's desire to maintain credibility with investors gives it a strong interest in the reliability of the auditor's work. Even so, there will always be some cases in which a client and an auditor find themselves willing to breach the public's trust for a short-term gain.

Some observers suggest that making the hiring of the auditor the responsibility of a company's board of directors, in particular the board's audit committee, can prevent complicity between management and external auditors. This arrangement is indeed a standard procedure in large corporations. Still, the ability of such an arrangement to enhance auditor independence hinges on the independence of the board and its audit committee. Unfortunately, there appears to be no simple mechanism for ensuring the independence of directors charged with overseeing a firm's audit relationships. In 1987 the National Commission on Fraudulent Financial Reporting found that among the most common characteristics of cases that resulted in enforcement actions by the Securities and Exchange Commission was weak or inactive audit committees or committees that had members with business ties to the firm or its executives. While such characteristics can often be seen clearly after the fact, it can be more difficult and costly for investors or other outsiders to discriminate among firms based on the general quality of their governance arrangements before problems have surfaced. While an outside investor can learn about the members of the audit committee and how often it meets, investors are less able to assess how much care the committee puts into its work.

The difficulty in guaranteeing the release of reliable information arises directly from the fundamental problem of corporate governance. In a business enterprise characterized by a separation of ownership and control, those in control have exclusive access to information that would be useful to the outside owners of the firm. Any outsider that the firm hires to verify that the information it releases is correct becomes, in effect, an insider. Once an auditor, for instance, acquires sufficient knowledge about a client to assess its management's reports, that auditor faces incentive problems analogous to those faced by management. So, while an external audit might be part of the appropriate response to the agency problem between management and investors, an audit also creates a new and analogous agency problem between investors and an auditor.

An alternative approach to monitoring the information released by a firm is for this monitoring to be done by parties that have no contractual relationship with the firm's management. Investors, as a group, would benefit from the increased credibility of accounting numbers this situation would provide. Suppose that a small number of individual investors spent the resources necessary to assess the truthfulness of a firm's report. Those investors could then make trades based on the results of their investigation. In an efficient capital market, the results would then be revealed in the firm's stock price. In this way, the firm's management would suffer the consequences (in the form of a lower stock price) of making misleading reports. The problem with this scenario is that while only a few investors incur the cost of the investigation and producing the information, all investors receive the benefit. Individual investors will have a limited incentive to incur such costs when other investors can free ride on their efforts. Because it is difficult for dispersed shareholders to coordinate information-gathering efforts, such free riding might occur and is just a further reflection of the fundamental problem of corporate governance.

The free-riding problem that comes when investors produce information about a firm can be reduced if an individual investor owns a large fraction of a firm's shares. As discussed in the second section, however, concentrated ownership has costs and does not necessarily resolve the information and incentive problems inherent in corporate governance. An alternative approach to the free-riding problem, and one that extends beyond the governance arrangements of an individual firm, is the creation of a membership organization that evaluates firms and their reporting behavior. Firms would be willing to pay a fee to join such an organization if membership served as a seal of approval for reporting practices. Members would then enjoy the benefits of reduced funding costs that come with credibility.

One type of membership organization that could contribute to improved financial reporting is a stock exchange. As the next section discusses, the New York Stock Exchange (NYSE) was a leader in establishing disclosure rules prior to the stock market crash of 1929. The political response to the crash was the creation of the Securities and Exchange Commission, which took over some of the responsibilities that might otherwise fall to a private membership organization. Hence, a government body like the SEC might substitute for private arrangements in monitoring corporate accounting behavior. The main source of incentives for a government body is its sensitivity to political sentiments. While political pressure can be an effective source of incentives, its effectiveness can also vary depending on political and economic conditions. If government monitoring replaces some information production by private market participants, it is still possible for such a hybrid system of corporate monitoring to be efficient as long as market participants base their actions on accurate beliefs about the effectiveness of government monitoring.

Given the existence of a governmental entity charged with policing the accounting behavior of public corporations, how much policing should that entity do? Should it carefully investigate every firm's reported numbers? This would be an expensive undertaking. The purpose of this policing activity is to enhance the incentives for corporate managements and their auditors to file accurate reports. At the same time, this goal should be pursued in a cost-effective manner. To do this, there is a second tool, beyond investigation, that the agency can use to affect incentives. The agency can also vary the punishment imposed on firms that are found to have violated the standards of honest reporting. At a minimum, this punishment simply involves the reduction in stock price that occurs when a firm is forced to make a restatement of earnings or other important accounting numbers. This minimum punishment, imposed entirely by market forces, can be substantial.[14] To toughen punishment, the government authority can impose fines or even criminal penalties.

To increase corporate managers' incentive for truthful accounting, a government authority can either increase resources spent on monitoring firms' reports or increase penalties imposed for discovered infractions. Relying on large penalties allows the authority to economize on monitoring costs but, as long as monitoring is imperfect, raises the likelihood of wrongly penalizing firms. The Sarbanes-Oxley Act has provisions that affect both of these margins of enforcement. The following sections describe enforcement in the United States before and after Sarbanes-Oxley.

## 4. GOVERNMENT ENFORCEMENT OF CORPORATE HONESTY

Before the creation of the Securities and Exchange Commission in 1934, regulation of disclosures by firms issuing public securities was a state matter. Various states had "blue sky laws," so named because they were intended to "check stock swindlers so barefaced they would sell building lots in the blue sky."[15] These laws, which specified disclosures required of firms seeking to register and issue securities, had limited impact because they did not apply to the issuance of securities across state lines. An issuer could register securities in one state but offer them for sale in other states through the mail. The issuer would then be subject only to the laws of the state in which the securities were

registered. The New York Stock Exchange offered an alternative, private form of regulation with listing requirements that were generally more stringent than those in the state laws. The NYSE also encouraged listing firms to make regular, audited reports on their income and financial position. This practice was nearly universal on the New York Stock Exchange by the late 1920s. The many competing exchanges at the time had weaker rules.

One of the key provisions of the Securities Exchange Act of 1934 was a requirement that all firms issuing stock file annual and quarterly reports with the SEC. In general, however, the act did not give finely detailed instructions to the commission. Rather, the SEC was granted the authority to issue rules "where appropriate in the public interest or for the protection of investors."[16] As with many of its powers, the SEC's authority with regard to the treatment of information disclosed by firms was left to an evolutionary process.

In the form into which it has evolved, the SEC reviews financial reports, taking one of a number of possible actions when problems are found. There are two broad classes of filings that the Corporate Finance Division of the SEC reviews—transactional and periodic filings. Transactional filings contain information relevant to particular transactions, such as the issuance of new securities or mergers and acquisitions. Periodic filings are the annual and quarterly filings, as well as the annual report to shareholders. Among the options available to the Corporate Finance Division if problems are found in a firm's disclosures is to refer the case to the Division of Enforcement.

Given its limited resources, it is impossible for the SEC to review all of the filings that come under its authority. In general, more attention is paid to transactional filings. In particular, all transactional filings go through an initial review, or screening process, to identify those warranting a closer examination. Many periodic filings do not even receive the initial screening. While the agency's goal has been to review every firm's annual 10-K report at least once every three years, it has not had the resources to realize that goal. In 2002 around half of all public companies had not had such a review in the last three years.[17] It is possible that the extraordinary nature of recent scandals has been due in part to the failure of the SEC's enforcement capabilities to keep up with the growth of securities market activity.

## 5. THE SARBANES-OXLEY ACT OF 2002

In the aftermath of the accounting scandals of 2002, Congress enacted the Sarbanes-Oxley Act, aimed at enhancing corporate responsibility and reforming the practice of corporate accounting. The law contains provisions pertaining to both companies issuing securities and those in the auditing profession. Some parts of the act articulate rules for companies and their auditors, while other parts focus more on enforcement of these rules.[18]

The most prominent provisions dealing with companies that issue securities include obligations for the top executives and rules regarding the audit committee. The act requires the chief executive and financial officers to sign a firm's annual and quarterly filings with the SEC. The signatures will be taken to certify that, to the best of the executives' knowledge, the filings give a fair and honest representation of the firm's financial condition and operating performance. By not fulfilling this signature requirement, executives could face the possibility of significant criminal penalties.

The sections of the act that deal with the audit committee seek to promote the independence of directors serving on that committee. To this end, the act requires that members of the audit committee have no other business relationship with the company. That is, those directors should receive no compensation from the firm other than their director's fee. The act also instructs audit committees to establish formal procedures for handling complaints about accounting matters, whether the complaints come from inside or outside of the firm. Finally, the committee must include a member who is a "financial expert," as defined by the SEC, or explain publicly why it has no such expert.

Like its attempt to promote audit committee independence, the act contains provisions regarding a similar relationship between a firm and its auditor. A number of these provisions are intended to keep the auditor from getting "too close" to the firm. Hence, the act specifies a number of nonaudit services that an accounting firm may not provide to its audit clients. The act also requires audit firms to rotate the lead partner responsible for a client at least once every five years. Further, the act calls on the SEC to study the feasibility of requiring companies to periodically change their audit firm.

With regard to enforcement, the act includes both some new requirements for the SEC in its review of company filings and the creation of a new body, the Public Company Accounting Oversight Board. The PCAOB is intended to be an independent supervisory body for the auditing industry with which all firms performing audits of public companies must register. This board is charged with the task of establishing standards and rules governing the operation of public accounting firms. As put forth in Sarbanes-Oxley, these standards must include a minimum period of time over which audit work papers must be maintained for possible examination by the PCAOB. Other rules would involve internal controls that audit firms must put in place to protect the quality and integrity of their work.

Sarbanes-Oxley gives the PCAOB the task of inspecting audit firms on a regular basis, with annual inspection required for the largest firms.[19] In addition to examining a firm's compliance with rules regarding organization and internal controls, inspections may include reviews of specific audit engagements. The PCAOB may impose penalties that include fines as well as the termination of an audit firm's registration. Such termination would imply a firm's exit from the audit business.

In addition to creating the new board to supervise the audit industry, the act gives the SEC greater responsibilities

in reviewing disclosures by public companies. The act spells out factors that the SEC should use in prioritizing its reviews. For instance, firms that have issued material restatements of financial results or those whose stock prices have experienced significant volatility should receive priority treatment. Further, Sarbanes-Oxley requires that no company be reviewed less than once every three years. Other sections of the act that deal with enforcement prescribe penalties for specific abuses and extend the statute of limitations for private securities fraud litigation.

The goal of the Sarbanes-Oxley Act is to alter the incentives of corporate managements and their auditors so as to reduce the frequency of fraudulent financial reporting. In evaluating the act, one can take this goal as given and try to assess the act's likely impact on actual behavior of market participants. Alternatively, one could focus on the goal itself. The act is presumably based on the belief that we currently have too much fraud in corporate disclosures. But what is the right amount of fraud? Total elimination of fraud, if even feasible, is unlikely to be economically desirable. As argued earlier, reducing fraud is costly. It requires the expenditure of resources by some party to evaluate the public statements of companies and a further resource cost to impose consequences on those firms determined to have made false reports. Reduction in fraud is only economically efficient or desirable as long as the incremental costs of enforcement are less than the social gain from improved financial reporting.

What are the social benefits from improved credibility of corporate information? A reduction in the perceived likelihood of fraud brings with it similar benefits to other risk reductions perceived by investors. For example, investors become more willing to provide funds to corporations that issue public securities, resulting in a reduction in the cost of capital for those firms. Other things being equal, improved credibility should also lead to more investment by public companies and an overall expansion of the corporate sector. Again, however, any such gain must be weighed against the corresponding costs.

Is there any reason to believe that a private market for corporate finance, without any government intervention, would not result in an efficient level of corporate honesty? Economic theory suggests that the answer is no. It is true that the production of information necessary to discover fraud has some characteristics of a public good. For example, many people stand to benefit from an individual's efforts in investigating a company. While public goods can impede the efficiency of private market outcomes, the benefits of information production accrue to a well-defined group of market participants in this case. Companies subject to heightened investigative scrutiny enjoy lower costs of capital.

In principle, one can imagine this type of investigative activity being undertaken by a private membership organization. Companies that join would voluntarily subject their accounting reports to close review. Failure to comply with the organization's standards could be punished with expulsion. This organization could fund its activities through membership fees paid by the participating companies. It would only attract members if the benefits of membership, in the form of reduced costs of capital, exceeded the cost of membership. That is, such an organization would be successful if it could improve at low cost the credibility of its members' reported information. Still, even if successful, the organization would most likely not eliminate the potential for fraud among its members. There would always be some circumstances in which the short-run gain from reporting false numbers would outweigh the risk of discovery and expulsion.

Before the stock market crash of 1929, the New York Stock Exchange was operating in some ways much like the hypothetical organization just described. Investigations after the crash, which uncovered instances of misleading or fraudulent reporting by issuers of securities, found relatively fewer abuses among companies issuing stock on the NYSE.[20] One might reasonably conjecture that through such institutions the U.S. financial markets would have evolved into an efficient set of arrangements for promoting corporate honesty. While consideration of this possibility would make an interesting intellectual exercise, it is not what happened. Instead, as often occurs in American politics, Congress responded to a crisis with the creation of a government entity. In this case, a government entity charged with policing the behavior of companies that issue public securities. The presence of such an agency might well dilute private market participants' incentives to engage in such policing activities. If so, then reliance on the government substitutes for reliance on private arrangements.

Have the SEC's enforcement activities resulted in an efficient level of corporate honesty? This is a difficult determination to make. It is true that known cases of misreporting rose steadily in the 1980s and 1990s and that the events of 2002 represented unprecedented levels of both the number and the size of companies involved. It is also true that over the last two decades, as activity in securities markets grew at a very rapid pace, growth in the SEC's budget lagged, limiting the resources available for the review of corporate reports. In this sense, one might argue that the level of enforcement fell during this period. Whether the current level of enforcement is efficient or not, the Sarbanes-Oxley Act expresses Congress's interest in seeing heightened enforcement so as to reduce the frequency of fraudulent reports.

How effective is Sarbanes-Oxley likely to be in changing the incentives of corporations and their auditors? Many of the act's provisions set rules and standards for ways in which firms should behave or how they should organize themselves and their relationships with auditors. There is reason to be skeptical about the likely effectiveness of these provisions by themselves. These portions of the act mandate that certain things be done inside an issuing firm, for instance, in the organization of the audit committee. But because these actions and organizational changes take place inside the firm, they are subject to the same informa-

tion problems as all corporate behavior. It is inherently difficult for outsiders, whether market participants or government agencies, to know what goes on inside the firm. The monitoring required to gain this information is costly, and it is unlikely that mandates for changed behavior will have much effect without an increase in the allocation of resources for such monitoring of corporate actions, relationships, and reports.

Other parts of the act appear to call for this increase in the allocation of resources for monitoring activities, both by the SEC and by the newly created PCAOB. Together with the act's provisions concerning penalties, these portions should have a real effect on incentives and behavior. Further, to the extent that these agencies monitor firms' adherence to the general rules and standards specified in the act, monitoring will give force to those provisions. If the goal of the act is to reduce the likelihood of events like Enron and WorldCom, however, monitoring might best be applied to the actual review of corporate reports and accounting firms' audit engagements. Ultimately, such direct review of firms' reports and audit work papers is the activity that identifies misbehavior. Uncovering and punishing misbehavior is, in turn, the most certain means of altering incentives.

Incentives for deceptive accounting will never be eliminated, and even a firm that follows all of the formal rules in the Sarbanes-Oxley Act will find a way to be deceptive if the expected payoff is big enough. Among the things done by the SEC and PCAOB, the payoff to deception is most effectively limited by the allocation of resources to direct review of reported performance and by bringing penalties to bear where appropriate. Any hope that a real change in corporate behavior can be attained without incurring the costs of paying closer attention to the actual reporting behavior of firms will likely lead to disappointment. Corporate discipline, whether from market forces or government intervention, arises when people outside of the firm incur the costs necessary to learn some of what insiders know.

## ENDNOTES

1. Patsuris (2002).
2. Alternative means of tallying the number of cases are found in Richardson et al. (2002) and Financial Executives Research Foundation Inc. (2001). By both measures, there was a marked increase in the number of cases in the late 1990s.
3. From the SEC Web page.
4. Holderness et al. (1999) present evidence of rising managerial ownership over time. They find that executives and directors, *as a group*, owned an average of 21 percent of the outstanding stock in corporations they ran in 1995, compared to 13 percent in 1935.
5. Shleifer and Vishny (1997) provide a survey of this literature.
6. This point is emphasized by Roe (2002).
7. Holmstrom and Kaplan (2001) discuss the role of the leveraged buyouts of the 1980s in aligning managerial and shareholder interests.
8. Roe (1994) argues that ownership concentration in the United States has been constrained by a variety of legal restrictions. While this argument might temper one's conclusion that the benefits of dispersed ownership outweigh the costs, the lever-

aged buyout episode provides an example of concentration that was consistent with the legal environment and yet did not last.

9. Demsetz and Lehn (1985) make this argument.

10. Henry Manne (1965) was an early advocate of the beneficial incentive effect on the market for corporate control.

11. Classic treatments of agency problems are given by Holmstrom (1979) for the general analysis of moral hazard and Jensen and Meckling (1976) for the characterization of corporate governance as an agency problem.

12. Lacker and Weinberg (1989) analyze an agency problem in which the agent can manipulate the performance measure.

13. Levitt (2000) discusses this point.

14. Richardson et al. (2002).

15. Seligman (1982, 44).

16. Seligman (1982, 100).

17. United States Senate, Committee on Governmental Affairs (2002).

18. A summary of the act is found in Davis and Murray (2002).

19. Firms preparing audit reports for more than one hundred companies per year will be inspected annually.

20. Seligman (1982, 46).

## REFERENCES

Berle, Adolf, and Gardiner Means. 1932. *The Modern Corporation and Private Property*. New York: Commerce Clearing House.

Davis, Harry S., and Megan E. Murray. 2002. "Corporate Responsibility and Accounting Reform." *Banking and Financial Services Policy Report* 21 (November): 1-8.

Demsetz, Harold, and Kenneth Lehn. 1985. "The Structure of Corporate Ownership: Causes and Consequences." *Journal of Political Economy* 93 (December): 1155-77.

Financial Executives Research Foundation Inc. 2001. "Quantitative Measures of the Quality of Financial Reporting" (7 June).

Holderness, Clifford G., Randall S. Krozner, and Dennis P. Sheehan. 1999. "Were the Good Old Days That Good? Changes in Managerial Stock 20 Federal Reserve Bank of Richmond Economic Quarterly Ownership Since the Great Depression." *Journal of Finance* 54 (April): 435-69.

Holmstrom, Bengt. 1979. "Moral Hazard and Observability." *Bell Journal of Economics* 10 (Spring): 74-91.

_____, and Steven N. Kaplan. 2001. "Corporate Governance and Merger Activity in the United States: Making Sense of the 1980s and 1990s." *Journal of Economic Perspectives* 15 (Spring): 121–44.

Jensen, Michael C., and William H. Meckling. 1976. "Theory of the Firm: Managerial Behavior, Agency Costs and Ownership Structure." *Journal of Financial Economics* 3 (October): 305-60.

Lacker, Jeffrey M., and John A. Weinberg. 1989. "Optimal Contracts Under Costly State Falsification." *Journal of Political Economy* 97 (December): 1345-63.

Levitt, Arthur. 2000. "A Profession at the Crossroads." Speech delivered at the National Association of State Boards of Accountancy, Boston, Mass., 18 September.

Manne, Henry G. 1965. "Mergers and the Market for Corporate Control." *Journal of Political Economy* 73 (April): 110-20.

Patsuris, Penelope. 2002. "The Corporate Scandal Sheet." Forbes.com (25 July).

Richardson, Scott, Irem Tuna, and MinWu. 2002. "Predicting Earnings Management: The Case of Earnings Restatements." University of Pennsylvania Working Paper (October).

Roe, Mark J. 1994. *Strong Managers, Weak Owners: The Political Roots of American Corporate Finance*. Princeton, N.J.: Princeton University Press.

_____. 2002. "Corporate Law's Limits." *Journal of Legal Studies* 31 (June): 233-71.

Seligman, Joel. 1982. *The Transformation of Wall Street: A History of the Securities and Exchange Commission and Modern Corporate Finance*. Boston: Houghton Mifflin.

Shleifer, Andrei, and Robert W. Vishny. 1997. "A Survey of Corporate Governance." *Journal of Finance* 52 (June): 737-83.

United States Senate, Committee on Governmental Affairs. 2002. "Financial Oversight of Enron: The SEC and Private-Sector Watchdogs." Staff report (8 October).

# UNIT 7

# International Human Resource Management

## Unit Selections

## Key Points to Consider

- How does the smaller world affect the practice of human resource management?

- What are some considerations of transnational firms in the human resource area?

- How would you expect organizations in the future to view the market for potential employees?

- How would you expect organizations to view compensation of international employees?

- Do you think there are differences in the way different cultures view sexual harassment?

 **Links: www.dushkin.com/online/**
These sites are annotated in the World Wide Web pages.

**Globalization and Human Resource Management**
*http://www.cic.sfu.ca/forum/adler.html*
**Labor Relations and the National Labor Relations Board**
*http://www.snc.edu/socsci/chair/336/group2.htm*

The world is changing and getting smaller all the time. At the beginning of the twentieth century, the Wright brothers flew at Kitty Hawk, and some 25 years later, Charles Lindbergh flew from New York to Paris, alone, nonstop. In 1969 the spacecraft *Eagle One* landed on the moon and Neil Armstrong said, "One small step for man, one giant leap for mankind."

Indeed, the giant leaps have become smaller. The world has shrunk due to transportation and communication. Communication is virtually instantaneous—not as it was during the early part of the 1800s, when the Battle of New Orleans was fought several weeks after the peace treaty for the War of 1812 had been signed. For centuries, travel was limited to the speed of a horse or a ship. During the nineteenth century, however, speeds of 60 or even 100 miles an hour were achieved by railroad trains. Before the twentieth century was half over, the speed of sound had been exceeded, and in the 15 years that followed, humans circled the globe in 90 minutes. Less than 10 years later, human beings broke free from Earth's gravity and walked on the Moon. The exotic became commonplace. Societies and cultures that had been remote from each other are now close and people must now live with a diversity unknown in the past.

A shrinking world also means an expanding economy, a global economy, because producers and their raw materials and markets are now much closer to each other than they once were. People, and the organizations they represent, often do business all over the world, and their representatives are often members of foreign societies and cultures. Human resource management in just the domestic arena is an extremely difficult task; when the rest of the world is added to the effort, it becomes a monumental undertaking.

Workers in the United States are competing directly with workers in other parts of the world. Companies often hold out for the lowest bidder in a competition for wage rates. This often forces the wage rates down for higher paying countries, while only marginally bringing up the wages of the lower paying societies—a development that is bound to have a direct impact on the standard of living in all of the developed countries of the world.

As more firms become involved in world trade, they must begin to hire foreign workers. Some of these people are going to stay with the firm and become members of the corporate cadre. In the global economy, it is not uncommon for Indian employees to find themselves working for American or European multinational corporations in, say Saudi Arabia. This presents the human resource professional with a problem of blending the three cultures into a successful mix. In this example, the ingredients are a well-educated Asian, working in a highly traditional Middle-Eastern society, for a representative of Western technology and culture. The situation involves three different sets of values,

three different points of view, and three different sets of expectations on how people should act and be treated. "A People Strategy that Spans the Globe" is a necessary approach to any organization doing business on a worldwide scale. As seen in "Changes Afoot in EU Pension Regulations," and "Don't Settle for Less: Global Compensation Programs Need Global Compensation Tools," there is bound to be a blending of ideas on such issues as compensation, benefits, and pensions. Not only on a regional level, such as the EU or NAFTA, but probably on a global level in the more distant future as organizations vie for top talent, no mater where they may originally come from.

American industry does not have a monopoly on new ideas in human resources. Other societies have successfully dealt with many of the same problems. While U.S. firms certainly will not adopt every idea (lifetime employment as practiced in Japan seems the most obvious non-candidate), they can learn much from organizations outside the United States. Human Resource Managers need to engage in "Learning From Our Overseas Counterparts" if they are going to meet the needs of their employees and contribute to the success of the corporation.

Faster and better communication and transportation are leading to a more closely knit social, cultural, and economic world, where people's global abilities can make the difference between the success or failure of an organization. But this closer world is also a more dangerous world. The recent events of the War on Terror have demonstrated the dangers associated with doing business abroad, outside of the confines of one's home country. Family and personal security have become a far larger issue than they were in the past and security is now a consideration for all individuals whether they are working domestically or outside of their home country.

# Changes Afoot in EU Pension Regulations

A European Court of Justice ruling may bring the
EU closer to a pan-European pension.

By Robert O'Connor

The European Union (EU) represents a dream that has worked. Founded by six countries as the European Economic Community in the 1950s, the EU has grown to 15 members and is poised to admit another 10. The EU has delivered peace, prosperity and a single currency.

But American businesspeople expecting to find a "United States of Europe" may be disappointed. Profound differences—legal, cultural and linguistic—remain from country to country. Among the most confusing of the differences are those that affect pensions.

Despite the establishment of the euro as the single currency in 12 of the 15 member states, EU countries still maintain their own tax regimes, including tax policies that cover pension schemes.

But things may be changing. In October 2002, the European Court of Justice (ECJ) declared that tax benefits for pension contributions should apply regardless of national borders. The court ruled in the case of Rolf Danner, a dual German-Finnish national, who moved from Germany to Finland and wanted to continue to pay into two German-based pension funds. Finnish authorities claimed he should be subject to taxes on these contributions. Danner argued that the contributions should be regarded, for tax purposes, in the same way as payments made to a Finnish pension.

The court ruled in favor of Danner, saying that EU member states would be wrong either to limit or disallow tax benefits on "contributions to voluntary pension schemes paid to pension providers in other member states."

Proponents of a borderless tax regime applauded the ruling, citing the lack of harmonized pension policies as the largest barrier to free movement of labor across borders. Companies could save money by offering one pension scheme for all their employees in different EU countries and could better recruit and relocate workers who start saving for retirement in one country and want to continue contributing to the plan while based in another country, proponents say.

Liza Hecht, a tax principal at Deloitte & Touche in New York, says the Danner ruling follows global thinking that has become apparent in international tax treaties. "I interpret the Danner case to be part of an overriding trend towards accommodating home country qualified arrangements while [an employee is] on assignment in a host location," Hecht says.

## Implications

Peter Ford, partner and head of pensions at the Norton Rose law firm in London, believes that the Danner decision may encourage job mobility, "in the sense that a French employee who gets moved to Germany may still be able to pay into his French plan and get the appropriate tax relief." But Ford also argues that the case will make it more difficult to create one plan for the entire EU. He notes that the decision does not remove the differences among the various national tax systems within the EU, and he sees no movement toward tax harmony.

But Harold Lewis, pensions partner at Eversheds law firm in London, says the ruling has made the establishment of a pan-European pension "a distinct possibility" within three or four years. Lewis describes the judgment as "a kind of policy rejection of tax authorities trying to defend their own patch." (See "Is There a Pan-European Pension Ahead?")

Alan Pickering, chairman of the European Federation for Retirement Provision, the umbrella organization for the European pensions industry, also takes a cautious

# Is There a Pan-European Pension Ahead?

The establishment of a pan-European pension would be within the spirit of the European Union. One of the guiding tenets of the EU is that there should be free movement of capital and labor. The European Commission, the administrative arm of the EU, has called for the establishment of a pan-EU pension. The commission has argued that tax restriction on cross-border pension contributions are in breach of European treaties.

The commission has submitted a directive for the consideration of the European Parliament that would standardize pension regulation throughout the EU. But this, of course, would not eliminate the tax differences among member states.

Alan Pickering, chairman of the European Federation for Retirement Provision, the umbrella organization for the pension industry, believes that the directive will make it slightly easier for multinationals to adopt a pan-European approach to their pension planning. The directive would be binding on all EU member states, which would be required to enact it into their national laws.

Pickering suggests that a succession of court cases could convince European politicians to take action on pensions out of fear that the European Court will do it for them. Without political agreement, there is the likelihood that the "courts will create a free-for-all" that would greatly diminish the power of the national tax authorities, he says.

Another concern is that a failure to resolve the issue will make "pension provision in Europe more expensive at a time when we ought to be making it as cheap as possible, given that we've got increased longevity and that we are having to chase every cent of investment return," Pickering says.

Mark Sullivan, European partner at Mercer Human Resource Consulting in London, doubts that the Danner ruling will be enough to open the door to an EU-wide pension. "That is still some way off," he says. "And the tax obstacles to achieving that are still considerable."

Cash-strapped governments could be expected to fight any changes that might threaten their sources of tax revenue, he says. Even wealthy Germany is struggling with budget deficits, he notes. Sullivan says he expects the new pension structure to be shaped more by judges than by politicians, who might fear that unpopular decisions will hurt them at the polls.

---

view on the prospects for pension change within the EU. Pickering, who is a partner in the London office of Watson Wyatt Partners, an employee benefit consultancy, says public pension provisions among EU states will continue to be reflected in differences in pension arrangements within organizations.

Lewis does not expect the national tax authorities within the EU suddenly to crumble and remove all barriers to cross-border pension contributions based on the Danner case. Much more likely, he believes, will be a series of court challenges to existing tax rules, possibly resulting in a snowball effect. Lewis warns that nothing will happen overnight. He notes that it can take up to three years to get a decision from the ECJ. To get to the court, petitioners must first exhaust all legal remedies in their own countries.

Another potentially important pensions case is pending in the United Kingdom. AMS Management Systems, a consultancy, has asked the Inland Revenue, the U.K. tax authority, for permission to enroll a British employee in a Dutch pension scheme. AMS is being supported by a number of multinational companies. Eversheds is advising AMS.

## Policy Adjustments

The amount of restructuring a large company will have to do to its pension program will depend on what it has done up to now, Lewis says. "My guess is that many multinationals have a patchwork of pension provisions, tailored to each particular country that the mobile worker happens to be working in for a year or two or three," he says.

These mosaics, Lewis says, should be relatively easy to dismantle and replace with schemes that would allow employees to be members in several states. Such arrangements would not be limited to people in the higher salary brackets, he says.

Pickering says that a U.S. multinational seeking to adjust to the EU's pension climate should take a step back and consider what it wants to achieve from its remuneration strategy within Europe. The company also should decide what role a pension plan should play within this package. "In developing a pension system," Pickering asks, "do we want to reflect corporate goals almost to the exclusion of local cultures? Or do we begin with local cultures and decide how corporate goals have to be trimmed in order to reflect those local cultures?"

Before businesses did this kind of planning, Pickering says, there were U.S. companies that, for instance, were providing private pensions to French employees—who also received state-funded pensions—that were on a par with the private pensions that they gave their employees in the United Kingdom, which has a more established private pension system.

The result, he says, was that the U.K. employees were probably under-pensioned, while the French employees were probably over-pensioned. "You do need to have due regard to social policy provision within each member state, which varies considerably and will do for quite a while," Pickering says.

Lewis says that a move toward a pan-European pension could generate huge savings for companies. The main benefit would come through the centralized management of investments, he says. Also, HR would be freed from having to comply with different national regulatory regimes, he adds.

Big companies are well placed to achieve economies of scale through the effective management of benefit programs and assets, Pickering says. The challenge will be for the smaller company that may have a big operation in one European country and satellite operations in others, he says. These companies are carrying most of the weight of regulation, he says.

## The Future

HR should keep a close eye on the developments that result from the Danner ruling, Hecht says. A pan-European approach to pension schemes would save U.S. multinational companies a lot of money and would give them much more flexibility in recruiting and moving expatriates from one member country to another.

Mark Sullivan, European partner at Mercer Human Resource Consulting in London, believes that HR will become more influential within organizations as a result of the Danner ruling. Benefits have a crucial impact on companies, he notes. "It is essential for the HR team to make sure they have benchmarked appropriately and have the right level of benefits in place to make sure they have the right skills to do whatever the job required is," he says.

Despite his caution, Pickering believes that a pan-European pension framework will be in place within five years. Large companies should be able to operate cost-effectively within that structure, he adds. "What I don't yet know is whether the nirvana will result from political foresight or guerilla warfare in the courts," he says. "But I think the landscape five years hence will be quite different to that which we have now."

ROBERT O'CONNOR IS A LONDON-BASED FREELANCE BUSINESS WRITER. HE PREVIOUSLY WORKED AS AN EDITOR AND REPORTER AT THE *BALTIMORE SUN*, THE *FORT LAUDERDALE NEWS* AND THE *WATERBURY REPUBLICAN*.

# A People Strategy That Spans the Globe

Human resources is key to the success of a company that is "only world famous in Denmark".

*Carroll Lachnit*

You're **Novo Nordisk**, a Danish company that does life-saving work—the treatment of diabetes, which the World Health Organization estimates will affect 300 million people worldwide by 2025. You are a pioneer in corporate social responsibility, rating company performance not just in bottom-line terms but also in its social and environmental impact and achievements. You already have 18,000 employees in 68 countries. So there's no need to worry about your ability to attract and retain employees, right?

Actually, there is, says Peter Møller, Novo Nordisk's vice president, business and organization. "Novo Nordisk is only world famous in Denmark. We have to make an extra effort to be able to attract the best employees."

Novo Nordisk also has ambitious growth plans—to double the number of employees between 2000 and 2010. And, Møller says, "we are a small company compared to our competitors, so outside Denmark, we have to be better to attract people."

Attracting and retaining the best people is one part of the company's five-pronged "People Strategy" which also targets customer relations, development of people, equal opportunities, and the creation of a winning culture. Novo Nordisk identified the five focus areas several years ago, using an analysis of how the company would develop, Møller says. "We identified the five focus areas, and determined they would be relevant for all units in the company, regardless of function or geography."

The People Strategy, along with an annual strategic-planning process and the guiding principles of Novo Nordisk's "Way of Management," directs all of the company's human resources strategies, whether they're being executed in India, Denmark, or the United States.

"Our challenge is to develop a global mind-set and at the same time hold on to our values and culture," Novo Nordisk CEO Lars Rebien Sørensen writes in an introduction to a guide to the People Strategy. Because a unified human resources strategy is key to helping Novo Nordisk succeed in the world marketplace, the company is the 2003 *Optimas* winner for Global Outlook.

When Møller and his colleague Lars Almblom Jørgensen, Novo Nordisk's executive vice president and chief of staffs, came to New York in March to accept the *Optimas Award*, Møller still seemed a little abashed at the fact that the company had won. "In all fairness," Møller had said a few months earlier, during the research process for the *Optimas Awards*, "the five focus areas we've identified as relevant for all the business units are not rocket science." But, he added, they're developed and pursued differently at Novo Nordisk, with top-to-bottom attention and follow-through.

Novo Nordisk arms each of the business units with a guide for making the People Strategy work. It spells out the five focus areas. It explains that year's target for each focus point, such as what percentage of employees expect to meet with a diabetes patient and talk to him about the illness and its impact, which is a cornerstone of the company's customer-relations focus. It shows how Novo Nordisk employees achieved goals in the focus areas. It also provides a "toolbox" for how the unit can meet its targets.

HR employees set the targets, and a draft goes up to the Novo Nordisk management committee. When the targets are approved, they're integrated into the company's balanced scorecard. Performance toward the targets of the People Strategy is factored into top management's compensation.

The emphasis on those targets appears to be effective. In 2002, 80 percent of Novo Nordisk's employees had a conversation with a person who has diabetes. Nirmal Kumar Jain, a regulatory affairs executive in India, said his meeting with a diabetes patient "made me feel that I should start contributing by whatever means possible."

# Learning from Our Overseas Counterparts

Adopt some practices that help keep your foreign colleagues flexible in the face of stringent workplace laws.

By Paul Falcone

**A**s U.S. citizens and employers, we all gripe about high taxes and the numerous workplace protection laws that make it challenging to manage difficult employees. That's especially the case in "employee-friendly" states like California, where courts and juries appear to assume that employers are guilty until proven innocent. And the grumbling continues like this: How are companies supposed to deal with restrictive and expensive laws like the Family and Medical Leave Act (FMLA), pregnancy disability leave and everything that comes with Title VII compliance?

It's a lot to deal with and keep track of as employment legislation constantly changes on the federal, state and local levels. However, take a gander across the pond, and you'll see that U.S. managers have it pretty easy in comparison. What challenges face our overseas management counterparts, and, more important, what can we learn from them in terms of how they deal with their own challenges?

## International Sensitivity

As unique as our problems appear, U.S. managers may be surprised to learn of some of the woes facing their overseas counterparts. Nothing helps you appreciate your situation more than viewing it through the comparative perspective of others. So let's briefly scan the globe and highlight some of the more salient issues that plague our management counterparts in foreign countries.

The European Union (EU) currently has 15 member states and is poised to accept another 10 in May. The EU gives new meaning to the term "work/life balance," tipping more heavily onto the "life" for many of its workers. For example, EU countries start with four weeks of vacation; however, in some countries that's just the beginning. In France, for example, employees are guaranteed five weeks of vaca-

tion per year, unless they are between 18 and 21 years old. Then they are entitled to a 30-day annual leave regardless of how long they have served in the company. Maternity leave is a minimum of 16 weeks (10 of which must be taken after the child is born) but can increase to 26 weeks for a woman's third pregnancy. More significant, the initial duration of unpaid parental leave in France is one year, which can be extended until the child's third birthday.

Maybe those sound like wonderful perks if you're an employee in the EU, but managing around four weeks of annual vacation and three years of child care leave (as opposed to our 12-week FMLA baby-bonding period) can certainly strain your business operations.

Try this one on for size: In Spain, workers who are laid off commonly receive nine weeks of severance for each full year of service. In the United States, it's a much more common practice to award one week of severance for each full year worked.

That means a five-year Spanish employee who is about to be laid off (or "made redundant," as they say in most other parts of the world) would be entitled to 45 weeks of severance. Under such financial constraints, a layoff may not be as attractive an alternative for your company becoming more economically competitive after all.

To make matters worse, certain EU countries such as Germany mandate a "social plan" in light of a pending layoff. In addition to objective selection criteria like years of service, performance track records and education or specialized technical skills, German employers also must consider a worker's age and number of dependents. Generally speaking, the more difficult it would be for a worker to find employment elsewhere or the more children that a worker has to support, the greater the level of job protection. Employers are also obligated to create a retraining plan to help those redundant workers re-enter the workplace with suitable skills to find employment elsewhere.

---

In Spain, workers who are laid off commonly receive nine weeks of severance for each full year of service.

---

Here's a twist to the high cost of employer-paid benefits: One in seven people in the EU works part-time. Because many part-timers are female, part-time employees hold the same employment status (including benefits) as full-time employees. Otherwise, the disparity in benefits could be seen as a form of sex discrimination. That's one of the reasons why employee benefits are evaluated at 70 percent of wages in France and 92 percent of wages in Italy (as opposed to 37 percent in the United States). Ouch!

And don't think these employment-related headaches are only limited to EU countries. Other parts of the world beyond Europe face employment-related challenges as well. In Japan, for example, female employees are entitled to a monthly (partially) paid absence called "menstruation leave." A great perk for employees, no doubt, but a challenge nonetheless for operational supervisors.

In Mexico, a Christmas bonus, consisting of at least 15 days' salary, is considered part of the salary. In fact, there are "13 months of annual salary" in many Latin American countries, just to make sure em-

ployees have enough money during the holidays to buy presents for their families.

## Lessons Learned

Now that we're all a little more *au courant* with some of the challenges facing our non-U.S. counterparts, let's see how successful managers abroad face their key day-to-day issues. Clearly the result of so many employee rights is the concern that an entitlement mentality may plague European workers. Because of the prevalence in the European Union of strong unions and works councils that are empowered with information and consultation rights on behalf of covered workers, employees may be more apt to challenge management's directives. To make matters worse, many European employers are required by statute to provide detailed employment contracts to new hires outlining the terms and conditions of employment. Employees have been known on occasion to refuse additional work responsibilities if those duties were not clearly outlined in the original written agreement.

To delicately work around such restrictions, many European managers attempt to create a work environment where employees can find meaningful ways to contribute. "There are a number of universal traits that make a good manager, including flexibility, credibility and active listening skills" according to Rensia Melles, director of clinical products, global services at FGI, a provider of international employee assistance program (EAP) services in Toronto. "There is an increasing need for global managers to develop relationships with employees—and the context of how this is done will differ from culture to culture. However, managers everywhere need to consider putting less of a focus on discipline and more emphasis on coaching as a means of creating change and motivating staff. This acknowledgment of the individual often takes the form of guidance, mentoring and training."

In essence, by giving employees the flexibility to reinvent their jobs in light of the company's changing needs and to take ownership of their work, there is less chance that workers will take a strict adherence to their job duties or otherwise look for ways of avoiding work.

Finding qualified staff to replace workers who are on leave can be time-consuming and costly, and regulated temporary services no doubt play a role in the process. "Since companies must comply with statu-

tory leave benefits, creative employers will take the opportunity to reorganize departments and realign resources with business needs. This is a good opportunity for change in the department and to motivate those employees on leave to return to new and challenging responsibilities in the workplace—possibly even earlier than originally planned," according to Deena Baker-Nel, senior manager of international assignment services at Deloitte in Los Angeles.

"Some companies meet with an employee before the leave even begins to discuss potential responsibilities upon return," says Baker-Nel. "Adding rotational assignments or new meaningful roles that employees view as critical to their career development can go a long way in motivating people to return early."

And because it's so costly to lay off workers and difficult to terminate for cause, many organizations forego the opportunity to shed individuals, even if it means going into an overbudget/overstaff situation. When facing the challenge of retaining substandard performers or genuinely "redundant" workers, employers may likely continue the employment relationship.

"In such cases, the company may have no choice but to rethink the individual's role," according to Heather Hand, senior vice president of global human resources at Sunrise Medical in Carlsbad, Calif. "For example, we were faced with a situation where a marketing director overseas had lost interest in her job. She rarely came out of her office and only dealt with her staff via e-mail. The cost of making her redundant was excessive, so we re-purposed her role in a way that she could focus more on her clients and spend less time managing people and dealing with creative services. We changed her title to director of affiliate relations, which allowed her to save face internally, and she tuned back in and became a solid team contributor. I don't know that we would have looked at that very same issue quite as creatively or strategically in the United States in order to come up with an employment solution that benefited both the employee and the company."

From time to time, it's important that U.S. managers increase their sensitivity of how others see the management world and thereby lessen their U.S.-centric view of things. U.S. challenges may seem unique, but there are other systems and ways of doing business that in some respects are superior to ours from a worker's standpoint and perhaps inferior from a managerial or competitive standpoint. In appreciating our differences, we can learn and share lessons that help keep our daily challenges in perspective.

Paul Falcone is director of international human resources at Paramount Pictures in Hollywood, Calif. He is the author of four books published by AMACOM, including *The Hiring and Firing Question and Answer Book* (2001) and *101 Sample Write-Ups for Documenting Employee Performance Problems: A Guide to Progressive Discipline and Termination* (1999). This article represents the views of the author solely as an individual and not in any other capacity.

# Sexual Harassment in the European Union: The Dawning of a New Era

James M. Owens, Glenn M. Gomes, and James F. Morgan

## Introduction

The European Parliament and the Council took a bold step toward prohibiting sexual harassment throughout workplaces in the European Union (EU) when it recently enacted amendments to the 1976 Equal Treatment Directive (European Parliament and the Council, 2002). The public policy objective of Directive 2002/73/EC (hereafter, "the Directive") is to harmonize the Member States' laws regarding the equal treatment of men and women. As Member States (currently 15 nations, soon to be 25) adopt laws implementing the Directive, sexual harassment will be recognized as a form of gender-based discrimination throughout the EU.

The Directive is a natural outcome of a series of policy initiatives over the last few decades aimed at realizing a fundamental principle underlying the EU— the equal participation of men and women in the labor market. Sexual harassment in the workplace did not receive serious attention by EU policymakers until the mid-1980s, when Rubenstein (1987) published the results of his study made on behalf of the European Commission. Finding that sexual harassment was a widespread problem, the Commission undertook a number of initiatives in the early 1990s to correct the problem, but progress was painfully slow and results minimal. In a more recent manuscript prepared by the European Commission (1998), evidence suggests that between 40 and 50% of women, and 10% of men, have experienced sexual harassment at some point in their working lives.

The EU's most recent efforts to eliminate sexual harassment in the workplace present significant challenges and opportunities for human resource managers in multinational corporations with interests in the EU. This article first identifies the major components of the Directive and, where appropriate, comments on significant similarities with U.S. law. Next, we offer informed speculation about how employers may wish to influence unresolved issues on the public policy agenda as they address the challenges created by the Directive. The article concludes with practical suggestions for employers who wish to seize the opportunities provided by the Directive for eliminating sexual harassment from the workplace.

## Key Features of the Directive

The Directive contains a number of key elements, including: (1) the nature of workplace harassment; (2) reference to preventative measures on sexual harassment; (3) the establishment of judicial and/or administrative procedures for enforcement purposes; (4) compensation for victims of discrimination and harassment; and (5) the establishment of national agencies charged with promoting equal employment opportunities.

### ■ Definition of workplace harassment

"Harassment" and "sexual harassment," as defined in Article 2(2) of the Directive, are now recognized as a form of discrimination on the grounds of sex and therefore are contrary to the principle of equal treatment of men and women. "Harassment" is defined to occur "where an unwanted conduct related to the sex of a person occurs with the purpose or effect of violating the dignity of a person, and of creating an intimidating, hostile, degrading, humiliating or offensive environment." In contrast, "sexual harassment" exists "where any form of unwanted verbal, nonverbal or physical conduct of a sexual nature occurs, with the purpose or effect of violating the dignity of a person, in particular when creating an intimidating, hostile, degrading, humiliating or offensive environment." The Directive also establishes that a person's rejection of, or submission to, harassment or sexual harassment may not be used as a basis for an employment decision affecting that person (Article 2(3)).

Interesting parallels can be drawn between the language of the Directive and definitions used in the United States. For example, Title VII of the 1964 Civil Rights Act prohibits employer discrimination "against any individual with respect to his compensation, terms, conditions, or privileges of employment, because of such individual's … sex…." (42 U.S.C. § 2000e-2(a)(1)(1994)). The Equal Employment Opportunity Commission (EEOC), the federal agency charged with enforcing the provisions of Title VII, states that sexual harassment involves "unwelcome sexual advances, requests for sexual favors, and other verbal or physical contact of a sexual nature constitute sexual harassment when submission to or rejection of this conduct explicitly or implicitly affects an individual's employment, unreasonably interferes with an individual's work performance or creates an intimidating, hostile or offensive work environment" (EEOC, 2002).

The concept of "unwanted" is a key element of the Directive's definitions, and closely mirrors U.S. sexual harassment law. In the landmark 1986 decision of *Meritor Savings Bank v. Vinson* (hereafter "*Meritor*"), the United States Supreme Court ruled unanimously that the employee's consent to sexual liaisons was not germane to the question of whether sexual harassment existed; rather, the proper inquiry is whether the behavior is *unwelcomed*. By employing the word "unwanted," Article 2(2) of the Directive appears congruent with U.S. law, and the crux of the determination is if the employee had a meaningful choice in being exposed to objectionable behavior.

The Directive also relies on the key phrase "intimidating, hostile, degrading, humiliating, or offensive environment." While the Directive does not provide guidance on precisely what constitutes such an environment, parallels can again be drawn by reference to U.S. law. The *Meritor* decision established the concept of a hostile working environment and that hostility could be shown when a behavior has the characteristics of being sufficiently severe or pervasive to alter the conditions of employment. Following that decision, the Supreme Court in *Harris v. Forklift Systems, Inc.* (1993) ruled that a victim need not claim psychological damage, but the working environment must take on characteristics of hostility.

Finally, in *Oncale v. Sundowner Offshore Services* (1998), the Supreme Court stated that the presence of sexual harassment could only be determined by considering the workplace's social or cultural context. For example, "a professional football player's working environment is not severely or pervasively abusive … if the coach smacks him on the buttocks as he heads onto

the field—even if the same behavior would reasonable by experienced as abusive by the coach's secretary (male or female) back at the office" (Oncale: 81-82). In other words, "in judging the severity of the conduct, attention to the cultural context in which the purported harassment occurs will guard against imposing liability on behavior that—although offensive to Miss Manners—does not offend Title VII" (Frank, 2002: 450).

In our opinion, if the EU adopts a definition of hostility similar to that used in the U.S., the concepts of "intimidating," "degrading," and "humiliating" may be used to establish the degree of severity or pervasiveness of the hostility. In any case, the reality of a social or cultural context cannot be ignored when arriving at a determination of a hostile environment, especially given the wide-ranging sociopolitical and cultural differences among the Member States (see, e.g., Timmerman and Bajema, 1999). In implementing the Directive, Member States should provide guidance to employers, employees, courts, and others on precisely what workplace conduct is unacceptable within the social context.

## ■ Preventative measures

Article 2(5) now specifies: "Member States shall encourage, in accordance with national law, collective agreements or practice, employers and those responsible for access to vocational training to take measures to prevent all forms of discrimination on grounds of sex, in particular harassment and sexual harassment at the workplace." It is interesting that the Directive merely "encourages" such activities. It does not legally require individual employers to take preventative actions.

While the Directive offers no specifics regarding the nature of effective prevention programs, guidelines already exist. Commission Recommendation 92/131/ EEC on the protection of the dignity of women and men at work (1992) contains an annex providing a code of practice on measures to combat sexual harassment. The Code of Practice encourages the use of clearly communicated policies, effective enforcement procedures, and training for all employees. It is interesting that the Commission Recommendation is similar to revised EEOC guidelines on the minimum contents of an effective prevention program (EEOC, 1998). In both instances, an explicit written policy against sexual harassment, clearly and regularly communicated to employees, is recognized as a necessary (but not sufficient) first step. Simply having a policy against sex harassment is not considered an effective prevention measure unless the employer actually implements the policy. There must be procedures for resolving complaints that encourage victims of harassment to come forward, and confidentiality should be protected to the extent possible. In all cases, effective sanctions and remedies, including protection of victims and witnesses against retaliation, must be provided.

## ■ Judicial and administrative enforcement procedures

The Directive obliges Member States to ensure that judicial and administrative procedures (including, if appropriate, conciliation procedures) are available to all persons who consider themselves wronged or victimized by harassment, even after the employment relationship has ended. The Directive does not address directly the proper burden of proof in these actions. Council Directive 97/80/EC on the burden of proof in cases of discrimination based on sex, however, applies to Council Directive 76/207/EEC and, by inference, to the Directive under consideration here. Article 4 of Directive 97/80/EC states that "it shall be for the respondent to prove that there has been no breach of the principle of equal treatment," and Member States may adopt rules of evidence that are more favorable to the plaintiff. Placing the burden of proof on the employer to show that harassment did not occur is in direct opposition to U.S. rules that require the plaintiff (in this case, the alleged victim) to prove a *prima facie* case. This issue of the burden of proof may be one of the most important challenges facing employers.

## ■ Compensation and reparations

When unlawful harassment has been established, the Directive prohibits limits on the compensation payable to the victim. Reflecting past rulings by the European Court of Justice (e.g., Draehmpaehl, 1997; Marshall, 1993), Article 6(2) now requires Member States to introduce measures "to ensure real and effective compensation or reparation … for the loss and damage sustained by a person injured as a result of discrimination." Moreover, the compensation should be "dissuasive and proportionate" to the injury suffered. There can be no fixed prior upper limit to the compensation, except in one instance: when the employer can prove that the only damage suffered by a job applicant was the refusal to take the job application into consideration, and there was no other actual financial loss. The desire to avoid unlimited economic loss may provide strong incentives for employers to institute procedures for eliminating workplace behavior that would expose them to such liability.

By way of comparison with the United States, Title VII provides that victims of sexual harassment be made whole. Title VII was amended in 1991 to permit compensatory damages (pain and suffering), and, where the discrimination was intentional, punitive damages. Congress placed limits on the compensatory damages depending on the size of the employer. The upper limit is $300,000 for employers with more than 500 employees. While these limits apply to Title VII, they do not apply to claims brought under the civil rights statutes of individual states, where awards can run into millions of dollars.

## ■ National "equal treatment" agencies

Article 8 of the Directive requires that "Member States shall designate and make the necessary arrangements for a body or bodies for the promotion, analysis, monitoring and support of equal treatment of all persons without discrimination on the grounds of sex." Whether created anew or a part of existing agencies, this administrative structure has the potential for serving as a key enforcement mechanism, especially if it also promulgates regulations for preventing harassment. For Member States that have national agencies already charged with defending human rights generally or safeguarding individual rights, these "equal treatment" bodies may form part of the existing agencies. Examples for such an administrative agency already exist. In the United Kingdom, these functions are the province of the Equal Opportunity Commission (EOC), a nongovernmental agency established under the Sex Discrimination Act in 1975 that deals exclusively with sex discrimination issues. (In the United States, these functions are undertaken by the EEOC.)

These bureaucratic entities are required to be competent at (1) providing independent assistance to victims of discrimination in pursuing their discrimination complaints; (2) conducting independent surveys related to discrimination; and (3) publishing independent reports and making recommendations on discrimination issues. In accordance with national traditions and practice, Article 8 also requests Member States to promote a dialogue between "social partners" that fosters the principle of equal treatment. The outcome of such a dialogue might include, for example, collective agreements, the monitoring of workplace practices, the establishment of codes of conduct, and the research or exchange of experiences and good practices. Employers are encouraged (but not mandated) to disseminate to employees and their representatives "appropriate information on equal treatment." Member States are directed to encourage dialogue with nongovernmental organizations that have a legitimate interest in fighting workplace discrimination based on gender. Finally, they are allowed to introduce and adopt provisions that "are more favorable to the protection of the principle of equal treatment" than established by the Directive itself.

# Shaping the Public Policy Debate

The Directive became effective on October 5, 2002, the day of its publication in the *Official Journal of the European Communities*. Member States have until October 2005 to enact the legislation, regulations, and administrative provisions and infrastructure that allow each to comply. This presents both opportunities and challenges. Employers will first have *opportunities* to influence public policy by engaging in the inevitable debate within each Member State over the nature of the national legislation implementing the Directive. The *challenges* will arise after such national legislation is passed.

We anticipate that the public policy debate within each Member State will be affected differently according to the degree to which anti-harassment legislation and court edicts already exist. In Member States where anti-harassment legislation has evolved in ways consistent with the Directive and where the regulatory bureaucracy is already established (e.g., the United Kingdom), the public policy debate over legislative mechanisms for implementing the Directive will likely be unprotracted and more or less routine. Conversely, in Member States with a relatively undeveloped legislative code in this area, or where the bureaucratic infrastructure responsible for promulgating and enforcing regulations may be nascent or immature (e.g., Portugal), the public policy debate may be more spirited and extended. In either case, it should be the role of the employer, as a vital social partner in the implementation process, to contribute meaningfully and assertively to whatever public policy debate ensues.

Employers will want to be heard on at least four important public policy areas: (1) the clarification of the *prima facie* elements of harassment and sexual harassment, including more specific definitions of such terms and phrases as "unwanted, "violating the dignity," and "intimidating, hostile, degrading, humiliating or offensive"; (2) the creation of an affirmative defense for employers; (3) the establishment of an official arbitration process for discrimination claims; and (4) the delineation of the powers, duties, and responsibilities of the "equal treatment" agencies mandated by the Directive.

## ■ Clarification of the elements of harassment and sexual harassment

Perhaps it is in the nature of "harassment" or "sexual harassment" that any definitions of these terms would contain broad, generic words and phrases that invite their own interpretive challenges. Two phrases are common to the Directive's definitions of harassment and sexual harassment: (1) "the purpose or effect of violating the dignity of a person," and (2) "creating an intimidating, hostile, degrading, humiliating or offensive environment." We anticipate that employers will want clarification of these words and phrases either in the implementing statutes or in the regulations promulgated by the equal treatment agencies. For example, exactly when is a person's dignity violated? Is such a determination based on a "reasonable person" standard, whereby an alleged harasser should have known, as a reasonable person, that the alleged harassing behavior would have the effect of violating the dignity of another person? Or is such a determination based on a "reasonable victim" standard, whereby any person

receiving the alleged harassing behavior could reasonably be assumed to have suffered a violation of one's dignity (cf., e.g., Kubal, 1999)? Similarly, what constitutes an intimidating, hostile, degrading, humiliating, or offensive environment? How are these words to be defined, and what standards are to be applied in defining them? Definitions are critical for establishing a *prima facie* case of harassment and sexual harassment and for defending against claims of discrimination.

## ■ Legislation providing for an affirmative defense

In the Directive, Member States are not required to include employer defenses within their national implementing legislation. It is possible to argue, however, that Article 8b(3) provides a basis for Member States to include employer defenses when it "encourage[s] employers to promote equal treatment for men and women in the workplace in a planned and systematic way." An excellent method of encouraging employers to enact policies and procedures prohibiting sexual harassment would be to give employers an affirmative defense. Unfortunately, Council Directive 97/80/EC clearly places the burden of proof on employers to prove that there has been no breach of the equal treatment principle. In essence, the employer is presumed to have violated the principle unless it can prove otherwise. To level the playing field in a way allowable under the Directive (and Directive 97/80/EC), employers should lobby for an "affirmative defense" within the national implementing legislation.

Member States could fashion statutes creating an affirmative defense by following the examples created by the United States Supreme Court in *Burlington Industries, Inc. v. Ellerth* (1998) and *Faragher v. City of Boca Raton* (1998). These cases created an affirmative defense for employers when they exercised "reasonable care" in preventing sexual harassment and, where sexual harassment is alleged to have occurred, they promptly corrected the harassment. An affirmative defense of this nature necessitates one additional element: that the employee alleging a breach of the equal treatment principle unreasonably failed to take advantage of any preventative or corrective opportunities provided by the employer. Such a requirement correctly allocates responsibility for preventing and correcting harassment to both the employer and the employee. This is consistent with Recommendation 92/131/EEC on the protection of the dignity of women and men at work, whereby the annexed Code of Practice acknowledges "employees' responsibilities" in preventing and discouraging sexual harassment.

## ■ Legislation establishing an official arbitration process

If the EU's experience is anything like that of the United States, the prohibition of workplace sexual harassment will lead to a significant increase in the number of claims requiring resolution within the legal system—inevitably costly for all parties. To minimize the risks and financial costs of trial, employers may wish to lobby for the creation of a system of binding arbitration. Whether such arbitration is allowable in employment cases under extant EU law is debatable (see, e.g., Sternlight, 2002). In the U.S., however, the Supreme Court has ruled that virtually all private employers can require applicants to accept dispute resolution via arbitration as a condition of employment (Circuit City, 2001). The arbitrator or arbitration panel is capable of enforcing all federal protections against discrimination. For the EU, Directive 97/80/EC acknowledges the possibility that such cases might be brought "before a court *or other competent authority*" (emphasis added), and a system of arbitration could serve as such an authority. Similarly, Article 6 of the Directive calls for "judicial and/or administrative procedures, including … *conciliation procedures*" (emphasis added). A system of arbitration would have the effect of lessening the anticipated increased pressure on the respective national court systems and would facilitate efforts to resolve discrimination claims (and other employment disputes) quickly and reasonably, but at a lesser cost than litigation.

## ■ The role and powers of equal treatment agencies

The Directive requires each Member State to create a mechanism for advancing the equal treatment of all persons, but the duties and responsibilities are broadly defined. As each Member State enacts harmonizing legislation implementing this part of the Directive, employers may wish to lobby for clarity regarding the precise powers of these agencies.

Until passage of enabling and harmonizing legislation in each Member State, employers should take an active role in the public policy process. Moreover, they must anticipate being called upon not only to take measures to prevent harassment and sexual harassment from occurring, but also to establish procedures for taking remedial actions once harassment has occurred (or is alleged to have occurred).

# Suggested Workplace Initiatives For Employers

The employer will be the EU's most important and direct guarantor of the principle of equal treatment between men and women in the workplace. In this section, we offer some practical suggestions for preventing sexual harassment and undertaking remedial measures once sexual harassment is alleged to have occurred.

## ■ Preventative measures

In anticipating what measures to take toward eliminating sexual harassment, employers need look no further than the Commission Recommendation 92/131/EEC on the protection of the dignity of women and men at work, particularly its suggested Code of Practice. While the Directive makes no mention of this Recommendation, in our opinion it is an essential companion document. Though not legally binding on Member States, the Code offers sound advice consistent with human resource management "best practices." The prevention of workplace harassment rests on a number of critical employer actions, including developing and effectively communicating unequivocal policy statements and assigning responsibility at each organizational level while providing training programs for all employees.

The most profound and effective measure for preventing sexual harassment is the dissemination of a policy statement stating unequivocally that harassing behavior will not be permitted or condoned by the employer at any time or in any fashion. Such a statement should include definitions of harassment and sexual harassment, examples of inappropriate behavior, and a statement of rights and duties for managers, supervisors, and employees. The policy adopted by the employer would inform employees of their right to report instances of sexual harassment and provide and explain the procedure they should follow to lodge a complaint or seek assistance with the process. Employees should be assured that the employer will take such complaints seriously and will address the complaints in a timely and (to the extent possible) confidential manner. The policy must also protect employees filing a complaint from retaliation. The range of sanctions and disciplinary measures to be taken against employees should effectively deter offending behavior and be specified clearly in the policy.

To increase the likelihood that policy statements will deter sexual harassment, the policy's provisions must be communicated effectively to all employees at every level. Copies of the policy should be given to every employee, and managers and supervisors should reinforce the employer's commitment to a harassment-free workplace by holding meetings with employees periodically to review the policy's essential provisions and convey a responsive and supportive attitude that will earn the employee's trust. If employees perceive management's commitment to be sincere and resolute, the probability that harassment will occur should decrease.

Managers and supervisors should be charged with the responsibility for implementing the policy and taking actions to ensure compliance. Employees likewise would be charged with the duty of complying. Such a policy could be integral to establishing an affirmative defense for employers (should the implementing legislation adopted by each Member State include provisions for an affirmative defense). Ongoing training—for managers, supervisors, and employees —is an essential element in the employer's arsenal of preventative measures. These training sessions should continuously reinforce the conditions that contribute to a harassment-free working environment, and should familiarize or reacquaint each employee with their rights and responsibilities. Such training should occur at the time of hiring and throughout an employee's tenure. Finally, employees assigned an official role in administering the policy's complaint procedures should receive specialized training.

## ■ Remedial measures

Employers will prefer to prevent sexual harassment and other forms of workplace discrimination. However, if the dissemination of a policy statement combined with ongoing training for all employees fails to accomplish this objective, employers must have processes for addressing incidents of harassment once they occur (or are alleged to have occurred). Procedures for remedying sexual harassment are as important as policy statements for employers seeking to provide equal treatment for employees consistent with the letter and spirit of the Directive.

Once again, the wheel need not be reinvented: Commission Recommendation 92/131/EEC provides sound advice and direction for employers seeking a system of remedial measures to address claims and instances of sexual harassment. The procedural mechanisms should include several facets of remediation: (1) an informal inquiry and complaint process, (2) a formal complaint process, (3) the availability of advice and assistance for employees, (4) an investigatory process, and (5) a system of disciplinary sanctions.

*Informal inquiries and complaints.*   Most employees probably prefer to resolve workplace discrimination problems in an informal way. Usually victims of discrimination, and especially sexual harassment, are content simply to have the offending behavior cease. Employers could encourage employees to resolve instances of harassment (or alleged harassment) informally among themselves through open communication and honest dialogue. Sometimes it may be necessary only

for an offended employee to communicate clearly to the offending employee the nature of the unwelcomed behavior, the fact that it makes him or her uncomfortable and may interfere with job performance. Where a policy statement has been communicated to employees who have also been part of an ongoing training program, this informal resolution process is often sufficient. If the offended employee finds it embarrassing or otherwise difficult to raise the issue directly with the offending employee, the employer might designate a counselor, employee assistance officer, or an employee liaison to provide the offended employee confidential advice and, when requested by the employee, to intervene informally on the employee's behalf. If informal methods are ineffective, the employee should have the ability to pursue a formal complaint procedure.

*Formal complaint procedures.*   The offended employee must be able to seek redress and remedy through a formal complaint process created and scrupulously administered by the employer. The employer must designate the person (or persons) with whom an offended employee may report an instance of harassment or file a complaint. Alternatives should be available in case the normal formal procedure is inappropriate (for example, when the person designated to initially receive formal complaints is also the person alleged to be the harasser). To ensure that all employees are aware of the formal complaint procedure—including the identity of persons designated to receive formal complaints, documentation required to establish a formal complaint, and appropriate time lines —it should be included as an integral part of the employer's sexual harassment policy. Indeed, the existence of an effective complaint process reduces the likelihood that a harassment victim will quit the employment relationship or, worse, seek legal remedies (Hogler, Frame and Thornton, 2002).

*Advice and assistance.*   The success of both informal and formal procedures for resolving sexual harassment complaints depends on the availability of a person within the organization charged with the responsibility for dispensing advice and providing assistance to aggrieved employees. Recommendation 92/131/EEC anticipates that this person will likely come from the personnel or equal opportunities departments. Alternatively, the designated counselor may be a member of the employee's trade union or a women's support group. Whoever is charged with this important responsibility must receive formal training in conflict resolution and must be intimately familiar with the organization's policies and complaint procedures. Appropriate resources must be budgeted for this position, and the person must be protected from retaliation for counseling or assisting anyone seeking advice or filing a sexual harassment complaint.

*Investigations.* Without question, the key to successfully resolving formal complaints of sexual harassment is the investigation process. The decision to investigate claims of harassment, and to do so reasonably, can no longer be viewed as simply a matter of managerial discretion (see, e.g., Morgan, Gomes, and Owens, 2001). Indeed, failing to investigate competently may be regarded as strong evidence that the employer approves, albeit implicitly, of the harassment, in direct contravention of the Directive.

Effective investigations should exhibit three attributes: (1) thoroughness, (2) impartiality, and (3) promptness. Thorough investigations involve interviewing the complainant, the alleged harasser, and relevant witnesses. The focus of the inquiry relates exclusively to the question of whether the alleged harasser engaged in prohibited behavior. Investigators must distinguish statements of fact from conjecture. Moreover, for the investigator to make determinations regarding the credibility of the parties and witnesses, the investigator must maintain unquestioned impartiality. The inquiry should be as short as possible, and reasonable investigations normally can be completed within a few days to a couple of weeks.

*Discipline.* The firm's policy prohibiting sexual harassment and protecting the dignity of employees at work should clearly (1) identify behavior that is unacceptable, and (2) specify the range of sanctions for employees who engage in such unacceptable behavior. The policy should prohibit retaliation against, and victimization of, persons bringing complaints of sexual harassment (or persons advising or otherwise assisting complainants), lf a complaint is valid, management must take whatever action is appropriate to ensure that the harassment ceases. When an allegation is found to be unsubstantiated, it may be prudent for management to reassign or transfer one of the parties to the complaint in the interest of reestablishing workplace harmony, especially if either party expresses a desire for such a transfer.

# Conclusion

With the recent approval of the Directive, the EU has taken a major step toward harmonizing public policy aimed at reducing sexual harassment in the workplace. As Member States pass implementing legislation, employers throughout Europe will enjoy new opportunities for advancing the principle of equality between men and women. In pursuing these opportunities, however, employers inevitably will face substantial challenges.

## REFERENCES

Burlington Industries, Inc. v. Enerth, 118 S.Ct. 2257, 524 U.S. 742 (1998).

Circuit City v. Adams, 121 S.Ct. 1302, 532 U.S. 105 (2001).

Commission of the European Communities (1992). Recommendation of 27 November 1991 on the protection of the dignity of women and men at work. Commission Recommendation 92/131/EEC. OJ L 49, 24.02.1992, p. 1.

Council of the European Communities (1976). Directive on the implementation of the principle of equal treatment for men and women as regards access to employment, vocational training and promotion, and working conditions. Council Directive 76/207/EEC. OJ L 39, 14.2.1976, p. 40.

Council of the European Union (1997). Directive of 15 December 1997 on the burden of proof in cases of discrimination based on sex. Council Directive 97/80/EC. OJ L 14, 20.1.98, p. 6.

Draehmpaehl [Nils] v Urania Immobilienservice OHG. Case C-180/95. European Court Reports, 1997, E 1-02195.

European Commission (1998). Sexual harassment in the workplace in the European Union. Directorate-General for Employment, Industrial Relations and Social Affairs, Unit V/D.5.

Equal Employment Opportunity Commission (1998). EEOC Compliance Manual. Retrieved November 1, 2002 at http:www/eeoc.gov/docs/retal.html.

Equal Employment Opportunity Commission (2002). "Facts About Sexual Harassment." Retrieved 10 March 2003, at http://www.eeoc.gov/facts/fs-sex.html.

European Parliament and the European Council (2002). Directive amending Council Directive 76/207/EEC on the implementation of the principle of equal treatment for men and women as regards access to employment, vocational training and promotion, and working conditions. European Parliament and Council Directive 2002/73/EC. OJ L 269, 5.10.2002, p. 15.

Faragher v. City of Boca Raton, 118 S.Ct. 2275, 524 U.S. 775 (1998).

Frank, M. (2002, February). The social context variable in hostile environment litigation, Notre Dame Law Review, 77, 437–532.

Harris v. Forklift Systems, 114 S.Ct. 367,510 U.S. 17 (1993).

Hogler, R., Frame, J. H., and Thornton, G. (2002). Workplace sexual harassment law: An empirical analysis of organizational justice and legal policy. Journal of Managerial Issues, 14(2), 234–250.

Kubal, U. R. (1999, Fall). U.S. Multinational corporations abroad: a comparative perspective on sex discrimination law in the United States and the European Union. North Carolina Journal of International Law & Commercial Regulation, 25, 207–269.

Marshall [M. Helen] v Southampton and South-West Hampshire Area Health Authority. Case C-271/91. European Court Reports, 1993, P. 1-04367.

Meritor Savings Bank v. Vinson, 106 S.Ct. 2399, 477 U.S. 57 (1986).

Morgan, J. F., Gomes, G. M, and Owens, J. M. (2001). The unintended consequences of outsourcing sexual harassment investigations. Journal of Individual Employment Rights, 9(2), 113–127.

Oncale v. Sundowner Offshore Services, Inc., 118 S.Ct. 998, 523 U.S. 75 (1998).

Rubenstein, M. (1987). The Dignity of Women at Work, Part I and II, COM, V/412/87. Brussels: European Commission.

Sternlight, J. R. (2002, July). Is the U.S. out on a limb? Comparing the U.S. approach to mandatory consumer and employment arbitration to that of the rest of the world. University of Miami Law Review, 56, 831–864.

Timmerman, G., and Bajema, C. (1999). Sexual harassment in northwest Europe: A cross-cultural comparison. The European Journal of Women's Studies, 6(4), 419–439.

Title VII of the 1964 Civil Rights Act, 42 U.S.C. § 2000(e) et seq.

The authors are professors of management. Dr. Owens recently co-authored a textbook on business law and has written widely on employment law issues. Dr. Gomes focuses his work on strategic management and business policy. Dr. Morgan, a specialist in employment law, has published several articles on workplace issues.

From *SAM Advanced Management Journal,* Volume 69, No. 1, Winter 2004, pages 4-11, 49. Copyright © 2004 Society for Advancement of Management. Reprinted with permission.

# Don't Settle for Less: Global Compensation Programs Need Global Compensation Tools

Al Wright

To drive higher performing workforces, businesses are creating compensation programs that more directly align with their strategic business and financial goals. The result is increasingly complex compensation strategies, taking into account factors of geography, job function, skills, competencies, and goal achievement, all driving multiple pay types including base pay and variable bonus and stock components.

Certain Web-based technologies can minimize HR administration expenses, while maximizing the positive impact on employee behavior. Tools that automate compensation planning, off-cycle compensation administration, and importantly, persistent employee communication are rapidly gaining acceptance, particularly among companies that have a global presence and need a Web-based solution that can support intricate multinational requirements.

## Compensation Planning Is an Increasingly Complex Business Process

As organizations grow in size and expand across the globe, they need to coordinate the allocation of salary increases and other forms of compensation to support long-term budgeting processes. The purpose of compensation planning is to ensure that salary increases are distributed equitably across the organization while staying within set budget guidelines. Yet, without the right tools in place, this can be an insurmountable task.

Each year companies set merit guidelines and budgets, balancing market factors, internal business factors, and the company's ability to pay. Then, managers are asked to rate their employees' performance and allocate merit increases along with other coinciding compensation programs such as bonus payments and stock option grants. Focal compensation planning periods have replaced, by and large, the practice of determining increases based on individual employment anniversaries.

Compensation planning is a business necessity for just about any company, but it can be a disproportionately difficult process for several reasons. First, the task of determining individual compensation often involves taking into account numerous company guidelines and compliance issues with regard not only to base pay, but to incentive pay (such as annual bonuses) and stock option plans. Each compensation program typically has its own set of guidelines for appropriate increases and awards in order to ensure that the organization is rewarding high performance. Salary increases alone can take the form of merit increases, adjustments to the salary range minimum, lump sum payments, equity adjustments, and promotions. In addition, each program has a separate budget or pool of available money or stock shares that managers need to administer. Internal equity among similar positions within groups and between groups must be taken into consideration as well. Finally, market pay rates and compliance for their U.S. and international locations need to be factored into compensation decisions.

## Compensation Planning History

Beginning in the 1980s, companies frequently relied on spreadsheets to administer focal reviews. Human resources generalists and compensation analysts were called upon to create individual spreadsheets for each manager that listed the employees for which the manager had direct compensation planning responsibility. Managers then input salary increases, bonus payments, and stock option share recommendations into their spreadsheets. Compensation departments then had the arduous task of aggregating the spreadsheets from multiple locations and in multiple currencies and at different management levels of the organization for additional input, review, and approval. Reconciling budgets proved problematic for large organizations.

Changes to employee data such as terminations or transfers complicated this process since the spreadsheets only contained static employee information.

The spreadsheet approach was so labor and time intensive for both line managers and human resources professionals that getting through the compensation planning process often took several months, hindering the organization's ability to focus on other important business issues. In addition, the lack of tools to assist the manager in making appropriate compensation decisions reduced their effectiveness in building a high performance organization.

# The Business Case for Automating Compensation Planning

For many organizations, the labor costs of manually administering compensation planning processes have become prohibitive. The degree of difficulty for creating and combining spreadsheets for hundreds, or even thousands, of managers increases to a point where such a process becomes impractical to administer. The Cedar Group estimated that in North America alone, companies experienced a savings of $5.29 per average transaction with an automated compensation planning system.[1] Multiply that potential savings for companies with 10, 20, even 100,000 employees, and the return on investment is clear, with many companies realizing a payback period in under two years.

In addition to squandering resources, labor-intensive manual compensation planning leads to missed budget targets and payroll errors resulting from employee status changes. The costs of these problems are considerable. In contrast, some organizations have experienced "instant" returns on their investment in automated compensation planning solutions.

For example, prior to deploying a fully automated compensation planning solution, a large telecommunications company struggled with payroll errors resulting from employee terminations, transfers and status changes during the compensation planning period. By the time compensation planning was completed, the employee information was so out of date that the resulting merit increases were erroneous. The payroll department had to correct all the mistakes at an estimated cost of $400 per error. Implementing an automated compensation planning system eliminated the payroll errors since the employee data was continually refreshed in order to keep it current. The savings to the company in avoiding the payroll errors more than paid for the new compensation planning system in its first year.

# Supporting Complex Compensation Plans

Automated compensation planning systems need to support base pay, variable pay and stock option plans across each geographic location. The main component of base pay is the annual merit salary increase that recognizes the individual's performance for the previous year. The amount of the merit increase is affected by the individual's performance rating and the corporate merit budget. Managers need the capability to enter merit increases as either a percent or an amount. Dynamically calculated "spending to the merit budget" information can be prominently displayed for the manager in an automated compensation planning system. Screen views that support the sorting of information can facilitate maintenance of internal equity for merit increases for employees with similar performance in the same position.

Associated with the merit increase is the lump sum payment. For high performing employees at the top of their salary range, lump sum payments can be awarded in lieu of a merit increase to their annual salary. In some organizations, employees can receive either a merit increase or a lump sum payment, but not both. Compensation planning systems can be flexible to support variations in merit increase and lump sum payment business rules.

Salary adjustments are often included in annual focal reviews, and these adjustments have several variations. An adjustment to the salary range minimum is often applied to an employee whose salary is below the minimum of the salary range. This "adjustment to minimum," typically does not debit the merit budget. In addition, equity adjustments are used to recognize an inequity in the employee's salary that cannot be corrected through a merit or promotional increase. Sometimes a separate adjustment budget is established. Compensation planning systems can support multiple adjustment types and the variations of their budget calculations.

Promotions sometimes occur during the focal review as well. Promotions typically include a change in the employee's salary grade to recognize the increased responsibilities and higher skill set required for a new job. Additional data is needed to support the promotion increase—including job code, job title, new grade and new salary range. Sometimes, in-grade promotions or reclassifications are also permitted in the focal review process. Compensation planning systems can facilitate accessing all the additional data required for both promotions and reclassifications.

Variable pay plans can differ greatly between organizations. Bonus plans vary from simple discretionary bonus payments determined by managers to formula driven bonus plans factoring bonus targets for positions, bonus guidelines based on performance ratings, and any number of corporate, business unit and individual objectives. In addition, many organizations have multiple bonus plans with differing eligibility rules. Due to the complexity of incentive programs, some compensation planning systems specialize in supporting just complex variable pay and incentive programs. Other compensation planning systems include variable pay support along with their support for base pay and stock programs so that the manager can plan the employee's total cash compensation.

Merit stock option plans are frequently included in focal compensation planning. An employee's stock option grant history is particularly helpful to managers for determining totals for vested and unvested stock option shares. Stock option guidelines typically recommend shares to be allocated to an employee based upon their position or grade along with their performance rating. Managers also need to allocate stock based on the available pool of shares. Stock pools are often calculated by multiplying a target number of shares per grade or position times an expected participate rate times the number of incumbents in the grade or position. Not all compensation planning systems include support for stock option allocation, guidelines or pool calculations.

# Integrating Market Data Into Compensation Planning

Many base pay programs incorporate the concept of merit guidelines. A matrix of performance ratings with associated merit increase guidelines is frequently provided to managers in order to assist them in making merit decisions that reward high performing employees within the annual merit budget. The employees' position in their salary range can also be integrated into the matrix so that for each portion of the salary range (e.g., quartile or tercile) for each performance rating, the manager has a guideline percent merit increase. Compensation planning systems can include merit guideline data in a decision support tool delivered at the time the manager is making the merit

decision. In addition, these systems can display the specific guidelines for the individual employee based on their location within their salary range and the performance rating selected so that managers do not have to interpret a guideline matrix. Additionally, for compensation programs utilizing bands rather than grades, the compensation planning systems can display the market target salary for the position in order to provide a context for the manager's merit increase decision.

# Supporting Global Compensation Requirements

For global organizations, such factors as rewards, salaries, incentives, and various forms of direct and indirect compensation must be aligned with the cultural and economic norms of each operating location. Effective global compensation planning depends on an understanding of environmental factors such as economic growth, inflation, unemployment, and prevailing pay practices in the countries where one operates. This leads many companies to ask the question: How do we create a compensation program that supports the way our company is structured, organized, and operated globally?

Because many companies have operations and offices outside the U.S., a global compensation planning system must support differing international compensation practices and requires that leaders think about compensation as a whole, regardless of the country location of the employees. The laws, customs, and philosophies regarding compensation vary tremendously from country to country, so exporting a U.S. style plan to other countries rarely makes sense. In fact, because of these variations, the Human Resource Certification Institute has developed the first Human Resource Certification for HR professionals with international and cross-border

responsibilities at multinational organizations.

For example, outside the U.S., most countries plan salaries in monthly rather than annual amounts. Further complicating the cross calculation between annual and monthly salaries, the number of months included in the annual salary varies by country. Seasonal bonuses paid in these countries are counted as "extra months of salary." So the number of months included in the annual salary is different from Japan, to Germany, and so on.

Additional compensation components, such as statutory increases, are required for compensation decisions in some countries. Compensation planning systems can cross calculate monthly and annual salaries as well as display the necessary wage information specific to the individual and country. In addition, accurately converting between a benchmark currency—for example, the U.S. dollar—and the employee's local currency is critical so that planning can be executed in local currency while budget spending can be aggregated in the benchmark currency. Compensation planning systems can be architected so that database field sizes accommodate the conversion of currencies with large exchange rate variances (e.g., one U.S. dollar converts to approximately 1.6 million Turkish liras.) Finally, merit budgets and merit guidelines vary per country due to economic conditions. Budget and guideline configuration for compensation planning systems can support these country specific variations.

Companies that adopt a compensation planning system for their global organization ensure equal standards and similar opportunities across geographic boundaries enabling leaders around the world to use an automated solution to determine their employees' compensation. This allows managers to evaluate employees in the same way, regardless of their location, as the process is applicable across business units, functions and international boundaries, while at the same time being appropriately calibrated to the local market in each country.

Furthermore, it allows employee compensation to be based upon a similar set of criteria, regardless of location. This simplifies the task for leaders who have to decide compensation for employees in several different countries with different currencies. This approach is quite different from organizations where each country has its own process, which makes it difficult to seamlessly move from one system to the next, and where valuable time is spent learning the special rules for each system.

Through reducing duplication and implementing best practices across the organization, costs are reduced and value is added in terms of consistency leveraging the capabilities of the organization on a global basis.

## System Flexibility Is Critical

One thing is certain—compensation plans change over time. Compensation planning systems can adapt to changes in plan components, eligibility, business rules, budgets, guidelines, access dates, calculations, and even screen presentations. Adding or removing base pay components, bonus plans, or stock plans is necessary to provide flexibility for typical compensation program changes. Creating eligibility flags in the database for each compensation component enables changing participant eligibility at a granular level.

Business rules such as minimum and maximum increases or awards can also be changed. Some compensation planning systems offer an administrative application for compensation professionals to quickly and easily change merit budgets, bonus and stock targets and pools, guidelines and system access dates. Calculations for values such as an employee's total compensation can be adjusted as needed. Finally, the actual screen presentations can be easily altered to support the changes in the compensation programs. In fact,

some compensation planning systems offer the flexibility to vary the screen presentation based on the employee population or an employee attribute such as Fair Labor Standards Act (FLSA) status.

## Compliance Issues

Compliance issues are demonstrated in several ways. Some organizations separate compensation planning for exempt employees from the planning for non-exempt employees—terms not even recognized other than in the U.S.—in order to prevent managers from using merit budget from one group for a different group. Compensation planning systems can present different screen presentations for different groups to accommodate different employee populations as well as differences in the compensation plans themselves. Regulatory compliance for protected groups (e.g., gender, age, and minority status) can also be reinforced with compensation planning systems. Presenting merit increase spending by protected group, for example, builds awareness with managers of possible adverse impact situations. In some European countries, data privacy of sensitive employee compensation data is a legal responsibility. Password protected compensation planning systems can limit data access to those who have a legitimate business need for the information.

## Completing the Compensation Solution

Compensation planning in common reviews is just one part of the compensation process conducted by managers. Off-cycle merit increases, adjustments, promotions, and bonuses are all common manager transactions that can be automated. Compensation applications can support focal planning and off-cycle transactions. Off-cycle compensation transactions can also require

varying guidelines and approval processes. Manager self-service applications that automate off-cycle compensation changes come with sophisticated rules engines and workflow to accommodate the business rule differences between transactions. Compensation planning applications can work together with manager self-service applications to report valuable "year-to-date" information so that managers can assess their merit and bonus spending throughout the entire year.

Communicating pay decisions to employees on a regular basis reinforces the desired behavior promoted by compensation plans—i.e., increased job satisfaction and motivation. Total compensation statements provide employees with a clear statement of the full value of their compensation and benefits. Online total compensation statements can be updated to regularly reinforce the wealth-building opportunities offered by a company, thus fostering the retention of top talent. Companies find that online total compensation statements are one of the most appreciated and used applications an organization can provide its employees.

## Implementation Tips

Organizations interested in deploying automated compensation management solutions in a manner that maximizes cost efficiencies should undertake certain strategies as they prepare for implementation. Among the most beneficial are the strategies listed below.

1. Plan sufficient time to implement an automated compensation planning system. Do not try to make a "last minute decision" which can compromise either the desired functionality of the application or the quality of the implementation.
2. Phase in functionality over time either by compensation component (base pay, variable pay, stock) or geographical region. Ag-

gressively manage "scope creep" to ensure the success of each phase.

3. Consider what is the best practice in the industry when reinforcing manager behavior with a specific feature or a business rule in the system. Often the best opportunity to improve a business process is when implementing a new application.

4. Check the frequency of occurrence for exceptions to corporate practices in order to validate whether they warrant being addressed in the software application from a cost and time perspective. Trying to create an application that supports 100 percent of all exceptions can be cost prohibitive. Supporting "rare exceptions" can dramatically increase the cost of the system.

5. Examine the ramifications of rounding for all calculations—especially when converting from annual to monthly or hourly amounts as well as when converting currencies. Also consider how rounding calculations can affect the user of the system. Unexpected rounding of values can confuse managers.

6. Validate all required data (especially management hierarchy data) with the Human Resource Information System or supporting systems. The accuracy of the data used within the compensation planning application is extremely important. A single piece of invalid data can jeopardize the user's confidence in the entire system. Plan time in the implementation schedule to correct data feeds coming into and out of the compensation planning system.

7. Test, test, and then test some more. Create test plans that include all calculations, business rules, and data entry validation checks. Test plans must include all country or organization specific business rules and calculations. Test each scenario carefully. Also test the technical network and server infrastructure as well as each user Web-browser/operating system version combination.

8. Carefully plan change management communication. Make time to gather input from all major stakeholders in all regions or organizations in approving the supported functionality and the implementation plan, as well as any pending business process changes.

AL WRIGHT IS A SENIOR SOLUTIONS CONSULTANT FOR WORKSCAPE INC.

---

[1]The Cedar Group HR Self-Service Survey, 2002.

# Index

# Index

# Test Your Knowledge Form

We encourage you to photocopy and use this page as a tool to assess how the articles in *Annual Editions* expand on the information in your textbook. By reflecting on the articles you will gain enhanced text information. You can also access this useful form on a product's book support Web site at *http://www.dushkin.com/online/*.

NAME: _____  DATE: _____

TITLE AND NUMBER OF ARTICLE: _____

BRIEFLY STATE THE MAIN IDEA OF THIS ARTICLE:

_____

LIST THREE IMPORTANT FACTS THAT THE AUTHOR USES TO SUPPORT THE MAIN IDEA:

_____

WHAT INFORMATION OR IDEAS DISCUSSED IN THIS ARTICLE ARE ALSO DISCUSSED IN YOUR TEXTBOOK OR OTHER READINGS THAT YOU HAVE DONE? LIST THE TEXTBOOK CHAPTERS AND PAGE NUMBERS:

_____

LIST ANY EXAMPLES OF BIAS OR FAULTY REASONING THAT YOU FOUND IN THE ARTICLE:

_____

LIST ANY NEW TERMS/CONCEPTS THAT WERE DISCUSSED IN THE ARTICLE, AND WRITE A SHORT DEFINITION:

# We Want Your Advice

ANNUAL EDITIONS revisions depend on two major opinion sources: one is our Advisory Board, listed in the front of this volume, which works with us in scanning the thousands of articles published in the public press each year; the other is you—the person actually using the book. Please help us and the users of the next edition by completing the prepaid article rating form on this page and returning it to us. Thank you for your help!

## ANNUAL EDITIONS: Human Resources 05/06

### ARTICLE RATING FORM

Here is an opportunity for you to have direct input into the next revision of this volume.
We would like you to rate each of the articles listed below, using the following scale:

1. **Excellent: should definitely be retained**
2. **Above average: should probably be retained**
3. **Below average: should probably be deleted**
4. **Poor: should definitely be deleted**

Your ratings will play a vital part in the next revision.
Please mail this prepaid form to us as soon as possible.
Thanks for your help!

| RATING | ARTICLE | RATING | ARTICLE |
|---|---|---|---|
| | 1. HR Is Dead, Long Live HR | | 34. Employers May Face Liability When Domestic Violence Comes to Work |
| | 2. The State of the Human Resources Profession in 2003: An Interview With Dave Ulrich | | 35. The Most Effective Tool Against Workplace Violence |
| | 3. What Is an Employee? The Answer Depends on the Federal Law | | 36. The Battle Over Benefits |
| | 4. Good As Gone | | 37. The Cutting Edge of Benefit Cost Control |
| | 5. 7 Steps Before Strategy | | 38. The Barbed Wire Straitjacket |
| | 6. Strategic Human Resources Management in Government: Unresolved Issues | | 39. The ABC's of Employee Discipline |
| | 7. Unquiet Minds | | 40. Three Strikes, You're Out: How to Play Fair at Firing |
| | 8. The Devil is in the Details | | 41. Temporary Worker, Permanent Loser? |
| | 9. The ADA's Next Step: Cyberspace | | 42. Big Companies Teach Business Ethics to Employees |
| | 10. Not In My Company: Preventing Sexual Harassment | | 43. Accounting for Corporate Behavior |
| | 11. The Aesthetics of Security | | 44. Changes Afoot in EU Pension Regulations |
| | 12. Aftershocks of War | | 45. A People Strategy That Spans the Globe |
| | 13. Too Old to Work | | 46. Learning From Our Overseas Counterparts |
| | 14. Can You Interview for Integrity? | | 47. Sexual Harassment in the European Union: The Dawning of a New Era |
| | 15. Does HR Planning Improve Business Performance? | | 48. Don't Settle for Less: Global Compensation Programs Need Global Compensation Tools |
| | 16. Tomorrow's World | | |
| | 17. Getting Happy With the Rewards King | | |
| | 18. Who Needs Superstars? | | |
| | 19. The "Write" Way to Enhance Business | | |
| | 20. In Praise of Boundaries | | |
| | 21. Fear of Feedback | | |
| | 22. What to do About E-dropouts | | |
| | 23. Who's Next? | | |
| | 24. Competitive Global Job Market Strains Employees | | |
| | 25. Seven Habits of Spectacularly Unsuccessful Executives | | |
| | 26. Equality's Latest Frontier | | |
| | 27. Limits to Diversity? | | |
| | 28. The Draw of Diversity | | |
| | 29. Plastic Paychecks | | |
| | 30. Merging Compensation Strategies | | |
| | 31. Top Pay for Best Performance | | |
| | 32. Ten Steps to Designing an Effective Incentive Program | | |
| | 33. Executive Compensation: Are Some Paid Too Much? | | |

*(Continued on next page)*

**BUSINESS REPLY MAIL**
FIRST CLASS MAIL PERMIT NO. 551 DUBUQUE IA

POSTAGE WILL BE PAID BY ADDRESEE

McGraw-Hill/Dushkin
2460 KERPER BLVD
DUBUQUE, IA 52001-9902

IıIııIıIIIııIIııııIIIıIııIıIIııııIıIıII

## ABOUT YOU

Name                                                                      Date

_____

Are you a teacher? ❑   A student? ❑
Your school's name

_____

Department

_____

Address                          City                          State          Zip

_____

School telephone #

_____

## YOUR COMMENTS ARE IMPORTANT TO US!

Please fill in the following information:
For which course did you use this book?

_____

Did you use a text with this ANNUAL EDITION? ❑ yes ❑ no
What was the title of the text?

_____

What are your general reactions to the *Annual Editions* concept?

_____

Have you read any pertinent articles recently that you think should be included in the next edition? Explain.

_____

Are there any articles that you feel should be replaced in the next edition? Why?

_____

Are there any World Wide Web sites that you feel should be included in the next edition? Please annotate.

_____

May we contact you for editorial input? ❑ yes ❑ no
May we quote your comments? ❑ yes ❑ no